Case by Case

Books by Ib Melchior

*Case by Case
*Order of Battle: Hitler's Werewolves
*Quest
Steps & Stairways (with Cleo Baldon)
Code Name: Grand Guignol
V-3
Eva
The Tombstone Cipher
The Marcus Device
The Watchdogs of Abaddon
The Haigerloch Project
Sleeper Agent
Order of Battle

Case by Case

A U.S. Army Counterintelligence Agent in World War II

Ib Melchior

PRESIDIO

Published by Presidio Press
505 B San Marin Dr., Suite 300
Novato, CA 94945-1340

ISBN 0-89141-444-4
Printed in the United States of America

To CLEO, *through whose eyes*
I saw it all again

To my grandson, TORBEN, *for the day*
he asks, "And what did you *do*
in the big war, Bedstefar?"

And to my XII CORPS *comrades*
who did not make it

XII Corps
Parent Unit of Counter Intelligence Corps Detachment 212

XII Corps was planned in 1921, but for more than twenty years it was merely an inactive part of the Organized Reserve, a "paper" corps.

XII U.S. Army Corps, to become known as the spearhead of Patton's Third Army, was, activated on 29 August 1942 in Columbia, South Carolina, and inactivated 15 December 1945 in Regensburg, Germany, after fighting through France, the Battle of the Bulge, Germany, and into Czechoslovakia.

The shoulder patch of XII Corps was an orange-red windmill on a shield-shaped background in blue. Because the first unit to be assigned to XII Corps in the twenties was an inactive reserve headquarters company from the Greater New York area, where the original settlers were Dutch, it was decided to use the old Dutch windmill design from the seal of the City of New Amsterdam and the colors of the Dutch royal house of Nassau.

Scaled down from the medieval coat of arms, the individual shoulder patches of the various army units are worn on the left shoulder as the ancient shield with its heraldic design was borne, and they are worn in the same spirit of valor and honor.

AGENT MELCHIOR'S WAR-TIME ROUTE THROUGH EUROPE

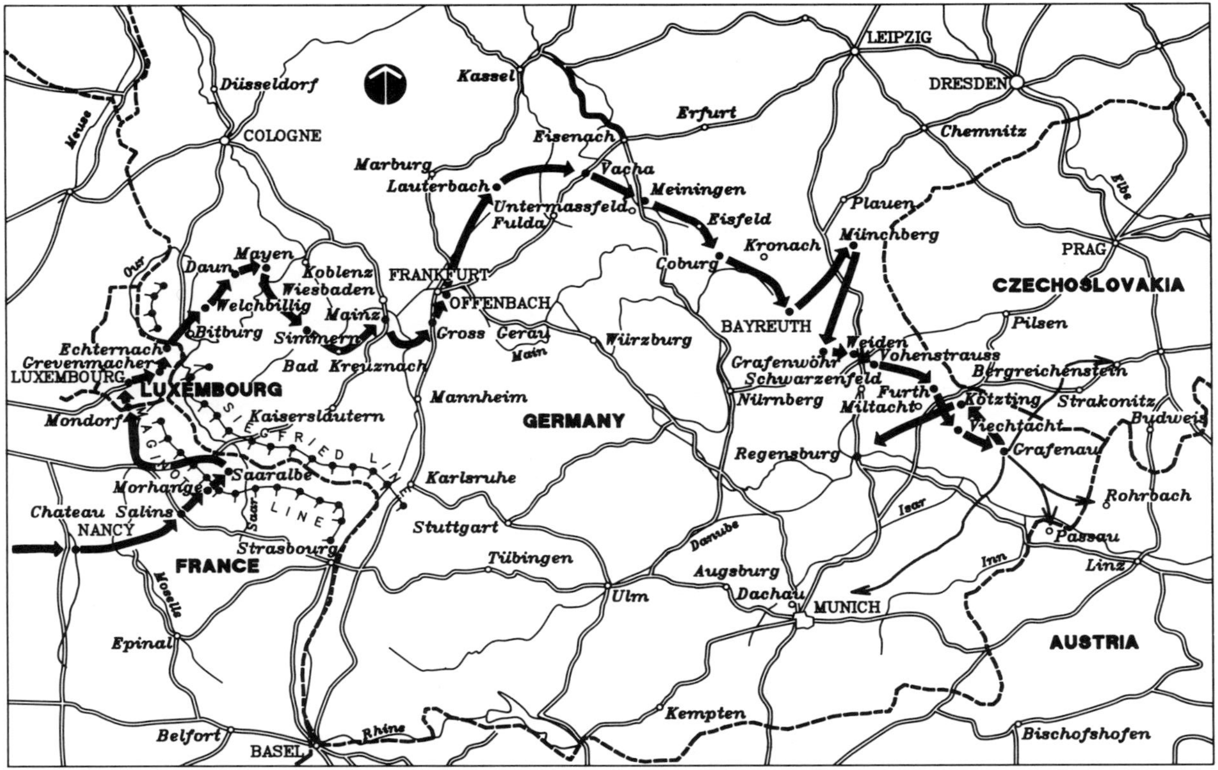

Düsseldorf
COLOGNE
Kassel
LEIPZIG
DRESDEN
Erfurt
Eisenach
Chemnitz
Meuse
Marburg
Lauterbach
Vacha
Meiningen
Untermassfeld
Fulda
Eisfeld
Plauen
Elbe
Kronach
Münchberg
Our
Daun
Mayen
Koblenz
Wiesbaden
FRANKFURT
OFFENBACH
Coburg
PRAG
CZECHOSLOVAKIA
Welchbillig
Bitburg
Mainz
Simmern
Gross Gerau
Würzburg
Main
BAYREUTH
Pilsen
Echternach
Grevenmacher
LUXEMBOURG
Bad Kreuznach
Weiden
Grafenwöhr
Vohenstrauss
Schwarzenfeld
Bergreichenstein
LUXEMBOURG
Mannheim
Nürnberg
Furth
Miltacht
Kötzting
Strakonitz
Budweis
Mondorf
Kaiserslautern
GERMANY
Viechtacht
MAGINOT
SIEGFRIED LINE
Regensburg
Grafenau
Saaralbe
Morhange
Karlsruhe
Rohrbach
Chateau Salins
NANCY
Saar
LINE
Stuttgart
Isar
Passau
Danube
Strasbourg
FRANCE
Tübingen
Inn
Linz
Moselle
Augsburg
Ulm
Dachau
MUNICH
Epinal
AUSTRIA
Kempten
Rhine
Belfort
BASEL
Bischofshofen

INTRODUCTION

One for us," the farmer's wife intoned, as she carefully placed an egg in a worn basket made of twigs, "and two for the war," she went on, as she put two eggs in a barrel of waterglass, watching them sink to the bottom of the clear preservative liquid in which they were to be stored. The eggs looked like tubby miniature submarines, diving erratically.

"Two for the war?" I wondered. "What war?"

It was the summer of 1936. I had just graduated from Stenhus College in Denmark, where I was born, and with a friend I was on a backpacking trip through Germany. We liked to earn our way as we went by doing odd jobs for carpenters, handymen, and farmers. I was standing in the kitchen of a farmhouse in Prussia, watching the farmer's wife sort the eggs we had just collected for her from the out-of-the-way roosting spots scattered throughout the farm. "One for us. Two for the war . . ."

What war?

Three years later I was to find out, when Adolf Hitler's Nazi troops invaded Poland and plunged the world into the most far-reaching and destructive war in history.

Throughout the next three years dire events tumbled incessantly from newspaper headlines. Both my native country and the country I had chosen to make my home were embroiled in a growing world conflict, and when on 7 December 1941 the Japanese bombed Pearl Harbor, I felt it was time for me to do something about paying *my* dues.

* * *

For the life of me I could not understand why I felt apprehensive. But I did.

The office in which I stood was cold and impersonal, spartan and somehow dismal. It was shaped like a railroad car, long and narrow. Behind a beat-up desk, placed at the far end, sat a Navy lieutenant (jg), stern, ramrod-straight, short brown hair neatly trimmed, eyes alert, lantern jaw thrust forward; any recruiting poster would have been proud to bear his likeness. I stood before him—not quite at attention, but close enough.

He pushed a piece of paper across the desk toward me.

"Did you write this?" he asked.

I looked at the letter. "Yes," I nodded.

"Good!" he said, the word sounding clipped with a note a finality—like the firing of a single round. He shoved another piece of paper at me and held out a pen.

"Sign this," he ordered.

I read the paper. It was brief and to the point. Above a place for the date and signature it read, "I hereby volunteer for hazardous duty, no questions asked."

I swallowed. What the hell was I getting into? The lieutenant glared at me, and much too intimidated to demur, I signed, acutely aware of the scratching sound the pen made as it traced my name, and somehow feeling apologetic for it.

"Good!" Once again the word was fired off. "Now, take off your clothes. Every stitch."

I gaped at him, hoping to see at least a glint of *I'm pulling your leg!* There was none. The man was grimly serious. He got up, and from a closet he brought out a large bag. "Put everything in there," he said.

As I began to undress, my mind whirled back to what I had done to get myself into this awkward, totally unexpected situation. . . .

It was a letter I had written in May 1942 when the Japanese attack on Pearl Harbor was still a fresh wound. I was twenty-four years old, and having been born in Denmark and educated there, I was still a Danish subject, awaiting my first U.S. citizenship papers. My native country was occupied by the Nazis, so I had written a letter—the letter that had ultimately brought me here to Lieutenant Harrison's office in Temporary Building Q in Washington, D.C.

Dear War Department:

Possibly this is not the correct or customary way of asking for information; in that case I ask you to excuse me and to be kind enough to submit this letter to whom it may concern.

My name is Ib J. Melchior, son of the Metropolitan Opera singer Lauritz Melchior. I am 24 years old and arrived in this country on Dec. 9, 1938. I have my First Naturalization Papers, being a Danish subject, and I am working on my final papers now, to which I am entitled, having been here more than three years.

I would like to know if it would be possible for me to get into the Army Intelligence Service. I think I could be of the most value to America, my new country, there, inasmuch as I possess knowledge that might be of value along those lines. At present I am employed as a stage manager at the Radio City Music Hall in New York City, and have been here for more than a year. However, I used to travel in Europe with an English theatrical company, The English Players, which I joined in the summer of 1937. It was a repertory company which had its own theater in Paris, France—Theatre de L'Oeuvre—where we performed plays in English. I was an actor and stage manager with that company and toured Europe with them, performing in fourteen countries, over eighty towns. I came to this country with that company as its Technical Director and put on a show on Broadway. Before that, I had done a lot of traveling in Europe myself, mostly on foot or bicycle, and I have a good knowledge of these countries, especially Denmark, Germany, and France. I speak English with a slight accent and furthermore I speak (read and write) Danish and German perfectly. Also French, having worked in that country almost a year, and Norwegian and Swedish, which are similar to my own native Danish. I have had a thorough education, finishing college in Denmark with a first degree and getting the degree of *Candidatus Philosophiae* from the University of Copenhagen, also with a first degree. Besides that, I have studied pre-medical chemistry, physics and anatomy.

I would be grateful for any information as to whether it is possible for me to get into the Army Intelligence and in that way serve my adopted country, and if so, how I should go about it. As additional information about myself I will state that I am six feet tall, dark and weigh 180 pounds, and my Alien Registration number is 1319232.

Hoping to hear from you soon, I remain,

Respectfully Yours,
Ib J. Melchior

Less than a week later I had received a letter of acknowledgment written on impressive stationery headed War Department General Staff, Military Intelligence Division, G-2, and signed by a captain in the MIS—the Military Intelligence Service. It read, "This will acknowledge receipt of your recent application for Military Intelligence work." That was it.

I was, of course, excited. It looked as if I might actually be considered.

I was more than a little surprised, however, when a few days later I received a second letter of acknowledgment, this time signed by a lieutenant commander in the Navy, and when a third acknowledgment letter arrived shortly thereafter, signed by a *civilian*, I was thoroughly perplexed.

I waited eagerly for the tap on the shoulder that would send me to Washington, D.C.—and Military Intelligence. But none came.

Instead, during the next several weeks I gradually became aware of strange looks—and quick look-aways—from friends and acquaintances; even my barber changed his usual friendly, chatty way to one of cautious professionalism. Most peculiar. I even received an occasional concerned note from people I knew in other towns, wanting to know if I was okay. I was, but I was also totally nonplussed.

Finally, a good friend took me aside and earnestly put the question to me: "What've you been up to? The FBI was around asking questions about you." And the light bulb above my head lit up brightly.

I was being investigated.

Then one day I had a telephone call from a young woman, who referred to my letter to the War Department. She asked a few questions, apparently to make certain she was talking to the *real* Ib Melchior. She then informed me that a couple of army officers, a Colonel Huntington and a Captain Brewer, would like to talk to me about my letter, and she set up a meeting in a little obscure hotel on Madison Avenue where they were staying.

I could hardly wait to keep the appointment.

Both officers were in civilian clothes when they received me in their hotel room; they were friendly and informal and quickly made me feel relaxed and at ease. They offered me a drink before we settled down for our talk—and after that I remember very little. The entire meeting is hazy and disjointed in my mind. I vaguely recall only one thing. The colonel casually asked me, "Tell me, Melchior, how would you feel about sticking a knife in a man's back?" I dimly remember that I was not the slightest bit startled by the, at best, unorthodox question. I had a friend whose parents owned a hardware store in Rochester, New York, and I insisted that they buy the knife from them. What my answer was I can't for the life of me remember—but then, I couldn't the day after either!

I returned to the hotel the day following the meeting to apologize for my peculiar behavior, but upon my query at the desk, the clerk stared at me blankly and said, "What officers?" Even the management professed never to have heard of a Colonel Huntington and a Captain Brewer. I never heard from them again either.

After a short while I received another letter, this time signed by a Navy lieutenant. It contained a detailed questionnaire the size of the Manhattan telephone book for me to fill out. I was asked when, at my earliest opportunity, I could put my personal affairs in order and report for duty. He didn't say what duty. My answer was, Give me a date and a place, and I'll be there.

Almost immediately I received a telegram stamped with the little red wartime star of officialdom instructing me to call a certain executive number in Washington, D.C.

I called and talked to a woman who instructed me to report in a week to Lieutenant Harrison, USN, in Temporary Building Q. "And," she added sweetly, "be prepared to be out of communication with everyone for at least three months. And, oh," she finished, "bring nothing with you but your toothbrush!"

When I reported to Temporary Building Q on the specified date, I was at once shown to the office of Lieutenant Harrison, escorted by a grim-faced MP. In response to my knock on the door, a man called, "Come!"

I opened the door and stepped in. Lieutenant Harrison, seated behind his desk, looked up. "Close the door," he ordered brusquely. He looked me up and down. "You realize," he said, a portentous note in his voice, "that when you crossed that threshold, you lost your identity!"

Resisting the urge to look around for it, I simply stared at the officer. It was the furthest thing from my imagination—not what I had expected him to say.

And now I stood before him, stark naked, clutching my only possession—my toothbrush—having just pledged myself in writing to "hazardous duty, no questions asked."

"About your identity," Lieutenant Harrison said to me. "Only I, and I alone, must know your true identity. For the next several months you will meet many people. To them, and to me from now on, you will be *Mel G-8*. That will be your only name. Is that clear?"

I nodded. I understood what he was saying—but *clear?* It was all very mysterious—and I loved it. My curiosity was at its peak.

"During that time," Harrison continued, "you will undergo special training. The people you will work with will try to learn your real name. *Do not let them!* You try to find out who *they* are, *their* real names, and report them to me. Understood?"

Again I nodded.

"You have your toothbrush?"

I held it up.

"Good. That's all," Harrison dismissed me. He pointed to a door. "Through there," he snapped. "You'll be told what to do."

I started toward the door, acutely aware that all I was wearing was my toothbrush. As I reached for the doorknob, Harrison called, "Good luck!—eh—what is your name?"

"Mel G-8," I answered.

I couldn't make up my mind if the look he gave me was one of approval or disappointment. I opened the door and stepped through.

The room beyond was large and filled with what to me appeared to be hundreds of people. All men. All stark naked. All more or less awkwardly holding on to a toothbrush. I knew exactly how they felt. I was gripping my own toothbrush so hard my fingers hurt; it was my only link to sanity.

Actually there were twenty-five to thirty men in the room, all of them politely carrying on a stream of small talk, a not inconsequential feat under the circumstances.

I entered into the spirit of things as best I could. Soon I was engaged in an animated, although somewhat artificial, discussion of the life expectancy of a "temporary building" such as Building Q with an impressively hung young man with a prominent appendix scar and another with an extremely hairy chest. All of us pointedly steered away from anything remotely personal.

The fate of Building Q remained undecided when everyone was issued GI underwear and fatigues and bundled into two large trucks. The trucks were closed up—hermetically sealed, it seemed—and we rumbled off. We drove for a good deal of the night. No one had the slightest idea where we were going.

It was not until a week later that I found out I'd ended up in the organization called Office of Strategic Services—the OSS, America's first wartime espionage service. The OSS had been created in July of 1942 by President Franklin Delano Roosevelt after two years of preparation, and FDR had named his friend and confidant Col. William J. "Wild Bill" Donovan, one of the framers of the organization, its director. OSS agents and operatives were recruited from both military and civilian ranks—anyone with special talents or knowledge. My letter of May that year reached the OSS brass as they were completing their formation, and we of the toothbrush brigade were among their first recruits. But for now, we were totally in the dark—both literally and figuratively.

When we arrived at our destination and were released to the outside world once again, we found ourselves in what appeared to be a large lodge resort with several outlying buildings of recent construction. It was called Camp B-2. Although we did not know it, it was actually Catoctin Manor in the Blue Ridge Mountains of Maryland, one of five OSS "B" camps. Our group consisted of thirty-six men ranging in age from eighteen to fifty-one and chorusing a Babel of accents. It was almost midnight, but we were at once plunked down for a lengthy examination, which consisted of a standard IQ test and what was called a confidential psychological evaluation.

I followed Lieutenant Harrison's admonition to the letter and didn't tell the fellow who was supposed to "evaluate" me a damned thing except my name, Mel G-8. It frustrated the hell out of him until he finally produced ID that proved he was indeed a psychologist doing his job. So I laid open my life for him. I told him about my education in Denmark, my theatrical work experience with the English Players all over Europe, my preferred leisure activities, my interest in track and the fact that I had won the hundred-meter dash in the interscholastic competition at Ollerup in Denmark.

I proved to him my knowledge of the languages I claimed to have mastered and told him about my travels in Europe, especially France and Germany, and I included a little incident that had happened on a backpacking trip, the one on which I encountered the farmer's wife and her eggs. My friend and I had worked for a carpenter for a couple of days, putting up what looked like fodder storage sheds on a large open field surrounded by woods. At the site of each shack was a hole in the ground covered by a large metal lid. Our curiosity finally got the better of us, and we asked what those holes were. "Oh!" said the carpenter conspiratorially, "those are the air vents for the underground airfield below!" And he told us that there was an underground special airfield installation *beneath* the field, with a hidden runway that began in a clearing in the woods and continued underground—much like a ramp to a hornets' nest. My examiner seemed interested; I often wonder what, if anything, was done about it—or if, in fact, it existed. If so, it might have been a field for the testing of early jet planes, to keep them from the public eye.

I had a lot of fun with a kooky set of Rorschach inkblots, and then, finally, came the big one. Resolved: You are driving a truck with a detail of twelve men in the back. You are on a narrow mountain road just big enough for your truck. On your right is a deep ravine, and on your left the cliff rises abruptly. You round a blind curve, and there in the middle of the road sits a baby. You cannot stop in time—what do you do?

There was, of course, only one answer, but it was not easy to voice it. Those who agonized over it and tried to find another way out, or those who hesitated too long, were flunked. Only operatives with the ability to make quick, firm decisions in a moment of crisis, however distasteful, were accepted into the OSS.

Early the next morning, at 5:00 A.M.—or 0500 hours as the military types among us complained—we were rousted from our bunks by a big, burly army captain in fatigues, with a Colt .45 automatic belted to his hip in *High Noon* fashion. He'd be our class instructor, he announced in a stentorian voice, for the next couple of months—or as long as we were able to survive the course. Most of us wouldn't, he stated cheerfully. "We have very little time to determine who is and who isn't fit to be one of us," he said. "You're in for a rough time. If you want out, *now*'s the time." No one reacted. I thought it was because we were all too damned tired. "Chow in fifteen minutes!" the captain finished.

Fifteen minutes later we assembled before the hut where we had spent the night, all thirty-six of us. The captain's name was Slater, something we had to find out for ourselves, like *everything* at the camp. We were told nothing.

Captain Slater took us to an isolated spot outside camp. On the way there we walked through a little makeshift cemetery. Some of the simple graves were marked with a plain wooden cross and a code name—like mine. One was just an open pit. Waiting. No one said a word, but I was sure everyone was wondering what the hell was going on. I was.

When we reached our destination two men were waiting for us. Civilians. They did not greet us, only watched us grimly.

Slater assembled us in a group before an earthen mound and took his .45 automatic from his belt. He realized, he said, that some of us had had little, if any, military training and knew nothing about guns. The one he held in his hand, he told us, was called a Colt M 1911 Al .45 automatic pistol. Seven rounds in the magazine. Standard issue. Patiently he explained to us that one end of the gun, the one with the little hole in it, was called the muzzle, and the other, the one with the hand grip, was, appropriately enough, called the *grip.* And he demonstrated by holding the gun up in front of him—pointing it at us.

"There is a big difference," he informed us, "whether you are on *my* side, at the grip end, or on *your* side, the muzzle end. Let me show you."

He suddenly opened fire. The live bullets whizzed through our group, zinging across our ears to slam with a deadened thud into the dirt mound behind us. Some of the men flinched but stood their ground, others hit the dirt, and a few took off. I think I was too petrified to move. Anyway—I stayed.

The whole crazy performance was witnessed by the two grim-faced civilians, who took notes in little black books. The following day our class was down to twenty-eight.

This was our initiation into the most grueling and fantastic training course imaginable. The course was compact and complete. Nothing that we might come up against or that could get us out of a tight situation in enemy territory was omitted. From communication to cryptography, from silent killing and "dirty" hand-to-hand combat taught by the fiery and justly famous Major Fairbairn of the Hong Kong police force, to terrain orientation. In this last, each trainee would be trucked alone in the middle of the night to a distant destination totally unknown to him, given a map on which all terrain features were correct—but all the *names* changed to Italian or German names!—and told to find his way back to the camp in a certain amount of time by orienting himself by terrain features alone.

We learned to fire every conceivable weapon, Axis and Allied, and how to use a knife effectively. We learned to drive every type of vehicle from motorcycles to big trucks from several nations: U.S. and British, German and Italian, Russian and French. We learned lock-picking and breaking-and-entering from experts—whoever *they* were—as well as other unorthodox subjects, such as practical bribery and effective lying. We became familiar with the handling of high explosives—dynamite and TNT, plastic, and foreign explosives such as gelignite and RDX. And the little omnipresent taciturn civilians with their black books were constantly with us, watching and observing and making their mysterious notations. If a man showed reluctance to crimp a highly unstable detonator cap onto a fuse with his teeth, he was apt not to be seen in class again.

We learned the distinctive smells of several poison gases and were made intimate with tear gas. We were all herded into a small, sealed shack where we donned gas masks. We stood in a circle with the sergeant from Chemical Warfare who acted as our special instructor, and a tear gas canister was set off in the middle of the circle.

The masks worked fine—until the sergeant took off *his* mask and shouted, "Masks off! Everybody! Now! And stay! As long as *I* do!"

And there we stood. Our eyes stung and teared, our nostrils smarted, and our skin burned. There was, of course, a door to get out. And a couple of the fellows quickly used it. In fact—sooner or later we all did. The sergeant was the last man out.

The whole program was designed to tear a man down to his basic survival strength and then build him up again to be able to face anything with confidence. It worked. After the first month I would get up in the morning and think, This is my last day alive on this earth. Today I fall flat on my face—and I'll never get up again. After the second month I would get up and think, Okay. Bring on Germany and Japan, and I'll lick them single-handed!

Gradually we progressed to simulated missions. One was to plan and carry out a thirty-seven-mile forced march with fifty pounds on our backs to a huge, guarded power stanchion that we were supposed to blow up. We reached our objective at the specified time, planted our simulated explosive charges, and got away undiscovered, returning to camp totally pooped, ready to drop. But we congratulated ourselves on a successful mission.

The first question our instructor asked was, "In case your original, your first plan had not worked, what was your alternative, your second plan?"

We gaped at each other. *Second* plan? We had no second plan. We'd naturally expected the first one to succeed.

Sorry, was the verdict. Mission failed. *Always* have at least one alternative plan when you carry out any mission. You'll do it again tomorrow!

Toward the end of our training we were required to run the notorious and dreaded Obstacle/Evaluation Course. We did not know *what* to expect. No one talked about the course. By design. All we knew was, it was tough.

It began inside a barbed-wire enclosure; the course was designed as an escape from this cage. First we had to find a way to scale the barbed-wire fence. It was usually done at a corner post where the wires could be used as a crude ladder—but not without leaving their painful little marks on hands and legs. Outside, a little distance away, stood a sentry with his back to the enclosure. He could not *see* you, but he was listening for you. The task was to sneak up on him and "kill" him silently before he detected you. Nearby was a motorcycle, usually of some foreign make, which you "stole"—after having fixed a minor mechanical problem—and then you were off to where the obstacle course began!

The start was at the top of a hill. You couldn't miss it; one of the ubiquitous observers waited there for you, his little notebook at the ready.

Here you picked up a backpack with forty pounds of Maryland rocks and an empty Mason jar, to double for the vacuum tubes in the radio you'd be carrying on a real mission. The jar had to be unbroken at the end of the course, or you'd have to run it again. And you couldn't take the jar out. For any reason.

The trail ran down the hill toward a wooded area below. It was quite steep. You ran—or stumbled—down the hill. Just as you reached a pile of broken masonry, a machine gun opened up in front of you. You dove for the cover of the rubble. Here you found a conglomeration of stuff: nails, old tin cans, bottles and jars, rags and paper, wire and tape—and explosives: dynamite sticks, plastic, primacord and detonator caps, fuses, matches, and other paraphernalia. The object was to fashion a makeshift grenade and hurl it at the machine-gun emplacement, silencing it.

My grenade was quickly made. A short length of red fuse, a detonator cap crimped onto it with my teeth, stuck into a bit of plastic high explosive, and stuffed into a small can half filled with stubby carpet tacks; the whole tamped down with rags, the fuse sticking out. Light the fuse—and hurl it at the machine gun nest. If it exploded, you were off. If not, you'd have to try again.

Here you also found a box with the parts for several field-stripped handguns all jumbled together—German 7.65 Walthers, 9mm Lugers and P38s, U.S. Army .45s, Italian Berettas, and British Brownings—with ammunition and loaded clips. You had to find the pieces to assemble one gun, load it, and pick one extra clip for it. It was up to you which you chose. I selected the U.S. .45. Its parts were the easiest to pick out. The gun assembled and loaded, I put an extra clip in my pocket. Fourteen rounds: I knew I'd need every one of them; at intervals throughout the course—usually the most unexpected and inconvenient ones—targets would spring up. You had to pump two rounds into each. Always two rounds—for stopping power.

At the wood's edge at the bottom of the hill ran a small stream with steep banks. It was about twenty feet from bank to bank, and a narrow log had been thrown across. The second you stepped onto it to cross the stream it looked like a strand of spaghetti. The trick was to go fast, run if you could. It was like riding a bicycle; the faster you go, the easier it is to keep your balance. But halfway across the log, an explosion went off close by, startling the hell out of you and buffeting you off balance, while a target popped up in the shrubbery on the far side of the stream. Two quick rounds. And don't miss.

On you ran. There were the standard fences and walls to scale, pipes to wiggle through, and obstacles to climb—all designed to tire you out for the more difficult hurdles ahead. And then, back across the stream again, this time without a log.

The banks here were less steep and formed a little flat area at the water's edge on both sides of the stream, which was eight to ten feet wide. A sign with a skull and crossbones painted in black on it proclaimed: *ACHTUNG! MINEN!* The streambed was mined; you could not wade across. You had to leap. It was only ten feet. What was the world record for broad jump? Twenty-six feet and better? Piece of cake. But then, the world's record broad jumper had not worn GI boots, nor had he carried a forty-pound pack on his back. Throw the backpack over first? The damned jar would break. And you couldn't remove it first. So you took as much of a running start as you could and started to sail over the water.

You needn't have worried about making it. When you were midway across, an ear-shattering blast slammed into you, and a geyser of water erupted from the stream to engulf you and catapult you to the far bank, where you landed in a heap. One of your friendly neighborhood observers had set off a small charge of TNT directly under you, which had been hidden in the water.

You struggled to your feet, your legs feeling like tubes filled with oatmeal mush. Ahead of you was a muddy embankment, rising some twenty feet. You wobbled toward it. When you started to crawl up, you'd slide right back down. Again. And again. But you had your paratrooper knife in your pants sheath. Use it. Jam it into the slippery slope. Pull yourself—and your damned pack—up the mucky incline inch by inch.

Then, on through the shrubbery at a run, with targets popping up where you'd least expect them. Two rounds in each. You did not stop to check your score. Every second counted if you wanted to finish the course in the prescribed time. There were trees to climb; in one instance you had to leap from a branch into space, grab hold of a rope some six feet away, and slide down to the ground. If you missed, that damned jar would probably break—if nothing else. There was barbed wire to negotiate and chains to swing you across mud-filled holes like an ungainly GI Tarzan.

And then, back across the ever-present stream again—this time, high above ground. Two tall trees stood on either side of the creek about fifty feet apart. Between them a steel wire had been stretched taut. A second, thinner wire was fixed five feet above the first, running parallel to it across the stream. All you had to do was climb up one tree, cross the creek on the wire, and climb down the other tree. Simple.

There were two conventional ways of doing it. Neither worked. Those who tried to hang on the lower wire, throwing their knees across it and pulling themselves along with their hands, soon found out that the weight of their backpack caused the wire to cut into their hands and made them so slippery with blood, they'd have to let go. The other way was to walk across on the lower wire while holding on to the one above, trying to balance yourself and keep the two wires exactly in line, one atop the other. If the wires spread apart, you'd find yourself hanging with your hands on one wire and your feet on the other, staring at the creek below you. One consolation—you wouldn't hang there for long. And with a forty-pound pack on your back, keeping your balance was an utter impossibility.

So there had to be a third way to do it.

There was. You'd take off your pack. Snap one of the pack straps onto the lower wire and let the pack hang on it. Snap the other strap onto your combat-boot strap—and as you carefully made your way across the bottom wire, holding on to the top one, you'd slide that pack along with you, with it acting as a stabilizing weight instead of throwing you out of balance. It worked for me.

Once on the ground on the other side, you ran along the stream, hugging the near bank as a machine gun opened up, spewing a staccato stream of live rounds that slammed into the dirt bank across from you. It certainly made you appreciate the importance of a defilade area.

When at last you left the stream, there ahead of you stood The Barn: your final obstacle.

The Barn held a "noodle test," an obstacle to test your smarts. Inside was a large, bare area. No one was there except an observer sitting at a small table in a corner. As he saw you enter, he conspicuously started a stop watch and made a note in his little black book.

A deep, twenty-foot-wide trench had been dug wall to wall in the dirt floor of the place, cutting the well-lit area in half. From the ceiling a long, heavy rope net was suspended, a transparent barrier that dipped into the center of the trench. A single, narrow plank had been placed across the trench, running through a vertical slit in the netting large enough to accommodate a man. In the far wall was a door marked EXIT.

The end of the course.

When I entered the test area, all this was taken in at a glance, as was a large sign by the foot plank: MAXIMUM LOAD CAPACITY 200 POUNDS.

It was not difficult to figure out. I weighed 180 pounds, the pack 40—20 pounds too much. There was no way I'd make it across the plank to complete the course if I had to carry the pack.

But there *had* to be a way, I reasoned, or the damned test would not be there. The possibilities raced through my mind.

Carrying the pack was out. So—because of the net—was throwing it across. Anyway, there was the jar; even if I *could* get the pack across by throwing it through the slit in the netting, the jar would not survive. And I'd have to hit the bull's eye on my first try. Fat chance. I could break up the pack, leave the jar, which had to remain inviolate, and take a few rocks across at a time, making several trips. Possible. But much too time-consuming. I'd never do it in the time allowed me. What then? Take the chance that the plank would hold me *and* the pack after all? Even if it did, they'd flunk me.

And then I saw it.

I ran to the plank, shrugging out of my pack. Lifting the end of the plank off the ground, I slid it through the shoulder straps of the pack. I lifted the plank higher, over my head, and the pack slid down it through the slit in the net to land safely on the other side. *I* was there as soon as I could get the plank down on the ground; I picked up my pack, the jar intact, and sprinted to the EXIT—and the finishing line.

They told me that the record for the course was twenty-seven minutes and a few seconds. Although I finished within the allotted time, mine was considerably longer than that!

But there was one more trial to conquer before our training at Camp B-2 was over: the House of Horror.

It was whispered about in camp in a mysterious tone of apprehension. Fun was made of it, but it was gallows humor. No one would—or could—tell us anything about what went on in the House of Horror. It was the final test at B-2. The guys left camp directly from the place, one way or another. But there were rumors. They were testing us to see how much pain we could endure if captured. One man had been taken away in a straitjacket—that sort of scuttlebutt.

My turn . . .

I was taken to the place by Captain Slater himself, grimmer and more sober than usual, I thought. I admit my heart was beating faster than normal. As we neared the building, I saw an ambulance parked nearby. Two medics were standing by. They eyed me dolefully as I walked past.

We entered the building.

The room was small and windowless. It was lit by a single naked bulb hanging from the ceiling. The only furniture in the place was a small table. On it lay a .45 and a fully loaded clip. One other door, opposite the one through which we'd entered, led from the room. Purposefully Slater walked to the table. He picked up the gun and handed it to me.

"You've done well," he said, strangely subdued. "But now, be careful. Real careful. You hear?" He glanced toward the door leading to—to what?

I swallowed. I nodded. He was getting to me. What the hell *was* behind that door? What *was* expected of me? An ambulance, for crissake!

Slater slapped me on the shoulder. There was a feeling of finality about it. "Good luck," he said. "I'll be waiting for you on the other side." He gave me a portentous look. "After I've gone—in your own good time—go through that door." He pointed to the door that led to the unknown, and left.

I took a deep breath. I checked my weapon. All was in order. I stared at the door, but my feet were leaden. The cliché we'd all bantered about so jokingly popped into my mind—"This is it!"—but it was no longer a joke.

This *was* it.

It's a common belief, another cliché, if you wish, that in a moment of crisis one's entire life flashes before one's inner eye. All through my life, triggered by the most unlikely events, I've stopped in my tracks and thought, What's a wet-behind-the-ears kid from Copenhagen doing here? And like a super-condensed *Reader's Digest* book, my life would flash through my mind with the velocity of the proverbial speeding bullet.

Enough. I had to go through that door. Now. The longer I waited, the more my imagination would conjure up terrible things that could happen to me, the more scared I'd be.

I opened the door.

Instantly the light went out.

I stood in stygian darkness. Petrified.

Automatically I dropped to one knee.

I listened. I listened so intently that I imagined my ears leaving my head, searching out the most infinitesimal sounds. But there was nothing. It was so quiet you could have heard a mouse pissing on a blotter.

I don't know how long I stayed like that. When each second is an eternity it is difficult to judge time. But finally I stood up. I strained to see. Slowly my eyes were getting used to the blackness. Dimly I could make out a faint sheen of light. It seemed to be far in the distance, but I knew it was an illusion. Slowly, cautiously, every nerve end pitched to its ultimate alertness, I started into the gloom beyond the little anteroom.

I took several steps. Nothing happened. I had gone perhaps ten feet. I was gradually getting bolder, when all of a sudden I felt something softly, tentatively touch my shoulder. I whirled toward it. Instantly I felt a slimy, wet "something" whisk across my face. Again I spun around—ready to shoot. But at what? Instinctively I groped around in the dark, and my hands came in contact with a cluster of slithery tentacles that clung to me. I lashed out; I flailed my arms at them. The more I struggled; the more I became entangled.

I stopped. I forced myself to stand stock still. Cautiously I felt around me.

From the ceiling hung a bunch of two-inch-broad cloth ribbons soaked in oil. Oil? What the hell was going on?

Whatever it was it had scared the stuffing out of me.

Either my eyes were getting more used to the darkness, or a faint light had been gradually turned on, but I could make out my surroundings. Faintly. I was standing in a long corridor so dark that the ceiling was lost in black shadows. At the far end the corridor seemed to make a sharp turn. It was at that point that the faint light seeped into the corridor. I swept aside the oily cloth ribbons and started down the passage toward the light, my gun held firmly locked against my abdomen, as I had been taught.

Suddenly I heard a small noise to my right. I wheeled toward it, just in time to see an indistinct figure leap at me. Instinctively—without thought—I fired. Two rounds. I knew they hit home. A terrible thought flashed through my mind. My God! Had I hit someone? This *was* supposed to be a training exercise, wasn't it? Had I *killed* someone?

The figure tore past me, turned, and came at me again. I almost pumped two more shots into the attacker. I stopped myself in the last split-moment. It was not possible. I *knew* I had not missed. Two rounds. It should have stopped him. I held my fire as the figure came at me again, and again brushed past me. It stopped and swung back toward me. I grabbed it.

It was a dummy hanging from a wire in the ceiling. It had two bullet holes squarely in its chest, the sawdust stuffing bleeding from the wounds. Bleakly I realized that it might just as well have been a man of flesh and blood. I would have fired. Automatically. As I had been trained to do.

But now I knew. I was in a "shooting gallery." The House of Horror was one giant, elaborate shooting gallery. I looked toward the light that spilled into the corridor.

I decided to have some fun.

It was like a huge carnival shooting arcade—except you were *in* the games. Targets would fly up, each to receive two rounds. Sacks filled with sawdust would lurch at you; trapdoors, loose floorboards, closed doors, and blind corners would bedevil you. At one point, as you kicked open a closed door, a man would face you, his gun at the ready. But—better not fire. It was your own reflection in a full-length mirror.

When at the end of the gallery I stepped out into the glaring sunlight once again and was met by a grinning Slater, I knew I'd made it.

There was a reason for the melodrama. A damned good reason. They wanted you to undertake the House of Horror test as uncertain, as keyed-up, and as apprehensive as you would be in a real life-threatening situation, or as close to it as possible. It was the best chance they could give you for survival. The bastards had probably concocted the gruesome rumors about the place themselves. As for Slater, I was ready to give him an Academy Award.

Our training at Camp B-2 had come to an end. In a short while we would be assigned to the proper OSS branch. There were three main branches. OSS-SO (OSS Special Operations), specializing in sabotage and collaboration with the underground in foreign countries, and OSS-SI (OSS Secret Intelligence), for which I was slated, specializing in espionage and infiltration, both operated in the field. A third branch, a Research and Analysis branch with several sections, was located in Washington, D.C.; it covered almost anything that could be imagined, including astrology! That made sense. Adolf Hitler had astrologers advising him what to do; our astrologers would tell *us* what they were telling *him!*

After completing the House of Horror test—which, after the initial fear, had been one of the most exciting experiences of the entire OSS training—we were driven to Quantico Marine Base in Virginia. Here we attended a crash course in parachute jumping; not the two months' training course offered at the parachute school at Fort Benning, but two days. It left us sore and tender in places we didn't even know we had. After the two days of training we were scheduled to make our five qualifying jumps—in one afternoon.

We piled into a truck and were taken to the base airfield, where we boarded a C-47 from which we'd make our jumps into a small clearing in a forest outside the base. The first jump would be from one thousand feet, with plenty of time to check your oscillation, orient yourself, and get control of your chute. The following four jumps would be from progressively lower altitudes until the final jump was made from a height of a few hundred feet, with no time at all before you hit the ground.

My first jump was great. It was a beautiful, sunny day. I drifted into the clearing. My oscillation had been checked, my drift was negligible, and I managed to yank down on my risers at just the right moment, all but stopping the descent of the parachute in midair. I hardly bent my knees when I landed. I loved it. Nothing to it, I thought. I was wrong.

The following jumps were a lot rougher. In one of them I hit a cross draft just as I was landing, which slammed me into the ground, knocking the wind out of me. Still, I wouldn't have missed it for the world. Our jump instructor had told us that there were two first experiences in a man's life that he'd never forget. The second was his first parachute jump. He was right.

A bonus to all this was the fun of watching the expressions on the faces of the Marine guards who checked us onto the base—again, and again—but never checked us out. Their eyes bugged bigger each time we arrived.

The parachute jumps had been like a graduation exercise. OSS basic training was over. Of my class of thirty-six, six of us were left.

There was only one more project to complete before I would be a full-fledged OSS agent. My field test.

> You will proceed to Hagerstown, Maryland. You will determine how to paralyze the town through sabotage, and you will ascertain how subsequently the Fairchild Aircraft plant in that town can be taken over by a company of paratroopers with the object of holding it for forty-eight hours. You will report your progress by radio transmissions to home base four times during every twenty-four-hour period as per attached time, frequency, and call letter schedules.

During World War II Fairchild was an important manufacturing plant for military aircraft such as the "Flying Boxcars," the C-82s, C-119s, and C-123s. The plant employed about ten thousand workers. The company had been founded in the 1930s by Samuel M. Fairchild, a nationally known inventor with an interest in aviation.

Settled in 1740 on land granted to one Jonathan Hager, Hagerstown itself, a typical little Maryland town of about thirty-three thousand souls, was situated on Antietam Creek in the Cumberland Valley in Washington County some seventy miles northwest of Washington, D.C. Besides the aircraft industry the town, among other items, produced sheet metal and sundry foundry products, and in the environs were slate and stone quarries. This was the town that had been selected for my final OSS test, my field test.

Because it was impossible to have the graduate agents go up against our real adversaries, the Gestapo and the German armed forces, in a "test" situation, which by the nature of the beast must embody a margin for error, the OSS brass had devised the next best thing. We would be sent on a mission to an *American* target, fully as important and as thoroughly and completely safeguarded as any enemy objective we might have to attack. We would pit ourselves against our own law enforcement agencies, the FBI, and armed forces security personnel. And these agencies did *not* know that we were not *real* saboteurs and spies. It was up to us to complete our mission successfully without being caught. It was about as close to reality as we could come without laying our lives on the line in an actual operation on enemy turf. In this case, if we were caught, we had instructions to ask our captors to call an executive telephone number in Washington, D.C., to verify our true identity. And someone would come, ignominiously, to pick us up.

Some agents, reluctant to admit failure, delayed that call as long as possible. There was, for instance, the Filipino officer who had been sent to a small town in the Midwest on his field test. His appearance immediately aroused the suspicions of the local constabulary, and they arrested him. When they found incriminating items on him, and he could not (or would not) prove his true identity, they thought they'd captured a real live spy and were determined to break him. When the OSS personnel finally arrived to pick him up, he was without front teeth, had a broken nose, and could hardly see out of his swollen eyes.

It was, of course, impossible to function without some incriminating objects in your possession or within immediate access. We had been issued a small, compact radio receiver/transmitter, the X-35, built into a case that looked exactly like a portable Underwood typewriter. Since possession of such communication devices was strictly illegal at that time, and no unauthorized amateur transmissions were allowed, the fact that we had to be on the air four times in any given twenty-four-hour period was like waving a red rag before a bull. With monitors constantly listening for such illegal activities and zeroing in on the location from which the transmission emanated, we could only hope we weren't nosed out before we had a chance to complete a transmission.

Add to this that we had to construct adequate antennae at all transmittal locations, and the chances that we'd get caught grew steadily higher. We'd use anything we could to serve as an antenna—long single wires or old telephone wires, metal clotheslines, or even bedsprings. Our messages had to be sent in Morse code, enciphered by using a double transposition cipher. A transposition cipher is one in which the letters in the clear message remain the same in the enciphered message, but are scrambled according to a special method known by both the sender and the receiver, which makes it possible for the recipient to unscramble the message. A double transposition cipher is simply doing this twice, making deciphering the scrambled message, called a cryptogram, more difficult for a would-be cryptanalyst. That is the cipher we would be using in the field. It was supposed to be "safe" from being solved for forty-eight hours, but that was, of course, before computers were as sophisticated as they are today.

I arrived in Hagerstown with my X-35 and a small bag with personal belongings and checked into a small, obscure hotel. I had devised a method for safety. I knew I would have to transmit at least once from each location I chose and figured it was impossible to tell how quickly the monitors would locate me. There could be a monitor truck right around the corner, for all I knew. So I'd rent a small room in the flea trap from the day clerk, and on the same floor, close by the first room, I'd rent a second room from the night clerk, using a different name. My theory was that if the transmission was discovered, and the room from which I had been transmitting was raided and I couldn't get out of the building, I could quickly go to the second room and become an innocent bystander. I never had to use this ploy. I always felt a little disappointed that I didn't find out if it would work.

Here I was in Hagerstown, the hometown of a vital war effort. I spoke with a foreign accent and carried identification papers that at best could be considered mediocre. And my mission was to determine how to "take over" the place.

It was amazingly simple. The people of Hagerstown were cooperative to a fault. Information was freely, sometimes even proudly, given. I had no trouble getting access to town records and plans, and I searched the files and logs at the town's Building and Safety Department, Planning Department, Public Works Department, and Water and Power Department, to name a few. Everywhere people were most accommodating and willing to help out a struggling young magazine writer who might say something nice about their town. Even the public relations people at Fairchild had been helpful, and pretty soon I knew every target point in detail—power stations, sewer system, water supply, transportation, communication, and defense—the works. I knew exactly how to paralyze this town of over thirty thousand people quickly and effectively and for a period long enough to take over and destroy the entire Fairchild Aircraft plant and the rail junction serving it. At least, that was my belief.

I kept up my schedule of transmissions and conveyed the results of my investigations to home base. It was, as I said, ridiculously easy—and also a little frightening. This was, after all, a time of war, and there *could* be the real McCoy out there.

I was sitting in my dismal hotel room and had just established contact with home base for the last time to advise them that my mission had been completed, when I received an emergency message: "QSP—QSP," which stood for "Accept my priority message."

At once I sent back: "QRV—QRV," "I am ready."

The message was brief, and I quickly deciphered it. I stared at it. "Mission considered successfully completed stop return to base soonest stop."

Back at base it was business as usual. I was told nothing, except to report pronto to Building Q in Washington.

At Q my orders were quick and to the point. "Pack your things," I was told. "You will be shipped to another camp this afternoon for special training and briefing. You have been assigned to a mission."

I was excited. It would be my first mission, my first mission in enemy-held territory. What would it be like? At the new camp I met my teammates, eleven young Norwegians, and I learned that although I had been trained and slated for SI work, *this* mission would be an SO operation: blowing up a vital heavy water plant operated by the Nazis in Norway. I would be the only non-Norwegian in the group. The reason for my participation was that during my original OSS questioning I had told them about my skiing in Norway. A group of us would go to a hotel located on the mountain "back" of Norway toward the Swedish border and then ski cross-country down to the Norwegian coast, using a route that followed a string of huts stocked with food, medicine, and other necessary supplies. That route had been chosen as the escape route for the sabotage team after the mission was completed. I was to be the guide.

For a couple of weeks we all went through an intense mission training and briefing, and a fiercely close relationship quickly sprang up among us. Finally we were considered ready and were flown to Westover Air Force Base in Massachusetts to board a plane that would take us to Iceland and from there on to the DZ—the drop zone near the heavy water plant in Norway that was our target.

We were sitting in the plane ready to take off when an officer came aboard. "Mel G-8?" he called.

"Ho!" I answered.

"Out!" he said, motioning toward the door. "Now!"

I was flown down to Washington, D.C. No one said a word. No one told me why. I was totally nonplussed. What the hell was going on?

I was put up in a hotel room with strict orders to stay put, not to venture out or communicate with *anyone* for *any* purpose until contacted by the OSS again; my meals would all be sent to my room.

And there I sat, in total seclusion, for one full week. Wondering . . .

Then I was summoned to Building Q and was finally told what had happened. The mission had been blown. Someone involved in the operation had compromised it. The mission, however, was too important to scrap, so the second-guessing began. It had to be assumed that the enemy was now aware of the mission and knew that we realized he was. Therefore he would assume that we would change the operation. So if we did *not* change it, we could still take him by surprise. However, *he* might anticipate that thinking and so still expect the mission to be carried out as originally planned—unless he thought that *we'd* think that *he'd* foresee that we'd anticipate *his* thinking and therefore—the rationalization could go on *ad infinitum*. The upshot of it all was that the mission was laid on as planned with only a minor change of timing to make the enemy think we *had* scrapped the whole thing and one important exception. The escape route had been changed. Once the raid had been executed, if the Nazis knew the escape route, and we had to assume that they did, it obviously could not be used. And because the sole purpose of my being on the team was knowledge of that original route, I was taken off.

Subsequently I was unofficially informed that the mission had been carried out but had been only partially successful. My eleven teammates had been caught—and executed—while I sat in a hotel room in Washington, D.C.

My first reaction was, Thank God I did not go! And then I had an overwhelming feeling of guilt for not having been with my comrades. It was a conflict not easily worked out.

During this time significant changes had taken place, changes that would completely alter my personal role in the war effort. The four big Allied powers in Europe had carved up the ETO (the European theater of operations) among themselves. I had been trained for missions in the Scandinavian countries, and all such operations now came under the jurisdiction of the SOE, the Special Operations Executive, the British equivalent of the OSS, which had served as the prototype for the OSS. I was therefore given the choice of transferring to British authority or entering the U.S. armed forces, remaining under U.S. authority, and becoming a citizen.

It was an easy choice.

I was inducted into the Army and sent to the U.S. Army Military Intelligence Training Center, Camp Ritchie, in the Blue Ridge Mountains of Maryland. Here I learned the Army way of doing things, quite different from the individualistic OSS approach. I received additional training in interrogation, interpretation, and investigation—on the theory of "set a thief to catch a thief," I assumed—cryptography and cryptanalysis, and the rudiments of several other intelligence disciplines.

Finally, in April of 1944, I was sent to England to await the invasion of the Continent: D Day.

The war for which the Prussian farmer's wife had saved most of her eggs was about to begin for me.

Because intelligence personnel are not used as combat troops, it was some time after D Day that I waded ashore on Omaha Beach. When in 1990 my wife, Cleo, and I decided to retrace my entire wartime route, road by road, village by village, town by town, and case by case, following a photocopy of an old, tattered military map, split in all the folds and water-stained in one corner, a map that I had carried and marked all through the campaign, Omaha Beach was the place we began our trip. In this year of 1990, forty-five years later, I was about to visit all the memories that still filled my mind and dip into the grab bag of remembrances, not knowing which ones would bob to the surface to be seized.

The D Day assault on the Normandy coast was carried out on five Allied beach sectors. Omaha Beach was flanked on the right by the U.S. Utah Beach and on the left by the British and Canadian Gold, Juno, and Sword beaches.

As I walked along the beach the sand was getting into my low-cut shoes. The last time I had made that walk, that had not been a problem; I had worn GI boots.

Omaha Beach was the same, yet it was not. Where forty-five years before it had been strewn with military equipment, crammed with soldiers, pocked with shell craters, and peppered with jagged, sharply pointed landing craft obstacles and the debris of war amid tangles of barbed wire, now it was dotted with colorful beach towels on which bare-breasted young women soaked up the sun, a beach where children and dogs frolicked merrily. The steeply rising stony bluffs and sheer cliffs immediately beyond the sand back then had been denuded of all vegetation that might have provided cover for an advancing enemy and obstructed the sight and fire lines from the massive bunkers and pillboxes that studded the bluffs. Now lush vegetation clad the then hostile and threatening heights in a mantle of peaceful green. But a short distance up the rise, out in the open, squatted the remnants of a concrete bunker. Within its dark interior a German gun could be seen poking its ugly snout through a slit, a gun that once took American lives. Cleo was close to tears.

Before we set out on our trek we paid our respects at the Normandy American Cemetery nearby. As I stood in the midst of the vast sea of stark white crosses and stars of David, I could not help reflecting that by giving their lives all these young men had made it possible for me to wade ashore on that beach unharmed. It was a humbling feeling. I must have gotten some sand in my eyes, for they began to smart. I was not the only one. Nearby stood a man my age with a younger woman—his daughter? His eyes were also bothering him.

We began our odyssey of remembrance, this time in a Ford Sierra instead of an open jeep equipped with a guillotine wire cutter. We drove through the little Normandy villages that I had passed through forty-five years before while still not assigned to a combat unit: Saint-Lô, Caen, and Falaise, then ravaged by war, now rebuilt and as charming and picturesque as ever, then on to Paris.

Paris, where I had lived and worked in the theater as a member of The English Players during 1937 and 1938, was much as I remembered it. Military Intelligence personnel had been billeted in a large building complex in a western suburb called Le Vésinet. Someone had told me that it was most appropriate for Intelligence to be assigned to that particular building. I thought it was because it was so big and comfortable; I later found out he was referring to the fact that it had once been an insane asylum!

Here, in Paris, I finally had been posted to a newly formed MIS (Military Intelligence Service) unit, MII (Military Intelligence Interpreter) Team 425-G, and assigned to work with CIC Detachment 212, the Counter Intelligence Detachment of XII Corps, spearhead of Patton's Third Army, which was about to smash its way into Germany.

CIC stands for Counter Intelligence Corps, a military organization, not to be confused with CIA, which stands for Central Intelligence Agency, a "civilian" organization. The CIA was not in existence during World War II but was formed after the war as a successor to the

OSS, which was dissolved at the end of the war. Military intelligence is the gathering of information about the enemy—his plans, his strength, his operations—evaluating it, and disseminating it. Counterintelligence is preventing the enemy from gathering such information about you and from carrying out clandestine operations against you. This was to be my work.

At last, after months of intensive training and impatient waiting, I was about to go into action.

CHAPTER 1

The weather was miserable—gray, inhospitable skies, cold rain, and wet snow—when we caught up with Corps in the city of Nancy, where XII Corps Forward, or Iceberg Forward, had been headquartered since 18 September 1944, and the rear echelon since the nineteenth.

Nancy, an ancient stronghold and the fifth largest city in France, located on the Meurthe River, had been liberated by the 1st Battalion, 134th Infantry Regiment of the 35th Infantry Division on 15 September. The town had suffered relatively little war damage. Iceberg Forward was housed in an art school, École des Beaux Arts, a large, two-story building, and here we reported to the commanding officer (CO) of Corps' Counter Intelligence Detachment, CIC Detachment 212, Capt. Benjamin T. Kinsey. Our team had been assigned to work with the CIC.

The first several days were spent in getting to know the guys in the detachment and learning the ropes. Our work would be that of CIC agents, because the detachment did not have enough men who could speak German. The detachment, besides the CO, consisted of thirty-six men, divided into six teams. Each team would work independently out of a different location as close to the front lines as possible and leapfrog each other as the front pushed on. Ours would be an additional team. Standard Operating Procedure (SOP) was that any extensive investigation would be carried out by two agents working together, and we were usually paired with someone who did not speak German. At least, this was the case during the first few weeks.

We were also given our identification as CIC agents and our insignia, which consisted of two U.S. officer's emblems worn on the collar tabs. We wore no other insignia of any kind except the XII Corps shoulder patch. No rank. No unit. Because our duties were such that we might easily find ourselves in a situation requiring the immediate and unquestioned assistance of available troops, we were empowered to request such assistance—if need be, *order* it—from any officer up to and including full colonel. Only general officers were entitled to know our true rank. To all others our standard reply to the inevitable question, "What *is* your rank?" was simply a firm, "My rank is confidential, but at this moment I am not outranked!" It was a vital ordinance; it saved the life of many a CIC agent in a tight spot—including mine, several months down the line! Some officers, unable or unwilling to see the necessity of this directive, resented it, because they might possibly be ordered about by someone of a lesser rank—unthinkable to some. Perhaps that is why certain military personnel insisted that CIC did not stand for Counter Intelligence Corps but for "Christ I'm Confused!"

In Nancy we also had our first taste of long-distance artillery shelling. The Germans had positioned a big 28mm railroad gun, dubbed the "Nancy Gun," somewhere to the northeast of Metz, and every night they would lob shells into the city, one every five or ten minutes. It was largely a harassment agent, but we all lost a lot of sleep over the damned thing. Shells were landing all around Corps command post as well as around our quarters.

I remember distinctly one evening when several of us were sitting in our quarters, reading, just shooting the bull, or writing V mail—that special GI mail that could be microfilmed, sent to the States, and printed on photographic paper before delivery. One of the guys, Smitty, Carlos D. Smith, wanted to make a telephone call. The telephone was on a stand close by one of the windows.

Smitty had just been connected and had not even had a chance to say hello when a shell landed outside, close enough to shake the whole building and shatter every window in the room.

Smitty's only comment was, "Jesus Christ! Hang up! Hang up! I'm being shelled!" And with those well-chosen words he slammed down the receiver.

Finally, we had been told what our mission was, what counterintelligence meant. Broadly stated, the wartime tactical counterintelligence operation consisted of detecting and combating enemy espionage, subversion, sabotage, and terrorism and hunting down high-ranking political and military leaders such as major Nazi party officials and members of the German General Staff, as well as war criminals, all of them automatic or mandatory arrestees.

It was not long before I was to become involved in my own first case, but not by design.

One evening after dark, with curfew in effect and no civilians abroad, I was driving in my jeep from a location in the outskirts of town to my billet. I was alone. Not unusual, we were, after all, in a friendly country, and Nancy had been cleared. As I drove down a side street, I saw the figure of a man standing in a doorway, urgently trying to flag me down. I stopped and backed up. The man, a young fellow with a downy lip, called to me from the shadows of the doorway:

"Monsieur l'officier!" His voice was a secretive half-whisper. "I must talk to you!" He looked furtively into the darkness behind him. "It is of importance," he finished.

I was intrigued. I checked to see that my gun was nice and loose in my shoulder holster, a gesture not lost on the young man. I dismounted and walked up to him. "What is it?" I asked. "It is about a radio," he told me in a conspiratorial voice, quickly glancing toward the dark staircase behind him. "An—an illicit radio. What the *Boche* call a *Schwarzsender*—a black transmitter."

"What about it?" I asked, at once alert. "What about a *Schwarzsender?"*

It was no secret that the Germans, when they retreated, had left behind several agents with clandestine radio transmitters, much like the one I had been taught to use in the OSS, to transmit information about the U.S. forces, strength, units, armor, deployment—that sort of thing—to the enemy forces facing us.

"There is one," the young Frenchman said urgently, "right here. In this house!" Again he glanced apprehensively into the dark.

"How do you know?"

"I heard it!" He poked his ear with a forefinger. "In code, in secret code, the messages are being sent. I heard them! Each half hour or forty-five minutes, I hear them."

"Do you know where the transmitter is?" I asked him. "Who is sending?"

He shook his head. "I do not know," he said regretfully. "I only hear." He frowned. "But—but I think—I think—"

"What?"

He shrugged and spread his hands. "There is a man," he said hesitantly. "On the second floor. He is—new here. He has not been here long. He—he keeps to himself. So—" Again he shrugged his shoulders and spread his hands.

"What exactly is it you hear?"

The young man glanced at his watch. "In a few minutes," he said, "you will hear it. If the *Schwarzsender* keeps to his schedule."

We stood together in the dark. Waiting. Listening.

The house was quiet.

We waited. The minutes went by.

Finally I turned to the by-now-anxious young man, about to speak, when suddenly a series of rapid, faint, irregularly spaced clicks and clacks interrupted the silence.

"*Voilà!*" the young man exclaimed with obvious relief.

The clatter went on for a short while. It did sound like code being transmitted on a hand-key set. I tried to identify it. It did not seem to be conventional Morse code, with which I was familiar. Something else. Something foreign in nature. It lasted for several seconds; then it stopped.

"You heard?!" the young man exclaimed excitedly. "You heard the *Schwarzsender*, just like I said, *n'est-ce pas?"*

I nodded. I was trying to collect my thoughts. *Something* was going on. If it *were* an illegal transmitter—and it certainly sounded as if it were, the classic rapid sending, although the operator's fist seemed unusually irregular, the short bursts of transmissions to avoid detection—it all fit. It was exactly as *I* had been taught in the OSS.

I was alone. It was against common sense as well as regulations to try to apprehend the clandestine radio operator by myself. I needed backup, and I needed it fast, not only as a security measure, but also to prevent a possible suspect from escaping by a back door as I was trying to get in the front; all good agents were taught to have at least two avenues of escape available. If I left the scene to get help, however, the operator might well be gone by the time I returned with reinforcements, having already transmitted several brief messages from that location. Again, that was standard OSS operation and would undoubtedly be true for an enemy operator as well. If the agent did leave, we would have lost him. But he was obviously there now, so now was the time.

But I did need backup.

Just then happened one of those coincidences that are so common in real life; in this case, given the circumstances, not too surprising, a weapons carrier came driving down the street. Quickly I turned to the young Frenchman. "Go to your room," I ordered hurriedly, "and stay there."

"But—" he began to object.

"Now!"

As I ran into the street, I saw him obey. Reluctantly.

The weapons carrier drew near, and I flagged it down. In the front seat next to a T5 driver sat a major. Engineers.

"Major," I said, "I need your help." I fished out my CIC identification and held it out to him. "I am a CIC agent," I continued, as he took the ID and looked at it. "I have an emergency situation. I need backup."

"Now look here," the major protested, peering closely at my ID card, "eh, Melchior. My men and I—"

"There's no time for that," I interrupted him. "How many men do you have?"

"Six," he answered automatically. "And my driver." He turned my ID over in his hand. "Look, eh, what *is* your rank?"

I held out my hand for my ID. The major gave it back to me. "My rank is confidential," I said, "but at this moment I am not outranked." It was the first time I'd used the phrase. It felt strange, a little exhilarating. The officer *did* outrank me, and then some. "Here's what I want you to do," I continued in a no-nonsense tone of voice. I pointed to the building where I'd heard the *Schwarzsender*. "I want you and your men to surround that building. Cover every exit. Stop anyone who tries to leave. Understood?"

Grimly the major nodded.

"I want your driver to come with me. I'll give you five minutes to get into position."

I looked at the officer. "Please give him your side arm."

"What?!"

"He'll need it," I said. "You can take his carbine."

Angrily the major complied. I knew I should have asked the major to accompany me, but I also knew I'd feel a helluva lot more comfortable with the T5. I was really not used to ordering majors around. And it might easily come to that, once we got the operation under way.

"Five minutes," I said. "Move out."

As the major and his men moved out to deploy around the target building, the driver and I went to the building entrance. There was no sign of the young Frenchman. Good. He'd obeyed my order. I turned to the T5.

"Now we wait," I said. "And listen."

"For what?" he asked.

"When you hear it, you'll know," I replied.

For a while we stood in silence, listening. Minutes went by, stretched almost to a quarter of an hour.

Nothing.

Were we too late? Had the operator finished, packed up, and left? By a rear door? Were we chasing a wild goose? A goose long since flown the coop? And then, there it was. A series of faint clicks and clacks in quick, irregular succession. I glanced at the T5. Wide-eyed, he was listening and peering into the dark.

"You heard?" I asked.

"Yeah," he said. "What is it? Sounds like Morse or something."

"Right. Where do you think it comes from?"

He peered into the dark. He pointed up the stairs. "Up there, someplace," he said. "Maybe—second floor?"

"That's what I make it," I said. "Let's go."

I drew my .45. The T5 had the major's gun in his hand as we cautiously started up the stairs.

I could feel my heart beat in my throat. Was there more than one agent in the room? Were we outgunned? Unlikely. Agents worked alone. Could I depend on the T5? Would I have to shoot? Kill somebody? Would I be shot at? Hit? It was a helluva time for all those questions to crowd in on me. I was committed.

The door to the apartment on the second floor looked fragile enough. With a well-aimed kick I splintered the door frame where the lock was engaged. As the door flew open and banged against the inside wall, the T5 and I burst into the room.

The man who stood in the middle of the floor was slight of build and seemed to be in his seventies. He was frozen in the process of shrugging into the suspenders of a pair of baggy pants. His expression was one of utter astonishment and shocked disbelief.

"Put your hands up!" I ordered. "High!"

At once he obeyed. With predictable result. As he stood reaching for the ceiling his pants bundled down around his bare, spindly legs. He began to tremble, staring wild-eyed at us.

My questioning quickly brought out his story. He had been a forced laborer for the Nazis. He had recently been liberated by the Americans and had returned to his native town of Nancy. The apartment belonged to his brother, who was in the hospital having been injured in a shelling. He himself, either because of the change of diet after his liberation or the unsettling times, had developed a bad case of diarrhea. Every half hour or so, he had to go—urgently. The toilet mechanism in the old building was shot, so he flushed it by pouring a pail of water into the bowl. He *had* noticed a strange clicking sound as the water ran down the old, often repaired pipes. Something stuck in them, no doubt. But he had thought nothing of it.

An old man with diarrhea and faulty plumbing, the sum of my first case! My illegal radio transmitter turned out to be a *Schwarzsender* with the runs!

The grin on the face of the T5 could not have been broader. My first inclination was *not* to face the major with the result of my emergency case, but I thought better of it. I felt I owed it to him.

To my surprise he grinned, shrugged, and commented, "You can't win 'em all!"

Win them *all?* This was my first case. So far I was O for naught. And I was sure I had done little to dispel the popular notion that CIC stood for "Christ I'm Confused."

It was little comfort that I felt I had conducted the case correctly. I had located the suspicious target; I had lined up necessary tactical support to carry out the mission; I had deployed them effectively; and I had discovered and apprehended my intended target. The fact remained that a little old man with the runs was hardly a case of earth-shaking importance.

I fervently hoped that my future cases would be of a little more significance. I need not have worried. Perhaps, had I known what my *last* case would be like, ten months and a lifetime of cases later, I might have felt better.

* * *

About a month after Nancy had been taken, Lucky Forward, the forward echelons of Third Army, moved into town. It was toward the middle of November 1944, and Iceberg Forward moved on to the little town of Chateau Salins (teutonized to Salzburgen by the Germans), which had been liberated on the tenth and where we had established our headquarters a couple of days later in the *Bürgermeisteramt*, the mayoralty.

Chateau Salins was a grim contrast to Nancy. The town had been shot up very badly, both by us, when the Germans dug in to resist our advance, and by the Germans once they were driven out. It was cold and rainy when we moved in. The town was practically demolished, and nearly all the inhabitants had left. Chateau Salins seemed like a ravaged ghost town. The troops had to use bulldozers to clear a path through the rubble in the streets; there was no power, no water, no heat. Most of the buildings had damaged roofs or no roofs at all; many of them were booby-trapped, and every window in town had been shattered. The once beautiful little church was fire-gutted and severely damaged both inside and out. When Corps moved up, the men were scattered all over town in order to find even half-adequate quarters. Iceberg Forward split into two groups; one was housed in the *Landrat* building, the district office, the other in a three-story, square stone building some distance away, with officers and men billeted all over the place—not an optimum situation. We considered ourselves lucky to have found our drab and drafty *Bürgermeisteramt*, which served our purposes just fine.

When Cleo and I rolled into Chateau Salins forty-five years later, the little town was once again whole and charming. The church, with its tall, slender tower stood proudly in the tree-dotted square, fully restored with a new blue roof, its interior neat and serene. The *Bürgermeisteramt* was once again the *hôtel de ville* and looked like a clean, newly painted version of the building in which we'd had our CIC offices. The mailbox was still in the same spot, and the windows had planter boxes with red flowers. A cheerful, peaceful picture of a grim and bleak memory.

On impulse we entered the mayoral office and showed the clerks photos of their town that had been taken during the war, including a shot of the building in which we now stood. They were greatly interested, and when they saw a photograph of the house in which the CO of XII Corps had stayed, a three-story building with part of the roof blown away and boarded-up windows, they told us that the house was still there, only a few blocks away.

It was. It had been restored and a tall, massive stone wall had been built around it. Belatedly, it seemed to us.

From Chateau Salins our CIC team moved up to a village some fifteen miles to the northeast called Morhange, which had been taken on the fourteenth. Here again we were subjected to harassing fire by the big Nazi railroad guns. Most of the damage inflicted by this shelling was done to the village itself, although one shell hit an artillery gas truck and an ammo truck, causing quite a fireworks display.

One night when we were asleep in the house we had appropriated for our quarters, one of these huge shells landed right outside. Large chunks of red-hot shrapnel shot through the house, in one room ripping a door frame from the wall, gouging the ceiling and walls with deep, ragged grooves and shearing all four legs off a wooden cot on which one of the guys was sleeping, depositing him in a heap on the floor—unhurt!

It was with a minimum of regret that shortly thereafter we leapfrogged to the little town of Saaralbe only ten miles from the German border.

Corps, which followed us to Morhange on Thanksgiving day, was less fortunate. They had put up all their road signs and directional markers but had not yet moved into the selected site, a casern on the southern outskirts of town, when the bombardment began. It quickly became obvious that enemy agents had been at work; the command post was bracketed. Some of the shells fell just short of their target; others passed directly over the CP buildings to be occupied and exploded beyond.

At 0300, however, one round landed about ten feet from a parked battalion maintenance truck. The resulting explosion hurled jagged chunks of shrapnel through the area. Several full gasoline cans on the truck burst into flames, engulfing a battalion medical truck and two one-ton trucks in a fierce conflagration. Streams of burning gasoline spewed from the tanks of the blazing vehicles and raced along the ground to become a running sheet of flame that ignited other vehicles parked in the area. In the original explosion one man, T5 Earl L. Benjamin, who had been standing guard duty, was instantly killed, and scores of others were severely wounded.

Saaralbe, the site of our new quarters, had been shot up, but not seriously damaged, although all the bridges across the Albe and the Saar rivers had been destroyed. We ensconced ourselves in a small hotel in the center of town within sight of the twin-towered, virtually unscathed church that dominated the area and hung out our CIC shield, much as a dentist newly arrived in town would hang out his sign.

Saaralbe was situated right between the Maginot and the Siegfried lines, and our territory also took in the little town of Sarre-Union, about twenty miles to the southeast, which had been captured on 3 December 1944. The following day I accompanied one of the other agents to that little town to check it out. Information had been disseminated to us that a large unit of M4 Sherman tanks was to pass through town on their way to the front. Sarre-Union was a simple, bucolic village with narrow streets and hairpin turns, many of which were more or less impassable, blocked with debris from previous fighting and shelling, and a route had been charted following the broadest and most direct streets through town. Some tight turns were, however, unavoidable. The M4 Sherman tanks are over nineteen feet long and close to ten feet wide, and in one spot they had to execute a ninety-degree turn in quite a narrow street as it reached the crest of a gentle upgrade in an undamaged part of town. I had stationed myself there with an MP to watch the passing of the tanks.

Everything went along fine. The lead tank came grinding up the grade, made an abrupt turn, knocking the corner off the building on the inside of the turn and clanking on down the straight road at full speed, leaving two tank track marks in the street. As they roared past, the next few tanks followed these marks until they became deep ruts, and each tank in turn knocked a chunk off the corner of the inside building. The massive iron and steel monsters that grated through the innocent, defenseless-looking little village, belching noxious fumes and leaving their marks of violence, seemed totally out of keeping with the surroundings.

Suddenly the MP grabbed my arm and pointed to the arching roadway between the deepening ruts just in front of us. Immediately we stopped the tank column.

There, in the middle of the road, sat a fully armed German anti-tank Tellermine of the type referred to by the Germans as the *Pilz*—the mushroom—because of its shape. More than a dozen Sherman tanks each weighing some thirty-eight tons had passed over it, a track on each side, without setting it off. None had touched it, but they had shaken the earth and compressed the unpaved roadway so deeply that the lethal mechanism had become visible.

The mine was removed, and once again, this time in safety, the tanks rumbled on to their destination of destruction.

The little incident taught me one thing: even the most innocent situation can hold a deadly surprise.

I was learning.

The house on the corner was still there when Cleo and I drove along the same route the Sherman tanks had taken. The damaged corner had obviously been repaired a long time ago, although the discolored patch still showed, but a new, deep nick had been gouged out of it, this time not by Shermans but probably by a modern-day truck no better equipped to negotiate the sharp, narrow corner than the U.S. tanks had been half a century before.

A little boy straddled a bicycle and curiously watched me taking pictures of a hole in the wall. When I told him that long, long ago another gash like that had been made in the same wall by a column of big American tanks, his eyes grew wide, and he looked at his familiar playground with newfound respect. A small bakery truck drove up, the driver tooting his horn, and was quickly surrounded by aproned housewives carrying baskets covered with colorful serviettes. A black cat scurried across the road on its own enigmatic errand; an old man came out to sit on his front steps, squinting into the sun, enjoying its warmth. A pleasant, innocent scene, far different from the one that had been played out forty-five years before.

Back at Saaralbe Cleo stood in the same spot across the river where I had been standing when I took a picture of the blackened skeleton of girders of a demolished bridge with the town's twin-peaked church in the background. She was steadying herself with her back to an old stone barn, as I had done, and shooting the same scene, except that the bridge had been rebuilt. It was fascinating to realize that in composing her shot exactly to match the one taken by me, Cleo was leaning against the same wall, and the same stones, that I must have leaned against so many years earlier.

It was one of the unexpected pleasures of the trip that we were able to find and photograph so many of the same places, many of them hardly changed. We found the little hotel we'd used as our CIC headquarters in Saaralbe, the Hotel de Commerce, and I duplicated exactly the shot I'd taken when our CIC sign hung at the entrance to the hotel. The church towers loomed in the background of both pictures, and the rooflines of the houses down the street were virtually unchanged. We went into the hotel, and I showed the proprietor the photos of his place that I'd taken during the war when the hotel had been the headquarters for American counterintelligence.

"It was a long time ago," he said.

We were working out of Saaralbe when on 16 December 1944, on Hitler's personal orders, the German army, which had been declared "without offensive capabilities," surprised us and the rest of the world by mounting a major winter offensive. In a battle of incredible violence, they achieved a lightning breakthrough, tearing a fifty-mile gap in our lines in the Ardennes and pouring men and equipment through it like water through a ruptured dam. Under the command of Field Marshall Walther Model, carrying out the audacious plan made by Field Marshall Gerd von Rundstedt, a quarter of a million men and eleven hundred tanks thrust into our territory with the bold aim of taking the Allied supply bases at Liège and Antwerp—a desperate campaign to be known as the Battle of the Bulge.

Patton's Third Army, including XII Corps, which was attacking to the west, about to enter Germany in force, was ordered to turn on its axis and attack to the north, ripping open the belly of von Rundstedt's Bulge and relieving the U.S. troops trapped inside. It was a Herculean task that only a general such as Patton, and his corps commanders such as our Gen. Manton S. Eddy, could carry out. It was one time we all fervently hoped that General Eddy's favorite saying would prove true: "Things are never half as good or half as bad as they look at first!"

As soon as we received our orders we loaded our stuff in our jeeps and trailers and set out for Luxembourg. It was the most grueling trip I ever endured. The weather was extremely severe, with temperatures below freezing. Snow and sleet and rain pelted us, making the going treacherous and arduous. The narrow, icy roads were clogged with an enormous volume of traffic: plodding infantry, armor, and supply trucks. A freezing fog lay like a clammy shroud over everything as we snailed through forests of snow-laden trees and across wind- and sleet-swept fields. We were freezing in our open jeeps. My knees were, I thought, as cold as the ass of a brass monkey sitting on the North Pole. I could have sworn that if I'd spilled some of the coffee I was sipping, it would have instantly frozen.

After hours and hours of driving we finally reached the little town of Mondorf right on the border between France and Luxembourg. Corps fulfilled its mission—incredibly—changing its direction of advance by ninety degrees, moving eighty thousand men with their equipment and supplies and eleven thousand vehicles and armor in four days and halting the German breakthrough north of Luxembourg city, an operation that Chief of Staff Gen. George C. Marshall called "a brilliant military achievement."

Upon reaching Mondorf, we turned into the first place that looked halfway possible for our purposes, some sort of official building, and began to thaw out. It was not long before we had our first customer.

Two MPs brought into our office a man in a sorry state—wet, bedraggled, and seemingly near exhaustion. There had been alerts that the Germans were dropping parachutist saboteurs behind our lines to create havoc among the relief troops, already fighting under most trying circumstances. Parachutes had, in fact, been observed in the area. The MPs had picked up the man wandering on the road. He claimed he was a Frenchman, but he had no papers at all. Next stop, the CIC.

There was no doubt that the man was French. Tears of joy ran freely down his mud-caked cheeks, and he kept pumping our hands and exclaiming, *"Ah, c'est rigolo ça! Les Americains!"*—Parisian slang meaning something like, "That's a scream! Americans!" He was dirty, disheveled, and scantily clad against the cold in cheap, patched work clothes. Between extravagant exclamations of delight at his success, he told us that he was a French slave worker with two years of backbreaking toil in a Nazi arms factory behind him. He'd escaped, he said, and for two nights and a day he'd run, crept, and stumbled toward his beloved France and the American liberators. And now he'd made it! His story, the method of escape, and the route he said he'd traveled checked against the maps and our terrain information; it all sounded perfectly plausible. And yet . . .

There *were* those reports of parachutists being dropped. And some of them were French.

I knew a little about parachute jumping, since I'd made several jumps myself. I took a look at the man's neck where the risers of the parachute sometimes slapped against the skin with the force of a whip when the chute was pulled out, but there were no telltale marks. I had him remove his shirt and looked closely at his shoulders where the harness jolt might raise red welts as the chute opened, but again there was nothing to see. The man seemed to be on the level—although harness marks and neck slaps *could* be avoided by the use of padding, easily discarded after landing. There was one last check to be made. I noticed that the man wore heavy, low-cut shoes, muddy and scuffed, and sometimes when jumping in such shoes, especially at night where landing is more difficult . . .

"Take off your shoes and socks," I ordered the Frenchman.

Slowly he pulled his feet out of the muddy shoes and peeled off his soggy socks.

I took one look.

"What specific acts of sabotage were you to carry out?" I asked the man sharply. "What were your orders? Were you to operate alone? Link up? Where did you hide your chute?" I shot the questions at him.

The man sat staring at his feet. He said nothing. There was nothing to be said. On each dirty foot and ankle were the clean outlines of a double-wrapped recently discarded bandage, just the kind of bandage a parachutist might use to support his feet when jumping, wearing low-cut shoes instead of giveaway boots, to avoid twisting an ankle in a night drop!

German thoroughness. Everything had been perfect, but the man had been betrayed by that one small overlooked detail. Before boarding the plane the saboteur had literally wallowed in mud to look the part he was to play even if he were picked up almost immediately after landing, which in fact had been the case. But as he discarded his chute and padding and bandages in the dark, he forgot to smear dirt on his feet where they had been protected by the supportive bindings.

With the signature of the parachutists literally stamped upon him, the man readily confessed to having been dropped behind our lines with the purpose of creating as much damage as possible before he journeyed south to take over underground activities in Marseilles.

* * *

I knew we had moved our CIC office into the first possible quarters we came to in Mondorf, to get in out of the cold, but I had forgotten just *how* eager we had been. Cleo and I had barely crossed the border when we made a left turn, and there was the building, looking nearly exactly as it had when it had become a welcome haven for our CIC team.

The place was now a fire station, but the square stone pillars of the broad gateway to the courtyard and the little square tower on top of the building were still there, as was the coat-of-arms crest shaped like the Chevrolet emblem (the center being the weapons shield) emblazoned in bas relief high on the building facade. Snow had covered the ground when I took some snapshots of one of my teammates; that was the only real difference, and the coat-of-arms insignia, which had been in color in 1944, was now painted the color of the building.

Our CIC team stayed in Mondorf only a couple of days before moving on to Luxembourg city into comfortable quarters in an apartment building. Iceberg Forward command post was handsomely and efficiently established in a large undamaged three-story concrete building big enough to accommodate the entire CP under one roof, a luxury not often available. The building belonged to an *ecole des jeunes filles*, a school for young girls, that, to the disappointment of many a GI, had suspended operation because of the war.

We were to stay in Luxembourg for the longest time in any town during the war while the Ardennes breakthrough was entirely contained and repulsed and the campaign put back on track. We didn't mind. The Luxembourgers were friendly and outgoing, and we spent Christmas in their city.

From here we worked cases in dozens of little towns throughout the tiny Grand Duchy of Luxembourg, and it was here that I was wounded by perhaps the strangest and most unusual Nazi weapon developed during the war.

CHAPTER 2

The city of Luxembourg was at that time rocked by occasional enormous, unpredictable, and irregular explosions, which struck the city in the most unexpected places. Arguments raged as to what they could be. They couldn't be bombs dropped by a plane—a plane couldn't fly high enough to remain undetected. Artillery fire was ruled out; there was no enemy artillery of sufficient range in place. Not even a railroad gun with the greatest range known could account for the explosions. Some speculated that the Nazis had developed some sort of major rocket or modified artillery shell. Others were of the opinion that the mysterious explosions were the work of saboteurs or were delayed time bombs planted by the Nazis before they left—such as they had done at Saint-Avold, when earlier in the month, on Saturday, 3 December 1944, heavy time bombs went off in five buildings, killing four officers and eighteen soldiers; seventeen more were missing and scores injured, all belonging to the 633d Antiaircraft Artillery (Automatic Weapon) Battalion. These time bombs had been ticking away for over a week after having been left behind in concealment by the retreating Germans.

One evening, shortly after we had established ourselves in the city, a tremendous explosion came from the area of the nearby main railroad station. Agent Flanagan and I went to take a look and possibly find out if it was indeed sabotage. If so, the ball was in our court.

We located the area, and once again the target made no sense whatsoever. The explosion had utterly destroyed an old, empty roundhouse and a few surrounding shacks in the marshaling yard, most certainly not the targets of a saboteur.

A few MPs were around to keep curious soldiers and civilians from wandering into the area and to see that no one touched the live, severed power lines.

Flanagan and I looked over the demolished roundhouse and examined the crater gouged out of the ground by the whatever-it-was, then we approached one of the MPs. Flanagan was a rather large, somewhat pompous person, and with great dignity he asked the MP, "And what exactly are these explosions like, soldier?"

At that very instant an explosion behind a row of railroad cars in the yard rocked the entire area, lit up the sky with a lightning flash, splintered the railroad cars, and threw us all to the ground, where we were showered with flying debris.

When it was over, Flanagan got up, brushed himself off, and turned to the dazed MP. "Thank you very much!" was his unruffled remark.

Not until after the war did I learn what these mysterious and destructive explosions were. We had been on the receiving end of the latest—and last—of Hitler's *Vergeltungswaffen*, his weapons of vengeance; not the V-1 buzz bomb or the V-2 rocket, both of which rained a terror of destruction on London, but the V-3!

The Germans had invented a weapon straight out of science fiction: the HDP Project. It was a weapon that defied imagination, one of the most extraordinary weapons of World War II, a colossal gun with a barrel 492 feet long, the length of a football field and a half! This giant gun had many names: HDP or *Hochdruchpumpe*, high-pressure pump; *Fleisiges Lieschen*, Busy Lizzie; the *Gleichdruchrohr*, the straight-pressure barrel; the *Mehrfachkammer-Geschütz*, the multiple-chamber gun; the London gun; the V-3; and most popularly, the *Tausendfüssler*, the Millipede.

Millipede was an apt name for the gun, because along the huge main barrel many pairs of short barrels protruded like the legs of a millipede. Each of these lateral barrels held explosive charges that went off *behind* the enormous projectile as it traveled the length of the main barrel, giving it a velocity that made it capable of reaching a target over a hundred miles away.

A prototype was built at Misdroy on Wollin Island on the Baltic Sea coast of Germany, using the Baltic as its test shooting grounds, and at Mimoyesque south of Calais in France two operational batteries, each of twenty-five guns, were built into a hillside, their fixed-trajectory barrels aimed at London and at each of the Channel coast ports where the invasion fleet, supplies, and troops were marshaling.

Although the Allies, despite extensive aerial photographic missions and intelligence operations, did not know the true nature of the construction taking place at Mimoyesque, the installations were bombed several times, the last time on 21 May 1944, only two weeks before D Day, by forty B-17 bombers that dropped 189 one-thousand-pound bombs on the area. Damage was done, but due to the extraordinary protection of the batteries, it was relatively minor. Although one of the batteries was put out of commission, the other was ready to go operational, with enough firepower to destroy the entire invasion fleet buildup—and London.

Blueprints, photographs, firing records, and other documentation chronicling the development and deployment of the guns exist at the German *Militarärchiv, Bundesarchiv* in Freiburg, Germany, and in the Imperial War Museum in London, including a test-firing report dated, Misdroy, 19 December 1944: "19 rounds fired. No mishap with device occurred. 60% of the projectiles flew well."

The Tausendfüssler was one of Adolf Hitler's favorite projects. In January of 1944 he had ordered Misdroy and Mimoyesque to proceed to completion "with all vigor and under all circumstances." In May of 1944, less than a month before D Day, there was an accident with the prototype gun at Misdroy, and on 16 May 1944, the Führer issued a flowery secret directive that read in part, "The long-range bombardment of England will commence in the beginning of June. . . . It will open like a thunderclap by night with a sudden long-range artillery attack." The Misdroy gun was rebuilt after the May 1944 accident, but too late to provide the necessary technical information for the batteries at Mimoyesque to go operational and prevent the invasion on 6 June.

In September 1944, after the Allies had landed in Normandy, the Millipede installation at Mimoyesque was overrun by elements of the Canadian First Army without the batteries having fired a single projectile. And in May of 1945, after exhaustive examination and documentation, the incredible Tausendfüssler batteries were blown up. Today, only half-destroyed tunnel entrances leading to the installation deep in the bowels of the mountain remain. The gigantic guns, which came within days of changing history, exist only as a memory and a collection of documents, charts, and reports, and strange, astonishing photographs.

However, two smaller versions of the Millipede guns were brought into action against U.S. forces during the Battle of the Bulge. One of these guns, which had a barrel "only" 197 feet long, was employed against Antwerp, the other against Luxembourg city. Projectiles from this mini-Millipede gun firing from an emplacement on a hillside near Hermeskeil inside Germany, a distance of some sixty kilometers as the missile flies, accounted for the mystifying explosions we were trying to figure out, but never did. Both these guns were destroyed by the Germans when they were in danger of being overrun by the Allies.

Before that happened, one day in December in Luxembourg city, I was walking down a street, when there was another tremendous explosion. I looked up and saw the tower of a church I was passing disintegrating in a thunderous blast. I leaped for cover, but not fast enough. A jagged piece of masonry plummeting to the ground hit a glancing blow to my right hand, with which I was shielding my face, ripping a two-inch cut into the back of it.

At my quarters I cleaned the wound, sprinkled some sulpha powder in it, put a field bandage on it, and thought nothing further of it. Had I gone to Corps Aid Station to see "Doc" Stokes, Capt. Robert Stokes, Assistant Surgeon at Corps Medical Detachment, two things would have happened: one, I would not have the faint scar still to be seen on the back of my hand, and two, I would have been awarded the Purple Heart.

There were two reasons I did not put in for that medal. First, my wound was a minor one, and second, and probably more important, because of a story that was being told gleefully at Iceberg Forward. It seemed that a staff officer, a "bird" colonel, was traveling in his jeep down a country road with his driver, when a single low-flying plane came streaking toward them. Thinking he was about to be strafed, the officer screamed for the driver to stop, flung himself from the vehicle before it had come to a complete halt, and tumbled down into a deep ditch at the bottom of which stood a barbed-wire fence. This precipitous maneuver put the rear of the colonel's anatomy in painful contact with the barbed wire, ripping open the colonel's pants and leaving an awkward red scratch. Meanwhile, the driver in the jeep cheerfully waved at the friendly plane, which wigwagged its wings at him as it flew over!

The intrepid, quick-acting officer applied for a Purple Heart—and got it. I always wondered how he felt wearing that medal on his chest when he met a soldier who had lost an arm or a leg, or both? I know how I would have felt had I put in for a medal for my superficial wound.

It would have been the same.

One of the missions to which I had been assigned while in Luxembourg was quite unusual. It was described in my team's activity report to MIS ETOUSA in this way:

> IV. Relations with Allied Agencies. (Par. 2, b)
>
> During Feb. 1944 agents Arnstein and Melchior in their capacity of French speaking, were used as liaison between Combat Team Darling and a Belgian unit under the command of Commandant Michet, located in Grevenmacher, Luxembourg.
>
> The assignment lasted one week.

Terse, to the point—and with no hint of the events that took place during that memorable week.

The name of the little town was Grevenmacher, but the GIs had another name for it—Booby Trap Town. And rightfully so. It was undoubtedly the most mined and booby-trapped town in all of Luxembourg. The town is located right on the banks of the Moselle River, with the Germans entrenched immediately across the waters. It had been booby-trapped by the Germans when they originally retreated before our advance, then by us when we drew back from the onslaught of the Bulge, and then again by the Germans as we retook the town. Grevenmacher was by now one giant booby trap, and no one had any maps indicating where the mines and traps were to be found. The town had been totally evacuated and was off limits to soldiers and civilians alike.

The area was held by two companies of Belgian troops under the command of a very friendly major, and it was because I spoke French that I, along with Felix Arnstein, had been assigned as liaison between the Belgians and the American unit to which they were attached.

We lived a comfortable life in the officers' quarters and—other armies, other customs—we even had a "footman" to take care of our chores. We did not complain. There were only two streets in town that had been cleared of mines and traps; one was the continuation of the road that led into town, the other was the street on which stood the four houses that served as our quarters. The Belgians had an elaborate system of guard posts along the river, to which access had been cleared, but the rest of the town was dead man's territory. It is a miracle that during the week I was there only five Belgian soldiers and one American were blown up; one German, who had ventured across the river, perhaps as a member of a reconnaissance patrol, also had run into a booby trap—ironically, a German one. It was an eerie feeling during the night to hear traps explode somewhere in town. Roaming livestock, mostly pigs, would set them off. The town was full of dead animals that had blundered into the traps set to kill men, and the presence of all those carcasses was beginning to be felt. But no one volunteered to go out and dispose of them. The town itself was dreadfully destroyed, and among the debris lurked hundreds of evil surprises.

Yet, even with this knowledge, we were bored enough, our urge to explore and investigate gung-ho enough, and our belief in our own indestructibility strong enough that every day we went out into town to find and disarm these infernal devices.

I knew a little about booby traps—enough that I should have known better. In addition to what I had learned in the OSS and at Camp Ritchie, I had attended a special course in booby traps at Shrivenham in England while I was waiting for D Day. Here we learned about and experimented with all types of booby traps. The damned things could be set off in any number of ways: push, pull, pressure, release, and electrically, and any combination thereof. The number of varieties was limited only by the imagination of the soldier who set the trap.

At Shrivenham we learned how to build the traps and how best to conceal them. As a graduation exercise we were given enough material to construct ten to twelve traps, with cherry bombs substituted for the high explosives we would use in the field. These fireworks bombs made a helluva noise and *could* do severe damage if you got close enough. We were given a stretch of land a hundred feet long that incorporated all sorts of obstacles and told to booby-trap the area, concealing our traps as best we could. When finished we were taken to a different strip of land and told to find and disarm the traps set there by someone else, while he tried to find and disarm ours. I was lucky, I set off only a couple of the traps and suffered no major damage. One of my fellow students however, did not fare that well; a cherry bomb went off inches from his face as he was peering closely at the mechanism, and he was quite badly burned.

We came away from Shrivenham convinced of only one thing: there is no sure way of knowing what will set off a booby trap. You never know *which* kind of trigger you are dealing with until the damned thing blows up in your face!

Yet here in Grevenmacher, AKA Booby Trap Town, we went out

of our way to look for these treacherous and deadly mechanisms. Why? They presented a challenge, and challenges are to be met, aren't they? Perhaps it was because we were young, and the young, in their arrogance, do not visualize their own demise. And, of course, it wasn't only curiosity and the thirst for adventure that made us wander around town in harm's way; we did have to make certain that no activities of CIC interest took place.

We did have some rather hair-raising experiences, and saw some unusual sights. One house we passed had the entire front wall blasted away; in the beautifully furnished room stood a big cupboard with fine china and crystal, all without a scratch or a crack, but stuck through the glass pane on one of the doors was a straw, punched there by the force of the explosion, like a pencil jammed through a sheet of paper! In another house we entered we found no less than five cleverly concealed traps. One of them was placed in a pot-bellied stove, set to go off if anyone touched the door or probed it for a trap. We discovered it by removing the top rings of the stove, then cut the detonating wire.

At yet another house we entered the kitchen through a window and carefully made our way to the door of the living room. After minutely examining it, we pushed it open—and stared at a long-dead German soldier, who had been careless in opening a desk drawer. He was lying on his back on the floor, greeting us with a mold-green smile and a yellowed parchment hand raised in a macabre "Heil Hitler!" salute.

The most sophisticated booby trap we found and disarmed also involved a desk—and a document marked GEHEIM (SECRET). The document was lying in full view on a desktop among other papers, all of them partly covered with plaster dust and debris from the damaged ceiling. Our immediate inclination was to pick up the sheet of paper, but we did not. Had we done so, I'd not be sitting here recounting the incident. We decided to "smell out" the place first. We carefully looked over the area without touching anything, and on the floor, mixed in with the dust and dirt, were traces of fresh sawdust. It saved our lives.

The trap was clever indeed. The use of a fake SECRET document, a marking almost guaranteed to make anyone pick it up, was an irresistible lure. And how could a single piece of paper lying on a desktop be booby-trapped? This is how: A thin wire had been taped to the back of the document. This wire ran down through a hole drilled in the desktop (hence the sawdust!), which had been lined with another wire. These two wires were connected to a battery trigger and a charge of high explosives concealed in the desk drawer beneath the hole. If the document was moved, the wires would make contact and complete the circuit—and the charge would explode. The beauty was, if anyone became suspicious and opened the drawer to see what was what, the same thing would happen. We were quite impressed with that one. It was fully on a par with another one I'd encountered earlier.

In this case a dead German officer was seen lying in a field, a holstered Luger pistol visible on his hip. The German Luger was a favorite souvenir. But such tempting treasures were often booby-trapped, so caution was the word. Close by was a burned-out German staff car with a rope hanging out the back, and near the body was an abandoned foxhole. The clever treasure hunter would take the rope, carefully tie it to the foot of the cadaver, string it to the foxhole, and jump in for protection before yanking on the corpse.

It was all very clever, except the dead German was not booby-trapped. The foxhole was.

Outside, at a main cross street, we found eight German S-mines called "Bouncing Bettys," an antipersonnel mine that when stepped on would explode five to six feet into the air and splatter the surrounding area to a radius of several hundred feet with a few hundred steel balls with enough force to penetrate a steel helmet.

A few houses down the street was a blackened, oily spot where a Belgian sergeant had run into one of the most devilish traps I've ever seen—and met a gruesome death. The flagstones of the sidewalk by the house were uneven, and the corner of one of them unobtrusively stuck up about half an inch, just where a drain pipe ran down the wall of the house. Plastic high explosives packed around a battery-operated triggering device had been stuffed up the bottom of this pipe and the opening sealed. From above, the pipe had been filled with gasoline. When pressure was applied to the uneven stone, contact was made and the trap exploded. When he passed by the house, the sergeant had stepped on the trigger flagstone; he had been showered with flaming gasoline as the pipe exploded. The ground was still black and littered with the partly burned bits of clothing the man had managed to tear off before he succumbed to the searing burns. His charred rifle stood perched crazily with the muzzle stuck into the scorched earth of a flower bed.

I was lucky on my trips through "Booby Trap Town," but I was even more lucky outside town. It was often necessary for us to drive the six to seven miles to the next town to contact our headquarters, and we usually used the highway. There was, however, a smaller road, which was about two miles shorter. Once, when a situation called for speed, I decided to take this shorter route and subsequently cut the driving time by several minutes. After that I often used this shortcut.

One day I was on my way back from headquarters, using the shortcut, when I heard a tremendous explosion in the distance in front of me. I drove on slowly until I saw an engineer who waved me to a stop. I asked him what was up, and he told me they were blowing up mines they had just dug out of the road. So far they'd found and removed twenty-seven mines. Most of them had been close to the road shoulders, and I always drove in the middle of the road. But in two places a string of three mines had been placed across the road. And I had driven that road not once but several times. My wheels must have passed right between the mines.

After my stint with the Belgians I returned to Luxembourg city, where a man contacted me with a fascinating tale to tell. He was an engineer, he said, who had been forced to work for the Nazis on the formidable Siegfried line. Built along the German frontier in the 1930s, the Siegfried line was a heavily fortified line of tank trap ditches, rows of antitank concrete "dragons' teeth," and other obstacles, with fortifications ranging from pillboxes to extensive, four-level underground strongholds with tunnel connections to outlying bunkers, an impressive obstacle to our advance that Corps would be faced with having to overcome within a short while, a task it was conceded would be both difficult and costly.

The man told me that he had made a secret copy of the German map showing in detail the stretch of the line on which he had been working, a section covering the approach to the town of Bitburg. He had been afraid to carry this map on his person and had hidden it in his house in Hinkel, a small village right on the Moselle River. He wanted us to have this map, but we would have to go get it; he could not. Hinkel was "off limits" to everyone. The German positions were right across the river, and the village had been evacuated.

A detailed map of the Siegfried line fortifications made by an engineer who had actually worked on the line with *Organisation Todt*, the Nazi construction organization in charge of the fortifications, would—of course—be most helpful to have, both in the planning and the assault stages of an operation to breach the line. I found out from the man where in Hinkel he lived and where in the house he had hidden the map.

And I was off. There was no time to waste. I knew that Corps troops already were probing the line; if they were to benefit from the map, they needed it *now*.

Hinkel was about an hour's drive away. It was bitterly cold, and there was snow on the ground. It did not make the going any easier.

I was nearing the village when I was stopped at a roadblock. A GI told me that the village was off limits. I showed him my CIC credentials and told him I had a job to do. He shrugged and said, "Suit yourself, sir. The place is under enemy observation."

It was a dilemma. If I waited till dark, I'd have a helluva time finding my way around, and I certainly couldn't look out for any traps, booby or otherwise. The village was badly shot up, and it would be all but impossible to wend my way through the ruins and rubble from the rear of town and end up in the right spot. And if I went in while it was broad daylight, I'd be an easy target. I decided to compromise. It was late in the day; dusk was around the corner. I would wait.

Half an hour later it was beginning to grow gray, and I drove toward the village of Hinkel. I was driving through a little patch of woods just before the road dipped down toward the river and the village, when I slowed my jeep to a halt. There on a tree before me a big sign had been tacked up. The two large eyes were crudely drawn, but the message was clear enough: Beware! The enemy is watching you!

Cautiously I drove to the edge of the wood and stopped the jeep. Before me lay the little village of Hinkel and the Moselle River. I could clearly see the opposite bank, enemy territory. It seemed merely a stone's throw away.

I dismounted. The road continued down to the river. The engineer's house was on the street running right along the river's edge in full view of the other side, where I could make out a strip of grassland and then a stand of small trees and bushes. If the enemy was there, that's where he'd be, in the woods.

Hugging the shadows of the badly damaged houses I made my way down to the riverbank street. I'd established that the house I wanted was about a dozen houses to my right. All was quiet. There was not a sound. No movement. I slid around the corner.

I began a crouched, broken run toward the house, darting from cover to cover—a doorway, a pile of rubble, a disabled vehicle. There was no sound from the enemy side. Perhaps it was already too dark for them to see. Or perhaps they weren't looking.

I was making it. I estimated I was better than halfway to the house, and so far nothing had happened. I broke cover to sprint the next leg—and they opened up. The lethal staccato sound of a machine gun firing its short, jerky bursts of death rent the evening silence. I was not aware of it, but I probably faltered in my headlong rush before I dove for cover behind a pile of rubble.

I could not stay there long. The cover was scant. Sooner or later they'd get to me. At a lull in the firing, I broke cover and made for a deep doorway I could see a little farther on. I ran as fast as I could.

I was only a few feet from the doorway when the machine gun opened up again. I leaped for the door as the bullets probed for me.

I knew that if I turned my head I would be able to see the muzzle flashes from the German machine gun. I did not look. I had a fleeting thought that it would establish a link between us, a link I did not want. Somehow, I felt that if I could not see the gun, it wasn't there, at least not specifically for me.

When I reached the doorway it was not as sheltered as I'd thought. I pressed against the wall, wanting to melt into it as the bullets searched for me. I'd managed a quick glance down the darkening street as I streaked for the doorway, and I thought I'd seen the house that was my goal, two houses farther on.

The firing stopped. Was it getting too dark for them? Two houses. If I were right. Only two houses. I felt unprotected where I was. I'd chance it. I'd come this far for the damned map. I wanted it. It was important. I broke cover.

Almost at once the firing resumed.

I raced along the snow-covered street, fearful of losing my footing. Curiously, I had no thought of getting hit. I remember being intrigued by the different sounds the bullets made as they slammed into different textures beside me. Plastered walls, naked stone, wooden fence—each had a distinctive sound.

And there it was, just as it had been described to me. I flung myself through the shell-damaged doorway. I was safe.

Slowly, cautiously, I made my way to the kitchen. The place was pitch dark, and I used the flashlight I had brought. There was the big cupboard my informant had described to me. I examined it. There was only an inch or so between the top of it and the ceiling. It was in that space the map had been hidden.

I pulled a chair over to the cupboard, found a broom, and raked the handle across the cupboard top.

Nothing.

Again I tried. And again, scraping the shaft vigorously across the wooden boards on top.

Nothing.

I suddenly felt very tired. Was I in the wrong house? Possibly. Didn't every house have a big cupboard in the kitchen? I flashed my light around the room. No. Everything was as the engineer had described it to me, down to the color of the kitchen-window curtains.

I tried again. I noticed that the top of the cupboard seemed like a lid that could be lifted off. I removed whatever dishes and pots and pans that were left on the shelves and struggled to pry the top section off. It would not budge. It must have been glued down. I tried to overturn the whole cupboard, but there was not enough room for it to tilt.

There seemed to be no way I could get to the top.

I looked around.

There was a hole in the back wall where the sink had been, apparently caused by a shell exploding outside. The sink was ruined; broken pipes stuck up out of the rubble. I walked over to it.

I was able to wrench loose a section of pipe about a foot and a half long. With it I knocked out the top two shelves in the cupboard. Then I went to work on the boards that formed the top of the cupboard itself. I poked and stabbed; I pounded and hacked at the hard wood. It took time, but presently I had made enough of a hole to insert my pipe and try to pry the boards loose. When I was able to get my hands into the opening I grabbed the wood, and with all the force I could muster I fought to break the boards.

Suddenly they gave way, almost sending me sprawling. I pulled the boards down—and there was the map, stuck to the dirty, grimy top boards made sticky by months of cooking moisture and grease. Eagerly I opened the map and shined my flashlight on it. It was everything I'd hoped it would be.

It was totally dark outside by now. I thought I could return to my jeep the way I'd come, rather than—as I had planned—taking the risk of negotiating the ruins and rubble of the village out of sight of the enemy, not knowing what disagreeable surprises might lie in wait.

Slowly I made my way out the front door. I waited, standing in the open. Nothing happened.

I could see clearly only a few yards in front of me. I felt confident that the enemy across the river would not be able to see me, to distinguish me from the black shadows and pools of utter darkness—if I did not move fast. Slowly I began to inch my way back. It seemed to take a lifetime, but I finally reached the corner, turned up the road to the woods, and reached my jeep.

The ride back to Luxembourg city didn't seem nearly as cold as it had before. Perhaps the map resting snugly inside my shirt kept me warm.

On 10/11 February 1945 Corps troops smashed their way through the Siegfried line on their way to Bitburg.

When Cleo and I visited Luxembourg city, it was once again a thriving, bustling metropolis with a distinct international flavor, and no signs of the damage suffered during the war. We checked into the modern and luxurious Hotel International in the hills of the northern outskirts of the city and enjoyed our complimentary champagne—markedly different from my first visit forty-five years earlier.

We stopped by the railroad yards, but it was impossible to pinpoint where the Millipede rounds had landed. Neither did I find the "church that fell on me," nor the apartment building where we had established our CIC headquarters.

When I had been in Luxembourg city during the war, I had found a snapshot left behind by the Germans showing a German officer standing on one of the many bridges that span the deep valley of the Alzette River, which cuts the city in two. For the fun of it I had had a duplicate photograph taken of me in the same spot by one of my CIC teammates, and now Cleo would take another one of me, on the same bridge, in the same spot. As I stood gazing down into the water below, I remembered yet another case in which I was involved while working as a CIC agent in Luxembourg, a case that earned my team a unit citation.

CHAPTER 3

Iceberg Forward had moved from Luxembourg city to the town of Larochette, also called Fels, in the central part of Luxembourg, on 24 February 1945, and we had moved on to Echternach, hard on the German border. The Ardennes breakthrough had been repulsed, and Corps troops were advancing into Germany, having crossed the rivers Nims and Prüm near Bitburg. Beyond Bitburg another river, the Kyll, badly swollen from the snow and rain, presented a further obstacle that could prove serious. PI (Photo Intelligence) had shown that there were no bridges left intact along the stretch of the river where Corps troops had to cross. The crossing would have to be made without the cover and support of armor unless a way could be found to get that armor across. PI was unable to provide further guidance, because what was needed in this instance was detailed knowledge of the condition of the riverbanks and the consistency of the river bottom, whether sand or rock, boulders or mud; the depth of the water in specific places; and the strength of the current under both normal and swollen conditions. Corps was faced with having to send out reconnaissance patrols to find these answers. Locations needed to be found where the banks were not too steep, the water not too deep, and the bottom firm enough to support armor, so that serviceable fords could be mapped. It would be a dangerous undertaking, probably with considerable loss of life, if success could be achieved at all.

Normally Photo Intelligence could come up with answers ranging from an assessment of the battle readiness of an entire town to the relief of a single infantry unit pinned down by enemy fire. In this case, however, the PI boys could supply only partial answers about the condition of the Kyll River and how to accomplish a crossing with minimum casualties, because those answers lay below the surface, inaccessible to their cameras. But there *had* to be a way, I thought, to get the answers other than using risky reconnaissance patrols.

When I was a boy back in school in Denmark and studying Swedish, I read a story called *"Där Finns Alltid en Tredje Utväg,"* "There Is Always a Third Way Out." If you are in an either-or situation where neither alternative would work, look for that third way out. I've done that all my life. In the story, which takes place in Lapland, little Svante is on his way home driving a horse-drawn sled loaded with a heavy wooden tub when he is pursued by a pack of hungry wolves. The horse cannot outrun the wolves while pulling the sled with Svante and the heavy tub, and Svante cannot fight the wolves when they catch up. It is an either-or situation: either Svante tries to outrun the wolves, or he tries to fight them. He is a loser either way. But there is that third way out: Svante cuts loose the horse so he can outrun the wolves, and he himself crawls under the heavy tub, safe from the wolves outside, until help arrives when his family is alerted by the horse coming home alone.

Svante's third way out was the tub. Where could *I* find a tub?

I had an idea. My father had owned a hunting estate in Germany before the SS confiscated it in 1939 when the war broke out. On this estate was a good-sized lake, where my father occasionally held a duck hunt. As a boy I spent my vacations there, and I had a *Faltboot* on the lake, a collapsible kayak that could be folded to carry as a backpack. During those duck hunts I'd paddle around the reeds along the shores acting like a hunting dog. As a result I knew every inch of that lake. And that was the answer—my third way out.

How to collect some good, applicable, and detailed information about conditions of the Kyll? We couldn't very well go over every foot of twenty-five miles of river ourselves. But who would know more about the river than the sports fishermen who had walked along its banks and stood in the middle of the stream, searching for the places richest with trout?

We contacted a fishermen's club in Luxembourg city, and for two days we interrogated every fisherman we could locate who had ever fished in the Kyll. We gathered a wealth of information and checked each report against the others. Finally we had a clear and detailed picture of a twenty-five-mile stretch of the river, including information about the width and depth, yard for yard, the bottom, the fords, and the banks.

A couple of days after our report had been handed in to G-2 (Military Intelligence), Corps troops crossed the Kyll River at the stretch described by us, and we knew the thrill of having substantially contributed to the success of our unit mission. We also earned a commendation from the G-2 on "a job, timely and well done!"

In the field, CIC often worked with other intelligence disciplines, and the Kyll River case is representative of such cooperation, with each discipline supplying part of the whole answer: in this case CIC the interrogation skills, and PI the expertise of that highly specialized function.

PIs, photo interpreters, were trained at military intelligence training camps (MITCs) maintained for the training of intelligence personnel for both the Navy and the Army. One of these was MITC Camp Ritchie in the Blue Ridge Mountains of Maryland. Here, under the expert guidance of the chief of training, Col. Shipley Thomas, officers and men for IPW (Interrogation of Prisoners of War), OB (Order of Battle), MII (Military Intelligence Interpretation), CIC, and PI received their special education and training. This was the MITC I attended, and among the intelligence disciplines I learned was PI.

The PI-to-be, already an expert in one or more fields such as military installations and equipment, industrial plants, railroad centers, vegetation, radio operation, engineering, and many others useful in PI work, would here become familiar with the different types of aerial photographs to be interpreted: high- and low-altitude photos; verticals and obliques, depending on the optical axis of the camera at the time of exposure; composites taken with a multi-lens camera and consisting of a vertical photo surrounded by four transformed obliques; controlled and uncontrolled mosaics, a series of overlapping verticals; and pinpoints, strips, and photomaps.

He would learn photographic laboratory techniques, and he would be taught to decipher and use the marginal information appearing on each photo, which showed negative serial number, time and place of exposure, altitude, camera focal length, and deviation from the vertical. Most important of all, he would practice stereovision.

Using a highly accurate stereoscopic device, the PI viewed a pair of overlapping verticals called a stereopair. Objects that appear flat on each single photo stand out in sharp, magnified, three-dimensional detail. Because the PI knows the scale of the vertical photo, based on the altitude at which it was taken and the focal length of the camera, the exact height of objects on the ground can be measured with astonishing accuracy. The steepness of hills and whether equipment can negotiate them, camouflaged buildings, relative sight lines, and many other undetectable secrets of the single picture are revealed through stereovision. Seasoned PIs were often able to develop the ability to do this by simply looking at the stereopair, without the use of a stereoscopic device.

Upon graduation the PI was assigned to a PI team, usually consisting of one officer and three noncoms with a special PI truck as organic transportation. This 2½-ton vehicle was a rolling photographic laboratory fully equipped to develop, print, and interpret aerial photos made into stereopairs, with a blacked-out darkroom, electric lights, running water, and all stereoscopic instrumentation.

Photo Intelligence became one of the most widely employed sources of information in military conflict and is officially credited with obtaining 90 percent of our military intelligence in World War II. No important defensive or offensive action was taken on land, sea, or in the air without the trail first being blazed by PIs. These PIs constituted in effect a corps of exceptionally efficient secret agents who covered infinitely greater areas of any enemy territory or endeavors than was ever before possible.

The first aerial photograph for military intelligence purposes was snapped in 1861 by the U.S. Army Balloon Corps. The camera was installed on a special kite. A plane was used for the first time by Wilbur Wright in 1909, and World War I saw the beginning of modern Photo Intelligence when hand-held cameras were employed to take pictures of enemy installations as a by-product of the Observation Squadron. And soon photo interpreting made Mata Hari obsolete: the famous "Big Bertha," the gigantic German gun that during the summer of 1918 was lobbing shells into Paris from ninety miles away, was located by PI.

The general area where the gun was concealed had been deduced by calculating the trajectory of the projectiles, but reconnaissance planes could spot no signs of activity in that area, and the gun's exact location remained a mystery. Finally a PI examining aerial photographs of the area discovered a line of footprints leading across a newly plowed field and disappearing into a dense patch of trees. Comparing photos taken at various times, he calculated the time these footprints were made. Knowing Big Bertha's firing schedule and the general activity in the area, he concluded that the footprints led to the big gun's hiding place.

He was right—and Big Bertha was quickly put out of commission.

When World War II broke out, the U.S. armed forces were ready with complete wings of the Air Force devoted to aerial photography, with mapping units, bomb damage recording, and last but not least, the photo interpreters. One of the most important PI assignments in London was the interpretation of photos of Hitler's Channel coast fortifications for the preinvasion aerial bombardment and collection of information about the installations for the invasion commanders. It was here the PIs worked out an ingenious three-step ruse. At an appointed hour three reconnaissance planes flew over the Nazi positions a few minutes apart, taking pictures. When they returned, the photos they had taken were rushed to the PIs, and shortly thereafter the exact locations of targets were disseminated to interested agencies.

This is how it worked. When the first plane approached the hidden German positions, an alert was sounded by the Nazis. The photos taken by this plane showed gun crews and other personnel streaming out of their barracks to man their guns. No matter how well they were hidden, the locations of the living quarters were thus given away.

The second plane brought back photos showing the direction in which the soldiers proceeded and the number of men in each crew. And the pictures from the third plane revealed the exact spots where the troops disappeared into the camouflaged installations. In this way the Germans were duped into revealing their well-concealed battery emplacements, antiaircraft installations, and defense fortifications.

The much-vaunted German efficiency, thoroughness, and precision were of great help to the PIs in their work on the Nazi west wall. Finding just two or three gun emplacements was enough to reconstruct the layout of the entire installation, because the Germans always built these positions according to regulation pattern. By the size of the personnel barracks housing the crews for the west wall's heavy guns, their type and caliber could be determined. And by tracing the shadows cast by barbed-wire patterns, hidden machine-gun positions could be spotted.

This may seem an almost incredible amount of information to be gained by interpreting an aerial photograph, but facts bear this out. On Kiska, one of the Aleutian Islands, PIs not only spotted all artillery pieces, but determined the caliber of each gun—with only *one* mistake. And on a small South Pacific island, the Japanese troops were estimated by the PIs as four thousand strong. They made an error, however. Capture of the island disclosed that the actual count was 3,967!

It was in London in 1943 that one of the great PI stories of the war broke. Around the tip of the Binnen-Alster, a body of water in the heart of metropolitan Hamburg, several choice military targets were located, including an all-important railroad center and a couple of vital industrial plants. The installations had for months been the targets of heavy bombing raids, but apparently to no avail. Strike photos showed heavy damage to the bombed area, but strangely, the efficiency of the targets was not affected in the least. For months this was a puzzle to everyone, until one day the riddle was solved by an alert PI officer—and a horse.

As this officer was examining the strike photos of the previous day's raids, he became aware of a feeling of familiarity, of déjà vu. About six hundred yards from the tip of Binnen-Alster a causeway spanned the water. This causeway was the main landmark used by the raiding planes to identify their target. On this causeway a lone horse-drawn cart could be seen. Looking at this cart, the PI suddenly yelled, "I've got it!"

Rushing to the files he dug out strike photos of the Binnen-Alster area for the last week, and in all of them the lone horse-drawn cart could be seen crossing the causeway. Horse-drawn transportation may be slow—but *that* slow?

It was easy to dope it out then. The real targets had been painstakingly camouflaged, and the Germans had built a fake causeway six hundred yards farther down. In their zeal for perfection and reality, the horse-drawn cart had been included. With the most careful attention to detail, a three-dimensional decoy canvas replica of the targets had been constructed on rafts that floated on the water between the camouflaged real causeway and the Binnen-Alster tip. This is what we had been bombing.

The strike photos following this PI discovery had a different story to tell.

This was Photo Intelligence as its strategic best. While stationed in Luxembourg, I had occasion to witness the climax of an effective job of tactical PI.

I was on a case in a little town called Remich right on the Moselle River in southern Luxembourg, in the XII Corps sector held by the 2d Cavalry Group. The Germans were dug in right across the river and had been harassing the troops with nightly shelling by two 88mm self-propelled (SP) guns. The unit was beginning to take casualties, but it had been impossible to locate and destroy the guns—that is, until the PIs got into the act.

The PI team with Iceberg Forward G-2 was PI Team 22, commanded by Capt. John Bourne. Aerial photos of the terrain opposite the 2d Cavalry Group sector were carefully studied, and tracks made by the 88mm SP guns were discovered all over the place. But wherever they went they would always disappear into a small, heavily wooded patch directly opposite the Remich waterfront. This obviously was where the guns were hiding during the daylight hours.

Orders went out to the 225th Field Artillery Battalion to destroy the two 88s, and as I happened to be in Remich I went down to the artillery observation point in the attic of a villa on the waterfront to see the fireworks.

An arty lieutenant was calling the shots. First, a few rounds of phosphorus shells *karrumped* into the trees in a tight pattern, the white clouds mushrooming up through the suddenly naked branches, and in no time the two SP guns came tearing out, hell bent for election.

There followed as effective a bracketing of moving targets as I'd ever seen. The lieutenant barked out his orders and directions; shell after shell screamed overhead, fired by the arty battalion to the rear of us. Before long the range was pinned down, and the SP guns were reduced to smoking scrap. Through my binoculars I could see wounded Nazi crew members struggle away from their mangled guns to safety. Others hung lifeless over the tangled iron wreckage.

Photo Intelligence can be divided into three main functions. The first is reconnaissance—to learn vital facts, both tactical and strategic, about enemy territory, positions, strength, installations, and artillery.

The second one is mapping. General Omar N. Bradley once said,

"The nation with the best maps will win the war." At the time of Pearl Harbor the United States had only one-fifth of the land area of the world mapped in enough detail to make the small-scale maps necessary to guide bombing squadrons, task forces, and armies into enemy territory. Much work was needed.

The third function of PI is to record the results of actions such as bombing raids and artillery bombardments and accurately assess the damage inflicted upon the targets.

Many camouflage subterfuges were invented in order to mislead the bombing missions and bomb-damage assessments. Tanks, trucks, and artillery pieces, for instance, were constructed of canvas and lumber, or as inflatable balloons right out of a Macy's Thanksgiving Parade, to fool strafing or bombing planes or to make up losses suffered by armored units in an air raid. A depleted unit would still seem to be full strength to the PI studying his stereopair, and thus the unit's striking power would be overestimated. Although the size, shape, and shadows of these decoys would be correct, the discerning PI could detect the ruse by comparing the relative tone of the real and the fake tanks and trucks, for iron and canvas reflect light differently.

Paint could also play an important role in fooling the PI. Shortly after the war, in Munich in Bavaria, I saw several big undamaged buildings still standing among the devastated structures in the ravaged city. These buildings were carefully painted to look exactly like burned-out hulks, with black tongues of painted soot licking up from the maws of apparently empty windows, showing the ravages of the assumed conflagration that had gutted the inside; yet there was hardly a scratch on these buildings and no damage to the interior at all. Their counterfeit cloak of devastation had saved them from further attacks.

The first phase of a PI mission was, of course, taking the necessary photos—not always an easy task. Raids and battles do not wait for perfect light conditions, nor are they carried out according to the convenience of the photographer. The photo plane must fly in all sorts of weather, through fog and smoke, in temperatures as low as fifty below, and at any time of day or night, sometimes with a speed of 400 MPH, dodging enemy fighter planes and flak while taking the desired pictures.

Most photos were taken to a stationary or mobile photo lab on the ground for quick developing, printing, and interpretation, but on special missions immediate results were essential, and the troop commander required up-to-the-minute intelligence. On such flights the plane itself literally became a flying photo lab. The pictures were taken and processed at once. The plane carried a PI who, without loss of precious time, could interpret the photos; detailed information was then radioed back, making instant action possible.

Night photo reconnaissance, using the equipment available at the time, was often successful when nothing could be learned by day. The enemy had a tendency to be less cautious in his camouflage discipline when he believed himself shielded by darkness. For this purpose the photo plane carried "flash bombs" set to explode at predetermined altitudes and capable of bathing several square miles of land or sea in day-brilliant lights. The camera shutters were set to trip automatically at the peak intensity of the flash. But most missions flown at night or in dense fog used infrared photos.

The PIs supplied their unit commanders with a steady stream of accurate information, both tactical and strategic, from providing photo interpretations that enabled the Air Force to destroy the elusive Italian cruiser *Trieste* when she was anchored off La Maddalena on Sardinia, to spotting the drying laundry of a camouflaged Nazi unit in bivouac in the woods of Bavaria, plotting a safe escape route for a trapped infantry company, or in determining the status of the bridges over a river about to be crossed. All this contributed to the fact that the PI deservedly earned the name "America's Secret Agent Number One"!

Through cooperation between CIC and PI, the Kyll River had been crossed. We were firmly on German soil now, and a big change had taken place. No longer were we the welcome liberators; we were now the enemy invaders. Friendliness, relief, and support had been replaced with animosity, resentment, and sullenness. We all felt it.

We were operating out of a small village called Welchbillig a few miles east of Bitburg. Iceberg Forward was still in Echternach in Luxembourg when we were summoned to a high-level conference that would result in a case that would take me deep into Germany, behind enemy lines.

CHAPTER 4

G-2 had a problem. An important piece of information had reached Corps: it seemed that a certain prominent scientist, a physicist, who at the moment resided in a town called Mayen and who reportedly possessed vital information about a major Nazi weapons project, might be willing to defect. Corps had been advised that the man was scheduled to be evacuated to a scientific research establishment in the National Redoubt, also known as the Alpine Fortress, the following morning. If we wanted to get him, it would have to be *now*. The trouble was, Mayen had not been taken yet and was still in German territory some thirty miles behind enemy lines. Someone would have to go in and get him. It was too late to mount an OSS mission, which would have been the normal procedure, so Corps was asking us to provide a volunteer.

There I was. I had had OSS training; I spoke German fluently; and I was available. I was the logical choice for the mission. Of course, I knew that in the army one never volunteers for anything if one wants to stay out of trouble. So, I volunteered.

I made only one stipulation—that I do it my way. That meant I'd stay in uniform, dog tags and all. That may sound crazy, but it was just after the Bulge, and the Germans had captured a lot of our equipment, including certain pieces of clothing. I'd wear a woolen cap, a big army mackinaw over my Eisenhower jacket, and a woolen scarf around my neck—all items of clothing the Germans had "liberated" during the Ardennes offensive and were using against the cold; a bastard American getup would not attract attention—I hoped. But I did not want to go in disguised either as a civilian or in German uniform and be stood up against the nearest wall if things went wrong. In my uniform I could always claim I was lost, and be treated like any prisoner of war (PW). I'd use my own jeep—muddy up the numbers and scratch the stars out. Jeeps were at that time commonly used by the Germans when they captured them, just as we occasionally used one of their Volkswagens. No sweat there.

At dusk that evening, I pulled the woolen cap over my ears, shrugged into my grubby, loose mackinaw, put chewing gum between my dog tags to keep them from rattling, tightened the scarf around my neck to hide my U.S. collar insignia, pulled on a pair of mud-caked paratrooper boots, and repeated the agreed-upon passwords so I could cross back over our lines—with or without my scientific quarry. And I was off.

I had no trouble crossing the lines; the situation was that fluid. I went in by a small logging path and joined the main road to Mayen once I was certain I was in enemy territory.

On my way to Mayen I passed a column of trucks loaded with Wehrmacht replacements. I waved and shouted a few ribald remarks about the *verfluchte*, the damned cold, in an open *Ami Klamotte*, an open American jalopy. They waved back, calling out a few choice remarks about their own freezing anatomy.

In no time I was entering the town of Mayen. It had been so easy that it made me uncomfortable. Something was bound to happen.

Mayen was badly damaged. The town was an important junction on the Andernach-Gerolstein railroad, vital to the rail traffic in the Rhineland-Palatinate, and as such had been the target of heavy Allied bombing raids. I had an address where my scientist was supposed to be but no town map, so I headed for the railroad station, where a town map was usually displayed.

It was still fairly early in the evening, but there were surprisingly few people in the streets. Later I found out that because of the constant air raids a couple of thousand townspeople had left their homes and taken refuge in some large caves outside town.

Only one place was teeming with activity: a big hospital building near the center of town, undamaged except for a few broken windows. The grounds were filled with people and vehicles; the place was obviously in the process of being evacuated; rows of ambulances were being loaded with patients on stretchers. The Germans, anticipating the imminent capture and occupation of the town, were transporting their wounded soldiers to the rear so they might be patched up to fight another day.

I steered clear of the place, but not knowing my way around I was forced to ask directions to the railroad station. Politely I was given directions, and presently I was at the railroad yards. The marshaling yards were a maze of corkscrew iron rails, shrapnel-shattered rolling stock, and jagged mounds of masonry rubble. But the station, though badly damaged, was still standing.

I parked my jeep, and because there was no way to lock it, I removed the rotor. Just in case.

The station was practically empty. And the people who *were* there didn't seem to be waiting for trains. Some of them were clearing away the debris from a recent air raid; others were huddled in small groups, possibly because this was the only place that offered at least some shelter. I felt conspicuously out of place, but no one paid me any attention. The place was sparsely lit, partly because of blackout rules, I surmised, partly because of a power shortage.

The cheerful travel posters and advertising bills that usually adorn railroad stations the world over were nearly all gone. In their place were Nazi propaganda posters, proclamations of wartime ordinances, and recruiting posters, most of them soiled and torn. There was a stirring scene of dreadnought battleships steaming ahead against a background of a huge *Kriegsmarine* (Navy flag): *Einsatz der Deutsche Kriegsmarine,* it proclaimed proudly, "Contribution of the German Navy"; from the wall stared the noble Aryan profile of a haughty Nazi airman superimposed on a Luftwaffe emblem. *Unsere Luftwaffe,* it said, "Our Air Force." There was a poster showing a group of grimly attacking infantrymen, *Infantrie, Königin aller Waffen,* "Infantry, Queen of all Armed Forces," and a prodding *Hier zu Uns,* "Rally to Us," a colorful bill showing a proud Hitler Youth waving a swastika banner, *Hinein in die Hitler Jugend!* "Into the Hitler Youth!" There was even a faded, hand-painted slogan on one wall: *Hitler Bringt Brot—Stalin den Tod!* "Hitler Brings Bread—Stalin Death!" And, of course, a portrait of a stern, godlike Adolf Hitler and the ubiquitous, drumbeat slogan *Ein Volk, Ein Reich, Ein Führer!* "One People, One Reich, One Führer!"

Finally, next to a sober admonition, *Feind hört Mit!* "The Enemy Listens!" I found a town map, still in good enough shape to be read.

According to the map, the street I sought was located not too far from the big hospital complex I'd passed earlier. The street was dark and deserted when I drove up, but I could still make out the white-chalked war slogan scrawled across the wall of the building next door—*Sieg oder Sibirien,* "Victory or Siberia," and on the ruins of a demolished building on the other side the pathetic, hand-scribbled sign, *Wir sind im Keller,* "We are in the basement," with an arrow pointing to a rubble-strewn flight of steps.

The place where my scientist was supposed to be found was a modest, four-story apartment house, seemingly undamaged except for a few shrapnel nicks. In the entry hall I pushed a button marked LICHT, which would provide a dim light for a short period of time, then turn off. There was a directory panel on the wall with the glass front broken. Only some of the names of the occupants were still there; my man was not among them.

I started up the narrow stairs. I had just reached the first floor above street level when the light went out. Cursing under my breath, I groped my way to the light button and pressed. The first thing I saw when the dim light returned was a yellowed porcelain nameplate on one of the two doors on the landing.

It was the name of my scientist. There was a bell button on the wall next to the door, and I pressed it.

Inside a rasping ring could be heard.

Then silence.

Again I pressed the button. Again I heard the rasping ring.

I waited.

I tried to decide if I should bang on the door and risk waking up the whole neighborhood. No. I was just about to press the bell button once more when I heard a man's voice from behind the door. *"Wer ist da?"* "Who is there?"

I took a deep breath. This was the moment I'd visualized. Laying myself open. Completely open.

"My name is Melchior," I answered, trying to make my voice sound confident. "Ib Melchior, *Herr Professor.*" I swallowed involuntarily. "I—am an American intelligence officer. I should like to speak with you."

There. I stood naked.

There was no reaction. Not a sound could be heard, except the beating of my heart in my ears. What the hell was the man doing? Getting a gun? Calling the police? What? Should I wait? Or should I get the hell out of there while the getting was good?

I waited.

Then slowly the door was opened, and a man wearing the long, wide-lapelled black leather greatcoat of an SS officer stood in the doorway. He stared at me, wide-eyed.

And the light on the landing went out.

I more felt than saw the German reach toward the wall behind him, and the light came on again.

I looked him over, just as he obviously was sizing me up. Late forties, early fifties, I guessed. Tousled, thinning hair; a tendency to a paunch. Bare feet in worn slippers, and a suspicious, strangely calculating look in his water-blue eyes.

"Who—who *are* you?" he asked. "What do you want of me?"

I explained to him who and what I was, that we'd been led to believe that he'd be willing to defect rather than work for the Nazis and that I was here to conduct him to our lines.

The suspicion never left his eyes. Neither did that strange look of calculation. Of craftiness. It puzzled me.

"Sie sind verrückt. You are crazy," he said firmly. "I am a loyal German. I have absolutely no intention of going with you. Anywhere." Again that calculating look. "If you are who you say you are, it is my duty to report you to the Gestapo, and I shall do so!"

"I have no doubt that you are a loyal German, *Herr Professor,"* I said earnestly. "But do you also believe in the Nazi cause?"

The scientist drew himself up. Deliberately he looked straight at me. "I am a loyal *Parteigenosse*, a loyal party member," he declared. But his affirmation sounded hollow, as if spoken for effect.

I was genuinely puzzled. The man's reaction and behavior did not make sense to me. If he did not believe me, if he really *was* a loyal Nazi without any intention of defecting, he'd have called the police up front. So why hadn't he? If he did believe me, and if he *was* willing to come over to our side, why all the denials and protestations?

Suddenly I understood. I'd heard of this loyalty affirmation by trial. In my interrogations. The man thought *I* was the Gestapo! Tempting him, testing his loyalty before he was sent down to some secret government project or other. If he professed a willingness to go with me, it would be the end of him.

"*Herr professor,*" I said soberly. "I *am* an American." I reached for my scarf; automatically the German drew back. But his eyes never left me. I pulled the scarf aside and showed him the U.S. insignia on my collar.

He stared at me. "There are many such 'souvenirs' in Germany," he said. But his craftiness seemed less assured.

I fished out my CIC identification and held it out to him. He did not take it, but he looked at it. Slowly he shook his head.

"They look authentic," he said, only the slightest hesitancy in his voice. "I congratulate you. But then, I know that the Gestapo makes the finest document forgeries in the world."

I had one more card to play, then—that was it. I unbuttoned my shirt and pulled out my dog tags.

"And these," I said. "They are dog tags. *American* dog tags." I gave a hard yank on the tags, breaking the chain around my neck. I held them out to the man. Uncertainly he took them, turning them over in his hand.

"Look," I said. "My name. My army serial number. My blood type. *American* dog tags."

The scientist looked at the tags closely. He tried to pry them apart, and the chewing gum holding them together stretched in sticky strands between the two tags. Wonderingly he stared at me.

"Chewing gum?"

"To keep them from rattling," I nodded.

"You *are*—American," he whispered. He suddenly looked apprehensive. He cast a worried glance into the landing behind me. "Come," he urged in a hoarse whisper. "Inside!"

We entered his apartment. He closed the door behind him and turned to me.

"You *are* American," he repeated, still speaking in a low, furtive voice.

"Yes, Professor, I am." I held out my hand for my dog tags. The German gave them to me, and I put them in my pocket. "Now, will you listen to me? Will you come with me?"

He stood staring at me. Slowly he shook his head.

"No," he said. "I can not."

"Why not?"

"It can not be done," he said, his voice low. "We will be caught, and . . . and . . . ," he searched for the words. "I—I am not a brave man." He gave a crooked little smile. "My imagination is too vivid to allow me to be brave. If we were caught, and we will be, I—I . . . no," he repeated. "I can not do it."

Briefly I contemplated him. I sincerely hoped we *would* make it, but there were no guarantees. And the man was right, if we *were* caught, he'd have to pay a heavy price. Too heavy, perhaps, for any man to have to pay.

"Would you come with me," I asked him, "if it was safe? Entirely safe?"

The man bit his lip in indecision. "I—I—. Perhaps . . ."

"There is a way," I said. "A safe way. If you do want to come with me."

The scientist gave me a look of curiosity.

"I can abduct you," I continued. "Kidnap you by force."

The man looked startled.

"I mean, we could make it appear as if I am taking you against your will."

For a moment the scientist stood staring at me. I could almost see the wheels of decision—or indecision—whirl in his mind.

"How?"

"Easy," I explained. "I'll hit you over the head. Lightly, of course. Just for show. I'll tie you up. Gag you. And put you in the back of my jeep. The top is up. You may not even be seen."

The man looked troubled.

"If, I say *if* we are stopped," I went on hurriedly, "you can denounce me. You can say you were abducted. You can show them your bruise, your bound hands. No one can blame you. You will be safe." I looked at him urgently. "How about it? Will you go with me, if we do it that way?"

The man stood silent, indecision on his face. "Look," I said. I did not want him to think too hard; there *were* flaws in my plan. "We don't have much time. Will you come?"

Slowly the man nodded. "Yes," he said. He sounded as if he were contradicting himself. "If—if you do this, I will come with you."

"Good!" I felt vastly relieved. It would have been damned awkward and much more risky if I *really* had had to knock the guy out and cart him off. "Get dressed. You need take nothing along."

The scientist looked down at his Wehrmacht greatcoat. "Everything is packed," he said. "For tomorrow. All I have is my uniform."

"That'll do fine."

"I am a scientist," he said, with a touch of bitterness in his voice. "But I am also a *Sturmbannführer*, a major, in the SS. It is supposed to be an honor."

He turned to walk toward a door that I presumed led to his bedroom. I followed him. While he got dressed I made small talk, trying to keep him from thinking too much about what lay ahead.

"You live here?" I asked.

"No," he answered me, as he pulled on his uniform trousers. "This apartment belongs to my brother. He is in the army."

On the wall were two enlarged old photographs, one of a man with a huge *Schnurrbart*, a handlebar mustache, and a stiff collar, the other of a round-faced, heavyset woman.

"Your parents?" I guessed.

He nodded, pulling on his jackboots.

"Where do *you* live?"

"In Frankfurt. I came here to pick up some things my brother had stored for me. Some personal things. For tomorrow."

I nodded. "When you are supposed to go—south."

"That is correct," he said, as he shrugged into his uniform tunic. He picked up his greatcoat, put it on, and placed his high-peaked cap with the silver death's-head and the Nazi eagle on his head. He turned to me, looking every inch the SS officer.

"I am ready," he said. But there was no enthusiasm in his voice.

I had spied a lamp that stood on a small nightstand. It had about five feet of cord. I picked it up, tore the cord from the wall outlet, and ripped it out of the lamp.

"Put your hands behind you," I ordered.

He obeyed, turning his back to me.

I quickly made an eight-loop with the cord, slipped it over his hands, and pulled it tight. I wound it around his waist and tied it securely in front.

"Okay, your choice," I said.

"What do you mean?"

"I can knock you over the head," I explained. "Or not. Your choice."

The man went visibly pale. He looked torn. Two fears apparently fought each other in his mind. The fear of being hurt, and the fear of falling into the hands of the Gestapo without every possible proof of innocence.

The Gestapo won.

I took his cap from his head. Wide-eyed, he watched me. I took my gun from my shoulder holster. He screwed his eyes tightly shut, waiting for the blow.

Quickly I struck him a glancing blow high on his temple just under the hairline, hard enough to tear the skin. At once he began to bleed. A scalp wound always bleeds excessively.

The man started, but stood his ground. Slowly he opened his eyes. He seemed surprised.

"Looks great," I grinned at him. "No one can possibly say you haven't been knocked out properly." I replaced his cap. A trickle of blood seeped from under it and slowly oozed down his cheek. I did nothing to stay it.

"That's it," I said. "Let's go."

The street was empty. I bundled the trussed-up and gagged scientist into the back of my jeep, where he huddled down into a corner, and we took off.

I had decided not to risk passing through the hospital area with all the evacuation activity but to get out of town the quickest way possible. I had plotted a route on the Wehrmacht map I'd been using that would take me to the main highway leading back to our lines by a slightly different routing.

We made it through town without incident and were soon barreling down a country road that would take us to the highway by which I'd come. My scientist hadn't moved from his huddled position in the back of the jeep and had not uttered a word. Not that he'd had much choice. I drove without headlights and had to peer into the darkness in front of me. Luckily it was not absolute; with my night vision I could see well enough.

Up ahead the road made a sharp bend as it passed through a stand of brush, probably where it crossed a creek. As I rounded the curve I thought I could make out some sort of obstruction on the road.

I strained to see—and suddenly I knew what it was.

A roadblock!

Two wooden X-barriers strung with barbed wire had been placed across the road. Two motorcycles with sidecars were pulled off the road nearby, and four soldiers, Schmeissers on the ready, stood before the roadblock.

German MPs.

One of them stepped forward. He raised his *Verkehrsanzeiger,* his traffic baton. The illuminated dot in the center of the disk on the end of the baton glowed malevolently red.

In an imperious voice he shouted, *"Halt!"*

I brought the jeep to a halt some eighty feet from the roadblock. I saw the MP noncom with the traffic baton start to walk briskly toward me. In a split-second I threw to the wind my carefully made decision to stay in U.S. uniform and not engage in any charades. With a trussed-up, knocked-out German scientist big shot in the back of my jeep, I did not think I'd be treated with kid gloves. As I hurriedly dismounted I leaned into the back of the jeep. I ripped off my woolen cap, tore the officer's SS cap from the scientist's head, slapped it on my own, and hissed to my petrified passenger, "Don't move! Keep silent! Put your head down—as if sleeping. *Do it!"*

There was no reply. Had he heard me? Understood me? Would he play it out? Or would he try to attract the attention of the MP—and save his own hide? There was nothing I could do. I'd find out soon enough.

I strode quickly toward the approaching MP. We met halfway between my jeep and the roadblock.

I glanced at the man's uniform: a single silver cord and orange piping bordering his shoulder strap. He was an *Unteroffizier,* a sergeant in the military police. His half-moon-shaped metal chest plate with the two prominent dots, the Nazi eagle, and the embossed word FELDGENDARMERIE, Field Police, daubed with luminous paint, glowed in the dark. He gave me a stiff-arm salute—*"Heil Hitler!"*

With a deliberate show of irritation I returned his salute. I knew what I had to do. The curtain was about to go up on one of the most important acting jobs in my life. And there was no script.

"May I—," the MP began. I cut him off at once.

"What the devil is going on here, Sergeant?" I barked. "I am Sturmbannführer von Stuelp. Gestapo. Get that damned roadblock out of the way!"

The sergeant snapped to attention. "I regret, *Herr Sturmbannführer*, but—"

"But!" I exploded. "Did you not hear me, *verdammt nochmal,* dammit all? Move! Now!"

The man was obviously frightened, but he drew himself up stiffly.

"I beg to report, *Herr Sturmbannführer,* I am under orders to let no traffic onto the highway. It is to be kept clear for a top-priority convoy, *Herr Sturmbannführer*. It is due any minute."

I stood glaring at the man while I listened to what he said, but only with a small part of my mind. I knew I had to keep up the bluff, once begun, and I knew I had to prevail. As soon as the man stopped talking, I'd have to light into him again. I could not allow him time to question *me*, to ask for *my* credentials. As long as he was occupied justifying himself, I was safe. But—how long could I keep it up? What would it take to make the sergeant, obviously a seasoned soldier, cave in? And he had to. He just *had* to.

"You hear me well, Sergeant," I snarled at the man, emphasizing each separate word, making my voice sound as dangerous as I could, rising in anger until I was practically shouting. "I am escorting Standartenführer [SS Colonel] Adolf Himmler to the front. The front, dammit! It is of the utmost importance that we get there as quickly as possible. And that means we take that highway." I stabbed a stiff finger at the road just visible beyond the barricade. "*That* highway, *do you hear me?"*

Pointedly I narrowed my eyes, as I glared at the man. "I hope I made myself quite clear, Sergeant," I said ominously. "That is Standartenführer Himmler who is waiting in the car." I nodded curtly toward my jeep. "Impatiently, I have no doubt." I lowered my voice. "I am certain you know Colonel Himmler's *uncle!"*

The MP looked shaken, but he stood his ground. *"Jawohl, Herr Sturmbannführer!"* I saw him eye my strange outfit topped by the SS cap with the silver death's-head. "May I—"

"You—may—not!" I shouted. "Delay is out of the question! Have I not made myself clear, *verdammt nochmal?* How dare you defy a superior officer?"

The MP sergeant was visibly shaken. "I have orders, *Herr—"*

"Orders!" I screamed at him. "To hell with your orders!" I drew myself up, shaking with suppressed rage. "Very well, Sergeant, I shall inform Colonel Himmler right now that you refuse to let him pass!"

Abruptly I turned on my heel, stopped short and whirled on the terrified MP. I held up the Wehrmacht map, taken along for show. Imperiously I stuck out my hand toward the man.

"Your pencil," I demanded curtly. "I shall want your name, your service number. For the record." I smiled maliciously. "The *Reichsführer SS* will wish to know exactly *who* delayed a mission in which he is vitally interested."

The MP stared at me, chalk-faced.

Suddenly the low, dull roar of many motor vehicles intruded upon the night silence. We both looked toward the road. Driving with blackout lights only, the convoy was bearing down on the road junction—a giant, growling shadow snake with a thousand slit-orbed eyes.

The sergeant wet his dry lips.

"If is pleases the *Herr Sturmbannführer*," he croaked. "The convoy is going to the front. Perhaps—if the *Herr Sturmbannführer* would care to join the—"

I cut him off curtly. "See to it. *Sofort!* At once!"

I turned on my heel and stalked stiff-legged back to the jeep. I climbed into the driver's seat.

"*Herr Profess*—," I began. Somehow my voice cracked. I began again. "*Herr Professor,* we are joining a convoy. We'll be in U.S. territory soon. Sit tight."

I started up. At the roadblock the MPs were pushing the barriers aside. The sergeant stepped out onto the highway and raised his traffic baton. The oncoming vehicles slowed down. The MP waved me on.

As we drove past him onto the road, joining the convoy, the sergeant peered curiously into the jeep at the dark figure in his black SS greatcoat huddled against the cold in the backseat. Reichsführer SS Heinrich Himmler's nephew himself! He snapped to attention and raised his arm in a stiff *Heil Hitler!* salute.

I returned it with an indifferent wave of my hand.

As I sat staring at the shadowy truck ahead of me in the convoy, intent on keeping the proper distance, I wondered if Reichsführer SS Heinrich Himmler actually did have a nephew. Why not? He did have an older brother.

I was suddenly aware that I was shivering with cold. The sweat of fear that had drenched me was drying on my skin. It was a small price to pay.

The next fifteen miles or so were about as eventful as watching the grass grow in your Aunt Tessie's planter box, as we slowly but steadily rumbled along in convoy. I was especially grateful for being part of that convoy when we passed through the little village of Ulmen, which had been all but deserted when I drove through only hours earlier but was now teeming with activity. But the ever-present German MPs along the route kept the convoy moving, waving it—and me—right through.

When we neared the point where I had to turn off to hit the logging path I'd taken going in, I sped up, driving closer to the truck ahead of me, making it more difficult in the dark for the truck following me to see what I was doing. When my little side road turned up, I stepped on the gas and quickly veered off the highway to disappear into the woods. No one followed me.

A short while later I arrived at Iceberg Forward with my charge, by now untrussed, ungagged, and unbelievingly relieved, after a safe and uneventful trip—courtesy of a German military convoy.

I did not know it at the time, but it later became apparent that my scientist buddy had been slated to be involved in a top-secret Nazi project. He had been working for Degussa, the prominent Frankfurt-based scientific research organization that had been manufacturing uranium for use in an atomic bomb being developed by the Nazis. My man was among those important scientists being evacuated to the Alpine Fortress, where the Nazis were set up to continue the development of that A-bomb. Their atomic pile was concealed in a huge complex of caves, formerly used to store wine, under a mountain located at Haigerloch near the Black Forest. This entire project was to be moved to the Alpine Fortress, and most of Germany's top scientists were slated to work on this priority project. I have no idea what happened to "my man."

The town of Mayen was taken a few days later, and on 12 March 1945 Iceberg Forward moved there, establishing their command post in the big, now empty, hospital in the center of town. A few days later we leapfrogged the village of Kastellaun and moved on to Simmern, a town that was to play a role in my years to come, a role just about to begin.

CHAPTER 5

Simmern is cozily nestled in the rolling, wooded Hunsrück Mountains some fifty miles west of the city of Mainz on the Rhine. It is a colorful little town that straddles the Simmerbach, a tributary to the Nahe River. The town, relatively undamaged, was taken on 15 March 1945. Our CIC team moved in the same day, to be joined by Iceberg Forward four days later. Corps command post (CP) was established in the *Landrat* building, the equal to a U.S. county courthouse, where the CP was to stay for three days before moving on.

As was standard operating procedure, immediately upon occupying the town, we ordered the population to turn in all cameras and binoculars. This was to prevent the locals from taking pictures of our equipment, buildings occupied by U.S. forces, signposts showing different units, and other subjects that might be helpful to the enemy forces opposing us. These items were collected in large bins, often bathtubs from bombed-out houses, gasoline was poured over them, and they were destroyed.

Shortly after entering Simmern I passed a bathtub heaped with that kind of contraband. On top of the pile I spied a beautiful, near-new Zeiss-Ikon, Konta 521/16, state-of-the-art camera. I picked it up. It felt so right in my hands that rather than consign it to the flames, I kept it for my own use; I had no camera of my own. Inside the housing the previous owner had scratched his name and address: Schönig, Altweidelbacherstrasse 21, Simmern. I thought nothing of it.

I was to use that camera all through the war, and I kept using it after the war was over. I took the first photographs of my two-year-old son, Leif, in New York when I returned and took pictures of the rehearsals of the "Perry Como Show" on CBS-TV, which I directed; when I moved to California in 1957 I recorded my son's first visit to Disneyland and shot the sets and actors on the first motion pictures I directed. And, of course, I took numerous shots of Cleo.

When next I happened to be in Simmern was in 1970, twenty-six years after the war. With my father, the late Wagnerian tenor Lauritz Melchior, I was touring Germany, visiting my father's old fellow opera singers, such as Hans Herman Nissen and Max Lorenz in Munich, Henny Trundt in Düsseldorf, Paul Schwartz in Hamburg, and Frida Leider, my father's favorite Isolde to his Tristan, in Berlin. It was an emotional journey; we all knew it was the final time these old friends would see one another.

My father and I were driving from Bonn to Mainz along the Rhine River. I was at the wheel; my father had never learned how to drive a car. It had been raining hard, and the great river, swollen with angry, raging waters, was overflowing its banks and flooding the valley. And then—suddenly—a sign: ROAD OUT—DETOUR.

And what a detour. Bumper-to-bumper traffic snaking at a snail's pace up into the Rhine mountains, following the only main road available, a detour of over a hundred miles. It was a bleak picture, hours and hours of tedious driving.

And then I saw a leaning signpost pointing down a narrow side road: Simmern. Quickly, to my father's surprise, I turned off.

It was a jump back a quarter of a century in time. Twenty-six years before, I had pushed along this same road in my jeep, and I knew it led through Simmern and right down to the city of Mainz. In the pitch darkness I followed it, driving through the town of Simmern, arriving at our destination less than two hours later.

In the glove compartment of our car lay the camera I had "liberated" in Simmern with the name of the town scratched into it!

When in 1990 Cleo and I were planning our trip to retrace my wartime route through Europe, I remembered the camera. How appropriate it would be if, forty-six years later, I could return it to its erstwhile owner. Even though it held many memories for me, the camera rightfully belonged with him. I wrote a letter to the mayor of Simmern, explaining the circumstances of the "liberated" camera and asking him to put me in touch with Herr Schönig, giving him the address that was scratched into the camera housing. I quickly got a reply.

He, Bürgermeister Bungenstab, the mayor wrote, had been astonished at receiving my letter. Herr Schönig, the elder, had unfortunately passed away, but his son still lived in Simmern; in fact, he worked at the mayoralty as a city architect. He would be delighted to get the camera back. He had used it as a fifteen-year-old, and he remembered his father scratching his name into it. Moreover, Mayor Bungenstab invited us to a special reception at the *Rathaus* in Simmern, at which time I might return the camera with proper ceremony.

And so, on 30 August 1990, we arrived in Simmern, checked into a charming little hotel on the bank of the Simmerbach, and later in the day attended a festive reception at the Town Hall. Press and radio representatives recorded the saga of the Simmern camera, and speeches were given by Mayor Bungenstab, by Herr Schönig, and by me. I told them how I had carried the camera with me all through the European campaign, photographing the ravages of war as well as the relief of peace, and how in the years that followed it had recorded for me many wonderful moments and places the world over. With flashbulbs popping and recorders whirring, I returned the camera to Mr. Schönig and said, "Thank you for the loan."

In my conversation with Herr Schönig after the ceremony, I told him of my attempt to find and rephotograph all the places I had photographed with his camera during the war. Unfortunately, I told him, the only picture I had from Simmern was one of me standing at the front door to a villa we had used as our CIC offices—a door with an intricate wrought-iron grille across a window in the door and a distinctive stone carving on a pillar next to it. But there was, of course, no way for me to find such a door in the whole town of Simmern—if it still existed. I had a copy of the photo along, and at his request I showed it to him. His eyes lit up.

"But that is no problem," he declared. "No problem at all. That is the front door to the house of my neighbor on the street where I live, two houses removed!"

So with the mayor, who proudly pointed out to us all the improvements, renovations, and new construction in town for which he was responsible, and with Herr Schönig leading the way, we all trooped to the house Herr Schönig pointed out. And there was the door—iron grille, stone carving, and all!

As I posed on the steps, as I had in 1945, I watched Herr Schönig, reunited with a small part of his past, delightedly examine his camera; I thought it in a small way was symbolic of another unification, that of his country, that of East and West. I silently prayed that that unification would bode well for Europe—and for the world.

Simmern had been relatively undamaged by the war, but this was not the case with the next town to which our CIC team advanced, the ancient city of Mainz, dating back to the time of the Roman Empire and the first century B.C. military settlement of Maguntiacum. Mainz is situated where the Main and the Rhine rivers join and is a major industrial center.

Iceberg Forward had moved its headquarters to Bad Kreuznach on 22 March and was billeted in the luxurious Palast Kurhaus, but we leapfrogged that town, going on to Mainz, which had been taken that same day. Mainz had been the target of several massive Allied air raids, and fully 80 percent of the inner city had been destroyed. That meant we had to find adequate quarters on the outskirts of town.

Our standard procedure in locating suitable accommodation for our team's use was to select an undamaged house that was still occupied by the Germans. We would order the occupants to get out within fifteen minutes, taking nothing but essential belongings, and leaving everything in the house—every door, every drawer, every cupboard—unlocked. As soon as the Germans were out, we'd move in.

There was an excellent reason for doing it that way, a reason that had become obvious from bitter experience. If you moved into a house, or any building, that was empty, it was liable to be booby-trapped. Favorite spots to place these devious, deadly devices were the bed, the toilet seat, an easy chair, the stove, or a picture of Adolf Hitler on the wall—in that order. Many a GI had blown himself up by flinging himself on a bed or plopping into an easy chair, by using a comfortable toilet seat rather than a slit trench in the cold outside, by trying to get warm at a friendly-looking stove, or by showing his contempt for the Führer by knocking his picture off the wall. A house occupied by a German family was not likely to be booby-trapped. As for leaving everything unlocked, it was not for looting purposes, but for safety: an explosive device, hastily planted, could easily be concealed behind a locked door or in a locked drawer.

Usually the Germans would comply with our order, however sullenly and resentfully. But not always. Some would weep and plead; some seemed too frightened to move and had to be prodded on their way. Outright resistance was, of course, out of the question. One of the teams in our detachment heard two shots when they came to take over a residential house. They immediately took cover, but when no other activity was heard, they entered the house to find a man and his wife who had committed joint suicide rather than submit to American demands. Once we moved on, usually a few days later, the Germans could move back in.

The same procedure was followed when whole units had to be billeted in a town. The CO of the Bivouac Detachment would round up the *Bürgermeister* and order him to evict everybody from a selected area of town, with all houses being turned over to the Americans, open and intact.

A Corps historian put it this way: "In France and Luxembourg, the public buildings and private houses were taken over with a degree of consideration for the feelings of the community; in Germany, the headquarters simply moved into the best buildings left standing in town, and kicked out what Krauts happened to be in the way."

By now our six-man team had garnered quite an entourage. With us traveled three young Ukrainian DPs (displaced persons) whose enthusiasm grew with every mile we advanced toward their homeland. One of them, a young man named Ivan, was an expert mechanic and kept our vehicles in perfect condition so we never had to waste time at a motor pool, and there were two cheerful girls in their twenties, Tony and Tania, who made it their business to wash and clean our clothes and to do household chores in the quarters we had taken over.

In addition we had been joined by a French chef, Andre, and his wife, Geraldine, who did our cooking for us. Andre had been the chef in a fine restaurant in Paris. His son had been carted away as a slave laborer, which had broken Geraldine's heart, and when the Germans pulled out of Paris, a general, who had taken a liking to Andre's cooking at the restaurant, pressed him into service as his personal chef. Geraldine had refused to stay behind and had been allowed to join her husband. As things got hot for the Nazi troops, Andre and Geraldine were left behind and were subsequently picked up by our team. Andre professed to being too distraught to return to Paris, but I suspected that he and his wife, against all odds, held the belief that somehow they could find their son. They were forever questioning other liberated DPs.

To transport all these people we had annexed a civilian car to go with our two jeeps, one with a trailer. This trailer was supposed to hold a blackout tent we had been issued, but that tent had been jettisoned long ago and had been replaced with other more pressing necessities, such as wine, champagne, and liqueurs, and clean bed linens. When we came to a house with good, clean linens we'd take them, leaving the old soiled linens behind as replacements. I often wondered what it would be like if the occupants of the string of houses throughout Germany attempted to straighten out the mess, exchanging sets of bed linen!

Feeding our eleven-mouth contingent presented no problem. The ration orders for each CIC team of six men were cut in such a way that the team could draw rations for the entire *detachment* of thirty-six at any railhead. When the time came for us to replenish our stores, Andre would simply give one of us a list of what he wanted, and we'd fill it. His meals were always great, and there were usually spices and condiments acceptable to him in the big houses we occupied; if not, he carried his own supplies in our trailer.

It all worked out splendidly. We were left free to do our jobs without having to worry about mundane chores, and our happy entourage lived well, always with a roof over their heads. It was obvious they enjoyed being with us, and we certainly enjoyed having them.

When we arrived in Mainz a few days after it had been taken, we sent out a young T5 whose name was Walter to find suitable quarters for us. Walter had been "raided." Because many of the CIC agents—recruited mostly from law enforcement agencies and the legal profession—did not speak German, we were constantly on the lookout for GIs who could speak the language fluently, for use as interpreters and in noninvestigative endeavors such as finding us new quarters. When we found such a man, we raided him, had him transferred to us.

Walter was a Jew, a Berliner, born and raised in Germany until, as a teenager, he was spirited out of the country to England by his parents, just ahead of the Gestapo. His father and mother had not been able to get out, however, and undoubtedly had been picked up and carted off to some concentration or extermination camp. Walter had never heard anything from them, or about them. He had eventually made his way to an uncle in Detroit, and when the United States entered the war, he'd volunteered for the army. Walter felt that his parents probably had perished at the hands of the SS, but when the war was over he planned to seek permission to go to Berlin to search for them. We'd pledged our help.

Walter drove around the suburb's streets looking for an undamaged house big enough to accommodate us all. He finally found a big villa surrounded by a low stone wall. He saw a thin plume of light blue smoke coming from the chimney, so he knew there were people living in the house. He went up to the front door and knocked loudly.

There was no response.

Again he knocked, more insistently. And knocked. And knocked.

Finally the door was opened. In the doorway stood a frightened woman. She stared at him—and her face went white.

He stared back. The woman was his mother!

And not only was his mother there but also his father—and sixteen other Jews, who had lived clandestinely in the big villa, hidden in the cellars by two Gestapo majors!

When the emotional reunion was over and we had settled in our quarters—in a different house, needless to say—we got the full story. The two Gestapo officers who had saved Walter's parents and the other Jews living in the big villa, as well as dozens of other Jewish people secreted in houses throughout the city, had long before decided that the brutal annihilation of the Jews was unconscionable and could not be tolerated. But—what to do? Had they voiced their feelings, had they complained or refused to carry out their orders, they would have been imprisoned—or, more likely, shot. So they kept right on doing their duty, arresting Jews whenever they were ordered to do so and turning them over for transportation to the camps. But whenever they learned of Jews about to be picked up by *other* Gestapo agents, they would get to them first and hide them in the various places they'd prepared for them. In that way they had saved hundreds of people.

We learned the whereabouts of the two SS officers and picked them up. We added our endorsement to the glowing affidavit in their honor signed by every man and woman we could find who had been saved by them, and it accompanied them when we forwarded them to the Army Interrogation Center (AIC). We hoped they would get the kind of treatment they deserved.

Although we did not have time for any in-depth interrogation of the two courageous men, we did get some fascinating information from them. It was the first time we'd run into Germans, let alone Gestapo officers, who had been actively working against the policies and actions of the Nazi Reich, and we were highly intrigued.

For the first time we learned some of the details of the miscarried attempt to kill Hitler at his headquarters at Rastenburg in East Prussia on 20 July 1944, when Col. Count Claus von Stauffenberg carried an attaché case crammed with high explosives to a meeting with the Führer. We knew of the plot; we knew that the explosives had been detonated; and we knew that Hitler had escaped virtually unscathed, although four others had been killed, including one of Hitler's doubles, a man named Berger. And we knew that heads had rolled in the aftermath. But we learned much more from these two men, who had been minor players in the plot known as "Operation Valkyrie." They told us of the bitter disappointment they'd felt when the leaders of the conspiracy, after overcoming nearly insurmountable obstacles, finally had succeeded in getting in touch with the Allies for support and recognition—only to be informed by the British foreign secretary, Anthony Eden, that *no* commitments of any kind would be made in advance of a coup, that they'd have to go it alone and take their chances. They told us that the Rastenburg incident was the *sixth* attempt to kill Hitler. Once the explosive mechanism failed; once the meeting selected for the assassination was canceled; three other times von Stauffenberg had actually carried his explosive-laden briefcase to conferences with the Führer, on 6, 12, and 16 July, only to abstain from setting it off for various reasons.

And they told us about some of the top-ranking German officers and officials who had been involved in the assassination attempt, a list that read like a *Who's Who* of Nazi brass and included Field Marshalls Erwin von Witzleben, Erwin Rommel, and Günther von Kluge; Generals Franz Halder, Ludwig Beck, Karl Heinrich von Stülpnagel (military governor of France), Alexander von Falkenhausen (former military governor of Belgium), and Hans Oster, who was in charge of intelligence personnel and could provide false credentials for the plotters to travel around in Germany and occupied territories and to foreign capitals; Admiral Wilhelm Canaris, head of the Nazi intelligence services; diplomats such as Ulrich von Hassell, former Ambassador to

Rome, and Count Carl Friedrich von der Schülenberg, former Ambassador to Moscow; and Friedrich Goederler, former mayor of Leipzig. There had been prominent clergymen conspirators: Count Clemens August von Galen, Catholic Bishop of Münster; Michael Cardinal von Faulhaber of Munich; Konrad Cardinal von Preysing of Berlin; the Reverend Dietrich Bonhoeffer; and Pastor Eugen Gerstenmaier, an influential leader of the Protestant ecumenical movement. Several civilian groups and organizations were involved in the plot, notable among them Count Helmuth von Moltke's group of dissidents known as the "Kreisau Circle," named after Moltke's estate, as well as a group of intellectuals in the faculty of Freiberg University.

Our informers told us that most if not all of these men had been tracked down and executed. More than five thousand victims were killed for allegedly participating in the coup, many of them dying in gruesome ways. Our two Gestapo officers had become so adept at preventing suspicion from being directed toward them that they'd come through the purge unharmed—had, in fact, because of their Gestapo positions, been able to warn and save some of their lesser fellow conspirators.

We spent hours talking with the two men. They were articulate and meticulously correct, neither arrogant nor subservient, treating us as equals exactly as we treated them. They impatiently thrust aside any plaudits for what they had done for Walter's parents and the other Jewish people, strongly emphasizing their conviction that their actions against the regime had been for the good of Germany. Ours was not a friendly chat but a guarded give-and-take exchange of information and points of view, and they obviously did not always agree with us. I had the feeling that they almost regretted being on the same side with us, the enemy foreigners. But they held nothing back. It was a fascinating session. I was sorry when dawn finally seeped in our windows, and it was time for us to send our charges on to AIC. I felt sure that our two Gestapo agents would be able to give the boys back there some highly interesting and valuable information.

While we were in Mainz, the 11th Infantry Regiment of Corps' 5th Infantry Division had crossed the swollen Rhine River in a surprise assault, using regular Army paddled assault boats and vehicle rafts assisted by a naval detachment of twelve landing craft vehicles piloted by Navy personnel. These landing crafts had been trucked at top speed across

France and Germany from the town of Toul, where the crossing had been practiced on the Moselle River; they were necessary to the operation because of the extreme width and depth of the Rhine and the forceful current of the season. A bridgehead had been established around Gross Gerau on the east bank, and on 23 March the first M-2 treadway pontoon bridge had been thrown across the rushing waters from Oppenheim by the 150th Combat Engineer Battalion with troops from the 995th, 996th, and 997th Engineer Treadway Battalion companies. The 972-foot-long bridge had taken eleven and a half hours to build. The crossing had been made without artillery preparation, air bombardment, or the dropping of airborne troops. The landing boats and rafts had slipped into the water so silently and under the cover of darkness that the enemy had been taken entirely by surprise. The astonishing fact is that this enormous and vital operation had resulted in only eight killed and twenty wounded!

The day after this first bridge went into operation, Gen. George Patton himself inspected it, although it was still under enemy artillery fire and air strikes. Patton walked across the bridge. Halfway across, the story has it, he stopped.

"Time for a short halt," he declared.

He stepped to the edge of the bridge and proceeded to relieve himself into the Rhine. Buttoning his breeches, he turned to his entourage and with obvious satisfaction said, "I've been looking forward to doing this for a long time!" Then he walked to the far side of the river.

It was time for us to move on.

After a tearful good-bye, we left Tony and Tania, Ivan, and the French chef and his wife behind. We had to. It was a strictly enforced rule that no civilians could be transported across the pontoon bridges. But we had made certain that good care would be taken of our companions. The French chef and his wife would be assisted in returning to wherever they wanted to go; the three Ukrainians would be placed in a DP camp until they could return home.

Headed for Gross Gerau, we crossed the Rhine on March 25. Just as we started across, a few artillery shells once again began to fall around the bridge, and the 81st Chemical Smoke Generating Company immediately laid a thick smoke cover over the area. Keeping our wheels on the narrow metal tracks presented a bit of a problem, but we made it without mishap.

* * *

Today the pontoon bridge, which among other purposes served to fulfill General Patton's dream, is but a memory along with the other bridges thrown across the river during the war. Today a graceful, permanent bridge spans the mighty Rhine, connecting Oppenheim on the west bank with Gross Gerau on the east. When Cleo and I drove across we had no trouble staying on course. There was no smoke, not even a hint of fog; it was a bright and sunny day. Only *I* remembered the smoke. I briefly contemplated doing a Patton, but thought better of it.

Our team's next stop was Offenbach on the left bank of the Main River, so close to Frankfurt that it was literally a suburb of that city. Although the town was heavily damaged, as was Frankfurt itself, we managed to find a nice, two-story house, which we took over. On 30 March Iceberg Forward caught up with us and moved into a nearby large public building just across the river from Frankfurt. It was in Offenbach that we were involved in an action that the official history of the unit calls "unique in the experience of XII Corps."

Iceberg Forward, in its rush to advance, had bypassed a large German SS unit, elements of the 6th Mountain Division, on the left flank, which was supposed to be protected by another corps. The SS troops were still full of fight. They broke away from the U.S. forces that were supposed to contain them and cut across the XII Corps rear in an attempt to join with other enemy forces on our right flank. In the early morning hours of 1 April we were urgently summoned to the CP. We were informed that the SS troops in our rear were threatening our main supply route; that Iceberg Forward CP had been cut off and isolated; that three senior officers, Major General Eddy (the CO), Brigadier General Lentz, and Brigadier General Canine (the G-2), on an inspection trip to a town called Lauterbach, Iceberg Forward's next stop, had been cut off; and that an attack in force on Corps command post itself was imminent.

Every man, from cooks to clerk typists, every staff officer, from ninety-day-wonders to bird colonels, were issued firearms and ammunition. The entire CP command was mobilized and formed into small units, each under the command of a soldier with actual combat experience, which resulted in full colonels taking orders from a combat Pfc who happened to be at the command post. We were formed up in a ring around the building, seeking cover wherever we could, peering into the darkness and waiting for the onslaught.

All of a sudden a volley of small-arms fire broke out, quickly intensifying in force. The din became indescribable. Who had come under fire? How soon would they reach us? It sounded as if the entire German army were firing at once. Tensely we waited for the attack, grasping our guns so tightly our knuckles grew white enough to show in the dark. But we saw no enemy. We received no fire. And gradually the din died down.

Only later in the day did we learn that the renegade SS troops had been nowhere near Offenbach, let alone our CP. The savage enemy fire had actually been the reports from a carload of ammunition that had caught fire and was burning in the Frankfurt rail yard just across the river, exploding in a barrage of detonating cartridges!

It was Easter Sunday, 1 April, April Fool's Day. That everyone at Corps CP felt a little sheepish is to put it charitably.

We could laugh at this adventure, but there was nothing to laugh about the next day when we went to a small town called Untermassfeld.

Untermassfeld had a huge, massive prison complex, forbidding and bleak—a Nazi work camp. Here thousands of inmates, mostly French and Dutch, were slowly being worked and starved to death. It was the first such camp I had seen. I was shaken and sickened.

Illness and malnutrition were rampant among the prisoners. The camp rule was absolute: No work—no food. The rations meted out were so minute that the inmates soon became too weak to perform what the guards considered a full day's work. The punishment was—no food. And the victims would slowly starve to death. It was no matter. There was a continuous supply of new workers available.

As I walked through the dismal corridors of the prison with a young medic from the liberating troops, it was like accompanying Dante on his journey through hell. The suffering and agony coated the cold stone walls and hung in the air like a stifling poison mist. In one cell I saw a man still lying on a couple of filth-soaked sacks spread out on the hard floor. At first glance he did not appear to be alive. A skeleton. A skeleton stretched over with soiled, pallid plastic skin. He lay immobile, flat on his back, and I could plainly see the curvature of his backbone through his sunken stomach. From deep in black sockets his eyes stared unblinkingly into nothingness, eyes that were disturbingly empty. His shriveled lips were drawn away from rotting teeth in a grotesque, grinning grimace. His spindly arms lay stretched out alongside him, each separate bone in them and in his parchment hands bared like gnarled twigs. It seemed impossible that he could be alive. I bent over him. The stench was almost unbearable.

"Who are you?" I asked. I spoke in French, hoping he would understand.

He did not move, but in the hollow of his eye sockets, as if possessing a life separate from the rest of him, his eyes moved toward me. And through his decaying teeth came a shuddery whisper: "*Sucre . . . sucre . . .* Sugar . . . sugar . . ."

Deeply shaken, I turned to the medic with me.

"He wants sugar," I said, my voice tight. "For God's sake, give him some sugar."

The medic shook his head. "It would kill him," he said matter-of-factly. "It is a wonder he is alive at all. We gave him some soup, but he'll be dead before the sun goes down."

The inmates who were still able to function were jubilant. On the prison press they printed a message of gratitude that they had composed. The little placard was printed on one side in French, on the other in Dutch:

2 April 1945
Our glorious American liberators
wrest us from the inhuman life of
imprisonment at Untermassfeld.
The radiant sun of liberty floods
our overflowing hearts with hope . . .

It was a shattering experience. It left me numb. I had no way of knowing that Untermassfeld was one of the more benign of the Nazi camps. Had anyone told me so, I would not have believed him.

I would have been dead wrong.

Untermassfeld is located about twenty-five miles northeast of the town of Fulda in what only a few months before had been East Germany. When Cleo and I, almost half a century after my first visit to the place, approached the town in our car, the enormous, ugly, squat prison complex on the outskirts of the town, dominating the landscape, was the first thing we saw.

It had been an eerie feeling to drive across the heavily fortified border between what so recently had been East and West Germany, with not a soul in sight. We were acutely aware of entering what a short while ago had been forbidden territory, as we drove past the looming guard towers and the forbidding control buildings, past the cement barriers, past the plowed once-mined death strips, and past the twisted barbed-wire fences that snaked across the countryside as far as the eye could see—all now totally deserted, grim architectural dinosaurs—realizing that only a few months before, people attempting to reach freedom had risked and sometimes lost their lives where we now drove through unchallenged.

The road into town led directly past the huge prison complex. In front of the main building a large, open gate led to a spacious parking area where several of the little light blue East German police cars were parked. We drove through the gate and joined them. I had decided that if I'd be able to get anywhere at all, I'd have to barge in.

About fifty feet in front of the fortresslike building, surrounding it, was a heavy wire-mesh fence with a sturdy wire-mesh gate. I dismounted and walked up to the gate and rattled it. At a control window in the building beyond, a couple of guards watched me with suspicion. After a few seconds they buzzed the gate open. On a path between two tall wire-mesh fences I marched up to the window and stopped. A guard behind it slid a pane of glass aside; two other guards stood behind him, hovering over his shoulders.

"Was wollen Sie?" the seated guard asked suspiciously. "What do you want?"

I explained to him that I had been to the prison in 1945 when it was overrun by the American troops, and I was interested in knowing if it still operated as a prison. I asked if it would be possible for me to see the inside courtyard.

The answer was a gruff "No!" I had expected it; I only wanted to see how far I could go. "Is it still a prison?" I asked.

Frowning, the guard nodded.

"What kind of prisoners are kept here now?"

"All kinds." The two guards behind him walked away, out of earshot. I could see them confer earnestly.

"How many are here?"

There was a slight hesitation. The frown furrows on the man's forehead grew deeper. "I can not tell you that," he said flatly.

"Is it still a work camp?"

"I can not tell you that."

The two other guards returned to take up their positions behind the seated man.

"Are they criminal prisoners?" I asked.

"I can not tell you that."

"Political?"

The East German guards exchanged glances. One of the standing guards broke in. "Are you a newspaper reporter?" he asked, unfriendliness in his voice.

"No," I answered him. "I'm only interested because I was here before."

"There is no one here who can answer your questions," the guard snapped. "You will have to go through the proper channels."

"Of course," I said. "I shall do so." I looked at the man. "I was merely interested in knowing if Untermassfeld is still used as a prison. I understand it is. Thank you."

I turned to leave. As I walked away I was aware of three pairs of eyes boring into my back. I marched between the tall wire-mesh fences to the gate. I reached it and tested it. It was locked. I waited. The buzzer did not sound.

For what seemed an age I stood at the locked gate. I deliberately did not look back. Finally the gate was buzzed open, and I walked out onto the parking lot where Cleo was waiting in the car.

As I walked toward the car, a uniformed guard—white tunic, dark trousers, and a peaked cap—came hurrying toward me, summoned by his comrades, no doubt. I stopped and greeted him pleasantly. He was slightly taken aback, but recovered quickly. "You can not stay here," he said brusquely. "You must leave."

"I didn't know," I apologized. "We are leaving right now. I was only curious if the prison was still in use."

"We can give you no information," the guard snapped.

"And I was interested in knowing what kind of political prisoners are kept here now," I finished.

He shot me a hostile glance. "I must ask you to leave," he said, his voice tight. "Now, please."

"Of course," I said. *"Grüss Gott!"* I used the friendly Bavarian greeting, a sort of "God be with you!"

He made no reply, only glared at me as I got into my car and drove past him, away from the forbidding prison.

Cleo glanced soberly at me. I knew she'd be glad to be through the gate and out on the road again.

On a napkin between us lay a piece of breakfast pastry. It was dusted with white sugar.

Sugar.

Suddenly memories came flooding back, and the Keystone Kops confrontation with the Untermassfeld guards didn't seem so funny.

After the Offenbach incident our CIC team had leapfrogged Lauterbach and moved on to Vacha, a picturesque little town with several romantic half-timbered houses and a pretty fountain in the town square. It was at this time that XII Corps was ordered to change its direction of thrust by ninety degrees and thus was deflected from driving north into the heart of Prussia—perhaps toward Berlin—and instead sent pushing east and south along the Czechoslovakian border, through Bavaria, and ultimately into Austria. As a result the front was fluid and constantly changing. I like to think that contributed to the monumental goof I was about to make.

Corps troops had just taken a small village, and Military Government, which had become operational as soon as we reached German soil, had requested that a new mayor or village leader, with whom they could work, be installed as soon as possible. Consequently I was asked to drive to the village, oust the Nazi village leader, and install someone I thought fit. It was a busy time, and I felt I could handle this small matter on my own, so against SOP I set out alone.

It was only about a ten-mile ride, and I had easily located the village on my map. I had to make several detours along the way because of road damage or blockage; most signposts had been knocked down or turned around, and when I arrived at the village even the sign that identified the place was gone. Not unusual. Instead a makeshift barricade had been thrown across the road, aimed at stopping or slowing down the advancing enemy armor. I made my way around the barricade and barreled into the village, my gooseneck wire cutter rearing from the front of my jeep as if asking for trouble. But none came. The streets were empty, completely deserted. Not even a GI was in sight.

Vaguely I wondered why, but I figured they were busy securing the area in front of them before setting up in the village.

A sign on the local *Gasthaus* identified the office of the *Ortsbauernführer*, the Nazi leader of the village, a sort of "mayor," and I swaggered into the place. I found the man cowering in the kitchen and heaved him out of office on his ear faster than you can say ex-*Ortsbauernführer*. I had him tell me where I could find a man who had been reported to us as being the most reluctant Nazi in town, the best we could do, and I looked him up and summarily installed him in the office of village leader. With him I went from house to house and collected a bunch of frightened villagers, brusquely ordering them to dismantle at once the Mickey Mouse barricade they'd thrown across the main drag into town. They hopped to it as if they had dynamite sticks up their collective butt. I told them to scrub off all the inane Nazi propaganda slogans painted on the walls, such as *Ein Reich—Ein Volk—Ein Führer,* "One Reich—One People—One Leader," and I generally threw my weight around before I left and returned to Iceberg Forward.

Back at Corps I reported to my CO, who was in the War Room.

"Fine," he said. "Did the company CO tell you when the Military Government boys can come up?"

"Didn't see him," I replied. "In fact, I didn't see anybody."

"You *what?*"

"Nobody there but the Krauts."

"What do you mean 'nobody there'? There's a whole damned company in that town."

"I didn't see a single GI," I insisted.

"Where the hell did you go?"

I told him the name of the village. He nodded. Right. "Show me on the map."

I did. I stared. The village I'd just turned upside down had a different name.

My CO looked at me as if I had two heads. "You went *there?*" he exclaimed. "Jesus Christ, you moron! That village hasn't been taken yet! It's still in enemy territory, for crissake! What the hell did you *do* there?"

Sheepishly I told him.

He shook his head. "That's one for the book."

It seemed I'd taken a wrong turn at one of the detours and blundered into the wrong village, a village still held by the enemy, and "taken" it, if not by storm, by drizzle.

When the village finally *was* taken, after a heavy firefight, we found out that when I had been there, the place had been bursting at the seams with troops from a Waffen SS outfit armed to their eyeballs. Ordering all the villagers to remain in their homes and stay off the streets, they had hidden in cellars and lofts, ready to strike. They had watched me, but apparently I'd seemed so cocky and arrogant that they were convinced half the U.S. Army was about to follow me—right into their ambush. Corps had known about these SS troops, and that was the reason the village so far had been left alone.

I took a lot of ribbing for that one. I was called a one-man *Blitzkrieg,* a poor man's Wrong-Way Corrigan, and a lot of less complimentary epithets. It had not been my finest hour.

But my choice for village leader stayed in office.

It does sometimes pay to be in the wrong place at the right time. If my little exploit doesn't prove that, the encounter of a certain master sergeant attached to a Corps IPW team does.

CHAPTER 6

Quite a few Germans and Austrians served in the Military Intelligence Service. They had come to the United States before the war, leaving their native countries because of the Nazis, and they had become U.S. citizens. Because of their intimate knowledge of the enemy country, the people, and the language, they were of great value, and most of them did a magnificent job. This particular master sergeant was one of them.

Sometimes, of course, it was quite amusing to hear their heavy accents, and this was especially true for our master sergeant, a man in his late thirties who had a deep hatred for the Nazis. This very capable man was a member of a prisoner of war interrogation team, an IPW.

On this particular occasion his team had been transferred from one unit to another and was to set up new quarters a few hundred yards behind the front. The sergeant went out in his jeep to scout the terrain and select a suitable location. On his way back he was challenged by a American soldier.

"Halt! And identify yourself!" the GI ordered, pointing his rifle at the sergeant.

"I am an Amerrican Sarjent," our man said imperiously, pointing to his stripes. "A Master Sarjent! I am on ze vay to mein unit."

That was enough for the GI, and despite his heavily accented protests, the sergeant found himself in the PW cage along with a batch of newly captured Germans!

The GI had acted quite correctly. Still fresh in everyone's mind was the utter confusion and disruption created by Hitler's supercommando,

Col. Otto Skorzeny, when in December 1944 he'd launched "Operation Greif" and sent his "jeep parties" behind our lines—captured U.S. army jeeps with German soldiers aboard who spoke "American," wore American uniforms, and carried U.S. identification, including dog tags. They'd created havoc. They'd helped our troops get lost by turning around the signposts at crossroads. They'd waylaid lone patrols; they'd cut communications cables, snarling our supply lines; they'd masqueraded as MPs and misdirected traffic, and they'd looped red ribbons around trees at safe roads, the standard warning that the road was mined, while removing these ribbons where they found them. It had been a time of dangerous bedlam and crippling suspicion. The rear area had been panicked by Skorzeny's phony and deadly GIs; everyone had been suspect. GIs were doubting and questioning one another; high rank had been no exception, even Gen. Omar Bradley had been detained and had had the devil of a time identifying himself to the satisfaction of the distrustful GIs. And because a rumor had started that Skorzeny and his commandos were out to kill General Eisenhower himself, the Supreme Commander had become a virtual prisoner in his office, in order to ensure his safety. The situation had been totally snafu!

The U.S. Army had combated the damaging state of affairs by instituting the strictest security measures, which had compounded the confusion even further. So when the vigilant GI heard the obvious Teutonic accent of our master sergeant, he thought, "Shit! Here we go again!" Taking no chances, he bundled the sergeant off to the local detention center.

The sergeant made the best of an annoying circumstance and used the time to good advantage. The German prisoners received him as one of their own, and he got more information out of them than he probably would have been able to get in an interrogation—certainly with less effort—before he was brought before his own astounded teammates to be interrogated! As a result of this incident, the sergeant thereafter occasionally had himself thrown into the PW cage, and he always emerged with much important information.

Interrogation by a CIC agent and an IPW differed only in the kind of subject usually interrogated. The CIC was primarily concerned with spies, saboteurs, war criminals, and subversives; the IPW concerned himself with prisoners of war. But often the two overlapped. For that reason our training at MITC Camp Ritchie had included a thorough course in IPW.

To the IPW the name of the game *was* information. Military information. Information about the enemy. He had been thoroughly trained to pry such information from prisoners of war who were usually most reluctant to talk or refused to do so altogether—without resorting to the kind of force and violence all too often practiced by the enemy. The tactical IPW's mission was to work as close to the fighting front as possible, so he could quickly interrogate any prisoner taken and get any vital information he unearthed to the commanders in the field. He spoke the language of his adversaries fluently, whether it was Italian, Japanese, or German. His quarters were often set up hastily in barely adequate locations and close to where the action was.

IPW Leo Handel glanced wearily at the luminous dial of his wristwatch: 2305 hours, just one hour since he turned in to get a little much-needed sleep. Dammit!

As he made his way to the blackout tent, he was dimly aware of the battle noises in the not-too-far distance. He automatically identified the crackle of small-arms fire and the occasional burst from a light machine gun or the *karrump* of an incoming mortar shell. He shook the mist of fatigue from his mind and gathered his wits. He had to be alert; a new batch of Kraut prisoners had just been brought in, and it was his team's job to interrogate the PWs and get every bit of valuable information out of them as speedily as possible.

Handel entered the tent and sat down behind the rough wooden table. He nodded to Sergeant Murray who stood at the door.

"Let's have him," he said wearily.

The German prisoner was led in. He stood stiffly at attention. His gray uniform was torn and dirty, and he looked almost as exhausted as Handel felt. The IPW fixed the man with an impersonal stare. "You are now a prisoner of war," he said in faultless German, "and your treatment here will depend largely on your conduct and cooperation. Is that understood?"

"Jawohl, Herr Hauptmann," answered the prisoner, promoting the IPW to captain and looking straight out in front of him.

"Your name?"

"Richter, Hans. *Unteroffizier*."

Handel glanced at the shoulder straps on the soldier's uniform. Yes, he was a sergeant as he'd stated; there was the elongated, horseshoe-shaped silver band denoting his rank. "What unit do you belong to?"

The PW hesitated. He was obviously ill at ease. He knew as well as the American IPW in front of him the importance of knowing what units the enemy had in direct opposition.

"*Herr Hauptmann,* I am allowed only to tell you my name, rank, and service number." The prisoner stood even more erect.

Handel looked hard at the German, sizing him up. He appeared to be a seasoned soldier, not just a civilian in uniform; no use trying to bully him into giving information. Another approach was needed. Again he looked at the shoulder straps on the man's uniform. A thin line of colored cloth tape encircled the edge. The color was black. That meant that the man was an engineer. Handel knew that each branch of the German army had its own color. White for infantry, red for artillery, orange for military police, and so on. Black was for engineers.

Handel nodded approvingly at the soldier standing at attention before him. "You have been well trained, soldier," he said gruffly. "Your commanding officer should be proud of you. What is his name?"

"Major Horst von Wetterling," snapped the PW proudly.

Handel made a slight nod to Sergeant Murray, who stood just inside the tent entrance, and the sergeant quickly went out. Handel slowly lit a cigarette. He spread out a map of the sector on the table in front of him. He was fully aware of the effect the aroma of the smoke had on the PW. Lazily he studied the map and the soldier, who kept standing at attention. The inactivity, the uncertainty obviously were getting on his nerves. Only a few minutes passed, and then Sergeant Murray returned and silently handed Handel a slip of paper. It read:

> **OB** Major Horst von Wetterling, commanding officer, 173d Engineer Battalion attached to 73d Infantry Division.
>
> **73d Inf. Div.**
>
> Commanding officer: Lt. Gen. Rudolf von Bünau (53)
>
> Composition: 170th, 186th, 213th Inf. Regt. 173d Arty Bn. 173d Rcn Bn. 173d AT Bn. 173d Eng. Bn. 173d Sig Bn.
>
> Home Station: Würzburg—Bavarian personnel.
>
> Previous campaigns: Poland, Saar, France, the Balkans, Southern Russia, Crimea and Caucasus. End.

Inwardly Handel smiled. The Order of Battle book had been useful once again. All this information from one name. Now to use it. He fixed his eyes on the PW.

"To what company of the 173d Engineer Battalion do you belong, Richter?" He delivered the question like a shot.

Startled, the PW stared at him. How did this American know his unit? Against his will, wonder, incredulity, and uncertainty crept into his face. He began to stammer something about being in the infantry.

Handel cut him short. "Stop lying!" he ordered sharply. "I know all about you. You are not the first from your unit that I have interrogated." He looked him squarely in the face. "Your unit of engineers is attached to the 73d Infantry Division, home station Würzburg, commanding general, General von Bünau. Now—out with it—your company?"

The PW hesitated only a moment. The American officer seemed to know everything already. There was little point in denying him the answer. Obviously someone must have talked before him. He could only hurt himself by being stubborn.

"Second company, third platoon, *Herr Hauptmann,*" he said smartly.

Handel thought quickly. He knew the exact organization of a German engineer battalion: about 850 men at full strength, an HQ unit, a signal section, two partly motorized companies, one fully motorized company, one motorized bridge column, and a supply unit; and he knew their equipment and their armament to the last detail. The second company was a partly motorized company whose main function usually was laying mines.

"How long have you been with the 73d Division?"

"Since Poland, *Herr Hauptmann.*"

It checked with the OB book.

"What was the mission of your platoon?"

The PW didn't answer.

"What was the mission of your platoon?" Handel repeated.

The prisoner stood ramrod straight. He was sweating, but he stubbornly remained silent.

Handel contemplated him. "Stand at ease," he ordered. The PW obeyed. "So," Handel said, "you won't cooperate." He nodded slowly. "Of course, I'll have to make a note of that on the report that will accompany you to the rear echelons." He sighed, resignedly. "You realize, of course, it might influence the way you—eh, the way you will be treated."

The PW moved uneasily.

"I'm going to turn you over to Sergeant Goldstein, now," Handel continued, nodding toward the waiting Sergeant Murray. "The sergeant is of Polish descent. His parents were killed in the ghetto of Warsaw. He'll take care of you."

He motioned to Murray. "He's all yours." He dismissed the PW and returned to his papers on the table in front of him.

The German PW looked frightened. Nervously he eyed the American sergeant who grimly approached him. What he saw apparently did not reassure him; he suddenly turned to Handel.

"One moment, please, *Herr Hauptmann.* I—that is, my platoon—we were to lay a mine field."

Handel looked up. "That's better, Richter," he said. He shoved a map toward the PW. "Show me where."

The German did. It was impossible for him to back out now. He described the field pattern and the safe paths as best he could.

"Your company has nine light machine guns and one 20mm anti-tank gun," Handel continued matter-of-factly. "Where are they placed to cover the field?"

The PW looked wonderingly at the American. Did he know everything? Now that he had started to talk, there was no way to stop. He showed the IPW the locations of the guns.

There were many other questions: about the other units of the division, about gun emplacements, and about troop deployment. The PW drew German army symbols on the map to show exact locations, and Handel mentally translated these enemy signs into American army symbols. The interrogation, once the PW was broken, yielded much information, which was quickly put into a report ready for prompt dissemination. Handel's job was done; he had the information he wanted.

Handel stepped out of the blackout tent. Outside stood the PW he had just interrogated—alone, smoking a cigarette. Handel went up to him, slapped him on the back, and said—this time in English—"Thanks. That was a damned good job. How about a cup of coffee?"

The PW answered, "Okay, suits me." And the two of them wandered off together, while the crackle of small-arms fire and machine guns kept up the infernal racket in the distance.

For this interrogation had taken place in Camp Ritchie in the Blue Ridge Mountains of Maryland, the Intelligence Training Center where the IPWs were trained, and the year was still 1943. The German "PW" who so convincingly had played the role of a combat engineer in the German army was in reality one of the many linguist instructors who were used in this training program. This was the last maneuver before graduation, the so-called "eight-day problem," in which the graduating IPWs were subjected to conditions as near as possible to those they would encounter in the field. Therefore the loudspeaker system was blaring forth simulated battle noises day and night for eight days, making real rest difficult if not impossible, and "prisoners" were brought to the graduating IPWs for interrogation at all hours.

The IPW teams had an important mission to fulfill on the battlefield. Our army had realized that there was no better source of fresh tactical information about the enemy units in contact than the newly captured prisoners of war. In order to get this information correctly and quickly, and above all accurately, certain intelligence officers and enlisted men received special training in prisoner-of-war interrogation at Camp Ritchie.

The training was thorough—and grueling. But once an IPW had finished the course, he knew considerably more about the enemy armed forces, his organization and armament, his officer corps, the missions of the various units, and the meaning of their uniform insignia, than he knew about his own. No details were left out. I went through that training myself at Camp Ritchie and was fully familiar with the vital mission entrusted to the IPWs. It was there that I met Leo Handel, who was to become a lifelong friend.

IPW Handel used the OB book to good advantage in his training interrogation. Order of Battle intelligence, OB, consists of carefully evaluated information about the enemy's army organization, strength, disposition, and individual units, collected by our intelligence agencies in as much detail as possible, sometimes down to the names of company commanders. This information, after thorough checking and editing by special OB teams, was printed in the Order of Battle book.

The purpose of this book, which was constantly being kept up-to-date by republication, was to furnish intelligence officers with a clear and accurate picture of the enemy army in all its aspects, from the function and composition of small units to the organization of the High Command. In this book could be found the histories of all main enemy units, including names and short biographies of their commanding officers and staff members. A thorough IPW in the field would augment his OB book with even more detailed and up-to-the-minute information about the enemy units immediately opposite his own sector.

The value of the OB book to the interrogator, whether IPW or CIC, cannot be exaggerated. It served not only as a check on the veracity of statements and claims made by the subjects but also as a source; the knowledge of one small fact would be sufficient to release a vast fund of information. For the commander in the field, the book was of tremendous value in facilitating the planning of military operations and in judging the enemy's local capabilities.

By far the largest number of officers and men at Camp Ritchie were being trained as IPWs, German, training that I also received. The schooling was as tough as it was thorough. First was a compact course in the organization of the American army, the British army, the French army, and the Italian army. Then came careful training in communications, sabotage, photo intelligence, and keeping intelligence records and in all the various other aspects of intelligence. Terrain intelligence was high on the list. Maps and the use of them were painstakingly studied and explained, and several times the trainees would undergo the same test I had in the OSS. They would be taken by closed trucks at night to some unknown district and handed a map of the area on which every village, stream, hill, or other terrain feature had been given a name either in German or Italian. It was up to the student to find his way back by picking out landmarks, studying the nature of the terrain, and comparing it with the map and orienting it. Asking the local population did little good for those who tried. It was difficult to make people understand that you didn't really want to go to Salerno or Bittendorf but to some little village right there in Maryland. And people were apt to become suspicious of someone with a heavy foreign accent and a foreign map asking directions.

But the real purpose of the IPW course was to impart a thorough knowledge of the German army, its organization and tactics, its maps and map symbols, and its documents and records of every description. The future IPWs learned German army organization directly from the training manuals of the German army itself, until they knew by heart the exact breakdown of every type of unit, including the number and types of weapons and all other equipment carried. Even such outlandish units as a *Nachrichtenhelferinneneinsatzabteilung* (female signal operations battalion), an *Astronomischer Messzug* (astronomical survey platoon), and a *Kraftfahrzeuginstandsetzungabteilung* (motor vehicle repair battalion) were studied and remembered.

They learned German army identification, from the colors of all the various services and arms and the insignia of all the ranks, to the individual emblems of specialized jobs in the German army, right down to the special insignia of the apprentice to the noncommissioned officer in charge of shoeing horses. And they learned German army abbreviations and German map symbols—and the Germans, being a thorough race, had thousands of them, from army group headquarters to bread-baking platoons, right down to the individual bicyclist who had a special symbol that could be varied to distinguish him as the Number One man or the Number Two man of his squad. Even messenger dogs and carrier pigeons had their own symbols. And, of course, IPWs would learn the art of interrogation—always remembering that PWs were to be treated according to the Geneva convention—all the little tricks and psychological devices and ploys that would make an unwilling man talk, that would break the stubborn prisoner.

The record of the IPWs' contribution and experiences on the battlefield makes exciting reading. It is not a history of a few spectacular achievements, although such do exist, but of a continuing flow of information of the utmost importance to the commander in the field.

Here is just one routine periodic report from one IPW in combat in Italy, Leo Handel. The intelligence officer's summary of the information his team had given to their field commander, covering a period of five days during which an American attack was launched, reads as terse military jargon, enlivened only by a few humorous touches:

Activities of 87 Mtn Inf Regt IPW Team
from 20 Feb to 25 Feb 1945

The PW interrogation center of the 87 Mountain Infantry Regiment was established night of 19 Feb at map ref 505152 (vic [vicinity] Vidiciatico). The setup consisted of an interrogation room, sleeping quarters for the interrogators and attached personnel, and one cage for incoming and one for outgoing PWs.

The first members of the master race to take advantage of the facilities provided arrived shaking from cold and recent experiences early morning 20 Feb. They had been captured on the right flank of the regimental sector, and as was determined later, did not know what hit them.

The enemy MLR [Main Line of Resistance] running from Rocca

> Corneta to Mt. Belvedere was held by the 5th and 6th Cos (W and E) of the 1044 Regt, 232 Div and reinforced by elements of the 14 (AT) Co of the 1044 Regt, which had constructed strongpoints and set up specially trained anti-tank squads equipped with AT close combat weapons. The 7 Co, 1044 Regt was W of the 5 Co and the 8 Co, 1044 Regt followed the 6 Co to the East. The 5 and 6 Cos had each appr. 80 to 100 men in combat strength on 19 Feb. Both units were virtually wiped out by the first impact of our attack. Most of the men who were not killed were regrouped, however, on our side of the fence. 40 men of the 5 Co and 43 men of the 6 Co were present and accounted for at the 87th PW cage.

All this detailed information about the enemy forces had been gathered through interrogation of more than one hundred PWs. Their statements had been checked and double-checked against one another and when confirmed had been speedily reported to the field commander for his disposition. But how do you get a man who is unwilling to talk to give you information of a nature obviously destructive to his own side?

Leo had several ways. One of them was the "P" method, a sort of three-step affair. If the prisoner persisted in his refusal to talk, Handel would appear to get increasingly angry and sharp with his subject. If the man still refused to talk, step 2 would go into effect. Handel would order his sergeant to grab the prisoner and follow him. He would lead them out behind the house or a nearby shed. Here he would grimly draw a rectangle in the dirt the size of a man laid out, six feet by two feet. He'd throw a spade at the PW and order him to start digging. A few minutes of working on this cheerful excavation, and contemplating its probable use, as often as not made the PW quite talkative.

Should it fail—and there were those who would brave Handel's anger and even face death—should the trench take shape with no signs of the PW caving in, the rare step 3 would be put into operation. Handel would turn to his sergeant in disgust and say in German, "All right, he's almost finished. I'll get the leader of that band of partisans who's been begging us for a Kraut. They'll take over. I'll be in the interrogation room. You know I can't stomach to watch." And he then turned on his heel to walk away.

Death might hold no terrors for the PW, but the prospect of death at the hands of a vengeful band of partisans was usually too much to face. Faced with the "P" ploy—P for partisans—the PW would talk.

So Handel got his information, nobody was hurt—and a slit trench was always in demand for other purposes!

Handel's summary goes on:

> The large number of PWs made it possible to obtain a clear picture of the situation. Two circumstances facilitated the compilation of intelligence: (1) A previous interrogation of a PW of 6 Co, 1044 Regt whose detailed statements proved to be correct. (2) The capture of the CO of the 6 Co, 1044 Regt (Lt. Kaiser), whose cooperation was secured.

This cooperation of Leutnant Kaiser, commanding officer of the 6th Company of the 1044th Regiment, was secured mainly because of the clever use of one speck of knowledge, which in the scheme of things seemed utterly unimportant.

It was Handel's wont, when entering a bivouac area previously occupied by the opposing forces, to gather all the papers he could find, including old hometown newspapers left behind by the troops. These papers were often gold mines of information that could be used to augment his OB book. From a previous PW, Handel had learned the name of the CO of the 6th Company, a Leutnant Kaiser, and in a local paper from a small town in the area from which the personnel of the 6th Company of the 1044th Regiment were recruited, he had read an article about a hometown boy, a lieutenant of the same name, congratulating him on the birth of a son, Karl Otto, born in January.

When a group of PWs taken in the 6th Company's sector included a lieutenant, Handel saw his chance. He walked nonchalantly up to the German officer and said, "Good morning, Leutnant Kaiser."

Startled, the German looked at him.

"And my congratulations on the birth of little Karl Otto," Handel continued. "Almost a year old now, isn't he? I hope your wife, Liselotte, is well."

In open-mouthed surprise, the young lieutenant stared at Handel. His sudden respect for American intelligence, whose knowledge was so complete that they could identify an obscure second lieutenant in the German army and know intimate details of his life, was so great that refusing cooperation seemed utterly futile.

Included in the information this officer supplied were the exact locations in the village of Castellucio of three 88mm self-propelled guns, which for some time had been harassing the American positions, taking a heavy toll in casualties and causing the headquarters to go completely underground. The locations of these guns were at once reported to Artillery Fire Direction.

Handel's paper collection often paid off. A newspaper story about a native son contained information that could be most useful if the man was brought before the IPW team for interrogation—not unlikely, since he did belong to a unit in direct opposition. Such knowledge never ceased to impress—and elicit cooperation.

Handel's report continues:

> Among arty targets pointed out by PWs on the first day of attack were a number of enemy installations in Castellucio. PWs reported on Feb 21 that our arty knocked out three 88mm SP guns in Castellucio.
>
> The enemy committed the first tactical reserves at 200400; one platoon of the 1 Co, 232 Rcn Bn was ordered to counter-attack W of Mt. Belvedere. The counter-attack was broken up before it got under way.

This enemy counterattack was broken up with the valuable aid of the IPW officer, who had learned of the plans from PWs whose statements about preparations and special activity had been correctly evaluated by the interrogator.

Handel often brought certain PWs to the forward observation posts of his outfit. With the enemy-occupied territory spread out in front of him, the PW could actually point out targets and installations on the terrain itself, thus assuring accuracy.

The report goes on:

> The first strategic reserves were committed in the early morning hours of Feb 21, when the Cos of the 1 Bn, 741 Regt, 114 Div were thrown in to regain lost ground. The presence of this divi-

> sion in the sector was not previously known. General Clark, who was notified about this new unit identification, ordered that one PW from this unit be evacuated immediately for strategic interrogation at higher headquarters.

When an officer such as Maj. Gen. Mark Clark, commanding officer of the U.S Fifth Army, takes personal interest in a little incident such as the capture of one German soldier, that incident is sure to be important. And it was.

The American offensive was geared to combat the resistance of units known to be in opposition. Here, suddenly, was identification of an entire new enemy division, the commitment of which to battle would certainly necessitate new plans and tactics. So this all-important PW was rushed back to Army for an exhaustive interrogation by a strategic IPW team.

Meanwhile Handel set out to confirm the presence of the new division and gather information about its deployment.

> The 3 Co, 741 Regt, 114 Div was committed N of Polla. PWs stated that the 1 Co was E of them, the 2 Co in reserve. The position of the 1 Co was confirmed later by paybooks found on the W slope of Mt. Belvedere. PWs of the 1 Co confirmed further that their Co was digging in on the NW slope of Mt. Belvedere.

It was while attempting to acquire information about this position on Mount Belvedere that step 3 of Handel's "P" procedure backfired. He had just told his sergeant that he was going to fetch the legendary partisan leader, to the horror of the digging PW, when one of Handel's fellow interrogators rounded the corner of the building and bore down on the little group. On his head was an Italian officer's cap, tattered and dirty; several cartridge belts were slung helter-skelter around his shoulders; a large red scarf was flowing from his neck; and from his bulging pockets protruded an assortment of knives and guns. In his hand he clutched a huge drawn sword—obviously the feared partisan leader in person!

"Let me at him!" he roared. "Let me have the bastard!" he shouted, as he clumsily charged toward them.

The sight was too much for Handel—he burst into laughter, and was soon joined by the sergeant and even the fierce partisan leader himself. The PW was not too dumb to catch on—and no information was forthcoming. But there were other fish in the net.

Handel's summary contains more information about the different units of the newly identified 114th Division:

> 153 PWs were captured by the 87 Mtn Inf between 20 Feb and 25 Feb and interrogated by this IPW Team. A large amount of documents was collected by various agencies and cleared through IPW. Some of them were necessarily outdated, but verified previously obtained intelligence. Among the intelligence obtained from documents were the following important items: (1) Identification and location of a new enemy infantry division. (2) Map Overlays and detailed plans of mine-fields in the vicinity of Corona. (3) Enemy arty maps indicating arty targets.

How many American lives were saved by that little item alone. What more can you ask than possession of a map showing areas the enemy has zeroed in on and intends to shell?

The activities of the IPWs were not limited to interrogations alone, however. Their ability to speak the enemy's language and their psychological knowledge of the enemy's character were often useful in other ways.

Thus, in April 1945, the Silver Star was won by Capt. Ferdinand P. Sperl, commanding officer of IPW Team 10, attached to XII Corps headquarters, for a daring feat.

Captain Sperl had learned through interrogation of several PWs that a group of German staff officers in possession of highly valuable documents was located behind the enemy lines opposite his sector. He volunteered to attempt to effect the capture of this group with the documents intact. Exposing himself to the gravest personal danger, Captain Sperl made his way through the German lines held by fanatic SS troops and made contact with the German staff commander. He succeeded in convincing this officer of the advisability of surrendering his group and the documents to an American task force. Captain Sperl then crossed the lines again, subjecting himself to possible capture or death, leading a task force that captured the staff group and the undamaged documents and returned them to our lines.

When the war was over and combat intelligence operations ceased, Counter Intelligence was charged with ensuring the security of Allied troops and bringing war criminals and Nazi leaders to justice. The IPW teams were on hand for conversion from combat to counterintelligence.

The G-2 Section of the XII Corps, doing occupation duty in Germany, had this to say about that arrangement in its Occupation Report of Operations: "The results were excellent; much worthwhile information and many leads to ultimate arrests by CIC were furnished."

Perhaps the best way to illustrate the opinion of our General Staff officers in regard to the achievements and contributions of the IPWs in combat is to quote the citation that accompanied the Bronze Star awarded Leo Handel, IPW, 87th Mountain Infantry Regiment:

> During the extensive operations of a regiment of mountain infantrymen against enemy forces fiercely defending their vital positions, Handel performed his vital duty as a member of the IPW Team with such devotion to duty and keen technical knowledge that the high efficiency of his section was maintained at all times. Through his tireless and intelligent efforts the success of the operations was speeded toward the final surrender of the enemy. He many times operated his station well forward in areas undergoing terrifying barrages of enemy artillery and mortar fire; but with tenacity of purpose he remained at his task, and by the tactful use of his superior knowledge and skillful methods of interrogation, he obtained much valuable information about the enemy's disposition and strength. His commendable work in the Intelligence section and personal initiative and bravery are truly typical of the highest traditions of the United States Army.
>
> By Command of Major General Hays

This was the IPW.

Not only military information was uncovered by skillful interrogation; other secrets were unlocked, and sometimes interrogation was hardly necessary.

This was the case in one of the most important nonmilitary revelations of the war, the discovery of a secret so vast, so astounding that the disclosure of it made headlines around the world.

CHAPTER 7

It was already dark and past the hour of curfew. The two MPs who patrolled the empty streets of the little undistinguished village of Merkers, between Vacha and Meiningen about fifteen miles southwest of Eisenach, were weary as they drove along, struggling to keep alert. Merkers had been taken earlier that day, 4 April 1945, by the 3d Battalion of the 358th Regiment, 90th Infantry Division attached to XII Corps. The mission of their outfit had been the usual follow-through in the wake of General Patton's advance tank forces as they barreled through Germany at breakneck speed. The task of the GIs was to clean up pockets of resistance and attempt to sort out German soldiers from foreign slave workers; of the latter there were many, for Merkers was the site of a huge salt mine.

As their jeep rounded a corner, the MPs spotted two women hurrying along the deserted village street. They stopped them. The women told them they were on their way to fetch a midwife for a farmer's wife who was in some trouble. This seemed a worthy reason to violate the curfew, and the MPs allowed the women to proceed. But just to be sure, they went along.

As they passed an entrance to the salt mine, one of the women whispered furtively, "That is where they have hidden it!"

The MPs' ears perked up. "Hidden what?" one of them asked.

"The gold," the woman answered, fearful now. "And—and all the money."

"Who hid it?"

"Die Behörden, the authorities."

"How do you know that?"

"It—it is being said," the woman answered.

Intrigued, the two MPs returned to the salt mine entrance. Some little local big-shot Kraut, they thought, had salted away his ill-gotten gains in the salt mine. How appropriate. Why not take a look? They entered the above-ground mine offices.

There were eight Germans present, all civilians, the guardians of the treasure. Politely one of them, a rotund, moon-faced individual, introduced himself as Werner Vieck, an official of the Nazi Reichsbank, and one of his co-custodians, a pale, gaunt man, as Dr. Paul Ortwin Rave, curator of the German state museums and assistant director of Berlin's National Gallery.

The MPs had stumbled upon the greatest treasure of the war. Now that its existence and hiding place were no longer a secret, the German caretakers talked freely and frankly about their charge. The mine, they told the incredulous MPs, held two hundred tons of gold bars; the German banker said it represented nearly all of the Reich's gold reserve!

In addition, they informed the Americans, there were three billion German Reichsmarks, probably the biggest hoard of German currency in the land, as well as great stacks of foreign currency: U.S. dollars and British pounds; Norwegian crowns and French francs; and monies from Spain, Portugal, and Turkey.

A detail of American officers and men went down into the mine. Besides the stacks of currency they found hundreds of crates and boxes, an enormous cache of priceless art: paintings by Rembrandt, Raphael, and Renoir, Van Dyck and van Gogh, and a "Venus" by Titian, all still in their ornate frames; a treasure trove of tapestries and engravings, including Dürers; and rare manuscripts by men such as Goethe and Schiller.

All this, and much, much more, was stored in chambers carved out twenty-one hundred feet underground. The Americans opened a few of the crates containing paintings and sculptures. On many of the cases they noticed stencils reading, Paris, Brussels, Vienna, and Amsterdam, but Curator Rave indignantly insisted that these were *not* stolen art treasures; they legitimately belonged to the Reich. They had all been removed from Berlin and stored in safety in the mine because the Russians were getting too close, he said.

The Americans asked about the gold, but bank director Vieck regretted that he could not show it to them; someone had lost the key to the specially secured chamber! Obligingly the Americans blew out the wall.

And there, in a salt-encrusted chamber, brightly lit by a string of electric bulbs running along the ceiling, was a mountain of gold. Thousands of bars, each bar weighing twenty-five pounds, each wrapped in a sack, each sack marked Reichsbank. And there were sacks of gold coins, many too heavy for a man to lift, and suitcases bulging with jewelry and precious stones.

It was a sight never to be seen again, and Generals Eisenhower, Patton, Bradley, and Eddy all examined the incredible treasure salted away by the Nazis in the Merkers salt mine.

It was not long after we had captured the great treasure of the Merkers salt mine that we suffered a much greater loss. On 12 April, President Franklin Delano Roosevelt died. We learned of it the following day. It was an occurrence that every GI felt as a personal loss; Franklin Delano Roosevelt had been our commander in chief.

XII Corps Forward was billeted in the town of Kronach, and here on 15 April, in a small garden in back of the command post buildings, a memorial was held. None of us who attended this gathering will ever forget the deeply moving, simple words of our CO, Maj. Gen. Manton S. Eddy, nor the manner in which they were delivered.

That memory was strong in my mind when Cleo and I, forty-five years later, stood in that same spot. The buildings had been remodeled, the garden was now a parking lot, but the memory was unchanged.

Somehow Kronach, lorded over by a massive, granite-strong fortress, Veste Rosenberg, once the headquarters of the legendary seventeenth-century Swedish king, Gustavus Adolphus, had seemed a fitting setting for a farewell to FDR. On the day of his death, Corps troops accepted the capitulation of another town dominated by a magnificent castle, the town of Coburg, whose commanding Veste Coburg, begun in the eleventh century and built on a hill overlooking the town, is one of the largest castles in Europe. The town itself had been badly shelled; when we entered the town, the white sheets of surrender flapped from many windows. The Adolf Hitler Haus on Coburg Square had been gutted, and several of the buildings of the castle itself showed the naked, scorched skeletons of fire-ravaged roofs. One of our missions in Coburg was to arrest the old duke of Coburg, a mandatory arrestee, who was in residence at the castle. We went there, but when we saw how frail and confused the old man was, we didn't have the heart to put him in a detention camp. He would not have survived. Instead, since we had no alternative, we let him stay at the castle and gave him a note suggesting to agents or units that might follow us that they leave the old man alone.

By 1990 both the town and the castle had been rebuilt. On Markt Platz, the 11th Armored tank on which forty-five years earlier I'd had my picture taken with a beautiful medieval building in the background had been replaced by a steaming sausage cart. The building, however, was still there, as were all the other picturesque old buildings, now free of surrender sheets, that ringed the square. The castle itself had been lovingly restored to its former splendor and perched jauntily and spectacularly on its hilltop, every building in fine tourist shape, the carefully kept up grounds ready to enfold in its operetta-like setting the throngs of visitors that swarmed through the woods up the hill. The old duke, of course, was long gone.

In Bavaria, land of hills and mountains, almost every town has a castle or fortress, a chateau or memorial on a hill towering over it, and this was true of the town to which we moved our billets from Kronach, the town of Bayreuth. But here it was not a medieval castle that crowned the hill but a monument to music, the famous Festspielhaus, Richard Wagner's shrine to his music and annual site of the world-renowned Wagner Festivals. Standing at the top of Festspielhaus Avenue, the imposing opera house was undamaged. The composer Richard Wagner personally laid the cornerstone to his edifice in 1872, and the inauguration of the Festspielhaus took place in 1876 before an august audience that included such luminaries as the composers Franz Liszt, Edvard Grieg, Peter Tchaikovsky, Gustav Mahler, and Saint-Saëns and other men of fame, including Friedrich Nietzsche—and Kaiser Wilhelm I himself. It had been the first performance of Wagner's *Ring of the Nibelung*.

Bayreuth had been taken on the fourteenth by the 11th Armored Division fighting with the 26th Infantry Division, and the town had been severely damaged during the fighting. Add to that the fact that the retreating Wehrmacht had stripped the town of food before pulling out, and Bayreuth was not a happy place when we pulled in. Their war experiences had been fully as bombastic as Wagner's operas. And here too the white sheets of surrender fluttered submissively albeit resentfully from the windows of shrapnel-scarred houses.

The traditional Wagner home, Villa Wahnfried, seemed to have escaped damage, but when I walked to the rear of the house, I saw that half of it had collapsed. In the wreckage of the large foyer stood Wagner's own piano, a big, black instrument with intricately carved legs and dated New York, 1876! Wagner's stirring opera *Parsifal,* created by him between 1877 and 1883, might have been composed on that grand piano. Miraculously it was undamaged, although covered with plaster dust and debris. When I touched the keys, I could not help but feel a little awed, particularly since my father, Lauritz Melchior, who was a Wagnerian *Heldentenor,* heroic tenor, and had sung in Bayreuth during the golden years between the First and Second World Wars, in 1923 had auditioned in this same entrance hall for Richard Wagner's son, Siegfried, undoubtedly accompanied on that same grand piano.

My father's last performance at Bayreuth was on 3 August 1931. Already the Nazi influence was being felt at the festivals. When Siegfried's widow, Winnifred, invited my father to meet the Führer, Adolf Hitler, whom she greatly admired, my father declined.

He left Bayreuth that same day. He was never to return.

And now, I stood in the ruined hall of Villa Wahnfried, tracing a crooked line with my finger in the plaster dust on Wagner's grand piano.

We set up shop in a large villa on the outskirts of town, following our usual routine of kicking out the German occupants for the time we were using their house so we'd be sure not to blow ourselves to Nazi hell on possible booby-traps. The villa had a large garden in the back, but it had been badly neglected; the shrubbery and flower beds were overgrown, the paths strewn with rubble.

I had taken a room on the ground floor facing the garden. One night, when I had just turned in, I thought I saw a shadow flit across my window. I was up at once, my gun—which was never far from my hand—held ready. But the shadow did not reappear.

Had I imagined it? Was I anticipating trouble because of the hostility in the air? Not until after dark the next evening did I get my answer. Once again the furtive shadow stole across my darkened window.

This time I was certain. Someone was out there. Who? Was I being watched? If so, why? I thought I'd better find out.

Being careful not to turn on any lights and lose my night vision, I quietly left the house, my gun in my right hand firmly locked against my abdomen, OSS style, a flashlight stuck in my belt, leaving my left hand free. There was an almost full moon and few clouds in the sky; visibility was more than adequate to get around.

Slowly, cautiously, I made my way to the back of the house and my window. I saw no one. I stopped. I stood stock still—and listened.

Nothing.

I was just about to move, when I heard it. A twig breaking? A stone grating against another stone? It was faint. It had come from the garden away from the house. Stealthily I began to make my way down the rubble-strewn path, through the weeds and broken masonry, to the bottom of the overgrown garden, careful not to make a sound.

I had gone perhaps fifty feet when I suddenly stopped. There in the darkness in front of me in a tiny clearing not ten feet away I could glimpse a figure hunched over on the ground, the back turned toward me.

Noiselessly I removed my flashlight from my belt. I aimed it at the squatting figure—and turned it on.

There was a short, sharp outcry. There, imprisoned in the beam of my flashlight, his face turned toward me, eyes wide in shock, mouth still open from the cry, sat a little boy, perhaps ten or eleven years old. He didn't move; he just squatted there in startled guilt, too frightened to try to run away.

I walked up to him. "What are you doing here?" I asked, my voice more brusque than I had intended. I hadn't realized how tense I'd been.

He didn't answer. He didn't have to. I saw.

On the ground before the kneeling boy was a small wooden cross, crudely put together. On the bare earth next to it lay a bunch of freshly plucked wildflowers.

I looked at the cross. A pet? A cat or a dog probably. It was not difficult to put together. The boy was grieving for his lost pet and had made the little gravestead in the garden, visiting it as one would the grave of a friend. But once ousted from the house in which he lived, and afraid of the new masters occupying it, he had restricted his visits to clandestine trips after dark.

I crouched down beside him and spoke as gently as I could. "Don't be afraid," I said. "I won't hurt you." I shone the light on the cross. "Who lies there?" I asked. "Your dog?"

He looked at me with huge, apprehensive eyes. He shook his head.

"No," he whispered. He held out his left arm toward me. The sleeve hung loosely from the elbow. "It is my hand."

I brought him in with me, and the next morning I took him to the couple who owned the house we now occupied and who temporarily lived with their neighbors. From them I got the boy's story.

His name was Dieter. He was ten. He came from Mainz on the Rhine. His father, his mother, and his sister had been killed in an air raid. He had survived, but his left hand had been badly mangled. With nowhere to stay in Mainz, he had been sent to live with his aunt and uncle in Bayreuth—in the house we had taken over for our CIC offices and quarters.

Dieter's hand had gotten worse. Infection set in, and amputation had become necessary.

When the boy found out, he was inconsolable. He simply could not face the loss of his hand. In his battered mind the loss of his parents and his sister, which he had not been able totally to accept, suddenly became fused with the loss of his own hand. After the operation he had insisted that the doctor give him the severed hand. He just could not bear to let go of it altogether. Somehow it had come to mean the loss of everything. His demand was, of course, not possible to meet, but Dieter persisted. When he was told his request was impossible, he'd retreated into a deep depression. He'd lost the will to live, and his condition worsened severely. Finally they hit upon an idea. They gave the boy a little box, securely sealed, and told him his hand was in it. He had believed them. And he recovered.

We made sure that Dieter and his uncle and aunt were taken care of as long as we stayed in their house. We told Dieter that any time he wished, he could come visit in the garden.

He did.

When Cleo and I arrived in Bayreuth in the late summer of 1990 we settled into a picturesque chateau called Schloss Tiergarten on the outskirts of town, which had been converted into a hotel. Bayreuth was back to its old colorful hustle and bustle.

We visited the Festspielhaus on the hill. It was closed for the season, but we walked all over it, and I remembered the two other times I had been there before. Once in 1930, when at the age of twelve I'd attended the Wagner Festivals in Bayreuth and for the first time heard my father sing an opera. I had roamed through the streets of Bayreuth, wearing my Bavarian *Lederhosen*, too young to be impressed by the dozens of famous men and women I met.

The second time I was there, fifteen years later, I'd been dressed in a U.S. Army uniform and had a gun in my shoulder holster.

Cleo and I drove along the little Bayreuth streets through which my father had driven in triumph after his last performance ever at the Wagner Festivals in 1931. The audience had gathered outside, waiting for him. They'd been an enthusiastic and exuberant lot. When my father got into his carriage they thronged around him; they unharnessed the horses, and a group of cheering young men drew the carriage down the Festspielhaus Avenue.

We went to visit Villa Wahnfried, now meticulously restored in its picturesque sylvan setting, and we watched and listened as a group of young schoolgirls were told of the great man who once lived there and his music that the whole world now listened to and loved.

When the following day we drove out of town, my mind was filled with memories, of a historical grand piano, dusty and abandoned, of my father's singing at the Festspielhaus, and of the hand of a little boy.

Dieter had been special, but throughout the war and during the occupation that followed, for us in our work the children were always especially hard to reach. It was not difficult to understand why.

If they were very young, they could not comprehend what went on; they were only aware of the stress, the fear, and the anticipation of awful things to happen. Once they were old enough to have had any schooling, or if they had belonged to one of the Nazi youth organizations, such as the pre–Hitler Youth Jungvolk, in which hatred and fear of the Americans had been drummed into them daily, they looked upon us with suspicion and hate. We were of necessity dealing with them on a vastly different level than the chocolate- and chewing gum–throwing GIs. In their minds we were out to take their parents away. Whenever we showed up, it meant trouble.

Perhaps the most harrowing, heart-rending episode in my work involving children—an incident I've never forgotten, and never will—concerned a mandatory arrestee, a man of sufficiently high rank in the notorious SS to warrant apprehension, special internment, and investigation. The man, however, was a simple, harmless fellow, totally apolitical, a printer who had his own little printing shop. The local SS corps had given him their business, and for business reasons the printer had joined their organization.

The SS had a program devised to increase the number of Aryan children born to the Third Reich. Each time an SS man fathered a child, he was promoted to a higher rank in the SS. Our little printer had seven children! For no other reason than his fertility, he'd reached an SS rank high enough to make him a mandatory arrestee.

It fell to me to pick him up.

They were all there when I arrived at the shop, the printer, his wife, and his seven children, the youngest less than a year old. They all instantly knew that something was terribly wrong. And when I informed them that I was there to arrest the man, pandemonium broke loose. No resistance, no anger, no rebellion—only abject grief and fear, pitiful pleading and beseechment.

"Please, please, please do not take my *Vati* away!" sobbed a little four-year-old girl, as she threw her little arms around one of my legs, turning her tear-streaked face entreatingly up toward mine. "Please, please, please do not hurt him!" she wailed.

The mother wept openly, at the same time trying to comfort the youngest children, who, while they did not understand, knew that something dreadful was happening. The other children, begging, sobbing, pleading, tugging in desperation at my sleeves and trying to kiss my hands in supplication, swarmed all over me in an avalanche of misery, fear, and anguish. The printer himself, pale and drawn and obviously deeply frightened, but concerned more for his children's torment than his own peril, tried to calm and reassure them. To no avail.

I attempted to explain to them that the arrest was only a routine matter, that no harm would come to their father, that he would be home again in a few days. My words fell on fear- and grief-deafened ears. I was not able to penetrate their shroud of terror and anguish. No amount of explanation and assurance could reach them. People taken away by the Nazi authorities were seldom seen again, and they expected no better from us, the enemy.

Still with me is the pitiful sight of the woman, cradling her wailing infant in her arms as she stood in the open doorway to the house staring after her husband, despair and bitterness etched on her face, and the sight of the wretched little faces of the children behind the tear-smeared window panes, looking betrayed and violated, their beseeching eyes filled with pain and grief as they watched me march off their father, convinced to the core of their anguished hearts that they would never see him again.

The printer was back home in less than a week, but I was not there to see the joy and jubilation at his homecoming. Instead I was about to descend to the other end of the emotional seesaw we were all riding.

It happened in Münchberg, a small village about thirty miles north of Bayreuth. Agent Bill Syring and I were there for a couple of days. We'd come up from Bayreuth, where the night before we had seen a USO show in the Festspielhaus that had featured a girl singer with a voice I am sure made Richard Wagner rotate in his grave at Villa Wahnfried. We were there to attend to some business, and we had taken over the mayor's office in the *Bürgermeisteramt.*

We were sitting there resting on our laurels, having just apprehended a Nazi big shot, a *Gauhauptstellenleiter*, an important state leader, when there was a knock on the door. On our "*Herein!* Come in!" the door was opened, and a girl slowly walked in. She was pretty, appeared to be in her early twenties, but her eyes were dark with suffering. We saw at once that she was a displaced person, a slave worker, probably Russian.

"Please," she said in a soft, trembling voice. "Will you help me?" Her broken German made her seem especially vulnerable.

We asked her what she wanted. She did not say anything—just looked at us with her big, tragic eyes. She walked—no, waddled—closer to us, her legs far apart, and lifted up her gaily colored skirt. High.

In utter shock I stared at her.

Between her legs was a large, blood-soaked rag. Carefully, painfully she peeled it away—and I gagged.

Where her vagina should have been was a huge, gaping, and festering wound. Blood and pus slowly began to ooze down her thighs, as she stood statue still, looking at us with her pain-filled eyes.

With the bitter bile still searing my throat, I croaked, "What happened?"

"The—SS," she whispered. "The SS—they—" She broke down and began to cry.

Within minutes we had a doctor in the office, and while he tended the girl so she could be transferred to a hospital, we got her story.

She was Ukrainian, and was forced to work for a farmer near Münchberg. An SS unit had been billeted on the farm, and when they were about to move out in the face of the American advance, they had first wanted to have their fun with her. All of them. In turn.

She had not been cooperative and had tried to fight them, so after they had had their fun, they had held her down, and to show their disapproval of her attitude and to make sure she would not give birth to a child fathered by the master race, they had cut out her entire vagina.

The emotional seesaw had shifted. My remorse, my self-guilt, for arresting that poor SS printer and inflicting such anguish on his family had changed to a raging anger at the goddamned SS troops, who deliberately and cruelly could inflict such inhuman suffering on a young girl.

We had her transferred to a U.S. field hospital, where they gave her the best care possible. But no one could make her whole again.

On 19 April 1945 troops from the 183d Field Artillery Group, attached to XII Corps, captured the town of Grafenwöhr, the site of a large Wehrmacht panzer and field artillery training school, and we moved the office of our CIC team to that town. A most sinister discovery was made here. A huge area of the training installation had been devoted to a colossal CWS (Chemical Warfare Services) dump. We found three million poison-gas projectiles and mines of all types, well hidden in the woods.

Our stay in Grafenwöhr was short. On 21 April the town of Weiden was seized, and we entered the town with the troops and set up shop in a house near the old town hall.

Weiden in 1945 had seemed just another drab and battle-scarred old town, neglected and run down during the years of war. The only bright spots in town had been the many white sheets of surrender that hung from the windows as limp signs of submission.

Not so in 1990, when Cleo and I drove into town. We turned up Unterer Markt, passing through the Nadelohr, the Eye of the Needle, the narrow gateway that cut through the tower of Das Untere Tor, the Lower Gate, which gives access to the Old Town.

In '45 this historic, fourteenth-century tower had slipped into sad disrepair; its walls were cracked and crumbling, its passageway gashed and marred by the passage of war, its roof destroyed. In 1990, the tower had been repaired and plastered and painted a pleasing pale gray with a darker gray for the beams of the half-timbered gatekeeper's house, and it had a new clock in the ornate, columned cupola that topped the steeply peaked, bright-red tile roof. It looked as if it had been built yesterday.

In Markt Strasse, the main street that runs through the old part of town, all the quaint, gabled fifteenth-century houses that lined it had been restored and sparkled with a painter's palette of muted colors, pinks and blues, yellows and greens; it was a cobblestone street running between two pastel rainbows of mortar and brick, a veritable fairyland town—incongruously surrounded by a skyline of the modern buildings of the new town.

The busy hustle and bustle of a prosperous town filled the street spilling into the square instead of the lines of solemn, dejected *Burgers* who had stood in the street in front of their houses when we had arrived in '45, hoping that by holding large white surrender bedsheets spread out between them, they could save their homes from being peppered by small arms fire from the GIs looking for snipers.

Cleo and I admired *Das Alte Rathaus*, the Old Town Hall, which stood on Markt Square, dwarfing the other buildings, brightly painted and festive in its picturesque, high-peaked majesty, its elaborate *Glockenspiel* charmingly chiming the melody of the hour as we drove up.

Weiden had held one other "distinction" in '45: it had been the gateway to Flossenburg, one of the most brutal, inhuman, and barbarous concentration camps of Nazi Germany. The camp was located only ten miles northwest of the town.

Flossenburg, established in 1938 as a "correction center" for political dissidents and later converted to a concentration camp, was primarily a work camp, where the inmates slaved in a busy granite quarry under the most grueling conditions—which kept the camp crematorium busy. Not only prisoners categorized by the Nazis as "undesirables" or "inferiors," such as political foes and Jews, but also prisoners of war, were interned at the Flossenburg hellhole in the early years. In 1941, 2,000 Russian PWs were imprisoned at Flossenburg; 102 survived.

The guards at Flossenburg had a reputation for being exceptionally cruel, sadistic, and inventive in their atrocities. It was here, we were told, that the infamous X-game originated. This is how it was played: The players formed two teams, and each team sent one of its members into the camp barracks to pick one inmate for use in their game. He was called "the pawn." The playing field was the size of a tennis court with a sort of cross beam gallows, looking like a miniature goalpost, erected at each end. The two "pawns" were stripped naked and hung by their wrists from the top beam of each gallows, legs spread out and anchored to the bottom of the upright posts. High in the air he hung, spread-eagled, forming a human X. The two teams would gather in the center of the field, each team with its favorite guard dog, usually a big German shepherd. Specially trained. At a signal from the SS referee, the two dogs would be turned loose. Cheered by the players, egged on with shouts and whistles, each dog would race for the opposing team's gallows posts and jump and snap at the spread-eagled "pawns" hanging above them.

The winning team? That team whose dog first ripped off the testicles of the opposing team's "pawn."

I was told it was a popular sport.

The Flossenburg game spread to other camps. After the liberation of Dachau, the *Stars & Stripes* of 3 May described the dogs, trained to jump for and tear off a man's male organs. "Many dogs now lie dead beside their kennels," the article reported, "where the doughboys shot them."

It was from Flossenburg that the notorious Death March began. When toward the end of April the Nazis realized that the camp was about to be overrun by elements of the 11th Armored Division, they were determined that the inmates of Flossenburg should not be liberated by the advancing Americans. The camp crematorium was working past capacity. The ovens could handle no more. So the camp commandant was ordered to march those inmates who could still walk to safer ground near the Czechoslovakian border and leave the rest to die.

During 16 to 20 April, fifteen thousand men had started out on what was to be truly a march of death.

For three days and three nights, without food, without water, and without rest, these already emaciated inmates had been driven, whipped, and bayonet-prodded on their torturous march, clad against the raw April weather only in thin, ragged striped camp uniforms. Those who were too weak and ill to go on and fell by the wayside were either shot, bayoneted, or clubbed to death by the Nazi guards—or simply left to die in agony. So shrunken were their bodies that they hardly bled when gutted by the German bayonets. The road shoulders along the route had been littered with abandoned corpses; for days after taking the territory we had to cope with the disposal of these pitiful horrors.

Toward the end of the nightmare march, some forty-five miles from the camp near the small village of Neunberg, the brutish SS guards, realizing that they could not prevent their charges from falling into American hands, had embarked upon a frenzy of killing, slaughtering hundreds. Of the original 15,000, half were now dead. Those who could staggered away into the cold countryside, crawled into the woods, into barns or other shelters, many there to die; others collapsed where they stood. The SS guards finally fled to safety before the American onslaught.

After overrunning the area, the Americans held a soul-shattering mass burial at the village of Neunberg. The villagers who had tacitly condoned the atrocities of the SS and ignored pleas for help by the survivors, were forced by the American unit that occupied the sector to dig up the shallow, temporary graves, furnish a coffin for each victim slaughtered within their township boundaries, and provide a proper burial, with every man, woman, and child in the village required to attend the ceremony.

The shaken U.S. Army officer in charge had given the assembled villagers a grim, unforgettable message in the name of the Corps commanding general. "Only God Himself," he said, "has the terrible might and the infinite wisdom to visit upon you, your cohort, and your leaders the dreadful punishment you deserve. May the memory of this day, and of these dead, rest heavily upon your conscience and the conscience of every German so long as you shall live!"

When Cleo and I, forty-five years later, traveled the same route covered by the Flossenburg Death March, we saw no signs of the past—neither the march nor the imprecation of the U.S. Army officer.

Although the GIs—and our own intelligence personnel—for the most part behaved responsibly and refrained from perpetrating atrocities such as those committed by the SS, I wish I could say that such behavior never occurred in the U.S. Army, that we always wore white hats, while the Germans always wore black hats. Regretfully, I can't. Lamentably there *were* incidents—albeit isolated incidents—of brutality, although nothing that could compare with the kind of inhuman cruelty carried out by the Flossenburg guards.

And thus it was, that while working in the area at the time of the Flossenburg Death March, I was nearly court-martialed.

It happened in a little village called Vohenstrauss about ten miles southeast of Weiden. We'd set up our offices in a two-story house, using the rooms upstairs on the second floor as interrogation rooms as well as our personal quarters. A huge pile of unevenly cut logs had been stacked outside by the occupants directly in front of the main entrance to the house, providing easy access to the firewood—as well as good protection from stray bullets.

One day when I returned to our offices from an outside investigation, the sergeant on duty downstairs told me that there was a PW upstairs waiting to be interrogated, probably a deserter, as he'd been picked up while trying to surrender. The sergeant also informed me that an MP captain was waiting to see me.

There was no captain downstairs, so I walked up to the second floor. On my way to my quarters, I walked by the closed door to one of the interrogation rooms. I stopped short—and froze.

From the room beyond came the faint sound of muffled thuds. A voice, unmistakably American, could be heard: "Talk, you fucking Kraut! Talk! Talk! Talk!" Each "talk" was accompanied by a dull thud.

I flung open the door. In a split second I took in the scene before me. It was not a pretty sight.

In the room stood a young MP captain. In his right hand he held a metal-tipped riding crop, affected by a few rear echelon officers emulating Patton. He was using its sharp point to prod at a large barely healed wound high on the right shoulder blade of a man standing before him. Stripped to the waist, his hands bound behind him, the man stood facing the wall, toes touching the baseboard. The blood from his opened wound ran in rivulets down his sweat-glistening back. His spasmodic breathing alternated with low moans.

"Talk!" the MP captain snarled. "Talk! Talk!" And with each word, using his free left hand, he rammed the man's forehead into the wall. Hard.

I felt cold rage well up in me. I did nothing to repress it.

"What the hell are you doing?" I cried sharply.

The captain glanced back at me. "Oh. Hi," he said cheerfully. "Just doing your job for you, is all. Figured you weren't here and could use a little help."

He dug the riding crop into the man's wound. In two strides I was at the captain's side. I grabbed the riding crop from his hand and in an instant of fury, broke it in two and flung it to the floor. Savagely I kicked it away.

Startled, the captain whirled toward me. Belligerently he began to protest.

I seized his jacket with both my hands and hurled him with all my might across the room.

He rammed backward into a chair, tumbled over it, and ended up in a heap on the floor. For a moment he sprawled there, staring at me in incredulous shock.

I stood silent, trying to calm myself. I had not meant to hurt the man, but my rage at his behavior had gotten the best of me. The captain climbed to his feet. "What the fuck is the matter with you?" he growled angrily. "You crazy or something?" He picked up the pieces of his broken riding crop.

"What the hell are *you* doing?" I shot back. "Torturing a PW? That man is *my* responsibility!"

I glanced toward the prisoner. He had turned around. I suddenly felt my rage return and surge red-hot through me.

The man was leaning wearily against the wall, favoring his injured shoulder. But it was his face. His forehead was a mass of bleeding holes where a nail, placed in the wall at exactly the right height, had been jabbed into his brow every time the captain slammed his head against the wall. His drawn and pale face was streaked with runnels of blood oozing from the wounds. His hands tied behind him, he was trying to blink the blood from his eyes. One spot on his forehead was so pitted with holes that a flap of bloody skin had torn loose and hung limply down over one eye. The man looked straight at me. His face was a mask of pure pain, the red-streaked mask of a clown made up in hell.

I turned back to the captain. "You—damned—bastard." It was difficult to get the words out.

Irate, the captain stalked up to the table. He snatched from it a *Soldbuch*—the soldier's paybook—which sometimes contained information about him. He thrust it out at me.

"Look you dumb asshole," he snarled. He jabbed a finger at a word in the booklet. *"Totenkopf!* Read it! Right there! *Death Head!"* He banged the *Soldbuch* down on the table. "You and me both know what those *Totenkopf* bastards were," he said heatedly. "Concentration camp guards, that's what! Murdering, sadistic swine, every one of them." He nodded malevolently toward the trembling PW. "That one probably belonged to that Flossenburg gang. Don't be a fucking bleeding heart for *that* Kraut shithead. This is a picnic compared to what *he's* used to dishing out!"

I picked up the *Soldbuch.* I only had to glance at it. "You goddamned dumb bastard," I said, my contempt, my disgust bitter in my mouth. "Didn't you read this? Or can you? That man belongs to the 1st SS *Totenkopf* Infantry Regiment, SS Panzer Grenadier Division *Totenkopf.*"

"That's what I damned well said," the captain spat at me. *"Totenkopf!* You think—"

"That man is an *infantryman,* dammit!" I interrupted, my fury barely contained. "He belongs to a Waffen SS Division *named Totenkopf.* He's a Pole, for crissake! A lot of foreign-born troops forced into the German army were put into the Waffen SS by the Nazis. That man does *not* belong to the SS *Totenkopf Verband,* you blasted idiot. *They* were the guards. He is no more a concentration camp guard than you are. Possibly less!"

"We'll find that out soon enough," the captain said icily. Before I could stop him he whipped the handle of his broken riding crop across the PW's bloody face. "Talk, you bastard!" he screamed.

My next action was pure emotion—no thought. I grabbed the captain by his uniform tunic; I literally propelled him out the door and hurled him headlong down the stairs.

My breath came in great gulps, my heart was racing wildly, as I stood at the head of the stairs watching the captain painfully pulling himself to his feet. In white-hot anger he glared up at me.

"You're in deep-shit trouble, you prick!" he snarled. "Striking a fellow officer! I'll see they throw the book at you at your court-martial!"

"I hope to God you *do* prefer charges," I said fervently. "I'd like nothing better than to see this whole stinking, rotten mess come out in a general court-martial!"

The captain picked himself up and limped from the house.

No court-martial was ever brought against me. I never heard of the captain again—and I never found out what he had wanted to see me about. But his outrageous behavior did have tragic results. On his way to the PW detention enclosure hospital, fearing what would happen to him next, the PW jumped from the jeep taking him there and was shot trying to escape.

It was one of the few such unholy incidents. The U.S. armed forces are made up of men. All kinds of men. Just like the population of the entire nation. Or the world. It would be miraculous if there were no rotten apples at the bottom of such a huge barrel.

The warden's office of the local jail in Weiden was a dingy, unexciting place. We had chosen this location for the drab and routine job of screening the flood of civilians, soldiers, and ex-soldiers fleeing before the Russians who daily streamed into our area because of the capacity of the jail to hold several subjects securely for further interrogation. It was here on 28 April 1945 that I heard a man utter the most startling statement I'd heard throughout the entire war.

"I am a werewolf!" he said.

CHAPTER 8

The Werewolf Organization was supposed to be a fanatic terrorist organization with the avowed purpose of "dealing death and destruction to the hated invaders," to quote from the propaganda leaflets they distributed all over Germany.

The reaction of most American officers in Germany to claims about the existence of such an organization was generally expressed by a contemptuous smile of disbelief and a dismissing shrug of the shoulders. There were bound to be subversive activities in a country occupied by the enemy, they said, but that was no reason to fall for the extravagant propaganda spread by a desperate people, headed by a lunatic propaganda chief named Goebbels, whose deranged brainchild the mysterious Werewolf Organization undoubtedly was. These "Werewolves" were supposed to be a secret organization of fanatic men, women, and children—SS, civilians, and Hitler Youths—sworn to fight the hated enemy by any means possible, and if need be gladly lay down their lives. It was a notion as absurd, these American officers claimed, as the name, dredged up from the medieval superstition that certain people, appearing normal by day, could transform themselves into ferocious, wolflike beasts at night. These creatures, called werewolves, would terrorize the countryside with their fierce and fiendish acts of murder and destruction. And that was exactly what the Nazi werewolves planned to do.

Dr. Goebbels screamed on the radio that every true German would be a werewolf with a fanatical belief in his cause, and that outstanding leaders were being trained to organize this murderous resistance.

But even this hysterical and mysterious daily radio program, which started off with a bloodcurdling scream, failed to convince the majority of Americans that the Werewolves actually existed.

Violent attacks on Americans and on German cooperators as well as serious sabotage against our supplies had, however, already taken place. The German mayor of Aachen, a large U.S.-occupied city on the Belgian border, had been warned by the Werewolves not to cooperate with the American Military Government; when he did, he was brutally murdered. American soldiers were found floating in the rivers, their throats cut; others were decapitated by guillotine wires strung across the roads. Supplies were destroyed mysteriously or disappeared, and equipment was sabotaged—all as the Werewolves had promised.

And now, here in front of me, stood a small, blond ex-Wehrmacht soldier with big blue eyes and a ruddy face, looking as innocent as a pot of cottage cheese, saying, "I am a Werewolf!"

But let me go back to the beginning of the case. His name was Josef Zingel. He was a Rhinelander, a discharged soldier trying to get home, brought to us for routine screening.

I was working at the job with CIC agent William G. "Bud" Hock, a young law student. It was customary for agents to work in pairs. After a while, you became more than a pair—you became a team. Bud and I were a team. The war was winding down, and we in the CIC had our hands full screening the thousands of subjects picked up by the MPs for various reasons: deserters and DPs, discharged soldiers and German civilians fleeing the Russians, politicians and party members. Among them might be saboteurs, spies, or mandatory arrestees. It was our job to screen out the suspicious characters for more extensive interrogation. It was a dull, routine job—for most cases.

This was not to be one of them.

Joe's papers were as good as could be expected under the circumstances of confusion and chaos, and Joe himself was eagerly straightforward and cooperative, but . . .

It is a peculiar thing, but when for months you have been interrogating all kinds of people, you develop a hunch as to whether or not they are telling the truth, a hunch that is seldom wrong. Bud and I both had a hunch that Joe was hiding something.

We gave him a pencil and some paper and told him to write down his military history for the last two years in detail: names, units in which he served, places, dates—the works. He clicked his heels smartly, cried a lusty *"Jawohl!"* and went to work.

When he had finished, we took his written record and compared it with the OB book, which was similar to the one used by the IPWs and was classified RESTRICTED.

Specifically, Military Intelligence Service described Order of Battle intelligence as follows:

> Order of Battle Intelligence consists of carefully sifted and evaluated information received from a great variety of sources on the organization, strength and disposition of enemy forces. This information, if complete and accurate, not only facilitates the planning of military operations but helps the commanders in the field to judge the enemy's local capabilities and to make their decisions accordingly.

When we compared Joe's version of his military history with the facts in our enlarged and augmented OB book, it didn't take us long to realize that our meek little Rhinelander was lying. His information was accurate and complete, but it is impossible to learn a life history in every detail without living it, and Joe had made two minor mistakes.

First, he stated that he'd served in a unit under a certain officer. The officer *had* commanded the unit, but, according to a German casualty list, he had been killed in action six months before Joe said he served under him. Second, he claimed that his unit had been engaged in a battle near a small town with a name very similar to another town where the battle actually had taken place—a hundred miles to the south. Close, but no cigar. These two small errors showed that Joe's history was *learned* not *lived.*

We confronted him with our discoveries, showing him the entries in the OB book that contradicted his statements—there is something about the printed word that lends credence to any claim. We told him that it was no use lying to us anymore; we could and would find out the truth. If he did keep on lying, we could only suppose he was a spy or a saboteur, and he would suffer the wartime fate of a spy. On the other hand, if he told the truth, it might just save his life, and we strongly suggested that he do so. Now.

And that is when Joe blinked his big blue eyes at us, and at the OB book, and said, "I am a Werewolf."

It was a startling story he had to tell.

He was a member of a Werewolf organization. He had come with them from Czechoslovakia, where the Nazis had run a school for Werewolves under direct command of Reichsführer-SS Heinrich Himmler. They had arrived in Germany at the beginning of April, some four weeks ago, and had set up their camp near a little town called Schönsee. The organization was commanded by a General Krüger and numbered about 350 highly trained military personnel and civilians. Of these, about 45 belonged to the Headquarters Unit Camp called Sonderkampfgruppe Paul—Special Fighting Group Paul, using the commanding general's first name, to which unit Joe himself was attached—the other units were distributed among three hidden operational camps. Slated to go into action once the Americans had overrun their positions, they were equipped with all types of small arms and had stocks of ammunition, high explosives, food, and other supplies to last for many months. Joe only knew the location of the HQ camp, and when we ordered him to show us on the map where the camp was located, he did. It was in an area already behind our lines! Joe's last contact with his unit, he said, had been on 24 April—four days before.

It was quite a yarn, but Bud and I believed him. We realized the importance of the information and immediately set out for Iceberg Forward in Schwarzenfeld. Here we saw the Assistant Chief of Staff, G-2, Col. John H. Claybrook, and told him our story. It was the first actual evidence of organized Werewolf activity, and Colonel Claybrook must have been a little incredulous, but he was the kind of man who believed in giving his agents in the field a chance to do their job the way they thought it best.

"Do you believe it, Melchior?" he asked me.

"Yes, sir, I do," was my answer.

"Stick with it, then," the colonel said. "What do you want in the way of support?"

"Two companies," I answered. It was what Bud and I had decided would be needed.

Colonel Claybrook raised an eyebrow. "Pretty steep," he said. "You're sticking your necks way out, aren't you? There *is* a war going on."

He contemplated us. "Okay," he decided. "You've got it. When?"

"Tomorrow—0500 hours, sir."

He nodded, and at once made contact with the XII Corps unit whose sector included the Schönsee area and ordered tactical support for Bud and me.

During the night and most of the following morning of the twenty-ninth, while Iceberg Forward moved on to Viechtach, Bud and I interrogated Joe further. He claimed to be a deserter from the Werewolves. We weren't entirely convinced of that, but in any case what was more important were the details about the organization he gave us. Besides learning inconsequential information—Krüger had only recently been promoted to general, but usually wore civilian clothes, his wife liked roses, and the unit, when it moved from Czechoslovakia to its present position, had used 124 horses to draw their wagons—we learned that the headquarters unit was located in a small forest between the villages of Schönsee and Eslarn; that the HQ personnel seldom left the area and when they did they were extremely careful not to leave any signs of their presence; and that the HQ unit was not to carry out any actual subversive activities, but only direct such activities by the other three operational units located in a semicircle around the HQ site. Communication was maintained by radio; agents were sent out from HQ to locate and report on possible targets; and even now the first such targets were being selected.

In the afternoon we drove to the headquarters of the 97th Infantry Division, in whose area Joe's Werewolf unit was supposed to be located, and arranged with the G-2 to have two companies of infantry search the designated wooded area. We gave the field commanders instruction on how we wanted the search conducted. Plans were laid to start the operation at 0530 hours on 30 April 1945.

It was a clear and cloud-free morning, and the ground was fairly dry when we began our search. We had placed the two companies opposite each other in two semicircles. They were to go through the entire length of the wood, infiltrating through each other and in this manner preventing the escape of anyone hiding in the forest. The soldiers had been given instructions to comb every inch of the wood, investigate any signs of a bivouac area, and arrest every enemy soldier and every civilian they found.

As soon as the operation got under way, Bud and I went to a nearby farm where we had set up a temporary barbed-wire PW enclosure, big enough to hold about seventy-five prisoners and guarded by twelve MPs with two machine guns.

The whole operation was being monitored by a sour, highly skeptical major from the 97th, who—dripping with rather inane sarcasm—found it irresistible to make snide remarks about our private war against an army of invisible werewolves. He wanted to know if we included vampires in our quest.

At 0900 the search was completed. The two companies of infantry departed while Bud and I looked over the result of their efforts. They had brought back exactly three Wehrmacht deserters, found wandering in the woods in search of some Americans to whom they could surrender, and three elderly civilian forest workers who had been engaged in sawing wood. That was the entire bag. They huddled, bewildered and frightened, in the PW enclosure, eyeing their twelve MP guards and the two machine guns apprehensively.

We dismissed the three soldiers as not being connected with the Werewolves, directing them to the nearest PW cage; there were hundreds of German soldiers roaming the countryside looking for a way to surrender or to get back to their own units. The war had moved fast here; changes had been rapid, and many of the enemy had been cut off from their units. But there was a chance that the forest workers, if not actually a part of the Werewolves, might know about them. We had to make certain, and quickly. Now that we had shown our hand, we had to complete our work before dark or give the Werewolves a chance to steal away during the night. Our major observer had a field day with his fatuous put-downs, but we refused to believe that there was nothing to Joe's story—we had to "stick with it." Besides, I had a disturbing picture of just how far my neck was stuck out by now. Obviously, drastic measures were needed.

We took the three elderly foresters into a small nearby field and placed them in a triangle, facing away from each other but within earshot, each man held by two MPs.

I walked up to the first one.

"Name," I said brusquely.

He told me.

"You belong to the Werewolves," I shot at him.

His eyes grew large with fear. He began to tremble. "No," he burst out. "No! *Du lieber Gott!* Dear God, no!"

"You know where they are." I spoke loudly, making sure the other two heard every word.

"No." The man was obviously terrified. I did nothing to calm him. I frowned in anger. "I know you are lying," I said icily. "Unless you tell the truth—now!—I'll have you shot as a spy."

The man said nothing, but he was literally shaking with terror.

I walked over to the second man, who had overheard the exchange. I stepped in front of him. He eyed me fearfully. I deliberately called upon my experience as an actor. I scowled angrily at the man.

"You too are a Werewolf, are you not?" My voice grated unpleasantly. My eyes bored savagely into his.

"N—no!" he stammered. *"Bitte, bitte.* Please believe me. I—I know nothing about them. Nothing!"

I made a show of removing my gun from its holster. "You lie!" I said, apparently able to contain my fury only with difficulty. Slowly I walked around the man to stand directly behind him. "Once more. Are you a Werewolf?"

"N—No!—"

"Do you know where they are?" The terrified man began to turn around to answer me. Roughly the MPs jerked him back.

"Don't turn around," I ordered him brusquely. "Just look straight ahead and answer my questions. Do you know where the Werewolves are hidden?"

"N—no—please, I—"

"Dammit!" I exploded. "I am getting sick and tired of your lying. If you don't tell me the truth—right now!—I'll shoot you on the spot! Now—for the last time—do you know where the Werewolves are."

"I do not! Please—I do not—"

I fired.

The shot rang out over the field and echoed through the forest. The two other men were kept from turning around to look by the MPs holding them. They had no doubt that their comrade was lying dead behind them. The SS would have killed him. Exactly like that. So they did not see that my bullet had entered the ground next to the prisoner, who was kept from crying out by a ham-sized MP fist clamped across his mouth.

I marched up behind the third man. I pushed the barrel of my gun into his back. I cocked the gun. The click could be heard throughout the field.

"Well?" I growled.

"Yes!" the man cried. "Yes! Do not shoot! I will tell you. I know. Please do not shoot!"

I did not remove my gun. "Talk!" I ordered him.

"We—we are not—not Werewolves," he stuttered. "We—we only worked for them. In—in return for some—some horses they gave us. We—we brought them fresh food. Milk. Bread. Vegetables. That is all we did. I swear it! Please, *Herr Offizier,* that is all!"

"Where *are* the Werewolves?"

"In the forest."

"You know where in the forest?"

The answer was barely audible. "Yes. Only—I think so."

"What do you mean, *think?"*

"We—the provisions we brought. We had to leave them. In a sack. Under a big tree." He rambled on, his nervousness making him speak in staccato sentences. "I—I know where that is. And—one day, one day when I was leaving. I saw someone come out from the thicket and pick it up."

"You will show us where."

The man wet his bloodless lips. *"Josef-Maria,"* he whispered. "They—they will kill me, if they—"

His mouth fell open, and his eyes grew wide as he saw his two comrades being led past him by the MPs—both very much alive. Thunderstruck, he stared at them. Then he turned to me with a look as if he were staring at the devil himself. A most satisfying look. I'd obviously played my part well. My audience had found me thoroughly believable.

But we had a problem. Our support troops had departed, and there was no time to recall them. All we had were our twelve MPs and the division observer, Major Know-it-all. With Bud and me, fifteen strong.

We left two MPs to guard the other prisoners, and the rest of us followed our reluctant informer into the forest—the same forest that had been searched by two companies of infantry only hours earlier.

Many German forests are laid out in squares, one hundred meters (sixty-five yards) on each side. They are harvested and replanted by the square, so the trees in any given square are all approximately the same height. Our reluctant guide took us to a tall fir tree standing by itself near the corner of such a square, thick with a stand of spruce trees twelve to fourteen feet high. He'd never been in there, he breathed, but that was where the Werewolves were—he thought.

The ten MPs, Bud, and I more or less encircled the hundred-meter-square stand of spruce, the division observer prudently keeping well to the rear. We took up positions behind stumps or logs or rocks. It was a pathetic if not ridiculous sight—our little force "surrounding" an area one hundred meters square, an area that supposedly hid four times that many fanatic Werewolves armed to the teeth with automatic weapons of all kinds! But it was our only course of action, short of losing them. We had to rely on bluff. When we were all set, we began loudly to shout to the Werewolves that their area was surrounded, to surrender and to come out with their hands up, or else.

There was no reply.

We kept up our shouts and threats for the better part of half an hour. The sun stood high in the sky, and the afternoon was well under way. There was little time to spare.

We finally realized that someone would have to go into the area and reconnoiter: Bud and I, of course. After all, it *was* our caper. Very cautiously we penetrated the spruce square, our guns drawn and our eyes and ears alert for the faintest suspicious sign. But as we went farther and farther into the stand of trees, crisscrossing the area without finding the slightest indication that someone was there, we were joined by the MPs. We became increasingly bold, and for two hours we tramped all over this little spot, examining practically every tree and clump of grass.

We didn't find a damned thing.

Suddenly a shot rang out. Immediately we all hit the dirt, but it was only one of the men, who had tripped over a root and accidentally fired his carbine. The nervous laughter bounced among the evergreens. Finally everyone tired of looking for what they termed imaginary Werewolves, and the division major, a self-satisfied I-told-you-so grin on his face, departed with the MPs and the three civilian prisoners, leaving Bud and me to our disappointment. It really did look as if we had hauled everybody out on a wild-goose chase. Not only were our necks way, way out, they were resting firmly on the block.

We decided that if the Werewolves were not there now, at least we could try to prove that they had been there and perhaps vindicate ourselves after a fashion. We got into our jeep and began circling around the spruce tree patch we had searched so thoroughly without success, looking for signs of previous camping activity—forgotten trash, abandoned supplies, perhaps. We did one complete turn. Nothing. We did a second complete turn. Still nothing. We did a third turn; by now we were at least three hundred yards from the original square and close to abandoning the search, when we came to a small alfalfa-covered clearing at the bottom of a rise. A small wooden hut stood in the middle of it. We stopped the jeep out of sight and crept back to the clearing to observe the hut, and we saw the peculiar shimmer of hot air rising from the chimney. Someone was in the shack or had been there very recently. We decided to investigate.

Very carefully we stole down the slope toward the hut, approaching from the side that was closest to being blind; only one small window faced us. Closer and closer we moved, our .45s in hand, hoping we would not be seen. We reached the cabin and made for the door. Then, in pure Dick Tracy fashion, we kicked in the door and burst into the shack, guns held ready.

Five people, three women and two men in Bavarian farmer's clothes, were sitting in shocked surprise around a table with a large tureen of soup in the center, spoons lifted halfway to their open mouths. They stared at us.

It was time to bluff.

In a brusque, matter-of-fact voice I said, "General Krüger! Front and center!"

Of the two men, one was about fifty years of age, the other was younger and a cripple. Before he could check himself, the older man started to get up.

We had bagged the Werewolf general himself.

But we were alone. Just the two of us—in the middle of the Werewolf lair. We had no idea how the situation might develop. There was need for no more than a glance between Bud and me. He did not speak German; I did. We obviously needed tactical support, so Bud at once took off, leaving me to guard the general and the other prisoners.

I knew that the only way I could keep the five from jumping me was to act totally confident, keep talking, keep them off balance—in one gigantic bluff. I told them that we had the entire area surrounded by troops. I dredged up from my mind every little detail Joe had told us; I asked about the general's wife, was she able to enjoy her favorite roses where she was? I congratulated him on his recent promotion and expressed my interest in how he had divested his organization of 124 horses by giving them to the farmers in the area. I tried to give them the impression that we knew all about them, when the truth was that we didn't even know where the general's Werewolves were holed up. And all the time I studied the five tense prisoners.

The general was dressed in a green embroidered Bavarian jacket and dark gray forester's britches; there was none of the Prussian ramrod military stiffness about him. Slender, with a slight shoulder stoop, his hair graying, he might have been any middle-aged, middle-class German. His long face with deep nose lines and bushy eyebrows held sad-looking eyes that regarded me steadily, but without emotion.

"I congratulate you," he said formally with the slightest hint of a bow. His voice was cultured, pleasant and unexcited. "We had not expected to hold on forever, but we did not look for capture as quickly as this."

The younger man, the cripple, had braces on his right leg and right arm. He stood awkwardly, and unsteadily with his arms raised. The general nodded toward him.

"Will you permit my staff officer, Leutnant Schmidt, to sit down?" he asked. "His leg cannot support him for long."

I nodded my assent. "As long as he keeps his hands on his head."

I contemplated the five prisoners. It was the women who fascinated me the most. All three were in their twenties, with strong, healthy bodies and faces that might have been pretty had they not been marred by a fanatic hate smoldering in their eyes and distorting the soft lines of their lips. And I listened. For any sign that Bud was returning. I heard nothing. How long had he been gone? I did not dare look at my watch, but it seemed like hours.

I continued with my monologue, designed to keep them from realizing the true situation. I hoped it would work. God, I hoped it would work! I told the general that we had thought his organizational plans, with three operational units located in a semicircle around his headquarters, remarkable, and I commented on how many of his HQ complement of forty-five were in the field as agents lining up targets for him. Then I expressed interest in his radio communication network—anything to make them think we were in complete command.

But as time went by, it was obvious they were beginning to wonder.

I watched the women. I guessed they were *Wehrmachthelferinnen,* German Wacs. But were they secretarial help, or were they trained for active field duty? No matter. I had to maintain my attitude of easy unconcern.

"General," I said evenly. "You may let your female staff take their hands down. Clasp them in front. They will be more comfortable, while my comrade arranges for transportation to the rear."

Krüger said nothing. Not one of the girls moved. They glared defiantly and malevolently at me. I was losing control.

Where the hell was Bud?

It became increasingly difficult for me to maintain my air of confidence. I could feel the moisture of anxiety ooze from my armpits and trickle down my sides. I knew that little traitor beads of sweat were forming on my forehead, but I did not dare wipe them away. I could only hope they would go unnoticed. The .45 in my hand seemed to have shrunk to the size of a peashooter—and no signs of reinforcement were to be heard.

For a moment there was silence in the little hut. The tension was so thick I fancied I had trouble breathing. A subtle change was taking place. I knew what it was. They were getting used to the situation. The shock was wearing off. They would be doing some serious thinking. I saw them exchange glances. I was losing control. And then I heard it. The rumbling and roaring of trucks, the clanging and clattering of half-tracks, the general racket of armored vehicles barreling into the clearing and grinding to a halt, mingled with shouted orders and the din of many men. The most glorious music my ears had ever heard.

The door burst open, and Bud came flying in. When he saw me still in one piece, he broke into a wide grin. He looked at his watch; he'd been gone less than eight minutes.

He'd been in luck. As soon as he'd hit the road coming out of the woods, he'd run into an armored Intelligence and Reconnaissance Platoon, and ordered the platoon leader to follow him. Thank God for that CIC rejoinder, "I'm not outranked now!"

We put the platoon leader in the picture, but we still did not know where the body of the Werewolves were hidden, and there was little chance that Krüger or any of his Walküries would tell us.

I had an idea. I walked up to the general, quite arrogant now.

"All right," I said. "We are ready to pick up your men." I stuck my face menacingly close to his and lowered my voice ominously. "But remember, General," I warned, "no tricks. We'll be right behind you. Get going!"

Krüger shrugged. There was obviously nothing he could do. He turned on his heels and started up the slope into the woods.

I walked right behind him. With the general leading, all we had to do was follow, right? And we did. Bud and I and the whole damned platoon.

The general took us along the same paths we had driven in our jeep. He took us to the same little spruce-covered square that had been combed by our two companies of soldiers and then searched by us for two hours. He walked into the thicket—and stopped. I motioned to the platoon leader, and he quickly surrounded the area with his troops—this time done properly.

I turned to the general. "Well?"

For the first time the man looked uncertain. But it was too late. There was nothing he could do, even though he suddenly realized that we had not known where his HQ was, that he himself had just led us to it.

He looked at me, resignation etched on his face. Then he drew himself up.

"Hauptmann Gebhardt!" he called. "Captain Gebhardt. Report!"

From somewhere close by came the distinct though muffled reply: "*Jawohl, Herr General!*"

"*Antreten,* report!"

"*Zu Befehl, Herr General!* At your orders, General!"

Ten feet away from us a man rose up among the spruce trees—out of the earth itself. He was a tall, athletic-looking fellow, and when he moved into full view it was an added surprise to see that he was also a cripple, his right leg being encased in a steel-and-leather brace. He seemed to get along quite well on it as he stepped forward to stand smartly at attention before the general. A nondescript jacket topped his German army trousers and boots.

He was immediately searched. It developed that he was the unit's executive officer, and when we went through the papers found on him we hit the jackpot—a complete roster of the HQ Unit, numbering seven officers and thirty-eight noncoms and enlisted men.

Gebhardt had emerged from an underground dugout that he called the command dugout. He acknowledged there were other dugouts in the area, and we ordered him to show us where.

He shook his head. He could not do that, he said. He knew only two other spots; there were others, he conceded, but their exact locations were unknown to him. This was for security reasons, he explained. Only one or two other dugout locations were known to every man. He, as executive, knew three. We'd have to find the others.

But there was another way to bag the entire Werewolf gang; we had, after all, the roster listing every man. We told the general to order his entire command to report to him at once. Anyone found after thirty minutes would be shot on the spot! At Krüger's direction, the order was shouted in a loud voice several times by Captain Gebhardt.

After a few minutes, the strangest spectacle began to unfold. All through the area small patches of the grass- and weed-covered ground began to move, lift up, and slide to the side. Out of the earth itself climbed the Werewolves, sometimes emerging literally at the feet of the astounded GIs, who stood with rifles at the ready.

Sullen, unwilling, the terrorists began to gather in the center of the area where Krüger, Gebhardt, and we awaited them. They were tense moments; we knew the danger. We knew we had a fanatic, a desperate and murderous Werewolf pack on our hands. Would they surrender without violence? Was the resigned attitude of the two German officers with us a cover for a sudden bold break? We sweated it out—relying on stern and confident handling. In thirty minutes we called the roster. All were present except four outside agents, including Josef Zingel—Joe, our informer.

When we examined the installation, we realized how it had been possible for two companies of soldiers, twelve MPs, and Bud and me to fail to discover the Werewolf lair in the two previous searches. The installation was entirely underground and unbelievably well concealed. It consisted of a command dugout that could hold six or seven men and several individual dugouts that held two or three, all constructed in the spruce-covered area in such a way as not to disturb the live trees. The entrances were for the most part located in the middle of a clump of trees. Each entrance was a two-foot-square hole in the ground. At about three feet down, this hole extended horizontally about ten feet and formed a cave large enough to accommodate three men. The cave walls and roof were reinforced with lumber, and there was a drainage ditch terminating in a sump pit under the wooden floor. The hole entrance was covered with a strong, close-fitting, boxlike lid on which grew the grass and weeds indigenous to the area, so that the dugout lid blended perfectly with the surrounding forest floor.

The lids could easily support the weight of a man; we'd trudged all over them for hours. Great care had been taken to destroy all evidence of habitation, such as bootprints, broken branches, downtrodden weeds, and discarded refuse of any kind, and to prevent paths forming in the area. When the accidental shot had been fired during our search, Bud had, in fact, hit the ground not two feet away from the entrance to one of the dugouts without noticing it.

Though the dugouts had all been constructed only a few weeks before, nowhere was there any loose dirt or other evidence of excavation. The Werewolves had taken some of it in sacks and mingled it with the dirt at the roots of wind-fallen trees; they had washed some of it away in a three-foot-wide brook that ran through the forest a short distance away, which also supplied them with water; the rest had been scattered on the dirt road that ran through the forest.

Existence underground, it seemed, had not been too bad. Most of the day was spent above ground in the surrounding forest, with sentries posted. Here sanitary necessities had also been taken care of, by lifting a chunk of sod, digging a small hole, and replacing the sod. Cumbersome, but effective. No fire or cooking had been allowed. Warm food and hot water came from the little forester's hut we'd raided. The dugouts were dry and well enough vented when the lids were left partly opened—they were closed only when there was danger of discovery. Light, when necessary, was provided by candles and compact battery sets.

The command dugout had a periscope device that ran up through the trunk of a tree, through which we had been under observation all through our search, and sounds could easily be heard in the dugouts. We had not been fired upon only because of strict orders by the general not to give away the position. Had we been successful in discovering the hideout, however, there would have been no reason for the Werewolves to withhold their fire, and it is highly doubtful any of us would have survived to tell the story.

Is the moral here that blundering pays off? It might seem so, as events developed.

As the prisoners were being processed for transportation to the nearest PW cage, the general turned to me.

"My uniform is in the command dugout," he said formally. "I request permission to change."

I frowned at him. Corps had a strict rule that officers were to be interrogated in the clothes they wore when captured. It was a sort of one-upmanship. A man in a dirty, bedraggled condition was apt to feel inferior to another officer in a spick-and-span uniform. But I felt good. Damned good! We'd been successful in our quest. Our judgment had been vindicated—and our necks were comfortably back in place. And besides, I was curious to see what the dugout looked like. So, against all rules, I agreed. On the condition that I and a GI accompany him.

There was only a fleeting hesitation before Krüger assented.

We descended the wooden ladder built into the access shaft. The dugout itself consisted of three rooms, two of them equal in size, the third at the end of the others, twice the size. Each room had a crude double-decker bunk, and along the unfinished lumber walls stood stacks of weapons, crates of ammunition, grenade boxes, batteries, and other supplies. In the room to the right I could see a radio transmitter/receiver setup that looked impressive. The dugout was lighted by rows of naked bulbs strung from the seven-foot ceiling. The general led us to the large room in the rear, obviously his personal quarters. Here, too, were stacks of crates, boxes, and batteries. A double-decker bunk stood against one wall, the lower bunk with a blue checkered curtain that could be drawn across it. Idly I wondered if it was Krüger or his female staff who required the privacy. At the other end stood a large table, heaped with papers and documents and with a large area map tacked up behind it.

While the general began to change into his uniform, watched by the GI, I went over to the table and started to glance through the papers before they were collected and sent back to AIC. It made fascinating and exciting reading.

In 1943 a school for guerrilla fighting and for combating guerrilla fighters was formed in Poland. During September of 1944, this school, which now also had a course in Werewolf recruiting, training, and operations, and was under the command of Col. Paul Krüger, moved to a town in Czechoslovakia called Thürenberg. In February 1945, an order from Reichsführer-SS Heinrich Himmler was received, stressing the importance of the Werewolf course. On 1 April, the school was closed and ordered to move to Germany with the remaining students and the cadre training staff, numbering somewhat over 350 men, and establish themselves ready to go into action after having been overrun by the enemy. By that time more than twelve hundred Werewolves had been graduated from the school, supplied with identification papers, and sent into Germany. The order from the High Command gave Krüger and his Werewolves their mission. It read: "To stay behind, evade capture, and then harass and destroy supplies of United States troops in the rear."

Upon receiving these orders, Krüger moved to the Schönsee-Eslarn area and divided his command into four units: the *Führungsstab*, or Headquarters Unit, and Operational Units A, B, and C, located in a semicircle about thirty to forty miles from Krüger's headquarters. Each operational unit consisted of ninety to a hundred highly trained Werewolves.

Besides these units, a five-man radio team was sent to the vicinity of Munich, more than one hundred miles away, to set up a radio relay station. Krüger's headquarters would send the general's orders to this relay station via a directional beam, and the station would in turn broadcast them to be picked up by the respective operational units. The headquarters unit would not do any transmitting from the concealment area directly. When needed, a radio team would be sent out to transmit from a different location each time to avoid detection and pinpointing by our radio direction finders.

It was necessary for Krüger to have agents outside to line up possible targets for him to choose from, and to obtain fresh food from the civilian population, who had aided the Werewolves in many ways, among others by housing and feeding the 124 horses owned by the organization. Joe, our informant, who had formerly been General Krüger's chauffeur, was one such agent, and so were the three "innocent" forest workers.

The document that I found in the command dugout was not the only startling thing we discovered. There was a motorcycle stashed away in one of the dugouts and a sedan automobile hidden in the woods some distance from the actual concealment area. The Werewolves had placed it there by bending down the larger trees and uprooting the little ones. Placing the car on logs, they had carried it over the bent trees into position, then replanted the small trees and released the bent ones. It was absolutely impossible to see this car unless you were right on top of it. We never did find out if our first wave of searchers had seen this car; it was, of course, not identifiable as a Werewolf conveyance.

Some of the Werewolves that belonged to Krüger's headquarters unit were in their army uniforms, but most of them wore civilian clothes, as did the general himself. Each member carried a very small gun, called a "Lilliput," that could be concealed in the palm of the hand. A most useful weapon for a Werewolf terrorist, it could fire eight 22mm rounds.

All members of the unit carried discharge papers signed by Krüger and other necessary identification papers, impossible to detect as forgeries because they were issued by bona fide agencies. The men had been aware from the beginning that almost certain death awaited them in their mission. Several of them held high rank in the Nazi party. General Krüger was one of them—a fanatic whose quiet temperament and cool self-control made him all the more dangerous.

As I was glancing through the documents on Krüger's table an official order with a recent date caught my eye. I picked it up.

I had positioned myself in such a way that I could keep an eye on Krüger and the GI guarding him. I was aware that the general had been watching me go through his documents. He seemed resigned, only moderately concerned. He knew, of course, that the papers soon would be examined in detail. But now—did the man seem to tense? It was more a feeling I had than a tangible action on his part. When I looked at him, his eyes were studiously averted and he was busy buttoning his uniform tunic.

I began to read. I sat up, suddenly urgently alert.

The order was a priority—top priority—augmentation to the standing mission of the Werewolves. Henceforth, it decreed, in order to create confusion and disruption within the ranks of the enemy occupation forces, primary importance and preference in the selection of targets should be the assassinations of high-ranking U.S. Army officers, preferably general officers, with special emphasis on the assassination of the Allied Supreme Commander, Gen. Dwight D. Eisenhower!

An analysis of the general's accessibility and whereabouts was attached. It seemed most plausible and minutely detailed.

Clearly this was information that Corp HQ must have at once. By now the rather sheepish-looking division observer had arrived with a couple of division CIC agents. Leaving them in charge, Bud and I took off for Iceberg Forward.

On the basis of all the documentation, maps, and other material we found at Krüger's HQ, the operational units A, B, and C were located and destroyed. Thus a powerful, highly trained, and thoroughly indoctrinated organization of Werewolves, who had all sworn to fight to the last for the Führer and his ideals, and who were equipped to do serious damage to American personnel and supplies, was annihilated. The plan to kill our general officers was derailed—and the assassination attempt against our Supreme Commander never came to pass. The Werewolves, Hitler's last hope, had been dealt a death blow. Late in the afternoon of that same day, Adolf Hitler took his own life in the bunker in Berlin; 30 April 1945 had indeed been an eventful day in the *Götterdämmerung* days of the Third Reich.

Reporting on conditions in the Corps zone of occupation following the events of 30 April, XII Corps G-2 stated, "Things were remarkably quiet. There were, it seemed, no more Werewolves."

We'd botched the search for the Werewolf lair; we nearly lost the Werewolf general when we had him; and we knowingly disobeyed a strict Corps rule by allowing the Werewolf general to change into his uniform—and it all turned out just fine. Had we not, the vital documents giving the Werewolves their final orders might not have been unearthed until too late.

So—what *is* the moral?

An important and dangerous Werewolf organization had been ferreted out and destroyed by a big bluff and a little knowledge, put to the right use at the right time.

Personally I was mightily relieved that our judgment in requesting the execution of the operation against the Werewolves had been vindicated—and I was even more pleased when the action earned me the Bronze Star.

Little things used at the right time can pay off big—occasionally something as inconsequential as a single letter of the alphabet can make or break a case—as I was to find out.

CHAPTER 9

Into our office in the little town of Viechtach wandered a small, bespectacled man in civilian clothes whose eyeglasses had the wrong prescription, judging from the way he squinted through them. Politely he asked if ours was the office of the American secret police. We were used to being called the American Gestapo, so his choice of words did not faze us.

On 29 April, Iceberg Forward had moved the sixty-some miles from Schwarzenfeld to Viechtach, which had been taken on the twenty-fifth. The move, begun at 0800 hours, had taken four hours. Iceberg Forward was open for business at noon, when Gen. George S. Patton arrived to confer with the commanding general of XII Corps, Maj. Gen. S. LeRoy Irwin, who had taken over from Maj. Gen. Manton S. Eddy. General Eddy had retired because of ill health.

We were in the process of screening the flood of discharged soldiers, civilians, and petty German functionaries, men and women, that was pouring into our sector, fleeing from the Russians. They preferred to be captured and dealt with by us Decadent Democrats rather than fall into the hands of the Barbarous Bolsheviks. Our bespectacled visitor was but one of them, albeit one who had sought us out voluntarily.

We asked him for his papers. As he was searching through his pockets, coming up with a collection of dog-eared cards and smudged, crinkled papers, he poured out his story to us. He was a war correspondent, he claimed. For a big Swedish newspaper. He had been born in Sweden of Swedish parents and was a Swedish subject. When he was a small child, his parents had moved to Germany; his father had represented a major Swedish steel producer, and the Krupps had been one of his prime customers. He himself had grown up in Germany and been educated in German schools and therefore—except for a few words—spoke no Swedish. His parents had returned to Sweden just before war broke out, but he had stayed behind to work as a journalist. He had landed a job as a war correspondent with one of Sweden's biggest and most important dailies in Stockholm, and because he spoke no Swedish had sent his editor his stories in German. He had been on the Eastern front when it collapsed before the Russian onslaught, and he had secured permission from American front-line troops to travel this far into Germany; he had the papers right here. He had come to us to get permission to travel on, with the object ultimately to join his family in Sweden.

I contemplated the little man. His story sounded plausible, just unconventional enough to be true—or, at least, partially true. Which meant, of course, it was also partially untrue. But which was truth, which fabrication?

His papers corroborated his story and seemed genuine, including an obviously authentic travel pass issued by an American front unit commander. There was no reason to suspect the man, but it *was* possible that his papers and carefully planned cover story had been issued to him by his masters to give him freedom of movement for whatever purpose, and it *was* possible that he'd been able to dupe a field officer into giving him a pass. It *was* just the sort of procedure a clever agent might adopt in order to get to the destination of his mission unmolested, realizing that without the proper permits he'd constantly be in danger of being picked up.

Besides, and I confess that was probably the main reason for pursuing the matter, it was the first time in the whole war I'd had even a remote chance to use my knowledge of the Swedish language. French, yes. German, yes. Even the few words of Czechoslovakian I knew. But Swedish, never. I'd be damned if I'd let that chance go by.

And then, there was that funny little feeling. The hunch. The man was too credible to be true. He had every loose end tied up. Didn't happen often.

"How long have you worked for that Swedish newspaper?" I asked.

"Three years, sir," he answered. "A little more."

"Most of the war, then," I commented. "Must have been difficult to file your stories, getting your stuff to Sweden?"

"Not at all, sir," the little man said, squinting amicably through his glasses. "It was—routine."

"How?" I asked. "You used the mail?"

"Oh, yes. It was no problem. Sweden is a neutral country. There is no difficulty with mail. It is quite efficient."

I nodded. "And I suppose then, that the paper could send their payment checks back to you? And you had no trouble cashing them?"

"No trouble, sir. No trouble at all. There are very good business connections between Sweden and Germany."

"Did the paper use many of your stories?"

"Oh, yes," the little man beamed. "Many stories. Many, what you say, eyewitness stories and descriptions."

I nodded. I handed the man a pencil and a piece of paper. "Here," I said. "Please write down the name of your paper for me. I'd be interested."

"Of course, sir. It is my pleasure."

"Please print it," I requested. "I want to be sure to be able to read it."

The man nodded. Meticulously he printed the name of the newspaper. He handed it to me. "Please," he said.

I took the slip of paper. I glanced at it. And I began to laugh. I laughed so hard I could feel the tears gather in my eyes.

Uncomprehendingly the little man stared at me through his spectacles. Then slowly the color began to drain from his pinched face, as he tried to figure out what was going on, realizing that something was terribly wrong.

I was finally able to stop laughing. "All right," I said. "Let's stop playing games. I want the truth, and I want it now!"

With total bewilderment, he gaped at me. "The—truth," he gulped. "But—but I *have* told you the truth." He pointed to the papers lying on my desk. "My—my iden—"

"Stop it!" I cut him off, all my merriment gone. "Stop lying. *Who* and *what* are you?"

The little man tried to wet his thin, dry lips. *"Ich—Ich verstehe nicht.* I do not understand."

"That's obvious," I said scathingly. I held his note up before his nose. "A war correspondent! A journalist who for three years plus has been sending material to his newspaper in Sweden! And cashing checks from that newspaper! And you don't even know how to spell the paper's name!"

The little man was deathly pale. His forehead above his spectacles began to glisten with the sweat of fear. "But—I—"

"But my ass!" I shot at him. You made a very stupid mistake, my friend. A very German mistake."

I shook the slip of paper on which he had written the name of his paper. I plunked it down on the desk before him.

"Look at it," I ordered him. "Look at what you wrote!" I stabbed a finger at the words he'd written—SWENSKA DAGBLADET.

The German stared at the paper, his face a frozen, perplexed mask. He looked up at me almost pleadingly. He didn't utter a word; just kept shaking his head in total incomprehension.

"You don't get it, do you," I taunted him. "Well, let me explain it to you. You wrote the name of your paper all right, the *Swedish Daily Paper*," I pointed to the first word on the paper. "But you used a *W* in *Svenska* instead of a *V*, which is what it should be." I glared at him. "You've never written a damned thing for that paper. You've only *heard* the name. You've never *seen* it written. On correspondence, on headlines, on checks, or anywhere else. You think because *W* is pronounced as *V* in German and *V* as *F*, it's got to be that way in every other language. Well, it's not! In Swedish a *V* is a *V*! If you'd been a correspondent for *Svenska Dagbladet*, you'd damned well know how to spell the name!"

It took an obvious effort, but at last the little man was able to tear his eyes from the paper. He stared at me, his eyes widening in horror and shock, as the ramification of his little error, one single letter, began to sink in. I could almost see the thoughts churning in his head. He'd been trapped. He'd been so sure of himself, and he'd been trapped by one tiny overlooked detail. What else had been overlooked? Where else could he slip up? He began to shake; he was falling apart. He sank to his knees and buried his face in his hands.

It was not difficult to get the true story from him. He was a Nazi agent, a graduate from one of the Reich's top-notch schools for secret agents.

We left it up to the boys at AIC to get the full story of his mission. We had not the time to do so. Screening subjects were stacked up three deep.

But we really hadn't taken too much time in catching our bespectacled journalist spy. The entire investigation—by the clock—had taken three minutes.

* * *

There was literally no limit to the imaginative schemes the Nazis would resort to in order to avoid arrest or to get preferential treatment. Pretending to be a war correspondent was just one of these. And then there were cases that required special handling, such as the case presented to us by a well-dressed, well-spoken gentleman and his male secretary, who showed up at our office demanding to see the commanding general. They were quite impressive. The secretary was clutching an expensive leather attaché case bulging with papers, and the gentleman himself was authoritative, exhibiting the haughty attitude of a German used to wielding a little power, when in the presence of subordinates. He summarily dismissed our offer of assistance, bluntly informing us that his mission could be discussed only at the highest level.

We informed the Assistant Chief of Staff, G-2, Col. John H. Claybrook, of the man's presence, and the colonel was intrigued enough to agree to see him. Fortunately this satisfied our visitor as well, although reluctantly, and I escorted him to the G-2 office at Iceberg Forward Headquarters.

Here, formally and somewhat overbearingly, the man proffered his case.

He had the honor, he said, of representing His Excellency, President Falkenstein, president of the recently formed New German Republic. This statesman, he claimed, had worked incessantly during the last two years of the war to form his new government and put a stop to the hostilities and dispose of the current Nazi hierarchy. Falkenstein had, in fact, on several occasions behind the scenes been successful in speeding up the surrender of a considerable number of German fighting troops to that end. He was, for example, directly responsible for the surrender of an entire armored division opposing our corps. He had ordered the commanding general of that division, in the name of the New German Republic, to surrender or face the consequences at a later day.

The man informed Colonel Claybrook that he and his secretary were emissaries from President Falkenstein, who desired at the earliest moment to confer with the Allied High Command with the object of ending the war and establishing his New German Republic as the ruling government of his country. He showed us several official-looking copies of letters, documents, and affidavits, among them a letter with the surrender ultimatum to the general who commanded the armored division that had, indeed, surrendered to XII Corps only days before. What lent a touch of authenticity to the whole affair was that the recent date of the letter corresponded to the date of the actual surrender of the division to us.

But despite a barrage of questions put to the man, he calmly insisted that he was there only to ascertain what kind of reception President Falkenstein and his proposal would receive, should he elect to approach the XII Corps commanding general as his first step toward establishing contact with the Allied Supreme Command. He was not empowered by the president to discuss anything further.

Bemused, the G-2, without in any way committing himself, turned the matter over to us, while telling president Falkenstein's emissary that he would take the matter under advisement. It was obvious to me that the G-2 wanted us to have a go at the enigmatic emissary.

Under the guise of taking down factual information that would be forwarded to Supreme Headquarters, Allied Expeditionary Force (SHAEF), we "interrogated" the man thoroughly, and it quickly became apparent that he was hiding something. But what? And how to find out? He was obviously not the kind of man to be intimidated. I sat him down over a cup of coffee, while we arranged for quarters for him and his secretary during their stay with us.

I treated him with the deference due an ambassador from a sovereign state. We put up the two of them in the most comfortable quarters the town could offer and assigned a local woman to wait on them, and we wined and dined them in the officers' mess; the G-2 even sacrificed a good cigar on the emissary. We did it up brown.

The emissary told us that he did not know exactly where Falkenstein was at the moment, but at the same time he assured us that he could get in touch with him as soon as it became necessary. And he constantly came back to the matter of security for the president. He demanded absolute guarantees that the man would not be harmed in any way, and he strongly requested some official document to that effect. It was becoming evident that what the emissary was really interested in was unconditional protection for the man he called President Falkenstein.

When I had determined his real goal, I began telling him how interested we were in his report and in his proposal, how eager we were to get in touch with the president himself, a man who obviously demanded respect and admiration, so we could mutually decide how best to implement the speedy establishment of the New German Republic.

I all but assured him that the Supreme Allied Commander, Gen. Dwight D. Eisenhower, would feel exactly as I did. That's what I thought he'd like to hear, and in this instance we aimed to please.

The next day, when we resumed our discussions, I thought the man was ready for the sixty-four-dollar question. I told him we had discussed the matter with the assistant chief of staff, G-2, and that this officer was indeed interested in taking the matter up with SHAEF. But I asked him very frankly to stop holding out on me, that we needed something concrete to convince SHAEF that this was indeed an important issue. I told him that it was imperative that we know the whereabouts of President Falkenstein. Now. I had expected an unorthodox answer from the man, but even so, his reply was a complete surprise.

"*I* am President Falkenstein," he declared.

Finally we could go to work on the man in earnest. It took some doing, but when he realized that his game had run its course and he had nowhere to go, he told us the real story. It turned out that he was a former *Unteroffizier,* a noncom tank commander in the armored division he had claimed to have forced to surrender! That, of course, explained his detailed knowledge of the surrender. He'd had a local printer print up all the documents he needed. He had been inducted into the armed forces, he told us bitterly, after having fallen into disgrace in his civilian job, the victim of a jealous and ambitious colleague.

When he told us what that civilian job was, we knew we had found a gold mine of information about an organization about which we knew little at the time. I felt certain that the boys at AIC would have a field day with him, once we sent him back for in-depth interrogation. The man, whose name was indeed Falkenstein, had been director of press and propaganda directly under the minister of propaganda, Dr. Joseph Goebbels!

Although we had given him no promise of immunity, the treatment he had received at our hands and the apparent unquestioning interest we had shown in his "Republic" had lulled him into believing himself quite safe. Exactly as we had intended.

But what had he wanted to accomplish with his outrageous charade? It was sometimes difficult to fathom the Nazi mind. Having worked so closely under the influence of Goebbels, he had been seduced by the Goebbels edict: The bigger the lie, the more eagerly it is believed.

He'd heard about Germans considered worthy by the Allies being installed in high positions such as mayors of big cities and important state officials, Falkenstein told us. He thought that if he could convince us that he had been *trying* to form his pro-Western government, we would consider him worthy for some kind of high position in postwar Germany, giving him the kind of power and leadership he wanted.

As for leadership, he got his wish—after a fashion. Falkenstein became the leader of a work detail in the internment camp where he was being held while his fate was being decided.

I never knew what became of "President Falkenstein," just as I never knew what became of Gen. Paul Krüger, the Werewolf general. Once our tactical work was done and we sent our subjects to the rear, to AIC, we lost track of them. It was one of my regrets. But there was no time to follow up. There was always a new case and a new subject waiting.

In the numerous cases I'd investigated and the countless subjects I'd interrogated, I had never used violence of any kind. I strongly felt that doing so would lower me to the standards of the Nazis, and I had vowed never to use physical force in my interrogations. Threats, tricks, cajolery—yes. Force—no.

The case of an arrogant Sudeten German official would become the exception to prove the rule. The man would make me break that vow—for the first and only time.

Driving a Citroën loaded down with household goods, boxes, bundles, and suitcases, the man came barreling into Furth, a German village hard on the Czechoslovakian border where my team was doing screening duty shortly before VE Day. He had a dark, sultry Czechoslovakian girl in her twenties at his side; he himself was about fifty, with a cruel mouth and mocking, water-blue eyes. His car was one of a long line of such conveyances headed west into our territory, fleeing before the advancing Red Army. Who were they? What reasons did they have for not daring to face the Russians? What were their plans once they were behind our lines? We had to know. All of them had to be screened and—if cleared—issued proper travel papers before being allowed to proceed.

While the MPs searched through the mountains of stuff heaped on the little Citroën, trying to keep their eyes off the voluptuous girl, who had draped herself over a nearby fence and was regarding the men with hooded eyes and slightly parted lips, we began to question the man.

He had no papers except an expired *Kennkarte*—the ubiquitous German identification card—that listed him as a minor post office official in Budweis, a town in south Bohemia. The woman—whom he said was his wife—had no ID at all. That was standard. Most of these people fled in such a hurry and amid such confusion that their affairs were rarely in order. Had their papers been in perfect order it would have been one case in thousands, and cause for real suspicion.

But there was something else about the man, which decided us to question him a little more closely than usual. He seemed too cocksure. His attitude was condescending and haughty—the bearing of a man used to command, and to being obeyed—not cringing and subservient, as were most of the little *Beamte* (civil servants) in Germany when confronted with authority. This was no petty post office official.

We took him to our office and had him stand before us. Automatically he placed himself at military parade rest. So, he was or had been in the armed forces.

We questioned him sharply. He answered our questions readily enough but never deviating from his "petty official" story. Things were bad in Budweis, he told us. Near chaotic. The threat of imminent Russian occupation was creating panic among the Germans in the city. Orderly and regular functions in the postal services had come to a standstill. He had thought it best to return to Germany while he could. He seemed totally confident and slightly condescending. We could get nowhere with him—and we had, of course, no proof that he was not telling the truth.

But I was certain he was not. That indefinable hunch again.

I looked coldly at him. "I don't believe your story," I said.

He shrugged, an almost insolent little smile on his thin lips. "It is the truth," he said.

"You realize, of course," I said, "that unless you tell us the truth here and now, we will send you to someone with more time, more—resources, who *will* get the truth out of you."

The German fixed his water-blue cold eyes on me as he raised his eyebrows. His smile grew a bit broader. "You are making a threat?" he observed. "Physical violence?" There was faint mockery in his voice.

"Forgive me, but now it is I who cannot believe you. I know American officers are too civilized to resort to that kind of—of Russian barbarism!"

I watched the self-assured, overbearing bastard stand before me—and something clicked. I stood up. Slowly I walked around the man. He stood stock still, never acknowledging my presence, totally sure of himself.

"So, you believe we won't lay a hand on you?" I asked casually.

"Of course," he answered. "I am an educated man. I never believed the propaganda ravings of Dr. Goebbels. They were designed for the more gullible."

"And you are not gullible."

"I am not." He seemed to draw himself up. "I have studied about America," he said. "I know what Americans are like. You are fair. You do not consider a man guilty before his guilt has been proved." He smiled his thin, unpleasant smile. "You are trying to frighten me. To intimidate me. You think I know something that I will tell you if I become afraid." Again he gave a slight shrug. "But, you see, you are wrong. I know nothing. And I have told you the truth about myself."

I began to walk around him again. "I'll tell you what," I said pleasantly. "You and I will play a little game." I stopped in front of him. He looked at me as one would look at a backward child being particularly exasperating.

"You will stand at attention," I continued, as I resumed my walk. Was there the slightest little start of a motion toward me? Was I getting on his nerves with my pacing? Things were happening that he did not understand; were they getting to him?

"The rules are very simple," I went on. "I will ask you questions. You will answer them. Truthfully. Every time you tell a lie—" I was back in front of him. I looked straight into his cold, water-blue eyes. "I will knock you across the room! Do you understand?"

He remained silent. The insolent smirk never left his mouth. He did not believe me.

I positioned myself directly in front of him. "Now," I said. "Let's begin the game. Do you come from Budweis?"

"Yes." He was humoring me.

"Is the Citroën your car?"

"Yes."

"Were you a member of the Nazi party?"

There was only a hint of hesitation. "I was."

"Good," I approved. "You'd have to be to work for the government. Did you work for the postal service?"

"Yes."

I hit him with all the force I could muster. The blow, brought up from my left hip, struck the man on the side of his jaw and sent him sprawling on the floor. In two steps I was standing over him. "On your feet!" I ordered harshly. "Our game has just begun. Get up!"

He sat on the floor. Unconsciously he put his hand to his face. There was a touch of bright red at the corner of his mouth. He was unaware of it. He stared at me. His smirk was gone. His arrogance was gone. His self-confidence was gone. I knew what went on in his mind. His world of logical certainties and unshakable beliefs had crumbled like a house of cards—from a single blow. He had been wrong. Wrong in his judgment. Wrong in his convictions. Where else was he wrong? What else might happen to him? Were the Americans like the Russians after all? Or—like his own?

"Get up!" I said again.

Slowly he rose to his feet.

"Now," I said. "Once again. Did you work for the postal services?"

For a brief moment he stood silent, looking at me. But he had nowhere to seek asylum.

"No," he said, his tone of voice quite different from before.

"What did you do?"

With pathetic pride he drew himself up. "I am Chief of Gestapo, Budweis," he said.

It was now merely a matter of asking questions. The ex–Gestapo chief's supposedly infallible convictions, his unshakable belief in himself, had been shattered. He had been convinced he could bluster his way through. The Americans were weak. *He* was strong. He could not fail. It had been a fatal miscalculation. We knew that he would provide AIC with a complete and detailed account of the activities of the Gestapo in his Bohemian town.

When we informed his young companion that her husband would be detained, she laughed. The ex–Gestapo chief was not her husband, she told us, she was only his mistress. She neglected to say his collaborator mistress, but that was only too evident. She decided to go back home to Budweis rather than face an uncertain existence in occupied Germany. I guess she thought she could find a more secure position with the Russian officers than with the Americans. She picked up her meager possessions and started back from where she'd come, this time on foot, a lone figure trudging against the flood of people pouring through our lines. And a flood it was—not only civilians and ex-soldiers, but whole German combat units, still battle able.

In a report to Corps, Agent Leo R. Dardas of CIC Detachment 212 gave a vivid description of how it was:

> We saw hundreds of Germans trying to give themselves up, and nobody would take them prisoners. I saw one man hold out his *Soldbuch* for half an hour to every GI that passed by, and nobody would bother with him. Everyone was taking so many prisoners that they got sick of it, and when Germans came along, they would just point to the rear and tell them to march. I saw a whole battalion of Germans marching back with no guards and a white sign on the front man saying, THESE ARE PWS, PLEASE DIRECT TO NEAREST CAGE. At one little town the burgomeister came in to our office with a fine-looking young man and said: "This is my son. I want him to give himself up." It was about 1700 hours and we were tired, so we shouted at him, "What's the idea of coming in to surrender at this time of day? Come back tomorrow morning at 0900 hours and have your son in full uniform." So, sure enough, the next day the burgomeister showed up with his son, resplendent in full officer's uniform.

Other columns of Nazi troops, crowded onto their own vehicles, many of them still fully armed and under the command of their own officers, rumbled through our sector on their way to the rear and internment—with a single, grinning GI acting both as guide and guard. German staff cars bearing high-ranking officers, trucks, and Volkswagens rubbed fenders with American half-tracks, 2½-tons, and jeeps on the choked roads. To ease the confusion, ramrod German officers wearing white armbands on their uniform tunics that read LIAISON OFFICER WITH U.S. ARMY shared the streets with American MPs, and field orders were issued in both English and German by American and German officers. No possible system of PW cages could take care of this flood of captives, and thousands of prisoners were simply herded together in large open fields and ordered to stay put until proper PW accommodations could be constructed. One field in our sector held over five thousand prisoners, some as young as fourteen years of age, the scrapings from the bottom of the barrel. Mixed in with the military rout were the German civilians fleeing Sudetenland. On foot, crammed into every conceivable kind of vehicle, pushing overloaded carts, baby carriages, or bicycles, they streamed across the border into Germany. They were ordered to stay off the roads, but it was like ordering the waters of a tidal wave to stay off the beach. The whole mess was a saboteur's paradise, a secret enemy agent's open sesame, which we had to try to stem.

Investigating a case that took me out of our own area of operation, I had the opportunity to visit the infamous concentration camp of Dachau, which was located a few miles northwest of Munich, only a couple of days after the camp had been overrun by the 42d (Rainbow) Division of Seventh Army on 29 April.

"When all other German prison camps are forgotten," *Time* wrote in May of 1945, "the name of Dachau will still be infamous." *Time* was right. Dachau has become synonymous with inhumanity and atrocity, with horror and suffering. And deservedly so.

Built by Himmler's SS in 1933 on the site of an abandoned World War I ammunitions factory, it was Hitler's first concentration camp. The SS guards were instructed, "Tolerance signifies weakness." They were quick to embellish on that concept. "Enter through the gate—leave by the chimney," became their greeting to new arrivals. And new arrivals streamed in every day. The Dachau dormitories, which in 1942 each held three hundred to four hundred inmates, by 1943 held a thousand, and by 1945, three thousand! Over seventy thousand human beings left Dachau "by the chimney"—or simply died. Some of them, the victims of unspeakable "medical" experiments, died in indescribable agony. Others—mere walking skeletons covered with ulcer-eaten skin—just starved to death.

When I walked through the gate at Dachau, inscribed with the mocking words ARBEIT MACHT FREI "Work Makes You Free," it was like walking into the forecourt of hell. Thousands of inmates, animated bags of bones hung with dirty, flimsy black-and-white striped uniforms, were still wandering around the camp. Within the first eighteen hours after being liberated 135 of them died of starvation or illness. Piles and piles of emaciated bodies, their mouths slackly open, their dead eyes staring unseeingly, were stacked like knobby cordwood around the crematorium. Inside, the ovens still held the ashes and bone chips of those who had left "by the chimney." The dormitory barracks were still filthy with the refuse of the inmates, who had been crammed into the confined space with hardly room to move.

But it was the stench that got to you. The stench of death and abysmal human suffering. The stench seared your nostrils and seemed to permeate your entire being. A stench never to be forgotten. It is still with me when I think back to those terrible sights—and smells.

The *Stars & Stripes* on 2 May 1945 described what was found when the gates to Dachau were opened:

> The extent of the horror at this camp is beyond description. There is no way to put into words the stench of thousands of corpses lying 50 to 100 deep in three large rooms in the crematorium or the death chamber. Buchenwald had just one block where 50 to 100 died each day. Dachau has six of these blocks.
>
> Only yesterday several thousand prisoners were killed by the SS and thrown into a water-filled ditch behind the camp. On the day of liberation 32,315 prisoners of thirty nationalities were still alive.

Most of these inmates continued to exist in the camp even after being liberated; there was simply nowhere else for them to go. It would take weeks before the machinery that would repatriate the various national groups could be activated. Meanwhile every possible effort was made to make their existence bearable, but often even this was in vain.

One group of pitiful half-dead men was found in the Invalid Barracks, where they had been isolated by the SS guards when they became too emaciated or sick to perform the work required of them. Here they were left slowly to die—given only one-half of an already starvation ration!

But the availability of food after the liberation had tragic consequences. Before U.S. Army doctors could intervene, hundreds of inmates died because their systems could not tolerate a normal intake of food.

Our business in the area was with the mayor of the city of Munich, a gentleman who told us he was as appalled as we were at the disclosure of the true nature and conditions at the Dachau camp. He had believed it to be merely a work camp.

We were less impressed with him when in the files of the camp commandant we found a letter from this same appalled mayor, bitterly complaining about the stench from the Dachau crematorium when the wind was strong in the direction of his city. He had strongly requested that on such days the damned Jews *not* be burned. "Smoke is made up of tiny particles of the substance being burned," he wrote, "in your case the Jewish cadavers in your crematorium ovens. It is intolerable that good German citizens who must breathe that smoke should endure being contaminated by such Jewish filth!"

His further tenure as mayor was short-lived, I believe.

In 1961 Dachau was opened as a museum, and a few years later a Jewish temple, a Catholic chapel, and a Protestant church were erected as monuments to the thousands who perished at the camp. In 1990 I finally revisited Dachau. It was an experience that left me shaken, angry, and frustrated.

Cleo and I entered the camp area through a special visitors gate—not through the ARBEIT MACHT FREI main gate. Ahead of us stretched a huge, barren rectangular area with large, gravel-covered rectangles marked off on the ground in two long rows. A big, clean, whitewashed building immediately to our left was the camp museum. This building, I remembered, used to be the camp *Wirtschaftsgebäude,* Housekeeping Building, which contained the camp kitchen and laundry, storage rooms, and the notorious shower baths where the SS guards would amuse themselves by flogging and torturing the prisoners. It now held a collection of blown-up photographs, which began with an explanation of how and why the Nazis had risen to power—an explanation or rationalization of why atrocities such as had been carried out at Dachau had become inevitable as a result of the raw deal Germany had been handed after World War I, when hundreds of real Germans found themselves out of work. From this, the exhibit progressed to depict Dachau camp life, showing some of the horrors in a strangely clinical, uninvolved, and impersonal manner, presented by the best modern museum display methods, the method almost more impressive than the content, all accompanied by logical explanations of why concentration camps such as Dachau became necessary. Here also was a tiny motion picture theater where a British film of camp life was shown, including graphic pictures of some of the atrocities inflicted upon the camp inmates.

What angered me most was what had been done with the camp itself, a place that I remembered stank of death, a bleak and filthy place, a place of horror. All the barracks had been razed; the gravel-covered rectangles bordered with concrete foundations marked where they had stood. But one had been restored—as a showpiece. Clean, spacious with spotless wooden bunks and a fine wood floor, the barrack had individual lockers for the inmates, a communal area with game tables and chairs for cozy relaxation, a separate washroom and toilet facilities. There was no mention, no hint of the overcrowded conditions in a barrack built to house a maximum of three *hundred* inmates into which three *thousand* had been crammed—the sick, the starved, the exhausted—three inmates to a bunk. No inkling of the unspeakable hardship—the horrendous filth caused by the issue of the ever-present dysentery that oozed and dripped from the top bunks through the lower two to the floor, the victims too weak to move. Should anyone die, his corpse would lie with his bunk mates until the prisoners were herded out in the morning to stand formation. Instead, the walls in this showcase barrack displayed large, nicely framed quotes from the writing of various famous authors, extolling a strict adherence to cleanliness and order! To the uninformed, all this said, "Well, this is not so bad"—and, in fact, I heard these very words spoken when Cleo and I stood in this miserable misrepresentation of the truth. I began to tell Cleo what it had *really* been like when forty-five years before I had stood in one of the real Dachau barracks. By the time I had warmed up, to my satisfaction, I had quite an audience.

Dachau had been sanitized and sterilized; everything had been scoured off—including the truth. We walked along what had been the Lagerstrasse, Camp Street, the main camp road, lined with stately poplar trees, planted years ago by the inmates. It was a somber day; the sky was full of weather and gusts of cold wind blew through the trees. We were headed for the crematoriums.

The two crematoriums were still standing in the far corner of the camp. It had been a bleak, a terrible spot. But now it was a lovely garden area, a park of beauty with flower beds and lush green bushes and trees that bowed gracefully in the wind. The larger of the structures, a pleasant red-brick building, looked like the main house of a prosperous farm, except for the tall, square chimney that pointed toward the leaden sky like an accusing finger. Although Dachau was not an extermination camp like Auschwitz, so many inmates died or were killed by the guards that it had been necessary to build a second crematorium, which held four ovens. When I had stood before this building, years before, there had been naked, emaciated corpses stacked high all around me. As I stood, filled with memories of this place of horror, I must have shown my thoughts. A gentleman and his wife came up to me. They told me they were originally from Estonia but had fled the country as children ahead of the Russian army and now lived in Brazil. They wanted to know if I had been to Dachau before. I told them yes, with the American army. And they asked me what it was like. I told them. But when I told them that where they were standing now, there had been a stack of dead bodies six feet high—they moved away.

Although I realize that it would have been impossible to show Dachau as the camp had *really* been, I was resentful and bitter at what it had been made out to be. My frustration threatened to choke me. I had to do something.

We went down to the neat, two-story building, the *Jourhaus*, that had housed the camp administration offices and SS guard rooms and through which ran the entry tunnel with the main ARBEIT MACHT FREI iron gate. It was in this building we'd found the mayor's letter. The gate was closed but not locked. No one was about. I opened the gate and went through to the other side. I looked at the neat, well-kept building, the clean, whitewashed wall. And I urinated on it.

It felt good. Damned good!

Numerous books have been and will be written about the abominable horrors of this concentration camp, but all of them together would only scratch the surface of the abysmal, hideous human torture suffered within the cruel barbed-wire fences that surrounded the hell called Dachau.

Back in the town of Dachau we quietly walked the streets until it was time for lunch. Somehow we could not face a hearty German meal. Instead we went to a colorful little restaurant on Erich-Ollenhauerstrasse. It was called Hong Kong.

We'd come away from the camp subdued and somber. My anger was still with me. It was not because of what I had seen—it was because of what I had *not* seen.

* * *

VE Day, 8 May 1945, found us in the little Bavarian town of Grafenau, where we had moved on 3 May. The town had been taken on 25 April after token resistance and scattered *Panzerfaust* fire, and compared with what we were used to seeing, it was virtually unscathed.

Nestled cozily in a shallow valley at the foot of Frauenberg in the Bavarian Forest, it was postcard picturesque. The cupola-topped church tower and the step-parapeted facade of the *Rathaus* (town hall) vied with each other for dominance of the skyline of the idyllic little town. It was here, on 5 May, in a ceremony in the garden behind Iceberg Forward Headquarters, that I was decorated with the Bronze Star for my achievement in capturing the Werewolves, with the Corps commander, Maj. Gen. S. LeRoy Irwin, pinning the medal on my chest. It was a most satisfying moment for me.

Corps' first encounter with Russian troops took place on 8 May near Susice in Czechoslovakia, in the midst of battle. A task force of seven Russian tanks was pursuing a column of SS panzer troops, just as a U.S. Army combat patrol consisting of an armored car and three jeeps from the 41st Cavalry Squadron was probing the area. In the heat of battle the Russians took the American patrol for the enemy and prepared to engage them in a firefight; the startled GIs identified themselves by shouting, gesturing, hollering, and shooting off flares. When the Russians responded with their own flares, the linkup had been made.

VE Day itself, not unexpected, was received with relief and satisfaction, but there was no celebration; we were all aware that there was still a war to be fought and won in the east. And we all knew we had a long and rocky road of "cleaning up" ahead of us. My own personal observance of the day consisted of asking a local printer to create special VE Day stationery for me, which would include a large U.S. flag in red and blue on the white paper. He did, but since he had no stars to set, he used round white dots in the field of blue, forty-two of them! I did not use the stationery.

Shortly after VE Day the CO of XII Corps hosted a gala banquet for our Russian Allies at Corps Headquarters in Grafenau. The menu was first class: fruit cocktail, sirloin steak, potato salad, green peas, green salad with thousand-island dressing, victory cake, and parfait rolls with chocolate sauce, all washed down with champagne, red wine, and beer. Lots of beer. The Russians were enthusiastic drinkers, a fact that was made apparent to me months later when I was at a gathering of Russians and Americans.

The Russians suggested that we hold a drinking match to see who were really the most robust fighting men. We agreed.

It was decided that the participants representing each country should drink their national drink. The Russians chose vodka. When they asked us what was our national drink, we answered—Coca Cola!

The bout began. Several rounds were drunk, and we were holding up very well, when the Russians huddled—and came up with an idea: "Now we switch. *You* drink vodka. *We* drink Coca Cola."

Why not? we shrugged. We figured we were way ahead.

So—the switch was made. For two rounds. Then the Russians, looking suspiciously at us, huddled again. This time their edict was quite definite. "We switch again," they declared emphatically. "Vodka better!"

They almost beat us anyway.

VE Day past, we settled down to occupation duty. It was a hectic time. A crisis case seemed to present itself every hour on the hour—but none more harrowing, more tragic than the one that began with the arrival at our office of two beautiful young women.

CHAPTER 10

Both girls were in their middle twenties; both were blonde, svelt, and attractively tanned, and their clothes, though dirty and bedraggled, were obviously of good quality. They seemed intelligent and cultured, a little haughty, probably the wives of minor diplomats or officials who had been stationed in Czechoslovakia. Agent William G. Hock—Bud—and I were all set to send them on their way after the usual cursory examination that constituted a screening.

The first young woman we questioned answered our routine queries satisfactorily. Her papers were as valid as any under the circumstances, and her *Kennkarte,* the German civilian identification card, seemed on the up and up. She was cooperative, but her face was hard. Perhaps it was only a resentful animosity toward the enemy that she could not conceal, but she was in complete control of herself, even a little arrogant. I did not like her, but it was not my job to like or dislike the subjects—only to screen them. Yet she left me vaguely uneasy. It was quite a different story when we began to question the second girl.

She was very pretty, her blonde hair pulled back tightly, held by a thin blue velvet ribbon at the nape of her neck, and allowed to cascade loosely down her back. Her tanned face was fresh and soft, but her troubled blue eyes were dark with fear. More than fear—suspicion, uncertainty. Even hate. And where her companion had been composed and answered our questions readily, this girl was hesitant and obviously nervous. Many subjects, in fact most, were nervous and ill at ease during an interrogation. That was normal. But my hunch—that something was wrong, crowded in on me even stronger than before. I glanced at Bud and met his eyes. And although he did not speak German well enough to follow the interrogation completely, I knew he felt it too.

There was—something. But dammit, it would take the whole bag of tricks to get it out. And time. Time that we did not have. There were hundreds of others waiting to be screened. But I couldn't let it go. Perhaps there was a way to get to her. A quicker way.

Her *Kennkarte* was still lying on the table between us. I picked it up. I frowned at it. I made a show of examining it minutely—and I watched the girl, sitting tensely before us, frightened and apprehensive.

I looked up—and smiled at her. I made my voice sound friendly and relaxed. "Very well," I said. "Your papers seem to be in order." I handed the ID card back to her. She took it. I watched her closely. But the reaction I had expected did not come. The tenseness in her face did not change. The fear in her eyes did not diminish.

Again I glanced at Bud. He was as puzzled as I. I had been sure the girl would relax, once her identification had been accepted. She had not. There was—something else.

Still she sat stiffly on her chair, clutching her handbag, twisting and untwisting the heavy strap in her trembling hands as she had been doing unconsciously all through the screening.

The bag!

I held out my hand. "Give me your bag, please," I demanded, my voice suddenly sharp.

There was a barely perceptible gasp from the girl. The blood drained from her face, leaving her tanned cheeks a sickly gray. But without a word she handed me the bag.

I gave it to Bud, who turned it upside down, spilling the contents out onto the table. The girl watched as if mesmerized.

A large comb. A purse with a little money. A small compact and a lipstick. A purple hair ribbon. A small pocket knife. Was that what bothered her? A weapon? Not likely. A handkerchief—embroidered. A fountain pen. A piece of paper with several safety pins attached, and—there it was! The one thing she undoubtedly had feared we'd find. A solid gold medal, twice the size of a silver dollar and many times as heavy, with a religious motif embossed on both sides.

We'd found the "something else."

It made sense. The medal must represent a fortune to her, her only means of starting a new life for herself, once back home, the only concrete hope in her nightmare world. It certainly could explain her nervousness. She had simply been afraid we'd "liberate" the only thing of value she possessed. It's what "her own" would have done. It had been as simple as that.

I handed her the gold medal. "Here," I said. "You'd better hold on to that."

She took the coin. Her fingers touched mine. They were cold as death.

I had been so smug in my belief that I had discovered the reason for the girl's uneasiness that I almost missed her reaction—or rather *lack* of reaction. She did not relax. She showed no sign of relief, as she clutched the gold medallion in her clenched fist.

I scooped up all her belongings, dumped them back into her bag, and gave it to her.

Perceptibly the girl relaxed. Some of the fear left her eyes; there was even the hint of a smug smile at the corners of her pretty mouth.

It was not her little treasure she had been worried about. *What* then? The bag itself? Something else in it? I was sure it was not the gold coin that concerned her. It was easy to verify.

"Let me see that medallion again," I asked her casually. "It looked very interesting." Quickly, obediently, she dug into her crumbled bag and came up with the gold medal. She handed it to me. *"Bitte!"* she said, "Please!"

She watched me as I made a show of looking over the medal, but there was no anxiety in her eyes, rather a certain expectation, a seeming eagerness to please her interrogator. Deliberately I put the coin in my pocket. Momentarily the girl looked startled, then she sighed almost inaudibly. It seemed more a sigh of relief than of concern.

I reached over and grabbed the bag from the girl. I poured out the familiar contents. Together Bud and I once more examined everything, this time much more closely. The little compact was pried open, the hollow tube of the lipstick was probed, and the fountain pen was tested and pulled apart. Nothing. I took the bag itself. I felt it. I tore the lining out—and there it was. A small piece of paper. I slipped it out.

The girl had uttered not a word. Ashen-faced, she sat rigidly in her chair, her eyes petrified with terror and shock.

Carefully I unfolded the paper. The first words I read were GEHEIME STAATSPOLIZEI—GEHEIME KOMMANDOSACHE! "Gestapo—Top Secret!"

Quickly I read it. It was a routine document. It dealt with the transfer of a certain SS-Standartenführer (Gestapo Colonel) Seiffert from Prague to Budweis on special assignment. It was dated two weeks earlier.

I looked at the terror-stricken girl. I was genuinely puzzled. It made no sense. Dammit!—it made no sense at all. Why would she be carrying a document like that? Secretly—and amateurishly—hidden in the lining of her purse, as if it were of earth-shaking importance? I gave the paper to Bud, who at once began to search our Mandatory. I glared at the girl.

"Who is this Colonel Seiffert?" I asked her sharply. "Why are *you* carrying his transfer orders? Answer me! *Now!*"

She winced. Her soft lips trembled. But she made not a sound.

Bud pushed the Mandatory Arrest and War Criminals Wanted List across the table to me. His finger stabbed a name: *Seiffert, A.* (37) *SS-Standartenführer*, Gestapo. Quickly I scanned the entry. Seiffert was a wanted man. A very much wanted man!

I began a sharp interrogation of the girl, nothing like my questioning of her earlier. What did she know about Colonel Seiffert? Why was she carrying top secret Gestapo orders? What was her connection with Gestapo, Prague? What was Seiffert's mission in Budweis? Where was *she* going? What were her plans?

Through it all she sat mute. It soon became apparent that we would get nothing from her.

I picked up the telephone and called the field hospital. I talked to several officers, even threw my weight around a bit, to no avail. Circumstances being what they were, I was told, they could spare no personnel for nonmedical purposes.

The girl sat staring at me. She could not understand the words, but she knew it was her fate being decided.

I finally gave up. I looked at Bud. "No go," I said.

A body search is a trying experience for everyone involved. The girl obviously had to be searched. Thoroughly. And that meant a full body search. Ordinarily such a search was performed by medical personnel—if available. But when conditions made such availability impossible, and time did not permit delays, it was up to us.

We went over every stitch of clothing the girl possessed. We found nothing. But things can be hidden in many ways, in the most astounding places. There are seven orifices in the female body. Each can provide a place of concealment. In wartime, hiding places for secrets could cost American lives, if not discovered. Systematically we began to go over every inch of the girl. She endured the humiliating ordeal in stoic silence. She let herself be manipulated like a mannequin. She seemed totally, inexorably resigned. It was a distasteful, degrading experience for all three of us. But it was necessary—and not in vain.

Taped to the instep of her right foot in such a way that it seemed almost like her own skin, we found a second *Kennkarte*. It had the same information, the same description, the same vital data as the other one carried by the girl. Only the name was different. It identified her as Maria Seiffert, wife of SS-Standartenführer A. Seiffert.

We both stared at the ID card. So that was her secret. She was the wife of a wanted Gestapo colonel. She had been so mortally afraid we'd uncover her secret that her actions in trying to conceal it had given her away.

I looked at the young woman standing naked in the middle of the room, her arms hanging dead at her sides, her head bowed. Dammit! Dammit all to hell! It had all been so unnecessary. She would have been perfectly safe—under her own name. We did not wage war on dependents.

I picked up her clothing and handed it to her. "Please," I said, as reassuringly as I could. "Please get dressed."

And finally she broke. She wept as she told us her story.

Miserably, haltingly, in sentences broken by pitiful little sobs, she talked. Yes, she was the wife of Colonel Seiffert. He was a good man, she told us, unshed tears brimming in her eyes. A good soldier. An officer to be proud of. A good German. She had used the false identity card because the Gestapo in Prague had instructed her to do so. *They* had issued it to her. That is why it could not be detected as a forgery—because it was not; it was the real thing. Except for the name. Fearfully she regarded us. She had been told, she said, that it was essential that the Americans did not learn her true identity. She had been told that all members of the families of Gestapo and high-ranking SS officers were put to death by the enemy. Perhaps tortured. She never doubted it. Had she not heard it said over the radio by Dr. Goebbels himself? Many times? She had had nightmares thinking about being killed. Or tortured.

She had been ordered to destroy her real identity card, but she had not been able to do that. It had been the final link to her true identity, just as the document pertaining to her husband had been her only concrete link to him. Not to be destroyed.

I had run into that sort of thing before, that peculiar Germanic trait that made it impossible for them to give up the last tenuous links to past power and glory. Or was it the fear of not being able to prove conclusively to officialdom their true loyalties, should the Nazis still prevail and once again seize power? After all, they'd been told often enough that that indeed would happen.

I watched her, as flat-eyed, lifelessly, she continued her story in a low, monotonous voice. Now, she had been caught. The wife of a Gestapo colonel. Using false papers. Trying to deceive the Americans. Now, she would be executed. She was convinced of it. That was what the Gestapo would have done.

"Where is the colonel now?" I asked her quietly.

Her expression did not change. She seemed beyond reaction. "I do not know," she whispered.

"When did you see him last?"

"Not for many weeks."

"What was the special assignment mentioned in the orders you were carrying?"

"I do not know."

"What were your husband's duties in the Prague Gestapo?"

"I do not know."

I do not know . . . I do not know . . . I do not know. The same answer delivered in the same flat tone of voice. Over and over again. There seemed to be no way of reaching her. To herself, her own person, her existence, her actions mattered no more. She was convinced that she was dead.

We both tried to persuade her that she would not be killed. That she would not be tortured. In fact, no harm at all would come to her. We told her that what the Gestapo had told her, what she had heard Dr. Goebbels say on the radio, was wrong. It was simply propaganda lies. She obviously did not believe us. Her own beliefs were too strong. We could not reach her beyond the flat, drawn mask of total resignation that enveloped her.

We explained exactly what *would* happen to her. A routine matter.

She would have to go before a Military Government court in the morning on the charge of using a false ID card. She might be fined. She might not. A travel permit would have to be issued to her, and she would be allowed to be on her way—with her friend, who was waiting in a local *Gasthaus*. But because *she* was a travel violator, apprehended using false ID papers, she would have to spend the night in jail, we told her. That was regulations. Not imprisoned by American troops. No. In the local German jail. Among her own people. In the morning she would be on her way.

She listened to us, silently, empty-eyed. I was not sure if she heard us. And I was not sure if the occasional, faint flicker of a smoldering ember deep in her eyes was hate—or despair.

We delivered the docile young woman to the local jail. It was late. We decided to wait until the next morning to question the other young woman once more. We had little hope of getting anything out of her, although with our new knowledge we might shake her up a bit. We were certain that both girls knew more than they had admitted. They were covering up—something. They were lying, we felt. But then—they *might* be telling the truth. We'd make one more attempt to find out in the morning.

In the morning I was awakened by the insistent ringing of the telephone. It was the warden at the German jail.

"Bitteschön! Bitteschön!" His pleading voice sounded panic-stricken. "Please! Please! Come to the jail. Please come at once!"

We were there in under ten minutes. The elderly jailer was waiting for us. He looked gray-faced and sick. Hurriedly he took us to a jail cell, the cell that held the colonel's wife. He opened the door. She was hanging from the bars in the little window high on the opposite wall—dead. Even in the lonely cell she had been forced to listen to the lethal words of Goebbels and the Gestapo. And she had believed.

In desperate determination she had hanged herself. Knotted tightly to the iron bars in the window and around her slim neck, a short towel torn into strips and tied together served as a hangman's noose. It was barely long enough to reach, so the young woman had to step up on the wooden bench bolted to the wall under the window to tie the knot around her neck. Unable to kick the bench away, she had stepped off it to hang from her macabre gallows until she strangled to death.

My stomach a leaden knot, my throat a swollen lump, I stood just inside the cell, my eyes inexorably fixed on the girl.

Blindly staring glassy eyes that seemed to strain to escape their sockets, a blackish, bloated tongue protruding obscenely between small, white teeth, purple-blue splotches on her puffy face and her bare arms, and grotesquely pointing stiff legs on the side of the rough wooden bench that had served as her gallows platform, the once lovely young girl had been transformed into a grisly apparition of horror.

"Oh—my dear God!" I heard Bud's shocked, hoarse-voiced exclamation behind me.

I wanted to turn away. I could not. Had we gone too far with her? Had *we* driven her to this? Black self-recrimination swept over me, but slowly I forced myself back to reality.

We had not killed this girl. The stinking, rotten lies of the Nazi bastards had killed her.

I stood, breathing deeply. Finally I once again began to think clearly. I felt Bud moving to my side. I looked away from the girl—and I saw it. Written on the oft-scrubbed, worn surface of the tabletop fastened to the wall was a message: *"Leb wohl mein Liebling. Weitermachen!* Farewell my darling! Carry on!"

A message, written in blood.

I walked over to the girl hanging from the barred window. I forced myself to examine her more closely. All her belongings routinely had been taken away from her by the jailer before she was placed in the cell. She had had nothing to write her pitiful words with, and no way to get at the only means of writing them—her own blood. But she had been determined. She had bitten open a vein on her wrist.

I glanced back at the pathetic message on the tabletop. The blood-ink had turned a dirty brown.

Farewell my darling . . .

I suddenly had to get some fresh air. Bud joined me. But we returned when Capt. Robert Stokes, Corps assistant surgeon, and a couple of medical orderlies arrived to remove the body.

My eyes were drawn again to the misshapen body hanging on the wall. In my mind's eye I visualized the grim desperation with which the wretched young woman had gone about her ghastly task. Again I felt a wave of pity course through me, and guilt still nagged at the edges of my mind. My eyes strayed to the message on the tabletop.

And suddenly the guilt-created haze that had obscured my thoughts was swept away.

What an idiot I was! I should have seen it at once. The girl, for all her youth and appeal, and seeming vulnerability, was the loyal wife of a war criminal, a dangerous Gestapo officer. And she'd admired him—and what he stood for. She had died only because in her own warped mind she had conferred upon us, her American enemies, the same unholy, inhuman ways of her own rotten system. She had been lying all the time! Undoubtedly she had known her husband's whereabouts. She might even have been in on his future plans, and judging from the man's record they would surely be worth discovering.

The proof was right there in front of me. On the tabletop. Written in blood.

For whom was that poignant message meant? Certainly not for her friend. It had to be meant for her husband. I had known that all along, of course, but in my shock and my misplaced pity and guilt, I had not recognized the ramifications of that realization. If the message was meant for her husband, she must have known it would be delivered to him.

Only one person could do that.

I heard Bob Stokes order his men to cut down the girl. I whirled on them.

"No!" I said. I hardly recognized my own voice. "Leave her!"

We used the telephone in the jailer's office, and twenty minutes later the other young woman, who had been waiting for her companion and for her travel permit at a local inn, was brought to the jail. We received her in the dingy prison office.

Still supremely self-confident, although obviously a little puzzled, she sashayed into the office very much aware of her good looks and the impression she made on the little group of Americans. With a nonchalance that bordered on insolence she waved a deprecating hand at a proffered chair.

"What do you wish with me now?" she demanded, impatience in her voice. "Why have I been brought to this—this place?" She looked around her with obvious distaste. "Surely, I am not under *arrest!*" The trace of mockery in her voice was brazen.

She seemed so damned sure of herself that it might be a cover-up for real, deep-felt apprehension, I thought. I fervently hoped so. I was counting on it.

I came straight to the point. "Where is Colonel Seiffert?" I snapped at her.

She was good. She didn't move a muscle—although her breathing seemed to quicken almost imperceptibly. "I do not know what you talk about," she shrugged, almost contemptuously.

I was taken aback. I had expected more of a reaction. Then I realized that the girl without a doubt had prepared herself for just that question. When her companion was detained, she must have reasoned that we'd found out about Seiffert. She was too clever to run away without a travel permit; that would only have metamorphosed suspicion into full-fledged certainty, and she would have been hunted down and brought back. All she really had to do was stay put—and keep her mouth shut.

I looked at her. I had a chilly feeling. There was a saying among the CIC agents that the Nazi women were ten times harder, ten times more ruthless than their male counterparts. It was true. I had run into them at concentration camps. This one—she would not break easily. It would take draconian measures. So be it.

I stood up. "Come with me, please," I said pleasantly.

We walked briskly down the dismal prison corridor. I glanced at the girl. She was a cool one, I thought with grudging respect. She must have wondered, but if she was the least bit concerned, she didn't show it.

The jailer waited for us at the open door to the cell that held her companion. His sallow face looked chalky. He averted his eyes from the girl coming toward him.

My mind was icy numb with the knowledge of what I was about to do. But, dammit! I had no choice. I *had* to know. I could not allow even the possibility of a deadly enemy agent such as Seiffert going into action in our sector.

Without a word I motioned the girl through the open door of the cell. She took one step into the cell—and stopped dead. Her hands flew to her mouth, and a choked cry of anguish escaped between her clenched fingers. Her eyes—forced wide open and black with horror—were riveted upon the grisly sight before her. For an eternal moment she stood rooted to the spot, then she slowly reeled back to sag against the stone wall. Her arms fell lifeless at her sides. She pressed her head back against the rough stone, her mouth wrenched open in a silent scream. Great rending sobs shook her, but she seemed unable to tear her eyes from the bloated, misshapen body of her friend hanging grotesquely on the wall before her, staring back unseeingly with frightful bulbous eyes.

I watched the stricken girl closely. I was acutely aware of my own heart beating wildly; cold sweat was running down my armpits.

The girl was beginning to hyperventilate. She was going into hysterics.

Now!

I stepped close to her. "You know Colonel Seiffert?" The question was like a shot, grating the silence.

She did not answer. She was totally unaware of me. Dread-possessed, she stared at the corpse.

I grabbed her shoulders and shook her. "Answer me!"

She was utterly oblivious to me, to anything but the turgid monstrosity on the wall. She could not wrest her eyes from the sight. She was on the verge of total physical collapse from shock. I stepped in front of her, blocking her view, and I slapped her face smartly. She focused her eyes on me as if seeing me for the very first time.

"You *know* Colonel Seiffert!" It was not a question now. It was a statement of damning fact.

She stared at me, her eyes glazed. She seemed no longer to have a will of her own; she no longer commanded her own mind. Her voice grated with emotion when she replied, "Yes." The answer was automatic. Disembodied, it floated in the deliberately narrowed ego-space between us. I was not even sure she was aware of having responded.

"Who is he?"

"My—brother—"

"*Where* is he?"

"I—I do not know—"

"You were meeting him. Where?"

"Munich. In Munich—"

"Where in Munich?"

"In—in a house. Next to the *Hauptbahnhof.* On Senefelderstrasse—"

I kept hammering the staccato questions at her, giving her no chance to collect herself.

"When were you to meet? When?"

"In May—"

"When in May?"

"Twenty-seven—"

"You—and your sister-in-law?"

She flinched at the mention of her companion. "Yes."

"What are your brother's plans?"

"Plans?—"

"What is he planning to do? His orders?"

"He was to—to fight. The *Amis*—"

"How?"

"He—he was to set up an—an organization to—to—"

"Sabotage? Terrorism?"

"To fight the enemies of the Reich—"

"And you and your sister-in-law were both part of all this?" Even as I asked the question I knew it was unnecessary. I suppose I asked it in an attempt to justify what I'd had to put the two young women through, I thought bleakly. It was sometimes difficult not to feel pangs of guilt, of self-reproach, even though facts and circumstances and reason had left you no choice.

The girl did not answer me. There was, of course, no need. For a while she stood staring at me, her eyes haunted. Then she whispered, "You—*you* did that to her." Her voice was dead. "You—killed her . . ."

"No," I said wearily. "Her own rotten conscience killed her."

When on 27 May, Gestapo agent SS-Standartenführer Seiffert came to the house on Senefelderstrasse opposite the main railroad station in Munich, prepared for a rendezvous with his wife and his sister, he was met by the American military police instead.

His terrorist group died before it was born.

During the first few days after VE Day we retained our offices in Grafenau and from there handled the many additional and sometimes unusual assignments brought on by the cessation of hostilities.

One such was described in a report to HQ, MIS, ETOUSA dated 19 May 1945 as follows:

> II Unusual Assignments (Par. 2, a)
> One of the assignments given CIC Det. 212 was to inspect several German Military Hospitals and check these places for possible Nazi party officials in hiding and for SS personnel.
> The hospitals checked were located in Engelberg, Fürstenstein,

Wegscheid, Hauzenberg, Rohrbach, Aigen, Bergreichenstein and 2 Hungarian hospitals in Coburg.

The job consisted of screening the patients and examining their papers. All SS personnel were tagged and persons of a suspicious nature were interrogated to determine their status. The co-operation of the chief doctor of the hospital was enlisted to facilitate the handling of the patients, and no problems were encountered.

One of our occupation jobs was to track down and seize the high-ranking Nazi leaders who had gone into hiding when Germany surrendered. Many of these were wanted war criminals, and some of them hid in the overcrowded German military hospitals, hoping to lose their identities among the thousands of wounded and sick German soldiers.

One of the hospitals we inspected was located in the little town of Bergreichenstein—now Rejstejn—near Susice in the Sudetenland area of Czechoslovakia; although it had been designated to become Russian occupation territory, we went in to check it out, since there were no Russians around and we'd had reports that several *Goldfasanen* (Golden Pheasants)—high-ranking Nazi officials, so named because of all the gaudy gold braid on their uniform tunics and caps—were known to be hiding among the patients there. When we got there, we found that the entire hospital staff and patient body were SS!

The chief of the hospital and his immediate staff of doctors were absolutely correct in their behavior, stiff and formal. But it was easy to see that no assistance would be volunteered, and it would be impossible for us to know exactly what to look for—or where to look.

So we went into our usual little act. We were very friendly, in no hurry to begin our unpleasant task. We produced a bottle of good Scotch and several packs of American cigarettes, worth their weight in gold, and handed them out generously. Not to be outdone, the former SS officers brought out a couple of bottles of excellent homemade apricot brandy, and we sat around the chief doctor's office enjoying these treats and making small talk. Soon we professed our admiration for the German military man, the soldiers and the officers, whose bravery and steadfastness were well known, and our contempt for the Nazi *Bonzen*, the civilian officials who had hidden behind their party standing and their gold braid and never lifted a finger to defend their Fatherland

and were now cowardly trying to hide among their betters. It never ceased to amaze me how that sort of bull could be accepted seriously by the Nazis, but it always was. I suppose that once you consider yourself a superman, you're are not surprised when *anyone* agrees with you.

When a couple of hours later, with an empty bottle of Scotch and a couple of dead apricot-brandy bottles on the table, we at last set out to inspect the hospital premises, the chief doctor himself insisted on accompanying us. He personally pointed out to us the patients whom he suspected of being deadbeat *Bonzen!*

Although this was fraternization with the former enemy, it was of a kind that paid off the right way. Our harvest of mandatories at Bergreichenstein was one of our richest.

This incident was our first case on Czechoslovakian soil, but not the first time Corps troops had entered Czechoslovakia. XII Corps' 90th Infantry Division holds the distinction of being the first Allied unit to cross the Czech border and cut the Third Reich in two, when on 18 April they pushed into the country near the town of Prex, and two days later the 2d Cavalry Group became the first American unit to enter Czechoslovakia in force, liberate a town (the town of Asch), and remain on Czechoslovakian soil.

Our hospital inspections also took us to Austria. It had been rumored that in one of the hospitals the staff members, even a couple of weeks after the surrender, still were running their operation strictly in accordance with the edicts laid down during the Nazi regime. Undesirables, such as the mentally retarded, the deformed, and the severely crippled, were being isolated in the basement of the hospital—and quietly killed, adults and children alike. The gruesome rumor turned out to be true. We put an immediate stop to it and installed an outsider overseer until the staff could be replaced.

When in 1990 Cleo and I were in Grafenau, we decided to visit one of these hospitals, and we chose Bergreichenstein in Czechoslovakia. We crossed the border at Bayerisch Eisenstein and headed for our destination via Susice.

On the way we stopped at a tiny village called Frantiskova Ves—one street, one little inn. It was lunchtime, so we stopped to get something to eat at the inn, a one-story, whitewashed building with a red tar-tile roof and planter boxes displaying red and white flowers perched on the outside windowsills flanking the door.

We entered the place and found ourselves in a small dining room. It was a toss-up which was most pervasive, the quaint, picturesque atmosphere of the place or the blue cloud of cigarette smoke rising from a group of four men loudly playing cards around a table. We were met with a battery of curious, startled looks as we walked in, before the men, one more colorful than the next, resumed their card-slapping, expletive-peppered game.

The innkeeper, a middle-aged man clad in gray pants, a blue-checked shirt, and a brown, button-front sweater showed up, his astonishment at seeing us apparent on his face. We asked if we could get something to eat. Since he spoke nothing but Czechoslovakian, which I do *not* speak, it became one of those conversations of gestures and sign language that always seem to work so well. We were soon enjoying a meal of excellent, thick-cut meats, sausage, and cheese, creamy butter, and homemade bread all washed down with—what else?—the local beer. The man seemed fascinated by our unexpected presence in his very local establishment unused to tourists.

After the card players had left, we were the only guests in the place, and I took some pictures of Cleo sitting at a table near the stove. I asked the innkeeper if I could take a photo of him with Cleo. He beamed his assent, but motioned for me to wait. He went into the back room, where I saw him carefully slick down his hair and brush his sweater. Briefly he disappeared around a corner, to emerge again with a bottle and two glasses in his hands. Ceremoniously he poured a drink for Cleo and one for himself. He raised his glass to her—and nodded to me. The resulting picture is a gem. When we left, the innkeeper followed us out to the car, where we said our good-byes. We felt we had gained a friend.

It had been a warm and friendly encounter, markedly different from my experience forty-five years earlier when I had driven through these small Czechoslovakian villages, and every house had been closed up tight, the streets totally empty of people.

From Frantiskova Ves Cleo and I drove to Bergreichenstein. The big, squat building that had been the SS hospital in 1945 was still there, but it was locked up tight, obviously no longer a hospital. We found a local woman who remembered the time of fifty years ago. The hospital had been closed shortly after the war, she told us, and the Germans left. It had since been a school and a warehouse, and now it was what she called a "merchants' building."

As I stood looking at the bulky, somehow forbidding building, the chilling memories of the past crowded in on me.

It rarely happened, but if by odd chance we'd find ourselves "between cases," we'd take the opportunity to look through the reports of possible subversive activities that had come into our office, deemed nonurgent when reported and filed for later action. From these reports we'd choose one to follow up.

On a May morning, having just finished a case, I was idly thumbing through our pending live-case cards when one of them, reported by an antiaircraft artillery battalion billeted near a neighboring town, caught my eye. I pulled it and showed it to Capt. Benjamin T. Kinsey, CO of the CIC detachment.

"What about this one?" I asked him.

He studied it for a moment, then shrugged. "A gunshot in the forest," he mused. "Unidentified." He handed the card back to me. "If you have nothing better to do, you might run over and see what it's all about." He gave me a sidelong look. "I think I know what it is that made you pick this one."

"You mean that 'no US troops in the vicinity' note in the report," I said.

"You got it."

It was a casual way to begin one of the most far-reaching cases we were ever to break—a case that reached all the way to World War III.

Our CIC office in a small hotel in Saaralbe, France, in 1944.

Left: Prototype of the Nazi super-gun, the *Tausendfüssler* (Millipede), with a 492-foot barrel. A smaller version bombarded Luxembourg City in December 1944 from deep inside Germany. *Right*: Interrogating a suspected saboteur during the Luxembourg bombardment.

"Alas, poor Yorick!" 1944: The town is Grevenmacher, Luxembourg, called "Booby Trap Town."

Left: At the doorway to our CIC team's office in Simmern, Germany, 1945. *Right*: At the same doorway in 1990. Only *I* have changed!

The Town Square in Coburg, Germany, in 1945. The white sheets flapping from the windows were a common sign of submission used by the Germans.

The same spot in Coburg Square in 1990. Few changes had taken place in the intervening years.

Captured Werewolves, with other German PWs, in a temporary holding area in Weiden, 1945.

XII Corps CO, Maj. Gen. S. LeRoy Irwin, decorating me for my role in capturing Gen. Paul Krüger and his Werewolf HQ unit. Grafenau, Germany, 5 May 1945.

Left: With William G. (Bud) Hock after capturing the Werewolves. *Right*: The Schareben forester family with Colonel Bauer's secretary/fiancee (kneeling). The small boy in a white shirt is *Forstmeister* Schoenberger's son, Otto.

Amid the rubble of Luftwaffe General Staff Officer Colonel Cornelius's ransacked encampment, I give special instructions to a Luftwaffe non-com.

The body of *Reichsamtsleiter* Anton Eckl, immediately after he took his own life. In my hands I am holding his suicide note.

The *Ehrenwaffe* (honor weapon) with which *Reichsamtsleiter* Eckl shot himself. An intricately carved Walther 7.65mm, it was a special gift to him from Adolf Hitler, and bore an inscription on the grip.

The farmer Zollner, pointing to where he had hidden his arsenal of guns in 1945. This was during my revisit to his farm in 1949, masquerading as a petty German official.

Former *Ortsbauernfüher* (Nazi village leader)—the farmer Zollner—greeting the Führer, Adolf Hitler, in what for Zollner was happier times.

The clearing near Saint Johannsburg with the tarpaulin bundle that held the body of the GI without a face. A crude, white-painted cross had been placed near the body.

On the magnificent riding horse formerly owned by General Wend von Wietersheim, commanding general of the 11th Panzer Division. Tom Winkler is on the right. Kötzting, Germany, 1945.

CHAPTER 11

On the surface it was no ball-buster of a case. A shot fired in the forest. Big deal. But Captain Kinsey had been right. Something was bothering me. It was reported that no U.S. troops had been in the area when the shot was fired, and per strict U.S. Military Government directive, *all* firearms should have been turned in by the German population. No exceptions. Consequently there should have been no shot fired in the woods. But there had been. If not by a GI—by whom? If by a German, why was a gun in his possession? And why was it fired?

Two prime possibilities suggested themselves. One, a local inhabitant had retained a gun against specific orders. If so—why? It was very risky, especially if you fired it. Two, a subject or subjects unknown had infiltrated the area after it had been secured. In that case—who? And why were they armed? What had been the purpose of the shot?

It could be as simple as shooting a rabbit for a meager household pot, or it could be something considerably more sinister. An execution of a suspected "collaborator"? Or someone stumbling upon something he should not have seen?

These questions obviously all had answers, and it was these answers I wanted to find.

Usually when investigating a case we worked in pairs, and this time I asked Franz Vidor to team up with me. Franz was a pleasant, easy-going young man of Viennese origin who had distinguished himself during the Battle of the Bulge. He agreed.

Before we left we inspected our files to find out all we could about the incident and the area, hard on the Czechoslovakian border, where it had taken place. There was not much. Apart from the fact that an unexplained shot had been heard, we learned only that a Nazi Luftwaffe general and several high-ranking officers from the German air force General Staff, which had been stationed in Prague, had surrendered in the same area some weeks before. With this skimpy information we set out for the antiaircraft artillery unit in whose area the shooting had occurred.

A freshly painted, black-and-white sign, in stark contrast to the cracked and weather-beaten open gate to a farmyard, pointed the way to the unit's Headquarters. We drove into the yard, where a conglomeration of rusty farm machinery and spotless military equipment rubbed shoulders, and parked our jeep. A GI on guard came over, and we were shown to the CO's office in one of the gray, drab buildings that surrounded the farmyard.

The CO of the outfit was a cheery-looking young captain who received us cordially. But when we stated the reason for our visit, he looked at us with a blank expression.

"Oh, that!" he finally exclaimed. "I'd forgotten all about it."

Franz and I exchanged glances. This was our big case!

The officer could give us no further information, except that the shot had come from the direction of a godforsaken place called Schareben somewhere up in the mountains. No one, to his knowledge, had ever been up there.

"Have you heard anything since that first shot?" I asked. "Any more shots?"

The captain shook his head. "Not as much as a loud fart," he grinned.

"I understand a lot of brass PWs were taken in this area."

"Before we moved here," the captain nodded.

"Do you have a detention enclosure?"

"Doesn't everyone?"

As a matter of fact, most everyone did. Every outfit worth its salt maintained such a compound to hold all civilians picked up without papers, travel and curfew violators, and discharged military personnel without proper documentation. There they waited for screening disposition. Often valuable bits of information could be gleaned in those places, and we had nowhere else to turn.

Our customary procedure was this. Usually among the detainees there would be a discharged *Unteroffizier*, a Nazi noncom, with a real rough "sergeant's voice." We'd single him out, take him aside, give him his specific orders—and let him take over while we merely watched. It was surprising how the Germans jumped to the orders given by one of their own. When we arrived at the detention enclosure, we had no trouble finding our noncom, a big, ruddy-faced bruiser of a man with his right hand missing and a voice that seemed to originate in his groin and rumble up through his barrel chest.

There were about a hundred men in the compound. Bellowing his orders, the sergeant lined them up. Scowling and cursing, he dressed his motley crew for inspection, informing them—as he had been instructed to do—that a war criminal wanted by the Americans was known to be hiding among them, and that the American intelligence officers had come to arrest him. He then smartly turned the inspection over to us.

Franz and I slowly walked along the rows of detainees mustered in the enclosure. A light, cold drizzle had begun to fall. Some of the detainees were huddling against the chilly wetness; they would be the civilians. Others stood stiffly at attention, oblivious to the weather; the ex-soldiers. A lot can be learned from very little. All you have to do is keep your eyes open.

We went from man to man and looked briefly, searchingly into the face of each one of them. The trick is to appear as if you know some deep, dark secret—and are ready to pounce. You look for all the little body messages that betray a man who has something to hide regardless of his outward self-control—the inability to establish eye contact, the little beads of sweat on forehead and upper lip, the slightly trembling hands, the arteries in the temples that beat a shade too frantically, the dry lips, anything that cries "guilt"! It was a crazy system—but it often worked.

The men standing before us were of all ages and all sizes. Some were well dressed, some in rags. Some were reasonably well groomed, others imbedded with the grime and filth of retreat and defeat. Ex-soldiers in stripped-down uniforms stood next to civilians in every conceivable kind of clothing—an embroidered Bavarian jacket, a fur-collared, ankle-length overcoat, a torn, once colorful ski sweater, a soiled but near-new belted tan trench coat, or no coat at all. They all had one thing in common: apprehension.

But no matter how open we kept our eyes, we found no information of value.

On the way back to the unit Headquarters to report our findings—or rather lack of them—to the captain, I felt uneasy. It was that familiar, disturbing uneasiness that gnaws at the edges of your mind, that nagging feeling that something has been overlooked, some little clue. But what the hell was it?

My mind was wandering. Clues. How the hell did you know when you missed one? The clues that broke cases weren't exactly neon signs that lit up when you got within a mile of them. They were stupid *little* things. They didn't stand out from the tedious sea of trivia like some Loch Ness monster rising from the calm surface of a lake. They were little things that could have perfectly reasonable, logical, and obvious explanations. They could be perfectly innocent. Or—they could not. A hell of a lot depended on that little word: *or*. Sometimes the difference between freedom *or* arrest. Joy *or* anguish. Life *or* death. All because of one damned little clue. Some little twisted detail.

I suddenly skidded the jeep to a halt. Franz looked at me.

"You too?" he asked quietly.

"Yeah," I said. My mind was racing.

"Yeah," Franz repeated. "I've had that funny feeling that we—that we overlooked something. It's been bugging me. I wish the hell I knew what it was."

I looked at him. "I think I know," I said. "The belt. The belt on that guy's trench coat. The crease was wrong!"

In a few minutes we were back at the detention enclosure. The big, burly German noncom did not allow his bewilderment or his annoyance at having to "perform" again to show on his grim, expressionless face. In no time he had the apprehensive detainees lined up for inspection once more. The uncertainty and puzzlement of the men at the repeat performance hung like an ominous mist over the formation.

The man in the tan trench coat stood at attention in the second row. We went straight to him. I stared at the belt on his coat. It was too big. An extra hole had been made in it to accommodate the leather-covered belt buckle. The leftover tongue was way too long, and halfway along it was a deep crease, the indented mark of the buckle where it used to be worn. The coat had obviously been worn by a larger man. Although soiled, it appeared to be almost new and of top quality. How had it come into possession of this detainee? How did he come by it here, in the middle of nowhere? Who was he? Where did he come from?

I stared at the man. Nondescript would describe him perfectly. Except for the trench coat. I suddenly felt uncertain. There probably was a thoroughly logical reason for that oversized coat. I was probably making a damned fool of myself. I hadn't learned to trust that "hunch" quite yet. And it was of little comfort that Franz had felt the same way. So we were both fools. Oh, well, I'd stepped into the mess, might as well wade through it.

"Take off your coat!" I ordered. The man looked startled, but obeyed.

I grabbed it from him and examined it. It was well made. I looked in the pockets. Nothing. I turned the collar inside out and peered at it. I turned to the German noncom.

"That man," I said sharply. "Bring him to the guard hut. *Sofort!* At once!"

I showed the coat collar to Franz. His eyes widened. The haberdasher's label in the coat read: *W. Nezval, Praha*

Prague!

It was from Prague that the Luftwaffe General Staff had fled the Russians.

It didn't take too much persuasion to get the man to admit that he was an *Oberleutnant,* a first lieutenant who had been attached to the Luftwaffe General Staff as a statistician—a dreary, dull job. He had fled the city as the Russians drew close with the commanding general and the other staff officers, but unlike most of them he had not surrendered to the Americans. He had correctly guessed that all General Staff officers, regardless of rank, had a high priority on enemy wanted lists. By losing himself in the flood of refugees, he had hoped to escape a lengthy stay in some PW camp. It had not worked.

The trench coat? It had belonged to his commanding general, who had given it to him as a sort of parting gift.

Where was the general now? And the other General Staff officers? He did not know. All he knew was that he and a few other officers had split off from the main group and together crossed into Germany from Czechoslovakia before going their separate ways.

We realized that the commanding general and most of his staff were the officers who had already surrendered some time before; apparently there were other Luftwaffe General Staff officers from the Prague area still unaccounted for.

"You know who the officers who crossed with you are?" we asked.

"I do."

"We want you to make a list of them," we told him. "Every officer from the General Staff who came over with you. Name. Rank. Is that understood?"

"It is understood."

The list was short. Only five names.

We had to ask. "When you crossed over, did any one of you fire a shot?"

He shook his head. "We had all discarded both our insignia and our weapons."

We returned him to the prisoner compound for routine disposition and walked back to our jeep. We might not have learned anything about the mysterious shot near Schareben, but at least we'd gotten a few more names to check against our wanted list.

Franz looked at me. "What do you think?" he asked. "Is it worth our while to take a look at that Schareben place?"

I shrugged. "We're here," I said. "Why not? Can't hurt."

We borrowed a couple of GIs from the antiaircraft artillery unit, just in case, and set out.

Schareben was not on our map, but a series of inquiries led us to a narrow dirt road that snaked up into the wooded mountains, little more than an overgrown trail.

The badly maintained trail was barely negotiable even for our jeep in four-wheel drive. The trip seemed to take forever. Suddenly the trail forked. An old, weather-beaten signpost leaned askew at one corner: SCHAR BEN, 2 km, it announced. A bullet hole had neatly obliterated the E in the middle.

The shot? The famous Schareben shot?

I stopped the jeep, and Franz jumped out to examine the sign. He shook his head. The edges of the hole were badly rusted; obviously the damage was months—or years—old.

Schareben consisted of two buildings and a few ramshackle coops and sheds. It was the home of a *Staatsforstmeister*, a state forester, and his family—wife, two girls, and two boys between the ages of nine and thirteen—who lived in the one-story main house. They were all waiting for us as we drove up, having heard our laboring jeep engine for the last kilometer or so. The other building was a two-story barn with a peaked roof. It was obviously also inhabited—a pair of muddy overshoes stood by the door—but no one showed.

The forester, a slight, balding man in his late forties with what was left of his dirty-blond hair shaved high above his ears and a small toothbrush mustache, beamed his welcome with excessive cordiality. With a flourish he introduced himself—Schönberger was the name, in charge of the Schareben Staatsjagdrevier, the Schareben State Forest and Hunting District.

I began to fear we were wasting our time. A gamekeeper. A hunter. Used to shooting game. He probably shot a deer now and then to augment his family dinners. He had probably fired the shot heard—if not around the world, certainly around the area of CIC Detachment 212! It was probably as simple as that. A boring exercise in futility.

Franz echoed my feelings. He looked around with chagrin. "This has all the earmarks of being as titillating as the tits on a ten-year-old," he remarked sourly.

We left the two GIs to keep an eye on the barn while Franz and I herded the entire Schönberger family into the communal dining/living room of the house. The room was stuffy, with a low ceiling and all the windows closed; it smelled of a mixture of cooked cabbage and old sweat. Ordinarily we would have separated the adults for interrogation, but in this case we felt it unnecessary to do so. This was not going to be an earth-shaking case. And we were anxious to get the thing over with.

"You are the *Forstmeister* here?" I began. "And you—"

"*Jawohl!*" the little man exploded, snapping to attention. "*Staatsforstmeister Schönberger, zu Befehl*!—at your service!"

"You own a gun?" I finished what I had intended to ask him.

"Three, *Herr Offizier,*" the man beamed happily. "Two shotguns. A Kettner, double barrel, and a Merkel, over and under. That one is wonderfully carved. Also a rifle. A Mauser."

"Have you fired any of them recently? Within the last couple of weeks?"

He suddenly grew cloudy. "How could I?" he said.

"What do you mean?"

"An ill luck has befallen me," he said resentfully. "My guns were taken from me."

"By whom?"

"By the *Amis.*" He corrected himself hastily. "By the Americans." He turned to a chest of drawers and opened one of them. He pulled out a slip of paper.

"I have here a receipt," he said, "signed by the American sergeant. Also with his rank." He handed it to me.

It was a receipt for three guns, property of a state official. It was signed by an infantry sergeant and dated 27 April, two days after Grafenau was taken and long before the mysterious shot was heard.

Shit! We were right back where we started.

I gave the receipt back to the little man. "Do you have any other guns?" I asked him. "Handguns?"

He looked shocked. "Other guns?" His face became indignant. "Of course not, *Herr Offizier,*" he said. "I would have given them to the soldiers. As they commanded me to do." The smile returned to his face. "It is only temporarily. It was explained to me. I am a state official, and I have my duties to perform. I cannot do that without my guns. I shall have them returned to me. Any day."

"Who lives across the street?" Franz asked.

The *Forstmeister* looked surprised. Then he smiled broadly. "In the barn. *Ach ja!*" He shook his head. "They are nobody. Refugees. They have no place else to go. I let them stay," he finished magnanimously.

"Who are they? How many?"

The little man frowned in concentration. "There are five," he said. "There is a woman. She is a fine lady. She is the widow of a Luftwaffe officer. And her son." He counted on his fingers. "There is Fräulein Ilse. Very pretty. And there are two ex-Wehrmacht soldiers, a sergeant and a corporal." Again he counted on his fingers. "*Ja,*" he said emphatically, "five. Two women, one boy, and two discharged soldiers."

"How long have they been here?"

"Oh, a long time. They came not long after the war was over."

"A shot was fired here," I broke in. "A few days ago. You must have heard it. Who fired it? Did—they?"

The forester suddenly looked gray. The family instinctively drew closer around him. "*We* did not," the man said firmly. "I told you that."

"Did *they?*"

He shook his head. "We—we heard it, naturally. One shot. I even said, Who could that be, shooting in the forest? In my *Revier?*" He looked at his wife. "Did I not say that, *Schatzi?*"

The woman nodded solemnly.

"Yes. I did." The forester looked at me. The matter was settled as far as he was concerned.

"Do you know if the refugees in the barn have any weapons? Guns?"

Vigorously he shook his head. The entire family followed suit.

"What *do* you know about them?"

"Nothing. Only what I told you."

"Names?"

He nodded. "The sergeant is called Bauer; the corporal is Joachim. The girl—"

I did not listen. I was busy fishing in my pocket for the list of names of the Luftwaffe General Staff officers our trench-coated informer had given us. There. It was headed by a *Colonel* Bauer and a *Major* Joachim! And following them was a Colonel Cornelius and two more majors, Schindler and Gruber.

We'd hit the jackpot, but we had no idea what the payoff would be.

Before we confronted the group in the barn, we needed backup. There was no telling who else might be in the vicinity. We kept one of the GIs with us and sent the other with the jeep to his outfit with orders to return with a detail of men.

While we waited for our reinforcements to arrive, Franz and I began our preliminary interrogation of the crew in the barn. The GI kept an eye on the forester family.

I had questioned stubborn suspects before but never a group so blindly obstinate as the five improbable refugees holed up in the Schönberger barn.

We told them that we knew their true identities; we brandished our irrefutable evidence before them—the list of Luftwaffe General Staff officers headed by Colonel Bauer and Major Joachim. But despite this, and despite looking and acting the prototype of a Prussian Junker officer, Bauer imperiously denied the evidence and insisted he was a discharged sergeant. He practically ordered us to believe him. It was, after all, *his* word against some inferior detainee, he claimed, unaware of the incongruity of that statement, the detainee being a lieutenant and he a professed sergeant. What was more, he claimed, his papers proved his true identity. He waved his *Soldbuch,* the soldier's paybook all enlisted men carried, and his discharge papers, all with the proper stamps and signatures, not difficult to get for a General Staff officer. It was there in black-and-white, he pointed out. Who would dare doubt the written word against that of some irresponsible nonentity? No contest, of course. He categorically refused to admit to what was obviously the fact—that he was indeed Colonel Bauer.

Joachim, to no one's surprise, followed suit.

The matronly officer's widow hardly deigned to open her mouth. When she did, it was to deny any knowledge of or connection with Bauer and Joachim, although her husband undoubtedly had served with them in the Luftwaffe. She had no interest in a couple of enlisted men; it was bad enough that circumstances forced her to share the shelter of the barn with them.

Her son had been brought up just right in the Hitler Youth. It was all he could do to keep from spitting in our faces.

It wasn't until we started on the young girl, whose name was Ilse, that we found an opening. We could see from observing both her and Bauer that these two were more than mere friends. Ilse was pleasantly plump with a sweet face and a disposition to match. She told us she had been a *Wehrmachthelferinn,* a German Wac, in Prague. It was obvious that she was quite smitten with the manly Sergeant/Colonel Bauer.

There was a commotion outside as the GI returned with our jeep. I went out to meet him, while Franz stayed with the suspects. A sergeant sat next to the GI, and the jeep was followed by a weapons carrier with a detail of men from the antiaircraft artillery battalion. I quickly gave the sergeant his orders and returned to the barn. We placed Bauer and Joachim under guard and took Ilse to a small, adjoining tack shed, which would serve as our interrogation room. We were well aware that the girl was our last chance to break the case, and we were determined to give it our best shot.

Ilse was obviously deadly afraid. We did nothing to dispel that feeling. We treated her in a cold, matter-of-fact manner. We explained to her that she was considered not a civilian refugee but a prisoner of war, as were the two soldiers. Her Wehrmacht discharge papers, dated within the last few weeks, could not be considered valid. We informed her that as a PW she was entitled to all Geneva convention considerations due that status, but also all the obligations—and the serious consequences of resisting such obligations. As a PW it was her duty *not* to withhold the name, rank, and serial number of any military personnel.

The girl listened in apprehensive silence, staring straight ahead.

We had put together a makeshift interrogation setup. A rough wooden bench served as a table, behind which Franz and I sat on bales of hay.

The girl stood awkwardly before us. Franz had fetched his musette bag from the jeep and brought out a sheaf of paper and a pencil, which he placed on the table. He would take notes. It always unnerved a suspect to see someone taking notes at the most unlikely times. The question would invariably arise in his mind—what was that all about? What did I say now? It was an effective trick to break down a suspect's self-confidence.

"Very well," I said sternly. "State your name, rank, and serial number."

She did. Easy. We knew that already.

"Now," I said. "Bauer and Joachim are both officers in the Luftwaffe, correct?"

The girl swallowed nervously. "I—I do not know," she whispered.

She was lying. We knew it. And she in turn had to be aware of that fact. Yet—she lied. The question was, why? What could possibly be accomplished by the ridiculous charade? All right, so it was evident that she and Bauer were more than just fellow refugees stranded in the Schareben barn, but was that enough for such histrionics? I doubted it. There had to be something else. We did not have time for a long, drawn-out interrogation session. A quick and deadly jab might do it, however. We had little real knowledge about the two men: first, they had been officers in the Luftwaffe in Prague, and second, they had fled that city to escape the Russians. Very well—let's use that knowledge.

I reached over and scribbled an *R* on Franz's pad. I said nothing to the girl.

Franz bent down and picked up his musette bag. He began unhurriedly to rummage through it. Ilse watched him tensely. Not a word was spoken.

Finally Franz brought out a bunch of large yellow tags, each with a string attached to it. Meticulously he began to write on one of them.

Still not a word was spoken.

Ilse had grown pale. Her large blue eyes were dark, filled with fear. They flitted uneasily from one of us to the other. We ignored her. She began to tremble.

Franz finished his writing. He stood up. He walked to the fearful girl. Without a word he tied the tag to a button on her blouse front. It hung like an evil tarot of death on her ample bosom.

"One last time, Fräulein Ilse," I said solemnly. "Will you tell the truth?"

"I—" Her voice broke. She cleared her throat. "I—have."

I shrugged indifferently. "Your choice," I said, my voice flat. I nodded to Franz. He went back to his bag and once again rummaged through it. This time he came up with a large red grease pencil. He returned to the girl and wrote a large red *R* on the tag around her chest.

I stood up. I looked at the girl with obvious pity. "I'm sorry," I said. I turned to leave.

"Please!" Ilse pleaded, her voice husky with alarm and incomprehension. She glanced down at the tag. "What—what means this?"

I turned back to her. I spoke kindly. "That is a PW tag, Fräulein."

She looked at me, fearfully questioning.

"You are considered a prisoner of war," I explained. "This tag will accompany you wherever you go from now on. It states your name, the time, the place, and the circumstance of your capture. It is routine."

Again she looked at the tag. She lifted her hand toward it, but she could not bring herself to touch it. "And—this red *R?*" she whispered. "What means it?"

I turned away from her. I hesitated. I played it to the hilt. Then I said, "Russia."

She had known, yet she blanched. "Russia," she repeated.

I turned back to her. I allowed my anger to show. "You chose it!" I said savagely. "It is your own doing." I stopped to let it sink in. Then I went on. "You will be turned over to the Russians. *They* will interrogate you, since you will not cooperate with us. You will be interned in Russia. Possibly Siberia. We have a quota of prisoners we must turn over to them. We give them the ones who will not play ball with us."

Ilse stared at me, ashen-faced. She swayed slightly on her feet. I noticed that Franz stood ready to catch her should she keel over. With open dread she stared at me. "And—the others. You will mark them with this red *R* too?"

"Yes." I turned to leave.

"Wait!" It was a cry of utter despair. I turned back to her impatiently.

"Well?" I snapped.

She stood staring at the PW tag. The big red *R* filled its yellow face. She clenched her hands before her in unconscious supplication. She squeezed them until her fingers showed white.

"Sergeant Bauer is Colonel Bauer, OQu IV," she intoned. "Deputy Chief of General Staff, Intelligence, OKL, Oberkommando der Luftwaffe,

Field Echelon, Prague." The damning words were delivered in a monotonous, lifeless voice. She added, "I—I was his secretary."

"Joachim?"

She nodded. "*Major* Joachim."

"You will repeat exactly what you have just said to Colonel Bauer's face." It was a statement, not a request.

"*Ja*," she whispered.

I looked at her. The tears were running down her cheeks. The goddamned war, I thought. She was probably a perfectly nice girl. If it hadn't been for those fucking Nazis, no one would have had to inflict all this anguish on her. Dammit all to hell!

I watched her for a brief moment. She looked utterly miserable. She could not know, I thought, that my "reluctant" disclosure of the Russian quota was pure fabrication.

The prisoners stood in a defiant group guarded by the GIs when Franz and I brought Ilse face-to-face with them. The girl was deadly pale, her eyes dark with despair, focusing on nothing.

I placed her directly in front of Bauer. The man fixed his blazing eyes upon her. She shivered. "All right," I said sharply. "Repeat exactly what you told us."

The girl's mouth worked, but not a sound emerged.

Bauer stood as if hewn in granite. His eyes bored into those of the terrified girl. The power emanating from him was an almost tangible thing. Starting at his bull neck, protruding from his tunic collar, his face flushed a deep angry red as he stood silent, immobile.

Twice the girl tried to speak. Twice the man's glaring eyes silenced her.

I let the drama play itself out. I knew what the girl was going through. Face-to-face with her comrades she had to betray them. She thought that by denouncing them she was saving them from a fate of unspeakable horror. Them—and herself. It was a soul-wrenching choice. Finally I spoke. "Well?"

"I told you nothing!" Ilse cried, a cry of pure anguish. "I only said what you wanted to hear. I was frightened. *I—told—you—nothing!*" She put her hands to her face. She sobbed.

Bauer moved not a muscle. But somehow his stance conveyed his triumph.

Franz and I walked toward our jeep. I was mad as hell. But stymied. Strictly speaking, it wasn't necessary to get confessions from the two officers. Our evidence was strong enough. They knew their identities could be checked out—in time. So why the playacting?

"Thick-skulled bastards," Franz muttered. "Damn them!"

I slowed down. "Two can play that dumb obstinacy game," I said slowly. "You want to play?"

"I hate to send a couple of suspects back to AIC without confirmed identification."

"Yeah," I agreed. "Repple-depple time." And there was something else that bothered me. Those other names on the list. That Colonel Cornelius. The two men had refused to admit any knowledge of such an officer. Bauer was no fool. Autocratic, pigheaded, yes. But no fool. He must know he was fighting a losing battle. That it would be only a matter of time before the facts would emerge. Then, why? What was it all about? Was he fighting some kind of holding action? Buying time? If so—for what? Had it something to do with Cornelius? With that damned shot in the forest? I made up my mind. Franz and I simply *had* to get to the bottom of the whole mess, right here, right now. I felt better.

"Let's have one more go at it," I said firmly.

"How? We've threatened the bastards with fire and brimstone. Or more specifically, the firing squad and the Russians. What the hell's left?"

"Forget about the phony crew in the barn," I said. "Let's go to work on our jolly *Forstmeister*. No holds barred."

The forester and his family seemed aghast if not downright incredulous when we told them whom they were harboring in their barn. But we were in no mood for any more parlor games. I glared at the man. "Pack a small bag. Necessities only," I ordered him.

The blood drained from his face. "But—why?" he croaked.

"You are coming with us," I snapped impatiently. "You are under arrest."

"But—but why?" His genial face was suddenly contorted with fear. "I—I have done nothing!"

"One," I said, "you are lying to American authorities. Two, you are harboring wanted General Staff officers."

"A capital offense," Franz added. "The firing squad, once the true identities of the people you have sheltered are firmly established."

"No—I did not know—I—*please!* I—"

"Of course," I suggested, "if you will tell us all you know. Now. With nothing left out. We might overlook your—forgetfulness."

He looked at me as if he were seeing the devil incarnate.

"Please," his wife whispered to him. "The children. Please!"

The man looked at the children gathered around him in the dreary, low-ceilinged room. He wet his bloodless lips. "What do you want to know?"

"The two men in the barn," I began. "They *are* Luftwaffe officers?"

Mutely he nodded.

The little SOB, I thought, he'd known all along. But I had to play it out.

"And you knew that those two men in the barn were high-ranking officers when you told us they were only noncoms!"

The man cringed. He took a step toward me. His eyes searched mine beseechingly. "You do not understand," he pleaded. "They—they threatened us. They said—" He spread out his arms to encompass his entire family. "They said they would," he gave a little sob. "My family . . ." He blinked at me, imploring me to understand.

"Where are Colonel Cornelius and the others?" I shot at him.

He started. I could almost see the wheels whirling in his mind. Should he tell all? Could he keep something back? Was it worth the risk? From whom had he most to fear? Us? Or them? But once he had begun to talk, it was impossible to stop. "I do not know," he said. "Somewhere in the forest."

"How many?"

"About—twenty, I think. They sometimes come here for food."

He had decided to play ball, trying to buy immunity for himself. Good.

"You still don't know where they are?" I asked.

With a quick glance at his wife, he shook his head.

It was time to play my ace in the hole. "Very well," I said. "Come with me."

"Come—with you?" he stammered. "But—you said . . ."

"Don't worry," I interrupted him "You are not under arrest. But you *are* needed as a witness. Against Bauer and Joachim. And Cornelius. We'll just put you in the barn until we return.

"Return? I do not understand." His eyes suddenly widened. "In the barn! With *them!*"

"We have to try to find Cornelius," I explained. "I hope it won't take too long."

"I—I will be left with them?" the little man asked fearfully. "Alone?" He swallowed. Hard. "Will they—will they know that—that—"

"That you ratted on them?" I finished for him. I shrugged. "Afraid so. You see, we tried to trick them into revealing their true identities. We told them that *you* had informed on them. Well—it's true now, isn't it?"

Aghast, he stared at me. "But—you cannot leave me alone with them!" His face had drained to a sickly gray. "They will kill me!"

He reached for his wife. She clasped the two youngest children to her. *"Gott im Himmel!"* she breathed. "Oh, my God!" She crossed herself.

"Sorry," I said. "Even if we keep you apart here, you'll still be thrown into the same detention enclosure with them down the hill. There are no—separate accommodations." I sighed. "If only you had been able to tell us where Cornelius and his gang are holed up, it might not have been necessary to hold you." I looked closely at him. "You are sure you have no idea?"

Terror-stricken, he shook his head. "I—I do not know! I swear it. In the name of the Holy Mother, I swear it!"

When the break came, it came from an entirely unexpected source. Suddenly the younger of the two boys stepped in front of his father. Big-eyed, big-eared, buck-toothed, and barefoot, his grimy *Lederhosen* looking as if he'd been born in them, he planted himself squarely before me. "I know where he is," he announced, staring straight up at me. "If you will promise not to hurt *Vati* and *Mutti,* I will show you. But only if you promise."

The woman looked thunderstruck. Her hand flew to her mouth. "Otto!" she exclaimed.

The forester put his hand on the boy's shoulder and drew him back to him. "He is only nine, *Herr Offizier,"* he said in quick defense of his son. "He did not know. He likes to play in the forest. To play at being a hunter. Like his father. Please do not be angry with him."

I bent down on one knee in front of the boy, so his eyes were on a level with mine. "Thank you, Otto," I said. "You can be of great help. To us. And to your parents."

Quickly we made our plans. The afternoon was wearing on, but we had no choice but to act at once. Tomorrow would be too late. Our quarry would surely have flown the coop.

Two men from our detail were assigned to guard the prisoners. Two men were given sentry duty, and two more were sent off to the battalion headquarters with orders to bring back reinforcements. On the double!

Gently I questioned Otto. With small-boy curiosity, he had followed Colonel Cornelius into the forest one day, pretending in his game of playing hunter that the officer was a wild animal, a lion no less, to be stalked to its lair without his tracker being discovered. Although Otto had not actually seen the bivouac area of Cornelius and his men, he had a good idea where it was.

In less than an hour two squads of men barreled into Schareben, and with Otto as a guide we took our search party into the woods. In silence we followed a narrow path winding up a steep slope among the thick evergreens. After half an hour's walk we came to a clearing where the slope leveled off. At one edge of the open area a large, bare rock formation thrust itself up through the underbrush. A perfect landmark. Otto pointed.

"In there!" he whispered, his eyes shining with excitement. "That is where the colonel went."

Quickly and quietly the squad leaders deployed their men. Skirting the open ground, the men cautiously infiltrated the woods lying ahead, while a disappointed Otto was ordered to stay hidden where he was.

Franz and I walked together, guns drawn, silently, carefully wending our way around clumps of underbrush and overgrown rocks. On both sides of us we could see the GIs stealthily moving forward, searching and probing.

We came to a heavy thicket. Franz circled it on one side, I took the other.

I was halfway around, when I suddenly stopped in my tracks. I stared. Dug into the ground directly in front of me was a big camouflage tent, so skillfully placed and concealed that it blended perfectly with the forest floor and the underbrush. One more step and I would literally have tumbled down on the heads of our quarry. At once I raised my hand.

All around me the GIs stopped in place, watching me tensely. I pointed to the hidden tent; their sergeant took over, and quietly, cautiously, the men surrounded the area, weapons ready. The damp air hung heavily among the silent trees. There was no motion to be seen, no sound to be heard.

As soon as everyone was in place I shouted at the top of my voice. "*Rauskommen! Los! Hände hoch! Los! Los!*"

At once the GIs took up the cry: "Come out! Hands up! Get going! Out! Out!"

The effect was instantaneous. The big tent in front of me heaved and shook with the sudden motion within. Bumps and bulges rippled across the mottled camouflage surface as the startled men inside leaped up and lurched against the canvas. A short distance away the astounding spectacle was being repeated at another hidden tent. I had not even seen that one.

From the two tents, men in field gray uniforms came tumbling out. For a moment all seemed utter chaos. Soldiers stumbled about in complete confusion, hands on their heads or raised high in the air, looking for the omnipresent enemy. So complete was the surprise that although the Germans were armed to the teeth not a shot was fired.

Quickly they were rounded up to form a group of bewildered men, huddled in the center of the small clearing between the two camouflaged tents surrounded by GIs.

I stepped forward. *"Achtung, Sondergruppe Cornelius!"* I called aloud. "Attention Special Unit Cornelius! Colonel Bauer, Deputy Chief of Intelligence, *Oberkommando der Luftwaffe,* has ordered you to surrender. You will obey his command without resistance!"

The prisoners shifted uneasily. I looked them over. "Which one of you is Colonel Cornelius?" I demanded.

A small, gray-haired man with steel-rimmed glasses stepped forward. "I am Colonel Cornelius," he said calmly.

Franz had joined me. I motioned the colonel over to us. I indicated the group of German soldiers. "Is that your entire command?"

"Yes."

"What is the size of your field unit?"

"Eleven officers, six noncommissioned officers, eight others."

"All from the Prague field echelon of the Luftwaffe General Staff?"

"Yes."

The sergeant from our GI detail joined us. The count is twenty-five," he reported.

I nodded. "It tallies." I turned to Cornelius. "Colonel Bauer is the CO of the *Sondergruppe?"* I asked.

Cornelius gave me a quick glance. He nodded. "Of course."

Franz looked the man up and down. "Why are you and your men camped out here, Colonel," he asked, "instead of in Schareben with your CO?"

Cornelius turned to look at him. A slight smile curled his lips. "Cornelius, Eugen," he recited. "*Oberst. Fünf—drei—neun—*"

"Oh, shit!" Franz interrupted him. "Save that crap!"

Cornelius at once fell silent, but the little smile remained.

"That's all, Colonel," I said curtly. "You may join your men."

Cornelius clicked his heels. With a slight bow he gave a military salute. He turned on his heel and with measured steps walked toward the group of men in the clearing. He had been correct. He had been courteous. Without knowing it, he had confirmed Bauer's true rank and position. And he had given me the unmistakable impression that he was mocking us.

I watched him as he walked away. He was an unusual officer, not at all like Bauer. He seemed more a scholar than a soldier, and he was in complete control of himself. I wondered what his function on the General Staff had been. His assignment? I had countless questions to ask him, but now was not the time, here not the place. Franz was scowling after the colonel.

"Hey! Do you see what I see?" He nodded toward the prisoners.

As Cornelius approached his men, one of them turned toward him. He stood attentively, as if awaiting any orders the colonel might give him. He wore the distinctive peaked Luftwaffe field cap and black jackboots. On his field-gray uniform tunic the Luftwaffe emblem, the flying eagle gripping a swastika, soared proudly over his right breast pocket. His epaulettes were those of a noncom, and the insignia of rank on his collar tabs showed three hashmarks, like stylized birds in flight, on a light brown background. A *Feldwebel.* An Intelligence noncom.

"How about it?" Franz suggested. "Nothing I'd like better than to deflate Bauer's overblown balls!"

"Why not?" I grinned. "Let's have a little talk with that eager-beaver *Feldwebel.*"

It was almost dusk when we returned to Schareben with Otto and our prisoners. Guarded by the entire detachment of GIs, the captives were marched to the open area between the two large buildings. They were ordered to fall in and stand at attention. From the gamekeeper's house the forester and his family were brought out to join Otto. They watched the activities with misgivings and awe.

When the prisoners were assembled, the little group from the barn was trotted out. Not one of them reacted visibly to the sight of the Luftwaffe PWs standing in formation, stiffly at attention.

In a loud voice I gave the order: "Feldwebel Bergman! Front and center! Make your report!"

From the ranks of ramrod prisoners the *Feldwebel* stepped forward. Conducting himself as if he were on parade, he smartly wheeled and marched to the center of the formation. Again he made a precise turn, and with firm, measured strides he all but goose-stepped to stand directly in front of Bauer, the self-styled sergeant. His hand shot up in a stiff-armed Nazi salute. His heels clicked together with the sharp crack of a shot. In a loud, firm voice he announced, *"Herr Oberst,* Colonel, sir! Heil Hitler! I beg to report that *Sondergruppe Cornelius* has surrendered!"

Bauer turned red as a boiled lobster. His eyes, glaring at the hapless *Feldwebel* with venomous malevolence, bulged dangerously in his crimson face. His massive body shook with barely suppressed fury and impotence. His fists clenched in rage at his sides. His tightly compressed lips worked in frustrated anger. But he said not a word. Suddenly he whirled about, and utterly disregarding the GI guards, he stalked stiffly to the hay-scented sanctuary of the barn, closely followed by the two grinning GIs.

It was a most satisfying reaction. Dammit—it was worth it!

That evening, when we returned to Grafenau, we brought along Colonel Bauer, Colonel Cornelius, and Ilse. She had finally admitted being Bauer's fiancée and had begged to be taken along. We could see no harm in it—and her presence might even mellow the hard-boiled Bauer—so we had agreed.

The G-2 of XII Corps, Col. John H. Claybrook, thought our catch was important enough to send his assistant G-2, Lt. Col. John W. Wilkin, to our billet, to contribute personally to the interrogation of the two colonels.

There were many intriguing questions wanting answers. How had the General Staff been operating? What had been its actions in the final days? Why were Cornelius, Bauer, Joachim, and the others hiding in the forest? Why did they not surrender with their commanding general and the rest of the group? What was their mission? Their plans? For almost six hours during the night we took turns questioning the two Nazi officers. They did not break. Stiffly they sat in their chairs, and stiffly they answered every question put to them with the same droning answer, until the guttural sound of their names, ranks, and service numbers reverberated in every cell of our brains.

At last, we gave up.

We were ordered the next morning to take the two prisoners to AIC, Third Army Interrogation Center in the town of Freising, and let the IPWs have a go at them.

But one nagging question would not leave me. They had been hiding out. *Why?*

The following morning we took off for Freising, just north of Munich. Our timing was perfect. As we were loading the prisoners in our two jeeps, each with a driver and a guard, Ilse was led past between two MPs. She turned a wan and drawn face toward Bauer and gave him a pleading look. He clenched his teeth, his face cloudy. He could not know that she was being taken to Military Government for proper papers that would allow her to travel home. He naturally feared something considerably worse.

He turned to me. "It looks bad," he said.

"It looks bad," I repeated. "Get in!"

We had a trip of over a hundred miles ahead of us, during which we would try to find out what we wanted to know. We hadn't called it quits yet. Halfway to AIC, just past a little village called Wallersdorf, we drove off the road down to a pleasant little lake, stopped our vehicles, and prepared to eat a good lunch. When the delicious aroma of real coffee drifted toward the eager nostrils of the troubled Bauer and the stoic Cornelius, they began to get restless. It was now or never. No amount of questioning or threatening would make those two diehards talk, so . . .

"Won't you join us in a cup of coffee and a bit to eat?" we called to them. Our invitation was promptly accepted.

For an hour and a half we sat there talking about all kinds of nonmilitary subjects—the beauty of the Bavarian countryside and the world importance of Germany's great sons. I told them of my admiration for German music, the gloriously melodious compositions of Beethoven and the grand, sweeping, and forceful operas of Wagner. Franz professed a great interest in the writings of Goethe and Schiller and the work of such towering artists as Holbein and Dürer, not to forget the contributions of a Gutenberg or a Kepler.

From German literature and art we drifted into history and politics. A bit of not too obvious flattery, although flattery seemed perfectly acceptable, arguing a point that had to be proven, and setting Bauer's mind at ease concerning Ilse, we little by little steered the animated conversation to the activities of the Luftwaffe General Staff. The discussion became more heated; the two Germans were caught up in a really fascinating discussion.

"This time," I argued, "the German military machine has been crushed for good."

Bauer snorted. "Germany will rise again, young man," the Prussian Junker countered. "She will grow strong again."

"But she will never be able to wage another war."

"And why not?" demanded Cornelius.

"I say she will *not.*"

"And I say she *will.* And I ought to know. I was—"

He suddenly stopped. He threw a quick glance at Bauer. There was a tense silence.

"Yes?" I asked, appearing to be oblivious to the sudden uneasiness. "You were what—?"

The two Nazis looked at each other. I knew what they were thinking. But they felt good. They had a nice lunch under their belts—and real coffee in their mugs. This was no military interrogation. What was the use of stalling any longer? Besides, they just couldn't bear to lose the point.

They talked.

When we resumed our trip to AIC we knew the mission that Colonel Bauer and Colonel Cornelius had been so jealously guarding. On the Luftwaffe General Staff, Cornelius had been in charge of the Office of Collection and Evaluation of Information for Future Wars, an office that had collected all available information and knowledge—both Allied and Axis—pertaining to the waging of war in the air in World War III—including stratospheric rocket warfare research!

The records were safely buried near Regen, and the mission of the hidden General Staff officers and their men was to safeguard and act as caretakers of this hoard of invaluable information once the immediate postwar turmoil had died down. To guard it—for the day . . .

The shot that started the whole thing? To break the monotony of canned rations for lunch, Cornelius had taken a shot at a rabbit.

He'd missed.

Grafenau was unrecognizable, as forty-five years later Cleo and I checked into a new, beautiful resort hotel situated in the hills overlooking the picture-postcard Bavarian town. The sleepy little town had turned into a teeming resort with flamboyantly clad tourists and vacationers tripping over one another in the souvenir shop–lined streets and cars parked everywhere. So much new construction and remodeling had taken place that the town held no familiarity for me, and as for finding my way to Schareben, I might as well have been stranded in uncharted territory.

Schareben was not to be found on any map, even my own from 1945. At the hotel, the tourist relations office, and the mayoralty, our inquiries met only with vacant stares. Finally an elderly gentleman clerk in a bookstore told us of someone who might know of Schareben, a regional mapmaker for the National Park Association, housed on the fifth floor of the striking, tall, step-gabled, and green-painted town hall. Walk-up, of course.

While Cleo wisely went sightseeing, I braved the climb and soon found a helpful young man who after much rummaging around in boxes and drawers came up with an old map that showed Schareben. As far as he knew, he said dubiously, it was still there. On the map we managed to locate and identify the small road that led from the town up into the mountains.

The narrow, wooded mountain road was deserted as we began our safari to Schareben. Consisting of little more than two ruts, the road grew steadily worse as it snaked up the steep rise. But slowly we coaxed our car onward, lurching along in first gear. After what seemed like miles we came to the fork in the road, now little more than a rocky trail about the width of our car. The SCHAR BEN road sign with the bullet hole was gone, and there was no replacement. But I felt we were on the right track, and after a couple more miles of bumping, swaying, and jolting over the rocky path, we burst from the tree-canopied trail into a small clearing, and I stared at a spot of the earth that time had forgotten.

There was Schareben. The same two houses. The barn, where Bauer and the others had been in hiding. The main house that had been the home of the forester, his son Otto, and the rest of his family. The sheds. All unchanged.

I stopped the car. For a long moment I sat in silence, gazing at yesteryear. The cast of characters of the case of so long ago suddenly crowded into the car with us—Bauer and Cornelius, Joachim and Franz, Ilse and Otto. The case of the hidden High Command had been one of intrigue and surprising twists. But changeless Schareben still had a surprise in store for me.

Although the pretty, sunlit clearing and the two buildings in it had not changed, Schareben was no longer a state forestry station. It now served as an end-of-the-road refreshment stop for hikers hardy enough to undertake the climb. One of the rooms in the forester's house had been turned into a small snack bar where the hikers could fortify themselves with a stein of beer and a *Stulle,* a simple cold-cut sandwich.

We entered the house and were shown to the dining room by the woman innkeeper. It was the same low-ceilinged room in which I had interrogated—and intimidated—the Schareben forester and his family a lifetime before, the same room where buck-toothed little Otto had stepped forward and defiantly declared, "*I* know where Colonel Cornelius is!"

There were two wooden tables with long benches in the room already occupied by a group of hikers enjoying their meals. There were two places left opposite each other at the end of one of the tables, and the woman indicated we should sit there. We did—while the Germans smiled and nodded at us, busily chomping on their *Stullen.*

On our trip we carried a little black book of miniaturized photocopies of the notes about my war experiences and many photographs to remind us how it was. Sitting in that stuffy room, in the smell of beer and tobacco smoke, Cleo wanted to be reminded of the details of the story that took place right there, so I handed her the black book. Keeping her hand over the photos of the German prisoners, Cleo sat, sipping a beer, reading about what had happened in that very room almost half a century before. We couldn't discuss it in front of the German hikers, but I quietly told her that the stove was the same, and the room unchanged.

Cleo and I were still working on our steins of beer and our *Stullen* when the hikers departed, enveloped in their cocoon of *Gemütlichkeit*, and we were alone in the room with the innkeeper, a woman in her sixties. I engaged her in conversation, and she told me that Schareben had not been a forestry station for many years.

"Did you know the *Forstmeister* who was stationed here in 1945?" I asked her. She looked at me with surprise, a cluster of empty steins held deftly in each hand.

"Forstmeister Schönberger," she exclaimed with animation. *"Ach, ja*! And a wonderful man he was, *gell*. I knew him well. And his lovely family."

"Do you know what happened to him?"

With no thought of putting the steins down, the woman let her face grow solemn. "He died, the poor man," she stated. "Already many years now."

"And his family?"

"Both the daughters married, *gell*. They moved away." She shook her head. "I do not know where they are. His wife, she also passed on." She began to cross herself with a hand filled with beer steins, but thought better of it. "And the two sons, they too left here. One moved to Passau." She frowned in thought. "I—I think he is still there. The other one left Germany."

"Which one was that?"

"The younger boy," she said. "The one with the crooked teeth. His name was Otto." She hefted the clusters of steins in her hands and turned to put them away.

"He went to America," she finished.

I sat there, staring after her, as she walked toward the kitchen. She had just given the final surprising twist to the convoluted Schareben case.

Little Otto, buckteeth and all, the key to the capture of the Luftwaffe hidden High Command and the retrieval of their vital records, was now an inhabitant of the U.S. of A.!

CHAPTER 12

From Schareben and Grafenau Cleo and I drove to the little town of Kötzting some fifty miles to the north, county seat of County Kötzting in Bavaria.

We thoroughly enjoyed our ride through the Bavarian countryside, a land of rolling hills and majestic, forest-mantled mountains towering over meandering rivers and streams, preening themselves in the mirror surfaces of clear, blue lakes fed by springs and creeks, of sun-drenched meadows and pastures and rich-green fields quilted among enchanted evergreen woods; a land dotted with picture-postcard villages, their pretty little houses ornamented with carved balconies, gables, and roofs and picturesque frescoes on whitewashed walls, planter boxes groaning with an abundance of colorful flowers on every windowsill, and gaily painted furniture on porches and stoops—all creating an image of charm and tranquillity.

Forty-five years before, when my CIC team moved its offices from Grafenau to the town of Kötzting, the look had been quite different. The houses in many of the villages had been roofless, their frescoes shrapnel-scarred, or they were burned-out hulks, their walls collapsed; others stood abandoned, their empty windows ringed with black soot, looking like the sad, mascara-smeared eyes of weeping women; the streets and roads had been deeply rutted by trucks and heavy armor; trees were splintered and meadows pockmarked by shell holes.

Kötzting itself had suffered relatively little damage. A monument to the battle of Sedan in the Franco-German war of 1870, the Sedan Lion greeted us as my unit rolled into town. The statue stood perched on a lofty, columned pedestal surrounded by a low picket fence. We set up our offices in a local bank building and established our living quarters in a hotel, Gasthof Karl Dreger, right next to it on Marktstrasse. At the bottom of the street on a small, cobblestone square stood the big, white official building, with its shuttered windows, red-tile roof, and tall clock tower crowned by a black cupola with a columned spire that dominated the town.

Kötzting had changed little in the intervening years, at least the parts around our former CIC headquarters. Gasthof Karl Dreger was still there, the street floor neatly remodeled, and the big, white official building with the clock tower still stood as imposing as ever at the foot of the street, the wooden shutters now gone from its windows, supplanted by the ubiquitous flower boxes. A little fountain and a few trees had been added to the cobblestone courtyard in front of the building as well as a couple of red-draped tables surrounded by white chairs under white beach umbrellas from an adjoining restaurant, making a cheery setting for an afternoon's coffee break. The Sedan Lion Memorial, unscathed in 1945, still stood on its pedestal, only the picket fence around it was gone. It had been joined by a memorial plaque to World War II's 11th Panzer Division. This crack division had been a direct and tough adversary of XII Corps, especially 2d Cavalry Group, for many months, all through Germany and into Czechoslovakia. They had surrendered to us in early May, just before VE Day—the entire division, including the commanding general, Generalleutnant Wend von Wietersheim, and had been held in the Kötzting PW assembly area. I still have in my possession the general's standard, a magnificent silver and silk embroidered flag that I "liberated."

Second Cavalry Group "inherited" General von Wietersheim's stable of blooded riding horses, stable boys and all, and we enjoyed many hours of horseback riding in the beautiful surrounding hills, courtesy of the 11th Panzer Division. We had also appropriated a number of Volkswagens, the German counterpart to our jeeps, complete with drivers—Wehrmacht soldiers who had screened out okay, had nowhere to go, and were only too happy to work for us, which meant adequate food and shelter—not always easy to find.

One such driver was Junior, so named because of his tender years. Junior, whose real name was Josef, came from Görlitz, *Wehrkreis VIII* (Home Area VIII), the home base of the 11th Panzer Division. His parents had been killed while visiting the nearby city of Dresden, where they had gone to fetch his father's ailing mother and bring her back to Görlitz to save her from the incessant Allied air raids. All three had perished in just such a raid, and Junior had nothing to go home to. He blamed the Nazis for subjecting German civilians to such bombing raids and for taking his parents from him. Or—so he said. In any case, Junior was fascinated by our work and insisted on helping us in raids. He actually did assist us at times, once by calling our attention to a man who was trying to get out the back way of a house being searched, and once by locating a stash of weapons in a chicken coop belonging to an "innocent" former SS man. So we sometimes let Junior help the troops watching a house being searched or let him assist in the search.

Junior was to be of help once more, when a friend of mine, Jack Plants, whom I had known in New York and who was stationed nearby, came visiting.

When Jack arrived, I had been on my way to a close-by village called Titling to investigate a man the Military Government wanted to appoint mayor of the town, replacing the former Nazi-oriented official. Titling was the site of a PW camp holding some fifteen thousand prisoners, so I felt it was important that a reliable man got the job.

I was delighted to see Jack. Since the case I was about to investigate was routine, I suggested that he accompany me on the trip to Titling. He readily agreed, and so that we'd have a chance to chat during the ride, I had Junior drive us in his Volkswagen.

The mayoral candidate was a well-to-do wood carver and furniture maker. His *Fragebogen*, the detailed questionnaire every German being investigated had to fill out, seemed okay; there were no red flags. He was forty-three years old and had served as a noncom in the Wehrmacht.

The man received us with the kind of bowing and scraping that always turned me off. With obsequious cordiality—and about as much sincerity as the wolf ingratiating himself with Little Red Riding Hood—he invited us in and offered us a schnapps, which we declined. We walked through the house in which he lived alone, his wife having died while he was in the service after a childless marriage. I saw nothing out of the ordinary. He showed us his workshop, which he was in the process of refurbishing in anticipation of resuming his profession.

Off in a corner, hanging on the walls and lying on the floor, was a conglomeration of old wooden tools. Curiously Jack inspected them, as I questioned the mayoral candidate.

"What are these?" Jack asked.

"Ach! Bitteschön, Herr Offizier," the man exclaimed enthusiastically. "Ah! If it pleases the officer, it is my collection of farm implements. *Antique* farm implements. From the olden days. I have collected them, *gell.* Through many years. It is my—my hobby. I much admire the way the wood is worked." He picked up a small tool that looked like a hand scythe. He caressed the carved wooden handle. "See? It is beautiful, *ja?"* He put it away. "You must excuse the disarray," he apologized. "It is all so dirty, now. Soon I will put it in order again. Then you must come and see them. They have been neglected, I fear. Of necessity."

While Jack kept looking at the old farm tools, I returned to my routine questioning of the candidate. He answered all my questions promptly without the slightest hesitation and with honeyed honesty—yet I thought I detected a certain tenseness that had not been there before. There was the faintest hint of a sheen on the man's upper lip. What the hell was going on? I felt uncomfortable. Was it the man's exaggerated fawning—or was it something else? I kept shooting my questions at him. Perhaps something would give me a clue.

Suddenly Jack called to me, "Hey! Come look at this."

I walked over to him. He stood looking down into an ancient scarred wooden butter churn from which he had removed the lid. I peered into it. Leaning against the side, standing on its tip, was a sheathed SS officer's dagger, the ornamental chain hanging down its side under the black handle with the Nazi eagle and the SS emblem. The blue cloth in which it had been wrapped lay bunched up around the metal sheath tip on the bottom of the churn where Jack had pulled it loose.

Bingo!

"I just wanted to look in the lousy churn," Jack muttered.

"Give that man a cigar!" I said. "Good job!"

"Just call me Sherlock Holmes," he grinned.

The German stood staring at the SS dagger, his eyes wide. The sheen on his upper lip had grown into little beads of perspiration. "What—what is that?" he stammered. "I never saw it before. I—I swear it! It is not mine. I never saw it before. Please believe me!"

"This is *your* house," I said coldly, "*your* collection of old junk. And you tell me you didn't know that SS dagger was there?"

Vigorously the man shook his head. "It is *not* mine. Please, *Herr Offizier,* I never saw it before! On the Holy Mother I swear it!"

"Then how did it get in *your* butter churn?" I asked sharply.

He wet his lips. He wrung his hands. He all but flung himself at my feet in his supplication. "I—I do not know—I do not know. Please, I—" He suddenly stopped. "Perhaps—Yes! That must be it!—Sometimes there were troops stationed in my house. While I was away. I know of this. My—my neighbors know of this. Waffen SS troops, perhaps. *They* must—one of *them* must have hidden the dagger there. In *my* butter churn!" He looked beseechingly at me. "You see? It is not mine. I was *not* in the SS. Never! I never saw that—that dagger before!"

I looked at the whining German before me. I knew he was lying. A little late—but now I knew. How to prove it? Fast? The case wasn't worth a lot of time and effort. I glanced at Jack. Sherlock Holmes? I had an idea.

I'd learned that one of the most effective tools in my bag of tricks was the bluff. I remembered my instructor back at Camp Ritchie saying, "If you ain't got the goods on 'em—bluff!" It was time to follow his advice.

"Very well," I said reasonably. "You may well be telling the truth." I saw the instant relief wash over the man's face. "But," I continued, "let's find out."

He looked at me. I looked back.

"You are clean shaven," I observed. "Do you shave every day?"

The man looked at me as if I'd suddenly lost my mind. He nodded. "*Ja*."

"After you have shaved," I asked him earnestly, "do you put anything on your face? Lotion? Powder? Anything?"

The man frowned in puzzlement. "A—a little talcum powder. Sometimes."

I gestured toward Junior, who was following the exchange with a mixture of excitement and bafflement on his young face. "Tell the soldier where to find it," I ordered the German.

Totally bewildered, the mayoral candidate did as he was told.

"Go get it," I said to Junior. *"Los!"* At once he took off.

"Now," I said to the German, my tone of voice utterly businesslike. "When you finish your furniture, do you ever use any wood stain?"

Uncomprehending, the man stared at me. From after-shaving powder to wood stain. What was I getting at? He nodded. "Yes. Occasionally."

"Do you have any of it handy? A dark stain?"

Again he nodded. He walked to a shelf and took down a small can. He brought it to me. I opened it. It contained a dark brown stain.

"Fine," I said. "Now, I need two brushes. One for the stain and one small one. Perhaps a detail brush. Soft." I looked him straight in the eye. "As soft as the tip of a cat's tail."

Mutely he nodded. He went to a work table with a drawer, opened it, and rummaged through a collection of small paintbrushes.

"Also a sheet of plain white paper," I called to him.

He nodded—and brought the requested items to me. I placed them on the table before me.

Increasingly perplexed and apprehensive, the man followed what I was doing. "Now," I said, pointing to an old calendar with kitschy pictures of the Bavarian countryside. "Let me have that one."

The German pulled it off the wall and gave it to me. I tore a page from it, and with the brush I smeared a streak of dark stain across the picture. The German followed my actions, totally mystified.

"Now, a can of your paint thinner and a clean rag, and we've got it," I said.

The German produced the needed items.

Junior came back with a small canister of after-shaving talcum powder. I took it and lined it up on the table with the other items: the paint thinner, the clean rag, the stain-smeared calendar picture, the sheet of white paper, and the fine paintbrush.

"All set," I said with satisfaction. I turned to the German. "Give me your right hand," I ordered him. "You *are* right-handed?"

Automatically he nodded—and pulled his right hand away. "What—what are you going to do," he asked worriedly. "What—why do you want my right hand?"

"Fingerprints," I said matter-of-factly.

"Finger—prints?"

"Yes, fingerprints. You've heard of fingerprints, haven't you?"

"Ye—yes," he answered uncertainly.

"Let me explain," I said. "In case you don't remember." I launched into a mini-lecture.

"No two persons have the same fingerprints," I began. "That is the pattern of the ridges and loops and whorls in the skin of your fingertips. When you touch something, an impression of your fingerprints will be left on the surface of whatever you touched. That impression can be brought out and compared with the known fingerprints of a suspect. It is a method of identification that has been used for decades by law enforcement agencies all over the world. But I'm sure you know that."

I reached for the can of paint thinner and opened it. "Now," I said, "here's what we're going to do. First we'll clean all the fingertips including your thumb on your right hand with the paint thinner and the rag. Then I will roll each fingertip in turn across the stain smear on the calendar page, and then across the clean white paper. That will give us a good set of your fingerprints."

I glanced at the German. He was getting markedly more nervous. He stared at my paraphernalia lined up on the table.

"Then," I went on, "we'll take the dagger from the urn, being careful not to touch it. We'll sprinkle it lightly with the talcum powder and brush it off with the soft paintbrush. Not all of the powder will come off. Wherever someone touched it, and left a fingerprint impression, the powder will adhere to the minute traces of oil from the skin and reveal an individual pattern of the print—the signature, if you will, of whoever touched it."

Again I looked at the German. He was getting a little green around the gills.

"I'm sure we'll find a print or two on the dagger," I assured him. "But—since you have never seen that dagger before, let alone touched it, it will—of course—not be yours, and you are therefore completely in the clear, and we can report that to the Military Government." I turned to the table. "Okay, let's get on with it."

I went to work on the—by now—highly apprehensive German mayoral candidate, and soon we had a fine set of dark brown fingerprints on the white paper.

I threw the rag to the man. "Use the thinner to clean your fingers," I said. "I'll get the dagger."

Almost somnambulistically the German went through the ritual of cleaning his fingers. He never took his eyes off me as I walked over to the butter churn.

For a moment I stood looking down into the churn. As if in thought, I rubbed a finger across the side of my nose—a spot where the skin is particularly oily. Then I bent down and dipped my hands into the churn.

Quickly I pressed a nice, oily fingerprint onto the hilt of the dagger, right between the Nazi eagle and the SS emblem. Then—carefully holding the dagger by the little knob at the top of the hilt with one hand and supporting it at the tip of the sheath with the other—I brought it up out of the churn, walked to the table, and carefully placed it next to the sheet with the man's set of fingerprints.

Mesmerized, he stared at it. It looked perfectly clean.

Again, holding the dagger by the knob on the hilt and the tip of the sheath, I pulled the dagger out of its scabbard. The blade gleamed wickedly in the light; the SS motto etched on it was clearly to be read: MEINE EHRE HEISST TREUE, "My Honor Means Faithfulness."

"Let's try the hilt," I suggested. "That would be the logical place to find a good print."

While everyone watched intently, I carefully sprinkled a thin layer of talcum powder on the hilt. Meticulously I gently brushed it off. And there smack between the Nazi eagle and the SS emblem—was a strong fingerprint. Smudged and crude, it still showed ridges and swirls. I held it close to the sheet with the candidate's prints. There was no way they could be compared.

The German stood utterly still, utterly silent. Was he hooked? Did he suspect he was being rooked? I felt he needed a little prod. I'd had no chance to arrange anything, so I hoped what I had in mind would work.

"Junior," I said nonchalantly. "You were with us the last time we did this, remember?"

For only a split second the young soldier looked perplexed—then he caught on. "Oh. Yes, sir," he said brightly. "I remember."

"Good," I said. I looked up at him. Smart fellow, I thought. Quick. "Then you remember what signs to look for, right? Your eyes are better than mine. Take a look."

"Yes, sir." He bent over the prints, making a show of examining and comparing them. The German candidate watched him anxiously.

"Well?" I prompted.

"There are some strong similarities, sir," the young soldier said slowly, frowning in concentration at the prints. Not only smart, but a ham to boot, I thought wryly. "The signs are there," Junior went on. "Some of the swirls on the finger I can make out seem to be identical."

"That's fine," I nodded. "The lab boys will be able to compare the prints in detail. Thank you. That's all."

"Yes, sir." The young Wehrmacht soldier stood erect and stepped back.

I looked at the German candidate. I scowled.

"Perhaps," I said slowly. "Perhaps under the circumstances, with this, eh, new development, you might like to—to rephrase your earlier statement? We'll have to detain you, of course, until the expert at the Army Interrogation Center laboratory has made a thorough examination of the prints we have here. You understand."

The man stood ashen-faced, obviously fighting with himself. His eyes flitted between us and the prints on the table.

"The facts, the truth *will* come out," I continued. "If you did make—an error, you can tell me now. Or we will have to send you back to AIC, for the boys there to work you over—you and the fingerprint evidence we have." I paused. The air was heavy between us. "However," I said. "However, it will, of course, go considerably better for you, should you, eh, 'voluntarily,' here and now, hand over that dagger to us and tell us your *real* rank. I hope you can see that."

He could. And he talked. He was in reality a major in the SS. He had gotten himself papers that showed him to be a discharged Wehrmacht noncom. They had served him well—until now. He was, of course, a mandatory arrestee. He would have to be interned and thoroughly investigated. He most certainly was not mayoral material.

Meanwhile, for the boys at Military Government, it was back to the drawing board. Their chosen candidate had proven himself not quite up to snuff—and he'd bought our bluff hook, line, and finger!

It was just about that time that we learned a bit of most important information: when we could expect to go home, now that the fighting in Germany was over! It was all determined by an elaborate computation of *points*. The more points you had, the quicker you'd be sent home.

On 11 May 1945, *Stars & Stripes,* under a banner headline, announced the point system and how it would work, computed as of R Day (Rating Day), 12 May, and reported on a form called the Adjusted Service Rating Card, which would indicate a soldier's ASR score. Points were awarded in four categories: one point for each month of army service since 16 September 1940; one point for each month of service overseas since that date; twelve points for each child under eighteen (with a limit of three children); and finally, five points for each combat decoration.

An enlisted man's "interim critical score"—the score that would make him eligible to go home—was eighty-five points. Officers and "essential personnel" (such as intelligence operatives) were handled individually according to need.

For days, everyone at Corps, in fact all over Germany, could be seen busily working with pencil and paper trying to figure his ASR score.

But for us in the CIC, the cases kept rolling in.

There was the case of the doctor in Cham, a former Wehrmacht doctor, who with the approval of Military Government was allowed to practice because the need for German doctors was critical. His practice flourished, until we found out why.

All members of the SS, and *only* SS members, with very few exceptions, had their blood type tattooed under their left arm. It was meant as a special privilege for quick identification in an emergency, but it became a certain giveaway of SS affiliation. Countless SS men and officers, trying to lose themselves among the masses, desperately wished that the telltale tattoo could be removed. Just cutting it off would not do, the remaining scar in the strategic place would be damning enough.

Our former army doctor provided an answer to the prayers of these SS members. He was so skillful a surgeon that he could remove the tattoo with only the smallest, practically imperceptible, scar. And his business was thriving.

He was caught only because he became too ambitious, too greedy. He sent out canvassers to round up business for him among the SS members still at large. We caught one of them, and he spilled the beans. We closed down the doctor's practice—and he had to satisfy himself with practicing medicine in a detention camp.

And there was the case that began with the arrival of two officers in unfamiliar uniforms who walked into our office one early morning. The two men introduced themselves as members of the Czechoslovakian Secret Police and ceremoniously showed us their ID.

"We respectfully request your assistance," the senior officer stated formally. "The official assistance of the American CIC. In a most serious case, which has led us here."

"All right," I said. "What can we do for you? What's your case?"

"We are on the trail of a most dangerous, most important Gestapo official, a very crafty agent," the officer told me solemnly. "A man of high position in the Prague Gestapo. A war criminal. A man with much knowledge of agents still at large in our country, and—" he looked meaningfully at me, "in your area. He is the key to much vital information, the only key we know."

"Why come to us?"

"Because," the Czech said, "we have tracked him here. He is in hiding here. In your *Landkreis. Landkreis* Kötzting."

For a moment I contemplated the man. If what he'd told me was true—and I had a hunch it was—it would be something we'd have to investigate. I nodded.

"Okay, we'll do what we can," I said. "And we'll start right now. With the county records."

I got up. The case brought to us by the two officers of the Czechoslovakian Secret Police was beginning in an altogether orthodox manner.

It was not to end that way.

CHAPTER 13

It was a strict Military Government regulation that all persons who had not been permanent residents in our *Landkreis* had to register at the MG County Office in order to be checked out and get proper identification papers. Constant checks, raids, and searches ensured that nobody without valid papers was at liberty for long. If the Gestapo agent hunted by the Czechs were in our area, he would have registered—under some name or other. He would not risk violating the law if he wanted to remain safe and inconspicuous.

I asked my teammate Tom Winkler, with whom I had worked on other cases, to join me and the Czech officers, and our first move was to make a thorough inspection of the residents' file and pull the cards that might conceal the identity of our quarry. It was not that difficult. The man's approximate age was known as well as the approximate date he'd have entered our jurisdiction, and we could, of course, at once eliminate by far the greater part of the entries—women and children.

One by one the Czech agents examined the data cards we selected. One by one they were ruled out for some reason or other. We were nearing the end of the files when one of the Czechs uttered a little cry.

"Wait!" he exclaimed. "This one!" He held up a card.

"What is it?" the senior officer asked sharply.

"Pittermann! Karl *Pittermann!*"

The two officers exchanged quick glances. The senior officer turned to me. "Pittermann," he said quietly. "It is one of the aliases our man has been known to use in the past."

"Then—you think he might have had old ID papers in that name, that he could have used when he registered here?"

"Exactly." He turned to his colleague. "What are the vitals?"

"Date of birth, 14 April 1903."

"Check."

"Place, Dresden."

"Check."

"Former occupation, salesman."

"Nice and neutral," Tom remarked.

"Height, 176 centimeters; eyes, blue; hair, blond."

"Check."

The two foreign intelligence agents looked at each other.

"It is he!" the senior agent said.

Pittermann had followed the golden rule: when assuming a false identity, use as much truth and fact as possible without compromising yourself, such as date of birth and hometown with which you are thoroughly familiar. That way there is less chance of being tripped up.

We carefully noted the rest of the data on Pittermann's card and went through the rest of the registration entries to make sure, but there was only one that fit.

Pittermann, Karl, salesman.

The entries on Pittermann's card gave us the information that he lived and worked at a farm in a nearby village.

The troops occupying *Landkreis Kötzting* belonged to Thoroughbred, 2d Cavalry Group, under command of Col. Charles H. Reed. Colonel Reed had formed a Special Security Patrol of hand-picked men that constantly roamed the area, on foot, in jeeps, and on horseback—a sort of special police force. Before we left for the village where Pittermann supposedly was hiding, we alerted this force to stop anyone attempting to leave the vicinity of the village and detain them on some innocuous routine matter without arousing any suspicion, then notify us. It was just a precaution.

Then, in the early afternoon, the four of us set out for the village.

When we reached the town, we drove straight to the *Bürgermeister*'s office. This worthy, the mayor, was a fat little fellow in his early sixties with a distinctly unpleasant body odor, sporting a corny handlebar mustache and a bowl haircut, who personally led the way, scraping and bowing into his office—a small room on his farm.

Yes, Karl Pittermann lived in his village, he beamed. He worked for the widow Breitbach, whose husband passed away only a year and two months ago and whose son was killed at the front—the *Russian* front, of course. Pittermann had been a godsend to the widow Breitbach, everyone agreed, and he, the mayor himself, had only the highest praise for the quiet, diligent addition to his village flock.

But his description of the man left no doubt of his real identity in the minds of the two Czech officers.

It was nothing unusual. Many high-ranking Nazis hid as common laborers.

Before we went on I told the mayor to leave us. Bowing and smiling sweatily, he left. I turned to the senior Czech agent.

"Okay," I said. "This is now *our* case. I'm sure you understand." He nodded grimly. "We must therefore ask you to wait here while Tom and I pick up Pittermann. We'll then turn him over to you. All you have to do is give us a receipt. Agreed?" The man frowned at me; although he said nothing, it was apparent that he was not pleased with the decision. We, on our part, had a certain responsibility for the two Czechs while they were in our territory. It wouldn't do to have a couple of Allied intelligence agents get into trouble in our backyard. And in a situation like this—one never knew. I stood up. "Come on, Tom," I said, the matter settled, "let's go pick up Pittermann. We'll—"

"Excuse please." It was the senior agent. "I suggest you do not."

Tom and I stared at him. Hurriedly he continued.

"Pittermann is clever, you must understand. Very clever. He knows he is being hunted. He will be constantly on the alert—and he is dangerous. He will undoubtedly be armed, and—"

"I doubt that," I interjected, slightly annoyed. I didn't need a lecture on how to handle an enemy suspect. "Pittermann probably feels himself quite safe here. He'd do nothing to jeopardize that safety, and to be caught with a firearm in a routine search would be a dead giveaway."

"No pun intended, I suppose," Tom grinned. "Anyway, so what? We shoot pretty straight."

"That is what I fear," the Czech said soberly. "If you kill Pittermann, he cannot talk. He *must* be taken alive. His knowledge must *not* be lost to us because of—because of a gun battle." For a moment I had the feeling he would have added "at the OK Corral," had he known the term.

"All right," Tom said. "So we'll be careful. We won't kill him."

"And can you also stop him from killing himself?" the senior agent asked softly.

"What do you mean?" Tom blurted. "Shoot himself?" He groped for a countermove. "We can wing him. Keep him from using his gun. If he has one, which I doubt."

"It will not be that simple."

"Why not?"

"Pittermann will not try to kill himself with a gun. That is too uncertain. He carries a poison capsule. Cyanide," the agent explained matter-of-factly. "We know this. If he feels he will be taken—" he whipped his right index finger across his throat, "*kaput*!"

"Where does he carry it?" I asked. "Do you know? Not in his pocket, I'm sure. In a ring? A button? Where? Perhaps we can prevent him from getting at it."

"No," the Czech officer said. "You cannot. The pill is not in a pocket. That is too unsafe. Not in a ring. Rings are too often—'liberated,' as you say. And not in a button. Buttons can be ripped off. No. The pill is already in his mouth. He keeps it there. In a false tooth."

"Must make it damned difficult for him to chomp on a steak," Tom observed.

"It does not interfere with normal eating," the Czech explained patiently. "The tooth that contains the poison is offset. Only by shifting his jaw—his bite—can he bite down on it and crush it."

"Jeez," Tom exclaimed softly.

"Like Himmler," I said.

"Himmler?" The Czech seemed surprised. "Heinrich Himmler? The Gestapo chief?"

"Yeah. Remember? After he was caught, back in May, when they were about to search his mouth, he bit down on a cyanide capsule he'd hidden in his teeth. Good-bye Himmler."

"So," said the Czech. He had obviously not known. "It is still a problem with Pittermann, who *must* be taken alive."

We were at an impasse. We finally decided that Tom should take the jeep and make a garden-variety routine inspection of the farms around the Breitbach place. A *strictly* workaday affair, obviously nothing but the usual bureaucratic rigmarole, it would create no suspicions of any kind but simply make certain that Pittermann was, in fact, there before we decided on a course of action to nab him—alive.

The Czechs and I would remain at the *Bürgermeister*'s office—out of sight.

When Tom had left, I called the mayor back. With elaborate gestures and much head-nodding, which made his comic-strip mustache bounce spasmodically, he insisted on treating us to *Apfelsaft*, homemade apple juice, and in a loud imperial tone of voice, decidedly different from the one he used with us, he shouted for his daughter to bring it. With *clean* glasses!

I looked the distasteful little man straight in the eye.

"Did you know that the man Pittermann, whom you recommend so highly," I asked him coldly, "is a notorious Gestapo agent?"

The fellow's face went ashen, his mouth fell open, and his ridiculous mustache began to twitch convulsively. I watched him. He had not known—or he was one of the world's greatest actors. But I had to know.

"Ges—Gesta—," he sputtered. "No. No! *Believe* me, *Herr Offizier*. Please! I—I—"

"I know," I interrupted him, not quite able to keep all sarcasm out of my voice. "Had you known, you'd have come to us at once."

"Ja!" The little man jumped at it. "Exactly so!" His relief almost overwhelmed him. "That is exactly what I would have done, *Herr Offizier*." He shook his head in reproving disbelief. "Imagine. Gesta—," he swallowed. "Such a man right here. And *no one* knew. Right here in . . ." He let the sentence die. There was a small commotion in the hall outside the office and the door was opened. Tom walked in. We all looked at him.

"Pittermann?" I asked.

Tom shrugged. "Gone. Flown the coop. Nobody home but the old lady. She's waiting outside."

"Bring her in," I said.

I rather liked the woman who entered the office. She was slight and looked to be about seventy, which meant she was probably in her late fifties. Her clear gray eyes met mine without a hint of apprehension, admirable considering she'd just been scooped up and unceremoniously whisked off to a confrontation with the "enemy" occupation forces.

I lit into her straight away. "Karl Pittermann lives at your farm?" It was more a statement of fact than a question.

"He does." Her voice was surprisingly strong.

"Do you know where he is now?"

"I do."

"Well? Where?"

"Where I sent him, I should think." She seemed to be enjoying herself.

"And where is that?" I was not about to fall for her game.

"The woods. Behind the farm."

"Why did you send him there?"

"Winter is coming," she said. "In four or five months it will be here. We must be prepared."

"Go on."

"Karl is working on the firewood stacks. Chopping wood for the coming winter. As my son used to do. And his father before him. It is necessary." She stopped. She had said her piece. I nodded.

"Thank you, Frau Breitbach," I said. "Someone will take you home. In a little while." I turned to the mayor, who had followed the scene open-mouthed, occasionally twisting his mustache sagely. "I am sure the *Bürgermeister* will be only too pleased to let you wait in his *Stube."*

Mustachio waving, the mayor nodded his head vigorously. *"Selbstverständlich,"* he beamed. Solicitously he led her away.

It was good news that the widow Breitbach had brought us. Pittermann was still about. And unsuspicious, we assumed. But—for how long?

News in a small Bavarian village had a way of traveling faster than a speeding bullet. How long before Pittermann was warned?

Quickly we analyzed the situation. It was not bright. So far Pittermann probably had not learned of our presence in the village; but if we did not take him before long, chances were that he would be warned and slip through our fingers. Even though the villagers, like everyone else, seemed cooperative and eager to please, we didn't trust any of them farther than we could throw a Gestapo agent. And if Pittermann decided to take off , even the security patrols would be ineffective against him if he were bent on evading them.

It was, of course, unthinkable to try to go after him in the woods. He would see us coming—and there was no way we could prevent him from biting down on his cyanide capsule. To wait until he came home to the farm early in the evening and take him there by surprise carried the considerable risk of losing him if he were warned. And chances were strong that by then he would be. Too many people by now knew that we were looking for him. And to Pittermann that could mean only one thing—get the hell outta here!

What to do? It was a real dilemma.

At that moment the mayor's daughter entered the little office carrying a tray with a pitcher of *Apfelsaft*—and clean glasses.

"*Grüss Gott*," she greeted us.

I watched her as she placed the tray on the mayor's desk and began to pour the homemade apple juice. A lovely, slender girl with long, golden blonde braids tightly rolled into round, serpentine disks at her ears, she looked to me to be barely eighteen. In her fetching, low-cut dirndl blouse and full, swirling skirt she made a most appealing sight. A real *Muckerl*, as the Bavarians would say—a real eyeful.

"*Bitteschön*," she said sweetly. "Please." And with a little *Knicks*—a little curtsy—she left the room.

I turned to the senior Czech intelligence agent.

"What would you say," I asked him, "if I told you that I could deliver Pittermann to you, unsuspecting, to within arm's length, in about an hour?"

The two Czechs stared at me as if I had suddenly turned into the Führer himself. But Tom spoke up.

"I don't know what our Czech friends would say," he stated firmly. "But I'd say you were nuts!"

"Perhaps," I said. "Perhaps not."

And for the next few minutes I outlined my plan for them.

While I made my arrangements, Tom got on the horn, and within a quarter of an hour one of Colonel Reed's special patrols, which we had requested cruise the vicinity, drove up to the *Bürgermeister*'s office.

We were ready.

It was a beautiful sunny afternoon as I started into the woods behind the Breitbach farm. I had shed my shoulder holster and gun and my .45 sidearm, and I was wearing the uniform shirt of a sergeant in the 2d Cavalry Group, borrowed from one of the soldiers, his cap perched jauntily on my head. Acting slightly tipsy—two or three beers' worth, perhaps—was easy; appearing to enjoy having my arm around the slender waist of the mayor's lovely daughter, occasionally stopping to do a little smooching, required no acting talent at all. To anyone observing us, I was just another GI out doing a little fraternizing.

And that is exactly what we must have looked like to Karl Pittermann, as we came upon him in a small clearing.

There he stood, a hefty ax in his hand, a pile of log chunks he had been splitting on the ground before him, a saw hanging on a tree nearby.

Karl Pittermann. Ex-Gestapo agent, war criminal, and fugitive. As advertised.

I gave the girl an obvious little "I'll show you!" squeeze, removed my arm from around her waist, and took a few steps toward Pittermann.

He did not move.

"*Sie! Mann!*" I shouted, my German atrocious. "What you do here?"

Pittermann looked from his ax to the wood to me. "I am chopping firewood," he said.

Arrogantly I swaggered toward him. "Who *erlauben?*" I demanded imperiously. "Who give permission? *Verstehe?* You answer. Now! Who give you ax? Who give you permission?"

I threw a quick glance toward the girl to make sure she was watching. She stood looking at us, wide-eyed.

"You have *Papiere?* Papers?"

Pittermann nodded.

"Herzeigen!—show me! *Los!"* I was swollen with self-importance. Was I overdoing it?

Pittermann must have thought me a harmless, fatuous ass out to show off for his girl, just what I wanted him to think. I was obviously unarmed and presented no immediate danger. For several weeks now, he had lived the life of a simple farmhand, taking no chances, following all Military Government edicts and regulations rigidly, calling as little attention to himself as possible, in an effort to go unnoticed in the great mass of uprooted humanity that blanketed Germany. And he had been successful. Now was not the time to jeopardize it all by being defiant. He played along. From his shirt pocket he fished out his ID card and handed it to me.

Haughtily I examined it. "This all?" I snapped at him. *"Das alles?"* More? More papers?"

"I—I have my work papers," Pittermann said obsequiously, playing his self-imposed role as a meek, law-abiding DP worker. "My local travel permit."

I held out my hand. "Show!"

"I do not have them with me."

I threw another glance at the girl and glared at Pittermann. "Where you have?"

"In my room," Pittermann answered. "At the farm where I live." He pointed. "Down there."

"I will see," I said curtly. "We go there. Now. *Los!*"

For a brief moment Pittermann studied me. I could almost see the wheels turning in his head. This was the crucial moment. What would he do? Would he accept my charade and consider me the amorous, drunk show-off I appeared to be? Or would he see through the ploy? Would he suspect? I was conscious of my heart beating; the missing gun under my arm was a gaping void. And Pittermann still held the ax in his hand.

Abruptly he turned and started down the path to the Breitbach farm. Luckily he had his back to me and did not notice my sigh of relief. I pointed to the ax in his hand. "You leave here!" I ordered him. He obeyed.

The little courtyard of the Breitbach farm was empty except for the widow, who sat next to the door to the house with a woven wicker basket in her lap, darning socks. The door was open. The woman looked up as we entered the yard, Pittermann in the lead, I—with my arm locked firmly around the girl—swaggering after him, then returned to her task.

Perhaps the man's annoyance and irritation with the insufferable *Ami* soldier and his deep resentment at having to submit to the bluster of a capricious blowhard had dulled the edge of his suspicious instincts. Without slowing his steps he walked through the open door.

The instant he stepped over the threshold both his arms were grabbed by the two Czech agents waiting in the house on each side of the open door, and his instinctive outcry was instantaneously choked off, as Tom rammed a rag into his mouth, preventing him from biting down.

With his entire body Pittermann fought to loosen their grip. Desperately, savagely, he twisted and strained against his captors. It took all four of us finally to subdue him.

Later that afternoon the two well-pleased Czech intelligence officers departed with their prisoner—minus one false tooth.

Pittermann turned out to be a perfect rat. Even before he was bundled off for Prague, he offered the Czechs the names and whereabouts of five other fugitive war criminals in exchange for immunity from torture and his life. They accepted the bargain.

I do not know if either party kept it. All I knew was that we had rid our *Landkreis* of a potentially dangerous adversary.

As for the mayor's daughter, I felt sure I could find a way to thank her properly.

* * *

In Kötzting another case involving a young girl began, but her story was not one of fun and games in the woods; hers was a case as shocking as any I can remember.

The girl came bursting into my office. She flung herself across my desk. Her wide, distraught eyes sought mine, and with a heart-rending sob she wailed:

"I have found him! *Ach, du lieber Gott!* Oh, dear God! I have found my father!"

CHAPTER 14

I helped the wretched girl to her feet, led her to a chair, and tried to calm her down. She was out of breath, and her dress was wet with perspiration. She had obviously been running. Her name was Lotte. Slowly, fitfully, she told me her story.

She came from a small nearby village in our *Landkreis*. A couple of days before American troops had moved into her area, her father, an influential farmer, had mysteriously disappeared. Since then no word had come from him, and he could not be found. No one seemed to have any information about him.

Then, about an hour ago, Lotte had made a trip into the forest near her village accompanied by a group of women and children in search of berries and mushrooms. As they were spread out in the woods filling their baskets, one of the children, a boy, had suddenly screamed in terror. Lotte and the other woman rushed to his side and found him staring at the ground in a petrified daze. There, through the loose earth where he had been digging up a succulent clump of mushrooms, grinned the face of a dead man, eyes open but caked with dirt, decaying lips drawn back from tobacco-stained teeth in a grimace of violent death. Lotte had kneeled at the shallow grave—and to her horror had recognized the decaying face of her father.

It took us only a few minutes in my jeep to reach the spot in the forest where the dead man lay buried. A small group of Germans silently ringed the grave, but they drew aside as Lotte and I walked up to them.

I looked down into the ghastly face, staring back at me sightlessly from dirt-filled eye sockets. The stench of putrefaction was strong in my nostrils.

"Uncover him," I said quietly.

No one made a move. Then a young man who had been standing with his arm around the softly weeping Lotte stepped forward. "I will uncover him," he said, his face grim. "He is *my* father."

Awkwardly he walked over to the grave. I found out later that he had lost his toes to frostbite at the Russian front when he was in the Wehrmacht. He knelt down and with his hands began to scoop the foul earth away from the corpse. One of the others knelt to help, and another, and soon the grisly body lay exposed in the makeshift grave. I turned to Lotte and her brother.

"Are you sure this is your father?" I asked. Decomposition made identification difficult. They both nodded.

"Ja," whispered Lotte. *"Es ist Vati.* It is Dad."

Carefully they lifted the dead man out of the hole. As they did, he slipped from their grasp and rolled over on his stomach. It at once became apparent how he had died.

I counted seven bullet holes in his back.

The young man, eyes burning with tears denied, knelt by the decomposing body of his father. His weather-beaten face was a sickly gray, and the knuckles of his hands showed white where he clenched his fists. Suddenly he stood up.

"Get out of here!" he ordered the other Germans brusquely. "All of you. Go! There is nothing more for you to see." He turned to his sister. "Go with them, *Lottchen*," he said gently, "and arrange for our father to be taken home."

I did not interfere. So far it was, strictly speaking, none of my business—nothing subversive, no security threat. But I stayed. Something about the case had alerted that acquired hunch that dwelled at the edge of my mind. I had no idea what it was, but I stayed.

The German villagers were drifting away through the woods, and soon I was alone with the son and the corpse of his father. Without a word the young man pulled a wicked-looking Bavarian hunting knife from its special pocket along the side seam of his *Lederhosen*.

He looked at me squarely, then he sank to the ground beside the body. After a brief hesitation he plunged the knife into the putrid flesh, probing for one of the bullets in his father's back. Soon the knife and his exploring fingers found what they were seeking.

He wiped the bit of dull metal in the thick moss on the ground and looked intently at it. Finally he whispered one word: "Luger!"

I held my hand out. Without a word he put the bullet into it. I examined it closely. It certainly looked like a round from a German 9mm Luger pistol.

The young man stood up slowly, his face dark with hatred. He stared in the direction of his village. "I'll kill him for this!" he said hoarsely, his throat constricted with malice.

"Kill who?" I asked, startled.

He turned to me as if he saw me for the first time. "The man who murdered my father," he said simply.

"You know who it is?" I couldn't keep surprise from my voice.

"I thought I knew. Now I am certain. I will kill him myself—the filthy Gestapo swine!" He turned on his heel and began to walk toward the village in his awkward gait.

"Wait!" I called after him. "I'll drive you."

It was my case now. If the man suspected of the shooting was a Gestapo agent or informer and was still at large, he was a definite security threat and a mandatory arrestee.

On the way to the village I explained to the young German that I was now taking over the case. He understood, and in turn gave me the background I needed. He himself was a former Wehrmacht sergeant—which explained his elementary knowledge of ballistics—with a medical discharge because of his feet. His name was Alois. His father had been a well-to-do, influential, and well-liked farmer, but not a member of the Nazi party, which had kept him out of public office.

As the American forces penetrated deeper and deeper into Bavaria, orders issued by *Gauleiters* and *Kreisleiters*, district and county leaders, had come down to every town, village, and hamlet to build fortifications, trenches, and roadblocks and to defend their homes to the last. Some villages had tried and had been wiped out, homes and farms destroyed in the ensuing battles, which could only have one outcome. Such an order had also come down to the village of Alois and Lotte, but their father had vigorously fought against the idea. His reputation as anti-Nazi had carried considerable weight at this time of imminent defeat, and as a result no roadblocks or other fortifications had been built, despite threats and cajolery by local Nazi officials.

One man in particular, the owner of the village hardware store, although not a Nazi official, had tried to force the villagers to obey the suicidal Nazi directives and had threatened them, especially Alois's father, with dire consequences if they persisted in refusing the orders. This man—Andreas Fischer—was the suspect.

Although he had no concrete proof, Alois was convinced that Fischer was in the pay of the Gestapo. Many little unexplained incidents in the past had pointed to it. Alois had returned to the village a couple of days after his father's disappearance and had at once tried to get hold of Fischer to confront him with his suspicions, but in vain.

I decided to bring about that meeting.

The village hardware store was closed, the doors locked, and although the shutters on every window were tightly bolted, Alois insisted that Fischer was there.

I banged on the door. *"Aufmachen!"* I shouted. "Open the door! American CIC!"

After our repeated banging and shouting, the door was opened by a drab middle-aged woman with fear in her eyes.

"Was wünschen Sie, bitte?" she inquired. "What do you want?"

"Is Andreas Fischer here?" I asked.

She hesitated for a moment, then nodded slowly. "Yes—he is here. But—he is very ill."

"Are you his wife?"

"No. I—I take care of his house for him."

"Can I talk to him?" I asked. "I am from the American Counter Intelligence Service. It is important."

She looked at me with apprehension. I knew that the Germans referred to us as the *Ami Gestapo.* It made us sound rather menacing. She glanced toward a flight of stairs leading to the upper floor. "I—I will ask." She walked to the stairs and arduously started to climb them.

While Alois and I were waiting, I opened the shutters of one of the windows to let in some light. The rays of the sun made a defined shaft of brightness through the dust in the air and came to rest on a large cupboard, gaily painted with colorful Bavarian motifs and displaying solid, ornate hardware, probably from Fischer's own store.

I turned toward the stairway as I heard someone coming down the stairs from the floor above. Slowly, laboriously, the hobbling footsteps descended. The treads creaked in protest as weight was placed on them, and I could hear wheezing, asthmatic breathing and an occasional muffled cough. Finally Andreas Fischer appeared. A short but corpulent man of indeterminable age, with a soiled woolen scarf around his neck, he did not look impressive, let alone dangerous. In a feeble voice he wheezed, "Please, may I sit down? I am a very sick man. My heart . . ." He pushed his worn felt slippers across the wooden floorboards toward a threadbare stuffed easy chair.

Alois stood beside me, fists clenched.

"You lie!" he suddenly spat out. *"Murderer!"*

Fischer's pudgy hands trembled as he reached for the support of the chair. His hooded, narrow-set eyes regarded Alois balefully. The three-day black stubble on his chin emphasized the pastiness of his face. "I do not know what you mean, my boy," he whined. "My heart . . ."

All at once, before I could do anything, Alois was upon the pitiful invalid. His huge fist blurred through the air and struck Fischer a savage blow on the side of his head. "You damned murderer!" he screamed.

The invalid flew backwards over the toppling chair, rolled head over heels, and struck the large cupboard, rattling the glasses and dishes stored there. Almost at once Fischer was on his feet. His fists clenched, his eyes blazing, he took one step toward Alois. "Swine!" he snarled venomously. "You will pay for that!"

I grabbed Alois's arm before he could strike the man again and propelled him outside.

"You idiot!" I snapped at him. "What the hell do you think you're doing?"

He glared at me, but said nothing.

"Go home. Stay there! I'll talk to you later." I turned on my heel and went back into the house.

Fischer was slumped in the chair. His hands were clasped tightly over his heart, and his raspy wheezing was ghastly to hear.

"I'll send for an ambulance," I said. "We'll take you to the hospital. You're a sick man."

"No, no," Fischer protested at once. "That will not be needed. I will be well taken care of right here."

"You need a doctor's care," I said firmly. "You'll have it."

For a moment he regarded me speculatively, then he whispered miserably, "*Ja. Ist gut . . .*"

I had my own reasons for wanting Fischer in the hospital. I could keep him isolated there while I tried to get to the bottom of this case—which in the end might turn out to be a non-case.

But it didn't take a Sherlock Holmes to see that there was something fishy about Fischer. His reaction to being knocked down had been reflexive, but entirely too quick for a feeble invalid. For that few seconds before he got himself under control his hands hadn't trembled, his voice had been strong, his stride firm. And his quick recovery from the heavy blow to his head was hardly that of a man at death's door.

At the hospital Fischer was given a thorough medical examination by an army doctor who was a friend of mine. It didn't surprise me that his report showed absolutely nothing physically wrong with the man that a good bath wouldn't cure.

Why would Fischer go to such lengths to feign serious illness? Was it to protect himself from rough interrogation? Or to provide himself with an alibi against accusations of some strenuous activities—such as killing and burying a man? It would be the perfect ploy to arouse the pity of soft-hearted GIs. But if Fischer *were* a Gestapo man and *had* killed Alois and Lotte's father, he himself was the only one who could establish that fact. Witnesses would be impossible to find, if indeed there were any. It would not be easy to get a confession from Andreas Fischer, and without that I had about as much chance to solve the case as Pruneface had to wake up one morning without a wrinkle. Still, I had no choice but to interrogate Fischer and see what might develop.

A thorough interrogation is a true ordeal, for both interrogator and subject. A man trying to lie successfully without any slipups has to have incredible willpower, memory, and stamina, and tremendous alertness not to break down or get himself hopelessly entangled in contradictions; he must have had excellent training, and even that did not always ensure success. And the interrogator must be razor-sharp, to pick up the slightest sign of inconsistency or hesitation and follow up.

I watched Fischer's reactions to every tough question I threw at him; I watched his Adam's apple, his eyes, his nostrils, his lips, the little arteries in his temples—all the places where a man might involuntarily betray himself. I saw nothing. Fischer was either an extremely clever and well-trained agent, or he was innocent and he actually believed himself sick. If he were guilty, he was an extremely dangerous man; if innocent, he really did belong under a doctor's care, even if his illness was psychosomatic.

I felt uneasy, beset by doubts. I couldn't get over the feeling that Alois had the true answer, however emotional his reasoning. On the other hand, I couldn't keep up my exhaustive interrogation if Fischer actually was mentally ill.

I decided to try one last ploy, and if I got no result, let the man go. I told him that I believed in his innocence. I spoke to him kindly. "You will stay here, Herr Fischer," I said solicitously. "And we'll do all we can to help you get well."

Was there a brief glint of triumph in his eyes? Or was it just—gratitude?

"Ach," he said contritely. "The Americans are so fair, so good to me. I should never have believed the Nazi lies." His voice was filled with self-reproach.

"And you shouldn't have quarreled with the father of Alois," I said mildly.

Fischer nodded vigorously, anxious to please. "You are right, *Herr Offizier*," he admitted. "I was wrong in doing that. But," he added quickly, "I did not kill him."

I nodded. "I wonder who did," I mused. "Any ideas?"

He shook his head regretfully. "No," he said earnestly. "It was a terrible thing to happen. Terrible."

"It seemed strange the way he died." I looked candidly at him. "Do you think—do you think he could have been shot by American soldiers?"

"Oh, no," Fischer said quickly, apparently horrified at the idea. "Americans would never shoot a man in the back."

I almost laughed out loud. Lulled off guard, Fischer had just fallen for the oldest interrogators' ruse in the book, the arch-cliché of the trickery employed in the trade. He'd dived headlong into a classic trap; the only innovation here was that he had dug it himself, in his overly clever, servile attempt to ingratiate himself with his "conquerors."

No one had told him that Alois's father had been shot *in the back!* As a matter of fact, no one had mentioned that the man had been *shot* at all until I deliberately said so. But Fischer's reaction to that bit of information showed me he'd known all along. The man had talked to no one but me and the doctor, and Doc had no knowledge of the case at all.

I fixed my eyes, hard and unforgiving now, steadily at him.

"In *the back?"* I said pointedly.

I let the question hang in the air between us like a cloud of arctic breath. For a split second Fischer stared uncomprehendingly at me.

Then his sallow face went deadly pale. He was no fool, this Andreas Fischer; the realization of his monumental gaffe cascaded over him. In silence I stared back at him. This time there was no mistaking his reaction; little beads of sweat began to form on his brow. He swallowed almost convulsively. I gave him no time to collect himself.

"When did you shoot him?" I snapped.

"I—I did not! I—"

"You did not? Why should I believe you?" I asked gruffly. "You have told me nothing but lies!"

"No—I mean . . . please! I did not shoot him!" Nervously his tongue darted out between his bloodless lips. "*They* did!" he rasped.

"They?"

It was only a matter of listening, then, to get the whole unsavory story. Fischer had indeed been an area undercover informer for the Gestapo. When he found that Alois and Lotte's father effectively opposed the Nazi edict to fortify and defend the village against ridiculous odds, he had requested the man's liquidation by the Gestapo. Under the pretext of discussing the situation amicably, he had lured his victim to his house. There, four SS men had been waiting for him.

Early the next morning, the five of them had taken the doomed man to a distant field near the forest and prepared to have a little fun.

There used to be a particularly disgusting form of rabbit hunting practiced in Germany. The rabbits were caught alive in nets placed over their holes when they tried to flee a ferret that the would-be hunters had let loose in their burrows. When a sufficient number of rabbits had been caught to ensure fun for all the hunters, these "sportsmen" would form a large circle on a field, and one by one the animals would be set free in the center. Seeing themselves surrounded by whooping and hollering men, the terrified rabbits would dash desperately around the circle while the "hunters" took pot shots at them. At last the frantic animals would try to break through the circle of death. They never made it.

On that fateful morning, the father of Lotte and Alois had been the rabbit.

With loathing I regarded the cringing creature before me.

I was sure of only one thing. I owed Alois an apology.

In the aftermath of the Fischer case, we searched his house for evidence of his Gestapo connection. Under the floorboards in the attic we found a collection of unusual weapons: an ornate SS officer's dagger with the usual inscription on the blade, MEINE EHRE HEISST TREUE! "My Honor Means Faithfulness!"; a Walther P-38 pistol; a SIG Saur P-220 7.65mm pistol; and two *Handgranaten 24*, the German stick grenades. Harbingers of things to come.

A short while after the Fischer incident the first planned raid involving the entire U.S. Zone of Occupation took place—Operation Tallyho. Operation Tallyho had been strategized several weeks before under the direction of Brig. Gen. Edwin L. Sibert, Assistant Chief of Staff, G-2, U.S. Forces European Theater, and the orders had reached us a few days before the operation was to go into action. As the CIC team responsible for the *Landkreis*, it was our duty to organize and carry out the raid in our territory.

The orders certainly had been clear. A date was set, and it was decreed that all firearms, all ammunition and explosives, all daggers and similar weapons, all equipment having belonged to the German armed forces, and all other contraband material were to be handed in to the American Military Government authorities by midnight of the date set.

Notices to this effect had been posted all over the zone, and copies had been given to all local German authorities for dissemination. But there had been no mention of the raid that was to follow the deadline.

For our part of Operation Tallyho we selected the county seat, the town of Kötzting, the most populous and important target, and divided the rest of the county territory among the units stationed in the various areas.

First we carefully divided the town into six equal parts, one to each CIC agent. We went through our files and selected priority targets, which we marked in red on our operations map, and organized a thorough patrol system to close up the town completely for as long as the raid would last. Each agent had at his disposal a Military Police noncom and four MPs or security troops. All roads leading out of town were guarded with roadblocks; motorized patrols swept the countryside; and the fields and forests were patrolled by security troops mounted on horseback or on foot. When Operation Tallyho kicked off at 0430, four and a half hours after the deadline to comply with the order to turn in all weapons and contraband, the German populace was taken completely by surprise.

My own area of operation was a part of the town that lay across the Weisser Regen, the little river that ran through Kötzting. The first house we entered was a large building housing about forty refugees from all over Germany. It had been red-lined because of the conglomeration of people that stayed there and the fact that such large, constantly changing groups were often favorite places of hiding for war criminals, mandatory arrestees, and other fugitives from justice who wanted to lose themselves.

Our procedure was to collect all the inhabitants in one room after having ordered them to unlock all doors, chests, trunks, closets, or other locked places. While I subjected each individual to a short interrogation, a so-called screening, and examined their papers, the MPs, supervised by the noncom, would make a search of the house.

In this first house, one of the refugees, a man of about forty-five, claimed to have come from Dresden, but although his papers seemed reasonably satisfactory there was something about them and the man himself that disturbed me. Moreover, his name had a familiar ring. And when I examined our blacklist his name was on it. It turned out that he was the chief of the German police in Prague, Czechoslovakia, listed as a war criminal. Faced with my knowledge, he admitted his identity and was taken into custody.

The next of our priority targets was a small house occupied by the owner and two refugee families—a woman with her little daughter and another mother with her two grown sons, one of whom had recently been discharged from the Wehrmacht. The reason for choosing this house was that a good many visitors from neighboring towns seemed to come there. This might, of course, be perfectly okay, but . . .

The residents were collected in the kitchen, and the soldiers began the house search while I screened the people. I found nothing out of the ordinary wrong with their papers, and their stories seemed logical and believable enough. I knew I would get no more information out of them without lengthy interrogations, for which there was no time, so I decided to join the search. The MP sergeant was in the attic with another GI. I went up to him.

"Anything yet?" I asked.

"Not even a slingshot," he said. "I've sent a detail to search the barn."

Climbing the stairs I had noticed that the floor of the attic was on two levels, one about a foot above the other. That meant a hollow space. I stamped on the solid floor planks.

"Have you looked between the floors?"

"Not yet."

We selected one of the sturdy floorboards, pried it loose, and lifted it up. The space between the two levels was filled with sawdust. Insulation. I felt around in it. Nothing.

We chose another board and freed it. More sawdust, more nothing. We decided to try once more. Again, sawdust—and a small corner of green paper. I pulled at it—and held in my hand an SS file folder. I opened it. It contained a sheaf of documents. The top one was stamped GEHEIM! "Secret!"

When we were through taking out all the papers, files, weapons, and equipment hidden in the sawdust between the attic floors, we could have armed a platoon of men to the teeth. We had boxes of ammunition and high explosives; uniforms and radio transmitters, batteries, and even a pair of military field binoculars. In the barn, buried under the dirt floor, heaped with straw, the GIs found a Wehrmacht-issue BMW R-750 motorcycle without sidecar and many gallons of American gasoline!

The documents were the records of a *Strafbataillon*, a Penal Battalion. These punitive battalions and regiments were made up of German soldiers who had been court-martialed for actual or imagined crimes against the state or the military such as treason, desertion, and sabotage, or insubordination or criminal behavior. Here the men served under the cruelest, most inhuman conditions and were considered totally expendable. The rate of survival in a penal unit was close to nil. The discharged soldier living in the house where the records were found had served as a cadre noncom in such a battalion; when ordered to burn the unit's records to prevent them from falling into enemy hands, he had purloined the most important ones and hidden them. Whatever his purpose was for doing this, whether as tools for later blackmail or to buy himself his freedom, if caught, we never learned. But we did fatten our list of war criminals.

For forty-eight hours straight we kept up the searches and the screenings of individuals.

In one house we found three German army rifles suspended in smoke-proof bags in the chimney. Another house boasted enough dynamite to blow up the building in which we made our headquarters. One family with three daughters, all married to German officers in PW camps, had a collection of the most murderous-looking daggers and knives salted away in the cellar, all beautifully oiled and wrapped in pieces of cloth to prevent them from rusting. After all, their husbands might come home some day and find good use for them. And to complete the list of weapons and contraband, in one house we found enough U.S. Army Post Exchange rations to supply a small unit for a couple of months!

During the night a man tried to steal through the guards and patrols ringing the town but was shot and badly wounded. He turned out to be an *SS-Hauptsturmführer*, a captain, and had belonged to the "Totenkopf Verband," the Death's-head League, the notorious concentration camp guards.

Tallyho was the first zonewide, large-scale raid, and throughout the American zone it netted us over eighty thousand prisoners and mountains of arms, ammunition, explosives, and military equipment carefully hidden away. The raid took place several weeks after the unconditional surrender of the German armed forces. Obviously a lot of civilians had had other thoughts.

There were other disturbing incidents—case in point was the girl named Wanda.

I was in one of the other towns in our *Landkreis*, close on the Czechoslovakian border, getting into my jeep after a meeting at the *Bürgermeisteramt*, the mayoralty, when a discharged German soldier came up to me to bum a cigarette. He was still wearing his uniform with all insignia removed, with his left sleeve pinned up where his arm was missing. I don't smoke, but I always carried a pack of cigarettes, a valuable commodity in many situations, so I gave him one.

Gratefully he accepted it. He lit it and then he said, "By the way, *Herr Hauptmann,* did you know that there is a girl lying in the ditch just outside town? I think she is dying." He took a luxurious puff on his cigarette. "Or dead."

I barreled out of town, following the directions the soldier had given me—and there she was.

She was lying in the shallow ditch, immobile. She was clad in a striped concentration-camp dress, her emaciated body angling through the flimsy cloth as she lay in the mud. By the size of her, she looked to be about thirteen years old, but her ravaged condition made it impossible to tell. Her feet were bare—raw and bloody from walking on the rough, stony ground without protection. But she was still alive.

I scooped her up, shocked at how little she weighed. I placed her in my jeep and rushed her to a nearby U.S. military hospital.

There she was cleaned up and her feet bandaged. She was dressed in a clean hospital gown and given some warm soup, the only nourishment the doctors felt her shriveled stomach could tolerate.

She spoke enough German to make herself understood, and slowly, slowly we learned her story.

She was a Jew. From Poland. She and her family, her father and mother and younger brother, had been sent to a concentration camp in Germany. Which one she could not tell us, so thoroughly had she erased the hellish place from her memory. But not what had happened to her there. That was so horrifying it was indelibly etched upon her mind, and no defense mechanism could deaden it.

Her name was Wanda, and she had been the subject of a medical/psychological experiment carried out under the Nazi Applied War Research Program, an experimental offshoot of the program spawned by the Section R experiments conducted at Dachau under the Chief Physician, Dr. Siegmund Rascher, who used the camp inmates for his hideous research experiments. Among them were the low-pressure chambers, designed to test how much depressurization an unprotected human being could stand flying at high altitudes. The human guinea pigs, placed in a vacuum chamber, were subjected to an ever-increasing vacuum until they screamed in agony and tore their hair out in a attempt to relieve the excruciating pressure in their heads; they tore at the seats restraining them and shrieked until their lungs burst. Another was the experiment of being subjected to freezing cold, to learn what would happen to pilots downed in arctic waters. The subjects were submerged naked in icy water until their abject screams of pain were silenced as they lost consciousness. Attempts at revival were done by using the warm, naked bodies of women prisoners placed close to the frozen man, the women instructed to stir sexual arousal in the victim to see if that would induce a more rapid recovery. Most of the victims died under these macabre manipulations.

All this we did not know as we cared for Wanda; only later did we learn of it. All we knew then was the experiment in which Wanda had been the subject, an experiment that made the others pale in comparison.

Question: How much horror does it take before a human mind seeks relief in madness?

The Nazi experimenters forced the girl, who was seventeen, to watch while they killed her father. They forced him to kneel. They put a gun to the nape of his neck and delivered their favorite *Genickschuss*, which instantly severed the spinal cord. They trussed his feet together and hung him on a meat hook, slit open his jugular veins and drained him of blood. That way the depleted body would burn faster in the crematorium oven, in fact, that way they could burn two corpses for one. Efficiency. And Wanda watched. They clamped a pair of large iron tongs into her father's ears and dragged him on the ground to the ovens. They tore out any teeth with gold crowns or fillings, and using a blood-smeared wooden ramrod they pushed the mutilated body into the oven and crammed a second body in beside it. And Wanda watched. They fired up and took the girl outside to see the black, oily smoke rising from the tall crematorium chimneys . . .

Wanda was in shock at the horror she had been forced to witness. But it was only a feeble beginning.

They now forced her—by what "persuasions" can only be imagined—to carry out all the atrocities she had beheld. First, on her younger brother, then on her mother.

And they observed her mind crumble—and made their "scientific" notes.

When the camp had been overrun and the gates opened, Wanda had run. Simply run. Without goal, without plans, without thought. She had run, her only aim to get away.

For weeks she had been wandering the roads in her threadbare concentration camp frock, begging for food from the German farmers when her hunger became too unbearable, hiding from anyone wearing a uniform, which terrified her because it reminded her of the concentration camp guards. Everywhere she had been turned away. We asked her if she had approached anyone in our town. She had. From her description of one of the farms where she had tried to get food, we recognized it as belonging to the *Herr Bürgermeister* himself. She had been told to keep on going. As she had everywhere else.

I immediately set out for the *Bürgermeisteramt* to confront the mayor.

"Did you know of the girl who came through this town?" I asked him point-blank. "A young girl close to starvation?"

With a puzzled frown he peered at me. "Girl?" he repeated. Then he suddenly grinned. *"Ach, ja!"* he exclaimed. "The concentration camp inmate." He nodded. "They told me about her. She was pestering everyone." With a conspiratorial mien he went on. "She came bothering us at my house, too. Last night. Why?"

"Why did you not give her something to eat?" I asked coldly. "Help her. . . . She was in very bad shape. Why did you not help her?"

With a puzzled expression he peered at me. "But—she was only a Polish Jew!" he said.

I could have decked him right then and there. But that would not have helped Wanda. My first inclination was to throw the bastard out on his ear. But—unfortunately—he'd been the best we could find for the job. If we got rid of him, who would we put in his place? I had a better idea.

I glared at the man with all the anger I could muster. It was not difficult. "You listen to me, *Mr.* Mayor," I said icily. "Here is what you are going to do. In a day or two that young 'Polish Jew' will leave the hospital. But she will need a lot of care, a long time to recuperate. And she will get it, *Mr.* Mayor—in your home! You and your wife will house her, feed her, give her clothing and shoes, and care for her every need, wait on her hand and foot, until *I* decide she can move on. Is that understood, *Mr.* Mayor?"

The man stared at me, his mouth open in disbelief.

"My—home—," he stammered.

"Exactly! *Your* home," I snapped. Narrow-eyed, I looked at him. "You can carry out my orders *to the letter*—or you can pack your things right now and change your comfortable office here for a crowded cell in a detention camp! What'll it be?"

Ashen-faced, he swallowed. "*Einverstanden,*" he mumbled meekly. "It shall be as you order."

It was. And incredible as it may seem, Wanda appeared slowly to recover.

But there were other miserable souls who strayed into the little town. By the time I was through with the *Herr Bürgermeister,* he and his wife were caring for five of them.

In not all instances were we the ones to give aid to these *KZ'ler*—the German term for the former concentration camp inmates, usually spoken with distaste, even contempt. At times these *KZ'ler* were most helpful to us, and they were almost fanatically earnest in their desire to assist us in apprehending Nazi leaders in hiding or war criminals, many of whom they had personally known in the camps. However, more often than not the information they supplied was distorted by their own personal sufferings.

Two of these former inmates had temporarily settled down in Kötzting and had taken it upon themselves to hand in regular reports informing us of everything that went on in our county that they thought might be of interest to us. Rumors, reactions of the populace, tips about subversive activities, newcomers to the area, people in hiding—in short, everything they ran across.

Weird, almost grotesque in appearance, these two characters, still wearing their concentration camp uniforms, had become a familiar sight; twice a week they ceremoniously presented themselves in our office and wordlessly, bowing deeply, handed us their report. We called them Pat und Patterschon after a Danish comedy team famous in Europe—forerunners of Laurel and Hardy—because one of the former inmates was tall, toothless, and thin, the other short, dumpy, and wearing thick-lensed, steel-rimmed glasses. In Danish the comedy team was called *Fyrtaarnet og Bivognen,* the Lighthouse and the Caboose. The name fit our informers. Rumor had it that the short one was a former science professor, but we could never get a word out of either of them about their earlier lives. We knew only that they came to our town from Mauthausen, the infamous camp near Linz, Austria, where 140,000 inmates died. It was in this camp that the camp doctor had taken two young Dutch Jews, two brothers, from a convoy arriving at the camp and had them shot—so that he could have a matched pair of paperweights made from their skulls. We often wondered what life in Mauthausen had been like for our *KZ'ler.*

As fate would have it, these two unlikely tale-bearers would bring us one of our most important cases.

One sunny morning I was sitting in my office reading their latest report without any great enthusiasm. We had decided that every lead had to be examined and if need be, followed up. However, wading through a couple of pages of fine, meticulously written Gothic script was not exactly my idea of an exciting pastime.

I was struggling through the disorganized writings when a startling little item buried in the cluttered script made me sit up: *In Kreuzbach, you will find Hitler's Right Hand . . .*

CHAPTER 15

My curiosity aroused, I reread the enigmatic passage in the handwritten scrawl. *Hitler's Right Hand.* Sometimes descriptions like that, given us by inmate or DP informers referred to ordinary Nazi party members, who in the eyes of these people (their judgment warped by what they had been through), had taken on immense importance. Hitler's right hand could be anyone from a farmer who might once have chased them away to the missing *Reichsleiter* Martin Bormann himself. But the statement intrigued me enough to want to follow through with an investigation.

I hoped it would not be necessary to question the two *KZ'ler* themselves. From past experience I knew how nearly impossible it was to get any detailed information out of them. Even if I'd wanted to, it was not possible to conduct a probing interrogation of the two former concentration camp inmates. Their years in the camps had conditioned them so that any firm command or demand sent them into a cataleptic silence. I didn't want to frighten or browbeat our voluntary informers; instead I hoped to get the information I needed from our own records.

Kreuzbach was a tiny village about five miles west of Kötzting and consisted of some forty houses and farms. I teamed up with Tom Winkler, and the first thing we did was to go through our files on Kreuzbach for any clues that might give us a hint of who this *right hand* might be.

Every nonpermanent resident of the village was supposedly registered; we had personal files on several others, including the *Fragebogen* questionnaires. We combed the files but did not find a single clue. Reluctantly we decided to try to get some further information from Pat und Patterschon.

The two men stood before us, their shoulders tensely hunched. They seemed so emaciated that I wondered where they got the strength even to walk. Already they looked trapped and terrified. I had chairs brought up and invited them to sit down so their eyes would be level with ours. The tall one looked down in his lap; the short one peered at me through his thick glasses, which probably were the wrong prescription, judging from the way he squinted sideways at me, or perhaps it was because one lens was cracked.

First I thanked them for their report and told them how much we appreciated their cooperation. Then I held out the page with the mysterious mention of Hitler's Right Hand, pointed to it, and asked, "What does that mean?"

Both men stiffened and stared at the floor. Neither spoke.

"What do you mean by 'Hitler's Right Hand'?" I asked, trying to sound as gentle as possible. "Who is he?"

I placed the page on the desk before them. They seemed to shrink away from it. The tall one began to tremble. They made not a sound.

I studied them. Had I been too direct? Had I sounded too forceful? The poor bastards had lived so long in those hellhole camps that they'd clam up at any hint of authority—retreat into themselves and just take it, as they'd had to do in the past. What could you expect, when a rough voice, a brusque command could mean death? Or worse? I spoke to them in a low, calm voice.

"Don't be afraid," I reassured them. "We just want to know *who* it is who is in hiding. How do you know about him?"

I looked away, fixing my eyes on the papers before me. It suddenly occurred to me that my inquisitive stare might be frightening to them—like dogs used to beatings, growing uneasy at a steady gaze. Quietly I continued.

"You don't have to tell us, of course. Nothing will happen to you if you don't. But we'd be grateful if you'd help us. Who is Hitler's right hand? Who told you about him?"

The short fellow apprehensively lifted his eyes to me. He looked clammy with fear. He blinked rapidly behind his thick spectacles, struggling to find the courage somewhere in his tortured, shattered spirit to speak. Finally he whispered hoarsely, "People . . ."

"What people? Who?"

The little man flinched and once again withdrew into himself, appalled at his reckless boldness.

"Please," I said. "There's no need to be frightened. No one will hurt you. Please believe me. Just—answer me."

But there was no answer. Both men stood mute, cowed—and unreachable.

I watched them with a mixture of compassion and frustration, but I knew there was nothing I could do. I called to the young MP who had brought the two men to our office and who had followed the proceedings attentively. He came over.

"Take them to the kitchen," I told him. "Get them something to eat."

"Yes, sir!" he said smartly. He turned to the two *KZ'ler*. "Come along, fellas." His young voice held a surprising amount of understanding.

Tom and I looked at each other. We both knew there was only one thing left to do. We'd have to examine every man in the village of Kreuzbach, without being so obvious about it that we'd frighten away a possible quarry. There was a way of doing it.

The following morning Tom and I, accompanied by a couple of noncoms from Colonel Reed's Security Patrol, arrived in Kreuzbach. We went from house to house, farm to farm, carefully impressing upon one and all—without being obvious about it—that we were merely conducting a routine check. This was nothing unusual; it was done periodically. Being visibly bored with the whole affair, we asked a few key questions with the least show of interest we could muster. As was usually done, men working in the fields, women searching for berries and mushrooms in the forests or helping in the fields were called back to their homes for a personal roll call and the area was criss-crossed by children, having a ball looking for adult members of their households so that no one would be overlooked.

Out of the hundred-odd people living in Kreuzbach only two proved impossible to find for their screening. The day was dragging on, and we were about ready to forget about the two missing subjects. We hadn't turned up one solitary fact of interest and didn't even know what the hell we were looking for. But we decided that if we did not follow through with the last two missing subjects, all the work we'd already done would be worthless.

We went back to the house of the first absentee. He was a young man of nineteen who early that morning had taken off on his bicycle for Cham, a nearby town of some size, to purchase some tools. We looked through his room without finding anything more incriminating than a battered old U.S. Army canteen—besides, we felt that this boy was a little too young to have been Hitler's right-hand man! Still, it was—of course—difficult to know what our weird informers had had in mind.

We ordered his father to see to it that the boy reported to us in Kötzting the next day. We sent the Security Patrol boys back to Kötzting, and Tom and I proceeded to the second stop, a farm on the outskirts of the village.

The place was just another typical Bavarian farm: a main house directly connected to the stables and a barn, a few sheds, and in a corner of the yard the ubiquitous dung heap oozing brown liquid over the cobblestones.

As we drove into the farmyard, a young girl sitting on a bench at the front door of the house darning a pair of heavy woolen socks jumped to her feet in alarm; her sewing basket fell from her lap, spilling the contents in disarray onto the ground. Quickly she ran into the house.

I brought the jeep to a halt before the house, and we dismounted. We were walking toward the door when it was suddenly flung open.

The middle-aged woman who stood in the open doorway, the young girl behind her, was heavy-set, obviously used to hard work. She glared in silent hostility at us. The girl, perhaps seventeen or eighteen, was suntanned, blue-eyed, and full-blown, with long yellow pigtails. She, too, regarded us with ill-concealed antagonism.

"*Grüss Gott*," I said, using the friendly Bavarian greeting.

There was no answer from either of them. Tom turned to the woman. "What is your name?"

Resentfully she told him.

"Who owns this farm?"

"My husband."

"Where is he?"

The woman shrugged. "In Russia."

Tom nodded toward the young girl. "The girl?"

"My daughter. Lise."

"Who else lives here?" Tom asked.

"Just us." The woman hesitated slightly. Her eye briefly flickered away from Tom's gaze. "And—my brother. Anton."

"He is the one the soldiers could not find when they were here earlier?"

The woman nodded.

"Where is he now?"

"In the forest. I do not know where." She gave Tom a withering look. "I told the *Ami* soldiers. He makes firewood. For the winter."

"When will he be back?"

She shrugged.

"How long has your brother lived here?"

"Always. Since I was married."

"He must have been away during the war. Like your husband. What branch of the armed forces did he serve in?"

"He did not." There was contempt in the woman's voice. "He was too old. He is almost sixty—no, sixty-one years old."

"And what does he do now?" Tom was doing the repetition bit. It always rattled a subject, especially if there was something to hide.

"I told you." There was exasperation in the woman's voice. "He works in the forest. He does some farming. I told you."

"And he has been here all through the war?"

"Yes." Again I noticed that slight hesitation, the flicker in the eyes. I knew that Tom did, too.

"He was never gone?"

"No."

Tom looked her hard in the eyes. He did not say a word. He waited. The woman licked her lips. "Only—"

"Yes?"

"He—he was away just for a month. In the *Volkssturm*. Near Cham." She suddenly flared in defiance. "He *had* to go! He had no choice!"

It made sense. The *Volkssturm* was Germany's last-ditch fighting organization, made up of young boys and old men.

"When did he get back?"

"About—about six weeks ago."

"And he lives here now?"

The woman glared at him. "Yes," she said with annoyance. *"Yes!"*

"I want to take a look at his room," Tom told her curtly. "Show me."

Angrily the woman turned on her heel and stalked into the house. Tom followed.

"Lise!" I called, as the girl started after them. "You stay here."

Resentfully she turned back to glare at me. But she stayed. She went over to the bench and sat down. Stiffly, silently she sat there, studiously ignoring me. She tried to seem unconcerned, but I knew she was apprehensive by the way she kept digging the toes of her bare sun-browned feet in the dirt between the cobblestones. I walked over to her. I tried to sound friendly and relaxed. After all, I was cast as the "good guy" in this combination.

"How old are you, Lise?" I asked conversationally.

"Seventeen." Her voice was flat.

"Your father is away?"

"Yes."

"How long has he been gone?"

"Three years almost."

"You must miss him."

She made no answer. I went on. "But it must be nice to have your uncle come around now and then."

Lise eyed me coldly. "He *lives* here," she said. "*All* the time." There was scorn and barely concealed triumph in her young voice. She wasn't that easily tricked!

"Didn't he ever go away?" I asked.

"Yes." The girl dismissed me with contempt. Not so smart after all, these *Ami* Gestapo people, she probably thought. "To the *Volkssturm*," she said. "For a month. My mother told you that."

"Was your uncle always a forester?"

"Always."

I looked at the girl. Was she telling the truth? I did not know. The young are better liars than adults. They're closer to the age of fantasy, when so many imaginary things seemed real. But if she were telling the truth, Anton didn't sound much like Hitler's right hand.

Lise turned away from me. She knelt down on the ground and began to pick up the contents of the sewing basket she had dropped when we entered the yard.

I bent down to help her. Something among the rags and balls of yarn caught my interest. I picked it up. It was a small white box with black printing on it. I shook it. It rattled. I turned to Lise, who was watching me with a puzzled frown. I scowled at her.

"Is there a gun in the house?" I asked abruptly. Lise gave me a disdainful smile.

"No," she said quickly. Too quickly?

"What's in this box?"

"Buttons."

"Where did you get it?"

"The box? My uncle gave it to me."

I looked closely at her. She stared back at me defiantly. I opened the box. It contained a collection of buttons. Different sizes, different colors, different shapes. I allowed my disappointment to show on my face. After all, buttons and bullets rattle alike. My letdown was not lost on Lise. She regarded me with a small derisive smile. The round was hers. I wanted her to think just that.

At that moment Tom and the farmer's wife emerged from the house. I knew at once that Tom had found nothing.

Tom was about to speak when I interrupted him. I spoke directly to the woman.

"We shall be leaving now," I said pleasantly. "We want to thank you for your cooperation and apologize for any inconvenience we may have caused you."

The woman gave a huffy snort.

"We need to talk to your brother," I went on. "Routine, you understand. Please ask him to report to our offices in Kötzting tomorrow. The CIC."

"The American Gestapo, yes," she said, her voice acid. "I will tell him."

I threw the little button box into Lise's sewing basket. "Here," I said. "This is yours." I turned to the woman. "*Grüss Gott*," I said, and began to walk toward the jeep.

Tom followed me. I knew he was taken aback at my abrupt departure with no real attempt at grilling the two women, but we had worked together long enough that he knew I must have a damned good reason. He said nothing, but climbed in beside me.

I was aware of the woman and her daughter staring after us until we disappeared through the farmyard gate.

For a short while Tom sat silent, then he turned to me. "What the hell was that all about?" he asked pointedly. "*My* gut feeling was that those two bitches are hiding something. What gives?" He looked askance at me. "On second thought," he said drily, "let me guess. The girl had the clap, and you were afraid of catching it by pissing against the wind."

I grinned, intent upon my driving. "Warm, but no cigar," I retorted. "Give me a minute, and I'll fill you in." I spied a little dirt road that led across a field and toward a forest-clad hill. Abruptly I turned off the highway and continued up the road. It quickly turned into a sandy, deep-rutted lane, and I engaged the four-wheel drive. I drove as fast as I could; I knew we did not have much time. Soon we were well into the woods nearing the ridge of the slope. I stopped; we dismounted and ran to the edge of the ridge where the trees ended. The slope down toward Kreuzbach was plowed earth and pasture. It was a perfect vantage point. We were hidden, but the farm we had just left lay in full view below us, bathed in the afternoon sun. Puzzled, Tom looked at me. "Now what?" he asked.

"Now we wait, and watch," I said. "Shouldn't be long." I turned to him. "Remember that little white box I threw into the girl's sewing basket? Just before we left?"

"Yeah?" Tom was still confused.

"She told me her uncle had given it to her. Anton. It came from a haberdashery in Berlin. It had contained a white dress tie!"

Tom whistled softly. "Bingo!" he breathed. "I'll be damned."

"You probably will," I readily agreed, "but why brag about it?"

"Why the hell would a lousy forest worker need a white dress tie?"

"Exactly. And how did he get it? At least the box?"

"*When* was he in Berlin?"

"And *why?*"

"If he did get the box from someone else, who?"

"I'd say that a lot of Hitler's right-hand cronies wore white ties." I looked at my teammate. "The box wasn't that old. But he probably forgot about giving it to his niece."

"All good questions," Tom observed. "Now, how do we get the answers?"

"I'm hoping the answer will be coming down the road pretty soon." I pointed. "Look!"

Down at the farm the woman and her daughter suddenly came hurrying from the house. Lise ran to one of the sheds and disappeared inside. Quickly she emerged with a bicycle, and at once she pedaled through the gate and on down the road toward the distant woods. Her mother stood for a brief moment staring after her, then she hurried into the house.

Tom looked at me. "So that's why you wanted it to look as if you'd given up on those two broads," he grinned.

"Looks like they bought it."

"*I* almost did, you bastard!"

We settled down to wait, huddled as comfortably as possible under the shrubbery. I was certain it would not be long before we made the acquaintance of the elusive Uncle Anton.

The earth smelled sweet and moist. The air was filled with the steady, soft hum of a host of insects, occasionally accented by the insistent whine of a curious fly. Dusk was beginning to creep over the land, that lovely time when the day settles down to rest, when they finally came into view.

"Here they come," Tom said. Instinctively he spoke in a whisper.

Below on the road Lise came bicycling toward the farm. She was accompanied by an elderly man clad in Bavarian forester's clothes, long woolen socks, knee breeches, and a gray woolen jacket. The two cyclists turned into the farmyard, dismounted, and made straight for the house.

Tom looked at his watch. "Forty-three minutes," he said. "He wasn't far away."

I stood up and stretched.

"Show time!" I said.

The farmyard was drowsy and peaceful in the setting sun. Even the scraggly hens scratched and pecked only lazily among the cobblestones. But they flapped frantically out of the way, squawking in protest, as we came careening into the yard and skidded to a dirt-spraying halt in front of the door to the house. Instantly we leaped from the jeep and burst through the door.

Only Lise was present in the *Bauernstube*, the combined kitchen–living room–dining room that is the hub of all Bavarian farmhouses. She was standing at the table frozen in shock, her eyes huge with fear. On the table sat a large, half-filled rucksack, and the girl was clutching a loaf of coarse bread in her hands.

"Where's your uncle?" I demanded, my voice sharp and commanding.

Lise stared at me, too startled to answer.

Suddenly the door to the rear of the house was flung open. I whirled toward it, my gun in my hand, firmly locked against my abdomen, pointing directly at whatever I might be facing. It was the way I'd been taught in the OSS. Holding your gun in your hand away from the body you are rarely able to hit anything in a crisis. Only by locking your weapon against your body do you have control; a fraction of an inch off your aim is a miss by a mile.

In the doorway stood Lise's mother. In her hand she held a large sausage partly wrapped in newspaper. Her face was hard; her eyes blazed.

"Your brother," I demanded curtly. "We know he is here. I want to see him. Now!"

The woman filled the doorway. She seemed totally unconcerned about the gun pointing directly at her. I was aware of Tom behind me, backing me up.

"He is not here," the woman said, her voice flat.

I gestured with my gun. "Over there," I ordered the woman. "At the table. With your daughter. Move!"

Reluctantly she obeyed. Tom and I were facing the two women. "Now," I said. "Where is he?"

Neither woman made a sound. I positioned myself directly in front of Lise, the weaker of the two. My eyes bored relentlessly into hers. She stared back, her suntanned face a sickly gray.

"Where is he?"

For a split instant her huge, frightened eyes flitted away from me. To the right. And up. Then she returned her terrified gaze to me.

I followed her glance. In the corner of the room, a narrow staircase. To the attic. The attic door stood ajar.

"Cover me," I snapped to Tom. I started toward the stairs. Cautiously I began to climb the steps, intent on the attic door.

Suddenly Lise cried out. "He has a gun!"

The thought—Is she warning me, or her uncle?—barely had time to race through my mind when the attic door quickly was opened a few more inches, and a shot rang out. Time suddenly went into slow motion. Below, the two women screamed. I was aware of Tom scrambling into position to cover the attic door. I was certain I could hear the bullet whizz by my head, but that was, of course, impossible. Another shot was fired from the attic door before I got off two shots of my own. Both rounds buried themselves harmlessly in the doorjamb.

And the attic door slammed shut.

Less than a second had gone by—in real time.

Tom was at my side. We stared at the closed attic door. Slowly we started up the steps.

We were nearly at the top.

Suddenly there was the sound of a muffled shot from behind the attic door. I bounded up the last few steps and kicked open the door. I threw myself back, and Tom and I flattened ourselves against the wall.

Nothing happened. Not a sound. No movement.

Warily I peered into the dim attic. Then I went through the door.

The body sprawled on the floor looked grotesquely out of place among the pieces of old furniture, wooden chests, and boxes that ringed the attic. I recognized the clothing. Knee breeches and a gray Bavarian jacket. Anton, Lise's uncle, was dead.

Tom joined me. We walked over to the body and looked down at the man. His unseeing eyes stared back at us from a blood-spattered face. The gun was still clutched in his hand. He had placed it in his mouth—and pulled the trigger. Crazily protruding teeth forced his torn lips apart, and from one corner of his mouth the blood flowed steadily, unhurriedly, to form a pool on the floor, pushing the dust before it.

I bent down and wrested the gun from the dead man's hand, turned the hand over, and looked at the palm.

"No wonder," I said quietly. "No wonder he couldn't let himself be seen by us. Look at his hands."

Gingerly I touched the palm. It was soft and full of blisters, some of them newly broken.

"Some forest worker," Tom concurred. "His hands must have been as soft as a virgin's ass."

I looked at the gun. It was a Walther 7.65mm. The entire blue-steel barrel was beautifully carved with intricate ornamentation—even the trigger and the trigger guard. It bore the number 211013K. I recognized the gun for what it was. It was a rare piece indeed, an *Ehrenwaffe*, honor weapon, given by Hitler personally to special friends and high-ranking Nazis. I showed it to Tom. He was impressed. "Holy shit!" he exclaimed. "*Some* forest worker!"

I looked at the inscription on the little plaque on the brown plastic grip. Half filed away I could still make it out: TO REICHSAMTSLEITER ANTON ECKL. FAITHFULLY, ADOLF HITLER.

Anton Eckl. *Reichsamtsleiter*. One of the top Nazi ranks. Eckl was high on our list. He had been the Nazi economics leader of Württemberg, Bavaria and half of Austria.

Our *KZ'ler* informers had not been too far wrong.

A piece of paper stuck out of the man's jacket pocket. I pulled it out. It was a note, hastily written on an old sheet of paper: "I can not face life in a concentration camp, Anton Eckl."

It was easy to piece together what must have happened. Eckl had gone into hiding at his sister's farm—if the woman below *was* his sister!—trying to lose himself as a humble forest worker. In time it might have worked, but he knew that right now he could never have passed inspection as such a worker because of his hands. In time, yes. But not yet. When he knew he would be examined, he'd had only one chance—to get away before he had to report to us. When he found himself trapped in the attic, where he'd gone to fetch a small suitcase—it was still lying on the floor beside him—he had realized that capture and exposure were inevitable and that he would be interned. He had visualized our internment camps as being like the Nazi concentration camps, and he must have known too much about life in those hellholes to want to try it himself. His only way to beat such a dreaded fate was to pull the trigger. He had feared suicide less.

How ironic and fitting that two former concentration camp victims should have been instrumental in the destruction of this man.

I gazed at the honor weapon in my hand. His Führer had given him a useful gift.

Today Reichsamtsleiter Anton Eckl's *Ehrenwaffe* lies on a shelf in a bookcase in my office. It is the only gun I kept of the many souvenir weapons that came into my possession during the war. After all, it does have a special history, a special meaning—for me.

The farm was still there when Cleo and I drove by forty-five years later. It seemed deserted. We stopped in front of it. It was a strange feeling to look at the place where I had come so close to being killed. Right there—but for the nervous trigger finger of a desperate fugitive—it could all have ended for me forty-five years before.

We did not go into the farm. I would have had nothing to say to whoever occupied the farm now. The hill was still there, still bathed in sun, still crowned with trees.

Nothing much had changed.

Working constantly with informers and saboteurs, spies and war criminals, as we did, made it difficult not to become callous toward deceit, disloyalty, and double-crossing. But even we were unprepared for the utter corruption and depravity of a case that began one summer morning in our office in Kötzting.

A man, in civilian clothes obviously once expensive but now threadbare and unkempt, came into our office, walked up to me, and announced, "I am Petkö. I am the son of the Gestapo chief of all of Hungary. Please arrest me!"

CHAPTER 16

I had been sitting reading a "Sad Sack" cartoon in the *Stars & Stripes,* and that was the first thing that came to mind: Sad Sack. The guy standing before me was typical of that snafued character—*asking* for trouble!

"Why should we arrest you?" I asked the wretched creature.

"Oh, if it pleases the *Herr Offizier*," he said quickly, bowing obsequiously, his voice best described as oily, "I have done nothing. Nothing at all!" He spoke with a thick accent; obviously he was not German. Anxiously he fawned on me. "May it please you, I will try to explain, yes? If you do not arrest me and question me like it has already pleased you to have questioned some of the others, they will become suspicious of me. Please, *Herr Offizier,* please understand. I am come here to be arrested!"

I had taken an instant dislike to the subservient little creep with his brownnosing manner, but I let him tell his story.

Petkö was Hungarian and came from the *Ungarerlager*, the Hungarian camp near the village of Miltacht in our area. Here, pushed off on a siding, stood four railroad cars that housed a weird, colorful collection of about a hundred Hungarians who, because of their undeniable Nazi ties, had fled Budapest before the Russians. The train never reached farther than this siding in Kötzting County, and since the strange passengers had nowhere else to go and spoke German badly or not at all, they had set up housekeeping right there in the railroad cars, like a tribe of gypsies, living by scouring the countryside for food, an activity that did not endear them to the local farmers.

We were well aware of this train and its unusual occupants, but since they so far had caused no major problems, except for their occasional rifling of fields and gardens, we had put off investigating them in favor of more important and pressing affairs. A couple of the train inhabitants had been brought to us by the Security Patrol at times for screening, having been picked up roaming the woods or the fields, but they said they'd only been looking for berries and mushrooms like everyone else, and it was hard to prove them liars. We'd usually sent them right back to their railroad cars after a cursory examination.

However, since we did know that these Hungarian refugees were all Nazis to a greater or lesser extent, we already had decided to investigate the whole crew thoroughly at an early date. Petkö jumped the gun on us, setting off a case that was to teach us the meaning of the word *treachery*.

Our decision to investigate the *Ungarerlager* had somehow become known among the Hungarians. Since they had nowhere to go they were pretty much forced to remain in the unorthodox camp. Several of them apparently had ample reasons for wanting to keep their pasts hidden from us, and they were all eyeing each other suspiciously for signs of informers. It had therefore become quite a badge of honor to have been detained and questioned by us, a sort of loyalty proof, and Petkö, holding the dubious distinction of being the son of Hungary's Gestapo chief, was afraid that if *he*, of all the refugees, were *not* hauled in at the start, the others might think he was in cahoots with us and likely as not do away with him. Therefore he respectfully requested to be arrested, and—of course—set free after an appropriate interval.

There were enough intriguing possibilities in Petkö's outlandish account to decide us to go ahead with the planned *Ungarerlager* investigation without delay.

Once again Tom Winkler and I teamed up. Tom was the obvious choice to conduct the investigation: besides being an excellent and imaginative interrogator, he had been born in Budapest and spoke Hungarian fluently. As a matter of fact, Tom and I between us could carry out interrogations in nine languages. Tom added Hungarian, Italian, and Romanian to my Danish, Swedish, and Norwegian, and we both spoke German, French, and English—and a smattering of Dutch and Czechoslovakian.

We sat Petkö down and began to pump him. The sleazy little man had a peculiar mind for intrigue. He wanted us to know that he was fully prepared to inform on his friends and to be of help to us in our investigation of the camp, provided, of course, that he himself would be shown a certain amount of "consideration," when his own turn came in earnest.

He leaned toward us, a conspiratorial look on his weasely face. "Perhaps," he whispered slyly, "perhaps I can even help you find out about the *great secret!*" He nodded his head vigorously. "There *is* a great secret at the camp—so great that even *I* have not been taken into confidence." He was obviously peeved. "But I *know* it is there," he finished importantly, "and I *can* be of help!"

Tom and I glanced at each other. The man sounded so corny as to be almost funny, and melodramatic enough for a ten-minute hiss. But Tom and I had long since learned from experience how closely *corny* and *melodramatic* are linked with reality.

Needless to say, we did not trust this unwholesome individual farther than we could throw the whole damned *Ungarerlager*, railroad cars and all; there was, however, such a promise of intrigue and clandestine goings-on in the man's double-dealing proposition that we slapped him in jail and set out for the freakish camp the following morning—to see what we could learn ourselves about Petkö's mysterious "great secret."

Tom took charge as soon as we arrived at the crowded *Ungarerlager*. The place was even more outlandish than I had pictured it. Multicolored laundry on clotheslines, strung from the railroad cars to nearby trees, flapped in the breeze, and heaps of trash protruded from beneath the cars. At an open space a big tent had been suspended over several crude tables and benches, with a community kitchen adjoining. We set up shop at one of the tables. Tom had found out who was the spokesman for the group and instructed him to order everyone to stay in camp for questioning. The leader, although raggedly dressed, had an imposing bearing. He stood erect, a huge man with fierce eyes, bushy black eyebrows and beard, and coarse black hair on his chest that showed through his open, torn shirt. His voice boomed forcefully out over the campsite, as he relayed Tom's orders. It was apparent that the man was used to command—and to being obeyed.

There was a carnival atmosphere over the whole area: people were babbling excitedly, milling around, laughing and seemingly enjoying themselves immensely. Perhaps their secret was that they were all totally nuts!

While Tom settled down to screening the Hungarians, I decided to take a good look around the unbelievable camp. The railroad cars were of the European type, with many small compartments set off a long corridor. Each little compartment housed an entire family. They were all stuffed with boxes, suitcases, and bundles tied with string and were incredibly cluttered. It would take an army a year to search through it all. Although some of these miniature apartments had been decorated with curtains and pictures cut out of magazines, there was a stale, sour smell throughout, and dirt was everywhere.

As I stepped off the last car, a woman was waiting for me on the ground. She said a few rapid words to a young girl standing beside her and pushed her toward me.

The girl was beautiful. Sleek, ebony hair cascading over her bare shoulders, large brown eyes, and full naturally red lips, she could not have been more than sixteen years old. She looked at me timidly and in broken German in a low voice she said, "My mother wishes to know what will happen to my father. He is our leader."

I at once saw the impressive camp chief in my mind's eye. Authoritative. Stiff-backed bearing. A high-ranking military man?

I smiled at the lovely child. "If he has done nothing wrong," I told her, "he has nothing to fear. Nothing will happen to him."

The girl quickly translated my reply to her mother, who grinned broadly and bobbed her head at me. Then they both turned and walked away. After a few paces they looked back and gave me a wide smile—which I returned.

I thought nothing of it. I couldn't know then what that smile of mine would lead to.

Meanwhile, Tom had finished his preliminary screening without any tangible results. There had been no mention of Petkö's secret, despite Tom's hints, and direct questioning on the subject was, of course, contraindicated.

"Why not let them hang themselves?" Tom said suddenly. "Let *them* come to *us*. Free Petkö, and see what happens."

Tom gathered all the camp occupants and made a little speech. He told the Hungarians that we had positive information that a couple of people on our wanted list were among them, that we were going to check up on all of them, and that we'd be back. Meanwhile the entire camp would be responsible for seeing to it that no one left the area.

Actually we hoped that someone *would* make a run for it. It would make matters so much simpler. But when the break came a few days later, it did not come in this manner, nor did it come from Petkö, our volunteer stool pigeon, whom we had sent back to the camp with orders to ferret out the mysterious secret.

Into our Kötzting office walked the wife of the camp leader and her lovely teenaged daughter. The woman insisted on seeing me and no one else, so the two Hungarians were taken to an interrogation room where Tom and I awaited them.

"Well?" Tom asked brusquely.

The woman wet her lips nervously. "If it pleases the *Herr Offizier*, I know it is my husband you will arrest," she said haltingly. "But—but I beg of you, do not take him away!"

Tom and I exchanged quick glances. Were they beginning to hang themselves?

"You don't think he deserves it?" Tom asked.

For a moment the woman stood silent, struggling with herself. "Perhaps," she said finally. "But it was not his fault. He *had* to join the SS, or he would have lost his position with the police. What would have become of us then? Please, please, do you not see?"

So that was it. The *Ungarerlager* chief was an SS police officer.

The woman looked directly at me. "We—we will bargain with you," she said, an almost imperceptible smirk on her thick lips. "The *Offizier* will like the bargain." She turned to her daughter. The young girl looked at her mother with pleading eyes, but she gave her a little push. "Now!" she hissed.

The young girl took a halting step toward me. Her big, brown eyes looked solemnly into mine, and a deep flush slowly crept over her lovely face. She looked utterly vulnerable. Her young voice was soft and low when she spoke.

"If you will please let my father go free," she whispered, "my mother says I am to do for you whatever you wish." She paused; her lower lip trembled.

Her mother stood leering and bobbing her head at me, and the picture of her grinning face at the railroad car in the *Ungarerlager* came to mind. I had smiled at her daughter then, and the mother thought I wanted her. She was selling her daughter for her husband's freedom.

I wanted to smash my fist into that grinning lecherous face, and perhaps I would have had Tom not intervened.

"We are not interested in such a bargain," he said coldly. He studied the woman for a moment, while I regained control of myself. "But," he said, "we might be inclined to go easy on your husband if you will help us find what we are really after at the camp."

"What is that?" the woman asked eagerly.

"Come now," Tom smiled at her. "Let's not play games. If you wish to help, do so. A woman in your position must know everything that goes on out there," he flattered her. "I'm sure you know what it is we want."

The two Hungarians exchanged quick, furtive glances.

"The—diary?" the woman whispered tentatively.

Tom said nothing; he just spread his hands.

"Karola's diary." There was fear in the woman's voice. "It is Karola's diary you want!"

"What do you think?" said Tom.

The woman launched into an agitated stream of Hungarian, while Tom listened to her. I watched them. Had we uncovered the mysterious secret of the camp? Was it Karola's diary, whatever it was, that Petkö had referred to? At last the woman stopped talking. Without a word Tom turned away from her.

"Get her out of here," he said in disgust. He picked up the phone and called the Security Patrol.

"Pick up a woman named Karola at the *Ungarerlager* and bring her here," he ordered. "And listen, bring along the pillow from her bed."

The diary was in a little flannel bag hidden in the stuffing of the pillow. Tom unwrapped it while the woman Karola watched sullenly. She was a large woman in her middle fifties. Stringy, graying hair framed a sharp-nosed face with burning eyes and a cruel, thin-lipped mouth.

Tom was thumbing through the little book. Arrogantly, defiantly, Karola was watching him, searching his face for any reaction. I saw Tom's brow knit as he read, totally absorbed. He swallowed a couple of times, and it seemed to me that he looked pale beneath his tan. At last he stood up, stared at the woman as if he couldn't believe what he saw, and without a word motioned me to follow him out of the office.

Outside he turned to me, obviously shaken.

"The woman is a fiend," he said, his voice husky. He handed me the little book. "This," he said, "is a diary of murder—the murders of countless Jewish children. The woman made a sport—a hobby, if you like—of killing Jewish kids in Budapest." He took the innocent-looking, flower-decorated diary and opened it at random. "Here. Let me read you one of the entries."

"I was walking along the Donau River," Tom began translating. "It was getting dark. Four little children were playing near the bridge, and I saw that one of them was a filthy Jew. I threw him in the river. Before he drowned he squealed like the Jewish swine he was. The other children ran away. They did not watch him die. They were frightened. Our young ones have still much to learn . . ."

For a moment we both stood silent, each with his own bleak thoughts. "Why should she want to keep such a gruesome, and self-incriminating diary?" I wondered. "Why did she not destroy it?"

"She was proud of it," Tom answered bitterly. "She would show it to special friends—like that bitch who wanted to sell her daughter. It was her link to past glory. And power. She could not bear to part with it."

"Perhaps this is the secret they were hiding," I suggested. "A war criminal."

"A monster," Tom corrected me.

However, as it turned out, we had not found the secret of the camp—yet. But Karola did her bit to help us find it, albeit involuntarily. We didn't hide the fact from her that one of her friends had informed on her, although we didn't say who it was, nor that she, Karola, undoubtedly would pay with her life for her bestial crimes. When her warped mind finally grasped the fact that she had been double-crossed, she became almost hysterical with fury.

"Who? Who?" she shrieked. "Who is the swine that betrayed me? Who told you where to find my diary? Who? I demand to know!"

"It should not be too difficult for you to figure out for yourself," Tom said, a mocking smile on his lips.

The woman stopped her raving. She stared at Tom. Her burning eyes widened, and her nostrils flared.

"No," she said slowly. "Not—not Gal. Was it Gal?"

Tom just smiled at her.

She bit her lip. "Of course! Who else? He was always jealous of me, the whoreson." Her eyes grew hooded. "Gal. Certainly. But two can play that game!" She was regaining her composure. "You know who this traitor who denounced me really is?" she went on vindictively. "He is *Gal!*"

"Gal?"

"Yes! In the *Lager*, and to you, he gives another name, but I know better. He is Csaba Gal!"

I did some quick checking. *Csaba Gal.* Minister in the Hungarian Nazi government. Confidant of the Hungarian Hitler, Ferenc Szálasi. Wanted as a war criminal. Priority arrest.

Bull's eye! The secret of the *Ungarerlager* was finally ours. Or so we thought.

Csaba Gal was promptly arrested and admitted his identity. That same afternoon our shifty informer, Petkö, came wandering into our office.

"What do you want?" Tom snapped at him. "We know your 'great secret' now, through no fault of yours."

Petkö looked worried. "Gal talked?" he asked.

"He told us everything we wanted to know. Now get the hell out of here!"

Petkö grew visibly agitated. "Please," he said. "Please believe me. I wanted to tell you myself, but—but I was afraid you would punish me if you knew I was involved. Please, *Herr Offizier,* I am telling you God's truth. I was against burying the papers from the start. Burn them, I said. I swear it! But—I *did* help you by telling you there *was* a secret, did I not? Please do not forget that it was *I* who told you that. It will be considered, yes?" he pleaded.

Tom and I looked at each other, hardly believing what we were hearing. Shocked, I realized that the identity of Csaba Gal was *not* Petkö's great secret. It was some buried papers. What papers? Buried where? By whom? For what purpose?

We had uncovered secret after secret at the *Ungarerlager*. Here at long last was the real one.

I don't know how Tom managed to sound quite bored when he said, "You're too late, Petkö. We've already made arrangements to dig up all the documents."

He gave Petkö a speculative look. "Of course," he said, as an afterthought, "if you want to come along and show us exactly where to dig, it might be a plus in your favor."

The boxes we dug up in the forest a few hundred feet from the

Ungarerlager were treasure chests of information: official state documents of the Hungarian Nazi government, papers signed in green ink by Ferenc Szálasi himself, revealing important, highly confidential deals and plots, secret records and files—all of it immensely valuable to Allied military authorities.

Ferenc Szálasi, a major in the Hungarian army, became the leader of Hungary during the last months of the war, replacing Adm. Miklós Horthy de Nagybánya. As head of the extremist Nazi Arrow Cross party, which stood mainly for chauvinism and anti-Semitism, Szálasi was named leader of his country in October 1944, with the blessing of the German Nazis and Hitler himself. Szálasi cooperated fully with the Germans, sending his Arrow Cross thugs into the streets to terrorize Jews and leftists and deserters as Hitler had sent out his SA and SS troops. Captured by U.S. soldiers in Germany, where he had taken refuge after the fall of Hungary, Szálasi was returned to his native country, where he was tried and sentenced to death by the People's Tribunal. He was executed on March 12, 1946.

The documents and papers found at Miltacht near the *Ungarerlager* helped speed him on his way.

Three months later, in June of 1946, Csaba Gal was hanged in Budapest. Tom Winkler witnessed his grisly execution. This is how he described the death of the war criminal to me:

> The uneven cobblestone pattern of the prison courtyard had been broken to force two heavy wooden stakes into the ground. No crossbar was fastened to either of these plain gallows, only a noose on each hung loosely down, secured to the top of the pole. Two men placed a small stool and adjusted a rope through a strong pulley at the foot of each of the two stakes. The gray dawn light lent an eerie indistinctness to the grim scene.
>
> There were two war criminals to be executed. The first one was brought into the courtyard. His hands were tied behind his back, but he walked quickly between the two guards to one of the gallows. His eyes looked unseeingly in front of him as he stepped up on the stool and tiredly leaned his back against the coarse wood.
>
> A Hungarian official stepped forward. In a droning, monotonous voice he read the criminal's sentence.

With incredible speed the noose was dropped over the condemned man's head. The rope from the pulley was tied to his feet with a quick knot, and as his assistant tore away the stool, the executioner gave a vehement pull on the rope. The criminal's neck lengthened visibly; his eyes seemed suddenly to come to life, straining to escape their sockets. Then his head was pulled askew as his neck broke—and he was dead.

A few minutes later Gal was led through the door into the courtyard. He took a few strides, and then his eyes fell upon the distorted body of his companion on the stake.

The blood drained from his face, and his mouth began to twitch convulsively. He took a couple of faltering steps, and then his legs lost their power. The guards took his arms and almost carried him toward the one empty post.

He began to whimper.

His eyes were riveted upon the misshapen body on the other post. Soon *he* would be like that. He didn't seem to be able to wrest his head away.

The Hungarian official was reading rapidly. And suddenly the two executioners flew into action. The noose was thrown around the prisoner's neck, and the rope tied to his feet. A quick, powerful pull—and Gal's whimpering pleas were cut short with a sharp rattle.

He was dead.

The unsavory occupants of the *Ungarerlager* near Miltacht were not the only Hungarians we ran into before the unconditional surrender of Germany in May, although they were decidedly the most preposterous. Already in April at Tirschenreuth north of Weiden, a large number of dejected Hungarians had surrendered with all their equipment and belongings, including their sleek horses and not so sleek women. And since it was, after all, a *world* war, we had run-ins with troops of other nationalities as well. White Russian mercenaries serving in the German army surrendered to us, exhibiting a distinct lack of enthusiasm for being captured by the Soviet troops; and at Zwiesel near Regen the 2d Cavalry Group in April captured thirty-five Japanese diplomats complete with wives and kids. They spoke English perfectly and were very polite. Later another group of about fifty Japanese diplomats was found in Grafenau.

With the exception of the Japanese, all the nationalities we encountered, both as allies of the Germans and as DP forced laborers, were looked upon by the Germans as German stock. It was an important part of the Nazi credo to prove that Europe, especially eastern Europe, was originally Teutonic—*German*. To this end they had established an organization called Institut für Deutsche Ostarbeit (Institute for German Work in the East), an institution that, besides dabbling in rocket, astronomical, and other scientific research, was dedicated to proving that other east European countries, such as Poland, were actually German.

Toward the end of the war, to be safe from the onrushing enemies, the institute moved from Kraków, Poland, where it had been headquartered, to the forbidding medieval castle of Zandt in Bavaria, complete with towers and turrets, ramparts and parapets, where the staff members continued their work.

When in 1990 I revisited the castle with my wife, it had lost much of its grim, bleak look. The gray, inhospitable walls were painted a cheerful white; the trees around the castle had grown tall to soften the hard, formidable lines of the medieval structure. Just as well, for the castle of Zandt was now an old people's home.

As I stood in front of the familiar yet transformed place, I wondered how many of its current inhabitants knew that nearly half a century ago one of the greatest art frauds of all time had been stored in large wooden crates in the basement, a magnificent and unique "forgery" that was described by Dr. Alfred Berlstein, then chief of the Slavonic Division of the New York Public Library, as a veritable "cultural timebomb."

CHAPTER 17

When the Institut für Deutsche Ostarbeit moved from the Polish city of Kraków on the Vistula River, the institute's home base for almost six years, and established itself in the castle of Zandt in Bavaria, the institute was headed by a Dr. Wilhelm Coblitz, who was a full colonel in the SA and a close personal friend of Generalgouverneur Dr. Hans Frank. The institute was under Frank's patronage. During his tenure as Nazi governor general of Poland, Dr. Frank sent fifty-five thousand Polish Jews from Kraków to the Auschwitz-Birkenau extermination camps. He was tried at Nürnberg and hanged on 16 October 1946 as a war criminal. Along with research material on such scientific subjects as rocketry and astronomy, mathematics and atomic power, all subjects designed to help the German war effort, the institute brought along equipment, files, records, and all documentation pertaining to its priority mission, that of proving—through a mixed application of truth and trickery—that the city of Kraków had been, was now, and always should be historically German: the absolute Germanification of Kraków.

When the Nazis first arrived in Kraków in 1939 they took over the renowned Jagiellonian University, founded in 1364 by Casimir III, the Great, and here they found the unique *Behem Codex*, a fifteenth-century illuminated manuscript, a famous and definitive source book for much of the culture and customs of eastern Europe, consisting of the medieval rules and regulations of the guilds of the Polish city of Kraków and their descriptions. Written in Polish, Latin, and German in 1505 by Balthazar Behem, bachelor of liberal arts from the Jagiellonian

University and Cancellarius of the city of Kraków (a kind of glorified city clerk), the *Codex* is illustrated by twenty-seven miniatures. Aglow with brilliant colors, these beautiful illuminations are the supreme achievement of Krakówian art, unfolding with wit and originality a vivid pageant of guild life and everyday life in this Polish city during the end of the Middle Ages.

The Nazis quickly recognized that with a few strategic changes, deletions, and falsifications the historical *Codex* could be used as a tool to alter the past to suit the Nazi ideology and "prove" that Kraków was, is, and always will be German. The original, priceless *Codex* was removed from the Jagiellonian Library and given to the Institut für Deutsche Ostarbeit, which was charged by Generalgouverneur Dr. Hans Frank with the task of performing the necessary transformation.

When we learned of the existence of the institute in our sector and raided its headquarters at Zandt Castle, we found that the skeleton staff remaining had nearly completed the destruction of their research records. Dr. Coblitz, who had stayed behind to supervise while the rest of the staff had dispersed, was arrested, but his codirector, a Dr. Drossbach, who had been in charge of the science department, had flown the coop.

We did find documents and records pertaining to the institute's scientific research, but it quickly became apparent that it had been rudimentary and was of no real value to us. We also discovered many crates containing art treasures looted from Polish museums and still bearing the museum markings; they were catalogued by Military Government officials for later return. And hidden in the basement we found ten large boxes each containing twenty copies of the Nazi version of the Kraków *Behem Codex*.

The book, *Der Krakauer Behaim-Codex* by Friedrich Winkler, was published by the Institut für Deutsche Ostarbeit in conjunction with Deutschen Verein für Kunstwissenschaft, German League of the Science of Art. In spite of the distortion of truth and fact in the text and the mutilation of some of the artwork, which had turned the *Codex* into a propaganda tool the Nazis hoped would convince the world of Kraków's germanity, the publication contained the most exquisite color reproductions ever made of the illuminations in the original *Codex*: twenty of the twenty-seven in full, glorious color, the remaining seven in black-and-white.

To reproduce the illustrations so faithfully and magnificently that it was difficult to distinguish them from the originals, a special process called *Farbenlichtdruck* was employed, using nine different color plates for each miniature and finishing them in gold by hand. So faithful were the reproductions that often even the Nazi eradications and "improvements" showed up. Experts who with magnifying glasses examined the illuminations in the Nazi book were convinced they were originals; there was no sign whatsoever of any printer's dots. One of the "improvements" or "corrections," for example, was made on the miniature accompanying the regulations for the Founders' Guild. In this illustration two aldermen are inspecting some big bells being shown to them by the master founder. The inscription STANISLAUS DE CRACOVIA adorned the rim of the big bell in the center. But because of the name's definite Polish flavor, the Germans removed the inscription.

The German text opens with this sentence: "The *Krakau Behem Codex,* to which this publication is dedicated, belongs to the most remarkable documents of German culture in the East. Its contents prove that Krakau is German." Kraków, of course, always was an integral and vital part of the area that is Poland; it was that country's coronation town from 1320 on and its capital until the end of the sixteenth century.

The belief that all culture of central and eastern Europe is of German origin or largely beholden to German influence is a pillar of German *Weltanschauung*. But the danger of this particular German propagandistic attempt lay in the minor elements of truth that lurked in Winkler's work. It is a fact, for instance, that in the fifteenth century and the beginning of the sixteenth century the urban culture of central Europe, including Poland, to some extent was German-influenced. Since the thirteenth century, many German colonists had settled in Poland, particularly in Kraków, bringing their customs and cultural traits with them. The step from this fact to claiming Kraków as German, however, is a giant one. It would be akin to claiming that New York was an Italian town because of the "Little Italy" neighborhood, or San Francisco a Chinese city because of the thriving Chinatown. But this is what the Nazi art historians attempted, hiding another basic fact, namely, that the German citizens, who formed only a moderate part of the city's population, were very quickly assimilated, so much so that toward the end of the sixteenth century Kraków was a purely Polish town.

Throughout the institute's insidious publication all questions of Kraków's *not* being German are arrogantly dismissed; not once was it acknowledged the Kraków was the capital of Poland when Poland was one of the leading powers in central and eastern Europe. Old Polish kings are mentioned, but with their names germanized and their nationalities omitted. However, to add to the seeming authenticity of the Winkler work, a long bibliography is appended containing names of well-known Polish art historians, among them the Jewish art historian Dr. Sophie Ameisenowa of the Kraków Jagiellonian University, who spent several years in German concentration camps. Dr. Ameisenowa survived and returned after the war to the Jagiellonian Library as chief of the Print Division. Concerning the Nazi *Codex* work, she wrote, "Of course I know of the German publication by Friedrich Winkler, who purportedly quotes me in a highly distorted manner, assuming that I died long ago in a concentration camp. I will settle that question with him some day."

Other Polish art experts are copiously and fallaciously quoted whenever their views could be twisted to correspond with those of the Nazis. Their contrary opinions are either not mentioned, minimized, or discredited. It is even insolently and scornfully stated that after the *Codex* was "taken into custody" by the Germans, all Polish-language titles and notes were carefully removed from the original manuscript, including the front page in Polish "with which the *Codex* unfortunately had been defiled."

This arrogance is amazing when it is realized that the manuscript in question was fashioned in Kraków, Poland, had been discovered there, and kept in the Jagiellonian Library there, and had *never* left the country until the Nazis appropriated it. There can be little doubt that the famous miniatures were created in Kraków, and that the artist who painted these illuminations, as well as Balthazar Behem himself were Polish.

The two hundred copies of the Nazi *Behem Codex* work found at Zandt Castle were supposed to have been distributed by the Nazis to the major universities and other learning centers throughout Europe, where the Orwellian historical "facts" would have been accepted as truth by students and scholars seeking knowledge as they consulted the work in the years to come. It is no wonder that Dr. Berlstein called the book a "cultural timebomb," which could have continued to wreak havoc long after the Nazis were gone had we not discovered the copies.

The priceless original *Behem Codex* was found in the U.S. Zone of Occupation shortly after the war, and Karol Estreicher, a Polish art historian, then a delegate of the Polish government, personally brought the cultural treasure back to its rightful home, the Jagiellonian Library in Kraków. I can only assume that the vandalism wrought upon the illuminations by the Nazis has been rectified.

The two hundred copies of the Winkler book we found were turned over to the American Arts and Science Authorities in Munich. They were designated as Nazi propaganda material and burned.

If the authorities had counted the books turned over to them, they would have found that they had burned only one hundred ninety-nine. I retained one copy. I still have it.

We did not stop our investigation of the Institut für Deutsche Ostarbeit with the capture of Dr. Coblitz, the recovery of the stolen art treasures, the prevention of the use of the fraudulent *Codex*, and the confiscation of the institute records, several of which helped convict Generalgouverneur Dr. Hans Frank at Nürnberg. We also wanted the missing Dr. Drossbach, not to intern him or prosecute him, but to question him about his scientific research.

We had an idea he'd still be in the area. It had been only a few weeks since he left Zandt village, we learned, so we asked around. Since most of the Germans were tight-lipped when it came to cooperating with us unless there was some personal gain involved, we concentrated on the displaced persons who had worked in and around Zandt and who were still in the area.

We found one man, appropriately enough a Polish DP, who had worked as a driver for the institute. He remembered Dr. Drossbach and his wife very well. He had on occasion taken them to the nearby town of Deggendorf, where they had visited friends.

We went to Deggendorf to the house of Drossbach's friends. When we knocked on the door, it was opened by a pleasant-looking woman around forty. We asked her name, and she answered, "I am Mrs. Dr. Drossbach." The doctor was there too, and meekly submitted to arrest.

In the room he and his wife occupied at their friends' house, Dr. Drossbach had two suitcases crammed full of selected files and records from his research work at the institute. As we gave the contents of the suitcases a cursory inspection, we came upon a large, official-looking sealed manila envelope marked STRENGSTENS VERTRAULICH! "Most Strictly Confidential, Drossbach."

Excitedly we broke the seal. Dr. Drossbach had been in charge of space and atomic research at the institute—what marvelous secrets might the envelope contain? We tore it open and eagerly spilled the contents onto a table and stared at it in utter disbelief.

It was the detailed, nothing-hidden photographic record of Dr. and Mrs. Drossbach's membership in a nudist colony.

There was nothing there we hadn't known before.

The hoard of art treasures recovered at Zandt was not the first such discovery. Corps had come upon other treasures, none more fabulous than the aforementioned find in the Merkers salt mines near the town of Vacha, with its enormous assortment of gold bullion and currency and invaluable cache of immortal art masterpieces, although a similar discovery in Regensburg was a close rival. Here in a huge vault under the Regensburg Reichsbank, Corps found a vast collection of art looted by the Nazis from all over Europe, including priceless paintings; suitcases bulging with precious stones, bracelets, rings, necklaces, and other jewelry and watches stolen from extermination camp victims and desecrated churches in the east; gold coins and bullion; twenty-two hundred pounds of silver bars melted down from stolen silver jewelry; and solid gold ecclesiastical items removed from churches in Czechoslovakia, including a gold tabernacle taken from a Russian Orthodox church in Prague. But the main value of the Regensburg treasure trove were the securities—three billion dollars' worth representing the greater part of Austria's wealth and an additional two billion dollars' worth in domestic German securities comprising the major assets of Bavaria—a pretty good day's work for the team led by Lt. John J. Stack, Jr., fiscal officer of the local XII Corps Military Government Detachment.

A treasure fully as valuable but of a decidedly different kind was recovered by the 2d Cavalry Group while stationed at Karlbach, close to the Czechoslovakian border, in a unique intelligence operation that could only be carried out with the cooperation of the enemy. It was learned through our intelligence that a large troupe of the world-famed Lippizaner horses, most of them irreplaceable brood mares and their colts from the Austrian Lippizaner Stables and the Spanish Riding School in Vienna, were quartered in a camp near a small town across the border in Czechoslovakia some ten miles behind enemy lines. The Russians were advancing fast toward the town; it was literally a question of hours whether the East or the West would gain possession of these fabulous snow-white horses, treasured by the world.

The Lippizaner horses are unique in the equestrian world. They derive their name from the Austrian imperial stud farm at Lipizza near Trieste, formerly part of the Austro-Hungarian Empire. The breed dates back to 1580 and was originally Spanish-bred offspring of Arab stock. Their forebears carried warrior knights into battle, and many of the incredible feats the Lippizaners can execute are an inbred legacy from days of yore when swift circling, leaps, and sidestepping were necessary maneuvers, today perfected to include the spectacular, world-renowned *capriole*, in which the horse soars into the air with his hind legs thrust out behind him. These, then, were the horses that were about to fall into the hands of the Russian army, where they most probably would have been put to use as draft animals.

Col. Charles H. Reed, CO of 2d Cavalry Group, realized the urgency of the situation, and after a quick call to Gen. George S. Patton for approval to cross the border into Czechoslovakia, one of the most audacious and unusual operations mounted by Corps began.

Through intelligence efforts a German Wehrmacht veterinarian captain serving at the camp where the blooded horses were stabled was contacted and agreed to come through the lines to discuss the possible rescue of the threatened Lippizaners. He did, and he gave an American task force, headed by Capt. Thomas M. Stewart, the information necessary to infiltrate enemy territory and reach the Lippizaner stables, acknowledging that the Germans preferred to turn the horses over to the Americans rather than having them fall into the hands of the Russian troops.

"Arrangements were made for me to accompany the German captain through the lines," Captain Stewart related, "avoiding all enemy troops, roadblocks and mines, and to attempt the release of the horses. I was to try to bargain with the German brass for the withdrawal of German troops from the area so that our men could go in and do the business. The German captain and I rode up to one of our cavalry outposts in a jeep, and from there we mounted horses brought by the German captain for this purpose. My mount was King Peter's private stallion."

Now the operation gets a little hairier. Captain Stewart succeeded in making his way deep into enemy territory. He met with and tried to persuade several high-ranking Wehrmacht officers to surrender the camp and allow him and his men to transport the entire stable of Lippizaner horses to 2d Cavalry Group territory—and safety. They agreed, but it would be up to him to get the herd through the sector held by German forces who knew nothing about the deal and could not be expected to condone it.

Captain Stewart returned to our lines and rejoined his waiting task force. Aided by the German withdrawal, he advanced with his men to the camp some ten miles into Czechoslovakia, and on 29 April, after a sharp firefight with a German patrol, unaware of the scheme, they reached the camp and the Lippizaner stables. Incredibly they managed to herd the entire troupe of horses through the lines to safety.

A small part of the war had been put on hold for a few hours with agreement from both German and American sides so that an irreplaceable living treasure could be saved.

Another unusual find took place during the hectic days around VE Day when thousands of refugees, DPs, newly discharged German soldiers, and others without roots were milling around in our area—all of them having to be screened before being sent on their way. Or interned.

Tom and I were doing screening duty one day when a man was brought before us with no travel permit—like thousands of others. He was a mature man. From his discharge papers it appeared that he was forty-seven years of age, a former *Feldwebel* (tech sergeant) in a *Nachrichtenabteilung* (a Signal Corps battalion). His papers were in order, as well as could be expected, and he said he was on his way to the town of Tüttlingen, southwest of us, near the Swiss border. His papers showed that he'd entered the army from Wehrkreis V (Home Base Area V), and that checked out. Wehrkreis V was the Stuttgart *Kreis,* and the little town of Tüttlingen was located in that area. Tom asked him what he'd done with his uniform epaulettes, and he said he'd thrown them away. That was standard. And he gave the color of the piping on them as *gelb*. That, too, was correct. Signal Corps personnel wore lemon yellow piping. We asked him a few more questions; he checked out.

The tattered remains of his uniform were little better than rags; he carried a small, battered suitcase, a rolled-up shelter half for protection against the weather, and a beat-up rucksack with his personal belongings, from which hung a collection of dented pots and pans that enabled him to cook the food he could glean from the land. He looked tired, but determined to get home. Exactly like thousands of others.

There was nothing that made the man suspicious, but Tom and I looked at each other. There it was—that hunch, again. Something was awry. What? By now we had learned not to dismiss that little hunch. Especially not if we both felt it.

So we put the man to the test. He passed with ease. We could not trip him up. But the hunch persisted.

So we searched him. Thoroughly. And that included the repugnant full body search, carried out by a medic. Nothing. No diamonds up his ass or his nose, as Tom put it.

We searched his belongings; we went over his clothing for secret pockets or lining stashes. We inspected the heels on his boots, his belt, his buttons, and the visor of his cap, a favorite hiding place for a lethal curved knife. Nothing. We inspected his old suitcase for a false bottom, a space in the lid or the side linings; we went through his rucksack, seam by seam. Nothing. We found an old tin, which contained only cigarette butts picked up after having been discarded by GIs. That too was normal. We looked in his mouth for fake teeth or a string tied to a rear molar. Small items, such as precious stones, could be placed in a pouch, tied to a string, and swallowed. He was clean. In short, we searched everything and everywhere, but we found nothing.

Finally we acknowledged that this time our hunch had misled us—and we told the man to be on his way.

As we watched him walk out of the interrogation room, his U.S. travel permit clutched in his hand, his pots and pans clanging from his rucksack, we frowned after him. That damned hunch was still clanging in our minds, louder than ever.

Of course!

The pots and pans! He seemed to carry an awful lot of pots and pans for the need of one man to cook a few simple meals.

We called him back. We looked at the pots, and we looked at the pans. To us they looked like heavy, beat-up tinware. But again, something told us we were on the right track, especially when I thought I caught a momentary glint of alarm in the sergeant's eyes as I turned one of the pans over in my hands. Or was that just wishful thinking on my part? But to satisfy ourselves, we asked that the tinware be examined by experts.

The cookware turned out to be pure platinum! A veritable fortune in pots and pans! The "sergeant" was actually a high-ranking Nazi official who knew that the only way he could preserve his fortune and his own safety was to smuggle it and himself out of Germany, into Switzerland. He had converted everything he had into platinum and cast his pots and pans, the humble possessions of a war refugee. And it *almost* worked.

For a long time his meals in an internment camp would be cooked in considerably less imposing pots and pans.

Other treasures on a lesser scale were retrieved throughout the war: a case in point, forty-one historical church bells stolen by the Nazis from Metzs and other French cities, which we recovered; and at the village of Tirschenreuth we made an impressive discovery. Tipped by a DP that a manure pile in a certain farmyard in the village held other things than cow pies and horse apples, we had the malodorous heap taken apart. Hidden in the center of the stinking mess was a large, heavy chest. When we forced it open we saw it was crammed with booty: jewels and watches, gold coins and bullion, foreign currency and securities—the enormous accumulation of loot acquired by a man who had served as an overseer of slave labor on the Nazi West Wall.

Once again a DP had been instrumental in helping us, but these displaced persons also caused us considerable difficulties. When we settled down to occupation duties, besides the hunt for saboteurs, high-ranking Nazis, and war criminals, we had another major problem to contend with: in our area of the U.S. Zone of Occupation, Corps found the appalling number of three hundred thousand DPs wandering around the countryside.

After years of degrading servitude as slave laborers under Nazi rule in a foreign country, taken from their families and homelands by force to toil in factories and on farms, their newly won freedom put these miserable people on the move. Many were striving to find their way home, others merely to seek better living conditions—to survive in a land that was hostile to them. The army took every opportunity to help those wishing to be repatriated, and trains and convoys crammed with humanity were constantly shuttling across Germany.

Often these liberated slave workers, having kept their eyes and ears open, were able to give us valuable information about their former "employers." We had benefitted from this before, and we fully expected to do so again. For that reason I made it a point to be on hand when a truckload of DPs, after having been deloused to prevent the spread of disease, was leaving Kötzting one afternoon in June '45, bound for a big repatriation camp near Regensburg.

As I walked among the excited men and women who were chattering away in a Babel of languages, a big but malnourished man plucked at my sleeve. Clearing his throat nervously, he said in broken German:

"Your enemy has weapons. The earth hides them for him. He means to kill!"

CHAPTER 18

I took the man aside.

He turned out to be a freed Estonian slave worker. For the past couple of years he had worked on a farm owned by a German farmer named Zollner, the *Ortsbauernführer*—the village Nazi leader—of a small village in Kötzting County. Our turf.

The Estonian was absolutely certain that the old man and his son, a recently discharged Wehrmacht soldier, had hidden guns and ammunition on the farm. Although he did not know with certainty, he believed their arsenal was hidden under the floor of the house.

The first and strictest Military Government order given to the Germans was all firearms, ammunition, and other weapons must be turned in to American authorities at once! If my informant was right and the Zollners had concealed a cache of guns and ammunition, it could be for one reason only. And that reason had to be countered without delay.

Early the next morning my teammate Tom Winkler and I and a couple of security guards drove to the Zollner farm to investigate the serious accusation made by the Estonian.

It was a typical Bavarian farm, but in worse condition than most. The large farmyard was completely enclosed by the main house and adjoining stables, coops, and barns. In the middle sprawled a huge, oozing dung heap right next to the well and pump that supplied the household with water. Trash and broken farm implements were strewn about, and the cow shed, that was connected directly to the living quarters, exuded a foul stench. In a corner stood a dung-stained, barrel-shaped manure wagon with a broken shaft.

We found the farmer and his wife in the farmyard in the process of filling a couple of wooden buckets with water.

As we dismounted, I looked over the former *Ortsbauernführer*. "A man of much importance," the Estonian informer had said. "Once he shook the hand of the Führer, Adolf Hitler." He didn't look it.

Indeterminate of age, perhaps around fifty, he had a shock of nearly white hair and a huge, unkempt mustache the same color but yellowed around the mouth from smoking. He wore a soiled once-white shirt of the kind on which the collar is fastened separately, but without the collar, and baggy pants held up by suspenders. One of the front straps was buttoned onto the pants, the other secured with a large safety pin.

His wife, presumably around her husband's age, was a drab and dumpy woman with lackluster mouse-brown hair pulled back from her face. She was clad in a formless short-sleeved dress made of cotton and printed with a flower motif. It hung on her like a sack.

As we approached the couple, a young man came from a barn and joined them. That would be the son, I thought, recently discharged from the Wehrmacht. To describe him would mean the repeated use of the word *average*.

A fourth member of the family, the farmer's daughter, a young girl of nineteen, was out in the forest gathering wild berries, we were told. She was expected to return any moment.

Before they had a chance to talk among themselves, we separated the two men and ordered the woman to stay away from them. We placed the son in a barn, guarded by one of the security patrol GIs, and instructed the other to keep an eye on the woman and to let us know as soon as the daughter turned up. Tom and I then took the farmer to the *Bauernstube*, the kitchen/living room, and went to work on him.

A partial cripple from the First World War, his right arm was slightly withered and deformed, but his glaring eyes seemed made of steel. His attitude did not bode well.

"You know why we are here," I said matter-of-factly.

"I do not know," the farmer firmly contradicted me. He shrugged. "You are *Amis*."

"We are here because of the weapons," I said curtly. I was watching him. He showed no reaction. Either he was good—or we were on a wild Estonian goose chase.

"What—weapons?" the farmer asked, mildly curious.

"The guns and ammunition you have hidden here," I said icily.

"Guns?" The man's bushy eyebrows rose in perplexity. "Ammunition? I know of no such things."

I looked at Tom. I knew he had the same feeling I had. The man was lying—but he would be tough to crack. Perhaps we could save ourselves some trouble.

"I think you do," I said to the farmer, putting as much menace in my voice as I could. I walked to the door and summoned the GI on watch in the yard. I turned back to the farmer. I tried a few more times to get him to open up. I assured him that we *knew* about the guns he was hiding and described the dire consequences he would have to suffer if he didn't tell us where. He merely shrugged and smiled an infuriatingly contemptuous smile, while he stubbornly denied knowing anything about "hidden guns."

For a moment I contemplated the obstinate man. Okay. We'd let him stew for a while. Sometimes when left alone with their own thoughts, even the most pigheaded subjects would talk themselves into confessing, rather than face the terrors their own imaginations conjured up. It was worth a try.

The GI came into the room and stood just inside the door.

"You stay here, understand?" I snapped at the farmer. "You don't budge until we come back." I turned to the GI. "Watch him," I said, and as I walked toward the door, I turned to the farmer once again. "I suggest you give some serious thought to what your answers will be when we return—and to the repercussions if you decide to keep lying to us!"

On the way to the barn where the son was being kept, Tom said: "My turn?"

"Be my guest," I answered him.

The son, having been left to his own devices for a while, not knowing what was going on with his father and mother, looked much more ripe for a successful interrogation. Tom waded right in.

"All right," he said crisply. "Let's hear your version of the story."

"What—what story?" the young man stammered apprehensively.

"Dammit!" Tom shot angrily at him. "Don't play games with me! You know perfectly well what we're talking about!"

The young man looked at him, fear and uncertainty building in his eyes. I knew what he was thinking. Had his father talked? And if *he* refused, what would happen to him?

"The damned weapons, you idiot!" Tom shouted at him. "The guns! The ammunition! I want *your* version of where you've hidden them. And I want it *now!"*

The man cringed before him. "I—I—"

"Well, spit it out! Now! We don't have all day." Like an angry bull he glared at the young man. "Or would you rather that we took you back with us, and . . ." He let the young man imagine the rest of the sentence. Petrified, he stared at Tom.

"I'm waiting," Tom said ominously. He stuck his face close to the cowering man. "Where are the weapons hidden? I think you had better tell me. Now!" He hammered the words into him.

Suddenly the young man put his hands to his head and gave an odd little cry. *"Hör auf!"* he sobbed. "*Bitte*. Stop it! Please! I will show you!"

Tom and I looked at each other. This was going to be duck soup.

The young man led us to a shed and pointed to a large stack of firewood at one end. "It is in there," he whispered. "I pushed it in there."

"Start digging," Tom told him.

The young man was half through the woodpile, when he straightened up. "Here it is," he said.

In his hand he held a rusty German bayonet with a broken point.

"I—I thought I could use it to cut grass," he explained lamely.

And that was it. That was all there was. We had him move the entire stack of wood, just in case, but there wasn't even a spent cartridge, let alone a gun or a small arsenal.

At that moment a young girl came running through the gate to the farmyard, a basket swinging from her arm. The farmer's teenaged daughter. When she saw us, she made a beeline for the house. I stopped her with a shouted command.

I walked up to her. Her name was Marerl. She had been running. Her breath came quickly between partly open lips; her clear blue eyes regarded me steadily. Her face was devoid of makeup—she didn't need any. Two long braids, the color of sunshine, fell across her shoulders. She was, in other words, damned attractive. But she was also a new subject for our interrogations—perhaps the last chance we'd have.

"Was wollen Sie hier," she asked, without the apprehension in her voice that was usually present when we confronted the Germans. "What are you doing here? Is anything wrong?"

"We have just arrested your father and your brother," I answered her bluntly.

She was startled. "Arrested? For what?"

"For hiding the guns and ammunition buried here."

For an instant her flushed cheeks lost some of their color—involuntarily her eyes flitted toward the house—but she caught herself quickly. The soft line of her lips became straight and firm as she said: *"Es ist nicht wahr.* It is not true! There are no guns here."

"We haven't dug them up yet," I said. "But we will." I gave her what I hoped was a stern look. "And you will show us where."

She shrugged her youthful shoulders. "How can I?" she said in wide-eyed innocence, "when there *are* no guns?"

But I had caught her quick glance toward the house. Had she been concerned about her father and her brother? Or about the guns?

We tried to break her. First I, then Tom. If the old man and his son had been stubborn, this snip of a girl was the personification of obstinacy. After a couple of hours of intense questioning, she was near tears, but she had told us absolutely nothing.

Was the Estonian informer wrong? Had he denounced his former masters for spite? To get even with them? It was not unheard of. But both Tom and I were convinced that something was rotten at the Zollner farm. And it wasn't just the ripe dunghill in the yard.

We were convinced that there *were* weapons hidden somewhere, and it was up to us to find them.

But how?

While one of the security patrol soldiers guarded the family, the rest of us made a thorough search of the farm. After all, a cache of guns can't be hidden under a thimble, and we had a better than fair chance of finding them. We searched the house, the stables, the barns, the sheds, even the malodorous outhouse. We found nothing. We broke up the flooring in every likely hiding place and had the young Zollner dig in the compacted soil beneath. Nothing. At no time did we even feel we were getting hot.

The family watched our efforts. Stoically. Silently. Apparently confident that we'd find nothing. They never betrayed their feelings—except the girl, Marerl. She glared at us with anger and defiance.

Good. That could be put to use. Any emotion out of the ordinary always could. One last time, I thought, one last time I'd try to break her.

I went over to her. Unceremoniously I grabbed her arm and marched her to a small tack room off the stable hung with old harnessing, bridles, and yokes. It smelled of wet leather and stale horse sweat. I closed the door behind us, pulled up a stool, and sat the girl down on it. I stood before her. She looked up at me, a mixture of defiance and mounting alarm on her pretty face.

"Now," I said to her solemnly. "It is just you and me. I'll give you a last chance to save the lives of your father and your brother."

She glared at me but remained silent.

"You know that hiding weapons is a most serious offense. If found guilty, your father and your brother could be condemned to death!" It was not true, but she could not know that. Under the regime *she* had lived in, it would have been the case.

Still she said nothing. I poured it on. I dwelt on the guilty horror her life would be if she refused to help us, knowing that her father and her brother had been executed because of her stubbornness. However, if she would cooperate now, I assured her, I'd plead leniency for the two men, and they would live. No one need know that she had talked, I told her. We would make it look as if we found the weapons by chance. Ultimately—of course—that would be the case anyway; whether she talked or not would make no difference in the long run—except for the fate of her father and brother. I looked earnestly at her. "You love them, don't you?" I asked her gently. "It is in your power to save them. Right now. You do not want to see them dead, do you?" I stepped closer to her. "Imagine how you'd feel if—because of you—they lay rotting in the ground along with the guns they'd hidden!"

Marerl had been listening to me in growing agitation. Suddenly she fell to her knees. She reached out and clutched my boots. "Please!" she wailed. "Please do not have them killed! *Bitte, bitte!*"

Gently I raised her to her feet. "We won't kill them," I said quietly. "Just tell me where the guns are hidden, and we can put all this behind us."

She pulled away from me. She looked me straight in the face—her eyes black with hate.

"Nie!" she whispered vehemently. "Never!"

I turned away from her. I did not want her to see the triumph in my eyes.

In her emotional distress the girl had slipped. She had not again insisted that there *were* no guns—only that she would not tell us *where* they were hidden! It was the first admission, although involuntary, that the guns *did* in fact exist. We had begun to think perhaps they did not. Now I knew.

But I was still puzzled. How could the Zollners keep on denying that the weapons existed? It must be obvious to them that we'd keep looking until we found them—tear down the damned farm around their ears, if necessary. And they had been strangely unconcerned at our thorough search so far. They must by now realize that we'd search until we did luck out, and the longer they waited to cooperate, the more severe their punishment would be. Yet they all seemed so damned confident that we'd find nothing—and so damnably smug about it. Why were they so cocksure?

Suddenly I knew why. It was so obvious, it was embarrassing.

The guns were *not* hidden on the farm itself! That's why they could keep on protesting their innocence. That's why they were so sure we'd turn up empty-handed. We had taken our Estonian informer too literally.

But—where, then?

The forest. It had to be the forest. That would be the only logical and safe place. The forest, which began a mere couple of hundred feet from the Zollner farm, was still easily accessible. It had to be the answer.

Tom and I put our heads together and quickly mapped out a plan; then we returned to the *Bauernstube* where the Zollners were kept under guard, forbidden to speak. I beckoned to the old man.

"Los!" I snapped at him. "*Mitkommen!* Come with us!"

Sullenly the old former village leader rose, and with a look of encouragement toward his family, he followed us outside.

We took him to the little tack room and plunked him down on the stool.

We said not a word.

The minutes went by. The silence, complete and inexplicable, began to eat at the old man's nerves. What did we want? What was going on? Why did we not say anything? But he was remarkably resilient. And he could not know that all we wanted was time.

After about ten minutes of total silence, I left—without having spoken a single word.

I went back to the *Bauernstube*. I pointed to the son. Tom and I had already decided that despite the cute bayonet trick he had played on us, he was the one most likely to fall for the plan we had devised.

As we walked out into the yard, I said, "Get a spade. And a pickax."

Puzzled, he looked at me, but he obeyed.

"Okay," I said. "Let's go."

"Where to?" His curiosity got the better of him.

"To the woods," I said matter-of-factly. "We're going to dig up the guns." I grinned at him. "It's all over, *Kamerad*," I said cheerfully. "Your father told us where the weapons are hidden. We just had a nice long talk with him."

The young man stared at me thunderstruck. "My—my father told you?" he stammered.

I nodded. "Sure. He finally realized it would be the best thing to do," I explained. "He knew we'd find out sooner or later. He's no fool, your old man. He knows when to fight—and when not. No wonder he was your village leader."

The young man nodded slowly.

"Okay, get going!" I ordered him.

We walked toward the gate, the young man carrying the digging equipment. Casually I asked, "What've you got out there?"

He shrugged. "Only small arms," he answered. "A few guns. Ammunition. We did not keep the grenades."

Tom opened the door to the tack room.

"Ready?" he called.

"Ready," I answered.

With the old man in tow, Tom came out of the shed. I turned to the son. "Let's go," I said. "You lead the way."

Obediently he began to walk toward the nearby woods; I was directly behind him, followed by Tom and the old man. We had decided to take them both to the hiding place. We felt that the presence of the father would back up the story I'd told his son—as long as we kept them from talking to each other.

It was a mistake. A mistake that almost cost us the case.

We'd walked a few hundred feet into the forest when suddenly the two Germans stopped dead in their tracks and stood staring straight into nothing.

We quickly realized that despite our keeping an eye on them, they had been able to communicate. The son had thought his father had told us where the arms cache was hidden—how else could we have known it was in the woods? His father, seeing his son with the spade and pickax headed for the forest, had thought *he* had betrayed the secret. Now they had found out that neither of them had told us anything! With looks, gestures, what-have-you, father and son had been able to reach each other. People who are intimately familiar with each other have ways of communicating that others do not even notice. We should have known.

But now the damage was done.

When we brusquely ordered them to go on, it was the old man who spoke up. There were no guns concealed in the forest, he claimed, his eyes blazing triumph. What his son had told us was not true. The boy had been frightened at our high-handed treatment of the whole family, and he had been confused. It was a misunderstanding. His son had thought *we* were going to show *him* where some guns were buried in the woods. Neither he nor his son, he declared, had any knowledge whatsoever of buried weapons in the woods!

He had us. It would be next to impossible to get them to show us the hiding place now, and it would be equally impossible to find it ourselves.

We had to act fast, or we would lose any momentum we did have. We figured we must be pretty close to the hiding spot, which would not be too far from the farm, and we were determined to find it.

It was *our* turn for a little intimate communicating.

I turned to Tom. "You take the old man," I said grimly. "Go take a look in that direction," I pointed. "See what you can turn up. I'll go that way with his son." I looked significantly at Tom, "It shouldn't take long."

I saw at once that he understood exactly what I meant. Good. Now, if it would only work.

Our guns drawn menacingly, Tom took the father and I took the son, and we went in opposite directions into the woods. We soon lost sight of each other.

The young Wehrmacht soldier was obviously frightened. Both Tom's and my attitudes had changed abruptly. We were now coldly hostile—not merely adversarial.

He was frightened—but would he break?

As we walked, I worked on his already frazzled nerves. Icily I pointed out to him that if I were to shoot him down now nobody would know the difference. I could easily claim he'd tried to jump me—or hit me with the spade: self-defense. And I threatened to do just that if he did not show me where the guns were concealed. And soon. I banked on him having seen how the SS troops acted in the field, so he would believe me. Finally, when I thought he was scared enough, I stopped.

"I've had it," I said in disgust. "I hope, for his sake, that your father is wiser than you are. You obviously would rather end up in a body bag than show me where your lousy guns are. Okay—if that's your choice . . ."

I stopped next to a pile of large boulders that formed a small cave. I gestured with my gun. "In there," I ordered. "Get in there as far as you can. *Los!*"

He stared at me uncomprehendingly.

"Now!" I spat at him. I leveled my gun at his eyes. Trembling and sweating, he obeyed. I glanced at my watch. It was about time.

"Turn your back to me," I ordered. "Put your hands on your head."

He began to whimper. "Please do not shoot me . . . Please do not shoot me . . ."

"Will you show me where you have hidden the guns?"

"I—please! Do not shoot! Please! Please! . . ."

At that moment a shot rang out in the distance—reverberating through the forest. Tom had done his part.

The young man started violently, as if the bullet had torn into *his* body. I cocked my gun.

"Well?"

"Ja!" he blubbered. *"Ja! Ja!* I will show you. Do not shoot me too. Please do not shoot me!"

He crawled out of the cave, stark horror distorting his face, his shoulders heaving.

We did not have far to go. The young Zollner led me to a smaller cave and began to dig the topsoil away.

Before long he had unearthed a nice collection of large tarpaper packages. I gave a long whistle, and a few minutes later Tom joined us with the old man. The farmer looked furious, but untamed. His son stared at him as if he couldn't believe his eyes, but no sound came from his bloodless lips. The old man's steely eyes were fired with hate as he looked at us—and at the pile of tarpaper-wrapped bundles at our feet.

We unwrapped the packages. When we were through we had an action-ready arsenal of five Mauser Kar 98k German army rifles, a double-barreled shotgun, a Luger P-08, a Walther P-38, as well as four Schmeisser MP-18/1 submachine guns, all well oiled and with plenty of ammunition for all types.

At a subsequent trial by the U.S. Military Government, both father and son were given stiff sentences at hard labor. But Marerl, the fanatically stubborn farmer's daughter, went free.

In 1949, more than four years after the Zollner case, I returned to Germany as a civilian, accompanied by a young American journalist named Will Sparks. Our purpose was to learn what the German people really thought after four years of occupation.

But how could American journalists get an honest and unbiased opinion of the situation? The people you talk to, for the most part, will tell you what they think you want to hear. Why make waves—and possibly be splashed in the process? So how do you learn the truth?

There is one way and one way only: you become a German.

Through my connections in the CIC I obtained papers identifying me as a German PW recently returned to Germany after having been released from a Russian PW camp. I bought myself an entire outfit of inexpensive German clothing and set out to mingle and learn.

In Frankfurt I met a young woman, a music student and a real Nordic beauty, who was engaged to an American, a minor official in Military Government. Why? Because she was tired of the drab existence in occupied Germany and wanted to live the life of luxury in her fiancé's native Boston, which she had heard so much about. Privately she was contemptuous of Americans, all Americans—including her future husband.

In Munich I made friends with a former Nazi tank commander who had fought campaigns in France, Belgium, Luxembourg, and Yugoslavia and was proud of his claim to have been commanding the first tank to cross the border into Poland. *"Mensch, das waren die Zeiten!"* he said with a nostalgic sigh. "Those were the days!" Now he was driving a limousine for American officers stationed in Munich. He longed for the days of Adolf Hitler and the Third Reich, when things were so much better, and he bitterly resented having to serve the American invaders. He regretted nothing of the past—only that Germany had lost the war.

It was with him that I one evening sat in a little *gemütlich* bar listening to the animated chatter and laughter of the Germans—and everyone there was German—as they emptied their steins of beer and munched on salted pretzels.

The door opened, and a young German woman came in, her arm linked with a man who was obviously an American, probably from the U.S. Military Government. All eyes shifted to the couple, and there was an awkward, though momentary, hush before conversation resumed and the couple was seated at the bar. After a drink or two, and a magnanimous round for the other patrons at the bar, the couple left—and once again there was a moment of silence.

One of the two buxom barmaids with obvious distaste picked up the glass from which the American had been drinking. *"Es ist genau wie vor unser'm Adolf,"* she said bitterly. "It is just like it was before our Adolf. The Jews and the foreigners have all the money." She stared at the glass in her hand. "Well," she said with determination, "no good German shall drink out of this glass!" And with that she shattered it in the sink.

The trip had been an eye-opener, and this was over four years after the war had ended.

There was one more investigation I wanted to make. I wanted to revisit the Zollner farm and talk to the old farmer and his family. I'd learned that both father and son had been released after serving only part of their sentence. What did *they* think?

Will and I wangled a Volkswagen and set out for the little hinterland village where the Zollner place was located.

What would it be like, seeing them again? It was only four years ago that I had placed a loaded gun to young Zollner's head and forced him to reveal the hiding place of the cache of arms he and his father had concealed so laboriously and sought to keep secret; I then had sent them both to prison. What had happened to them in the intervening years? How did they feel now?

There was always the possibility, as Will soberly pointed out to me, that their hatred toward the *Amis* who had tricked them, caught them, and jailed them, would be so overwhelming that they'd risk everything on a blind act of revenge. And it was likely that I would be recognized.

How would it feel to stand eye to eye with a man you had once threatened to kill, I thought? Most important, how would that man react when once again you appeared on the scene, this time unarmed and without the protecting authority of a uniform?

I was about to find out.

We had concocted a story about being officials of sorts from the state office, inquiring into the condition of German prisoners of the U.S. Military Government after their release from prison. We had no idea if such an office did, in fact, exist, but neither would the Zollners—we hoped.

We reached the village shortly after noon, parked the Volkswagen outside the Zollners' gate, and walked in, our official-looking briefcases under our arms. The farmyard looked as ramshackle and disreputable as before, the run-down barns and sheds had not improved, quite the contrary if that was possible, and the dung heap was still there, looking and smelling no different; but this time a flock of loudly protesting geese flapped out of the way as we approached the open door to the farmhouse.

After much pounding on the door and shouts of *"Holla!"* a toothless old woman timidly appeared in the doorway. Without her teeth I hardly recognized her as the farmer's wife, and she gave no sign of recognizing me.

Officiously, as behooved any minor German *Beamte*, I asked for the farmer—I pulled a document from my briefcase and consulted it importantly—the farmer *Zollner*.

At that moment a barefoot old man stepped out of the barn behind us and walked toward us. Withered, stoop-shouldered, his right arm held a little awkwardly, he was still lean and tanned, and obviously not feeble.

Zollner.

I felt a surge of adrenaline as I watched the old farmer approach us.

It was immediately apparent that I was not recognized. It was not surprising. A man looks different in uniform, and I had put on a few pounds in the intervening years.

With a properly overbearing attitude I introduced myself and Will, who merely acknowledged the introduction with a nod. He had relegated himself to a silent role, his German not good enough to pass for native. I explained why we were there, and Zollner accepted it readily, if not enthusiastically. Another meddlesome *Beamte*, he probably thought. There were so many of that ilk in Germany that a man like Zollner would accept another one with resignation and indifference. We had counted on that.

He motioned us into the house.

Seated in the same dingy *Bauernstube* where four years earlier the frustrating interrogation of the Zollner family had been played out was a strangely disconcerting experience. I was thankful I had my role as a German *Beamte* to hide behind as I looked at the old farmer sitting across the table from me waiting for my questions. The large room still had a massive wood-burning stove squatting in one corner; rough wooden benches along the walls, on one of which sat the farmer's wife, her hands idle in her lap; a bulky, graceless cupboard; and a scarred wooden table with four chairs, where Zollner and I were seated. Will sat on a bench behind me.

I made a show of consulting the papers I'd pulled from my cheap, battered briefcase.

"You have a son," I said, "and a daughter."

"My daughter is married," Zollner said. "A year now. She lives in Regen. My son has left home."

"Then you and your wife are alone here?"

"We have a farmhand. He is with the cows."

I nodded. "You were sentenced to five years' hard labor," I continued in what I hoped would sound like a routine interview. "How much of your sentence did you actually serve?"

"Three years and two months," Zollner answered. "My son served only two and a half years."

"I see." I meticulously entered the information on my bogus form. Have to stay in character, I reminded myself.

"You were once the leader of your village," I went on. "Has your conviction and your jail term impaired your standing with your fellow villagers?"

Zollner erupted into a short, mirthless cackle. *"Binna Preiss!"* he chuckled (using the colloquial Bavarian term for "I'm a popular neighbor"). "They all know my—my 'crime.' The weapons I hid from the *verfluchte*—the damned *Amis*. Should they think less of me for that?" He snorted.

"No. They admire me, and they know I am a good German." He suddenly looked aggrieved. "But I have suffered from the foreigners."

"How were you treated in prison?"

"What good is complaining now?" Zollner shrugged. "Food was bad. But the jailers were German. They, too, knew what was my 'crime.' And they eased my stay. The hard labor they gave me was only mending the prison uniforms."

"And your son?"

"He was young. And strong. Life in the Wehrmacht had toughened him. He was not hurt—but he learned to know who were his friends."

He looked at me. "As I told you, he is no longer here. The farm became run down while we were in jail because of those *verdammte Ami* officers who arrested us." He spat on the already filthy floor. "My son is now in Munich," he continued with a conspiratorial air, "where they know how to deal with the foreigners who think they are fit to rule Germany!"

He nodded in thought. "Too bad the *Amis* found our guns," he mused. "They would have been useful. Someday." He gave his cheerless cackle. His eyes twinkled. "For shooting rabbits, *ja?*" He laughed.

We joined him. We were becoming fast friends.

I returned to my "questionnaire." "Do you think your sentence was just?" I asked.

"Just!" Zollner spat the word. "The American judge was a Jew. Can you expect justice from a *Jew?*"

"What about the American agents who arrested you?" It was my sixty-four-dollar question.

Zollner lost his friendly smile. *"Zum Teufel damit!"* he exclaimed angrily. "The devil take them! One of them was a Jew, of course, the other—" He stopped. "Wait!" he said. "I have the names right here. Anna, my wife, she wrote them down. At the trial." He opened a drawer in the table and rummaged among the cutlery and kitchen utensils kept there. Presently he came up with a piece of dirty, crumbled paper. He peered at it.

"The Jew," he said. "His name was—Winkler. The other was—was" He squinted closely at the paper, brushing it with his hand as if that would make the words easier to read. "It was—M E L—" He frowned at the writing and tried again. "M E L—"

"C H I O R," I finished for him. "*Melchior.*"

It took a few seconds, then the old man stared at me with utter astonishment.

I was aware of Will stirring slightly behind me. I placed the balls of my feet under my chair, my hands on my knees. I was in a position of perfect balance for any quick movement that might become necessary. I looked the old man straight in the eyes.

"Do you not recognize me, Herr Zollner?" I asked quietly. "I am one of the agents who arrested you. I am *Melchior*."

There was a shocked outcry from the woman across the room. Out of the corner of my eye I saw her hand fly to her toothless mouth. In the same instant Zollner sprang to his feet, the heavy chair crashing to the floor behind him. Face ashen and drawn, steely eyes boring into me, knuckles white where both hands gripped the edge of the open drawer in front of him, Zollner stood in explosive silence.

Suddenly one of his huge, callused fists plunged into the depth of the drawer. He whipped out a huge knife, with at least an eight-inch blade.

For a few seconds he stood frozen, his eyes locked on mine. Neither of us moved.

I saw the rage in Zollner's eyes change to resolution. His hand tightened around the handle of the big knife until the veins stood out. He began to lift it—

I was a pulse beat away from leaping out of my chair when suddenly there was a choked cry from Zollner's wife. She lunged to her feet, rushed to the table, and put her hands on her husband's arm.

"No, Otto!" she shouted. "No! He is not worth it! He is not worth it!"

For a brief moment the two Germans stood before me like a motionless tableau—then the knife clattered onto the table, shattering the tense silence.

Zollner's eyes burned into me. "*Ja*," he muttered. "*Er ist es!* It is he!"

For a full minute not a word was spoken. Then I said, "Do you feel you were unjustly treated? You grossly violated the law by hiding those guns. And you knew it."

Zollner scowled sullenly at me. "I was not going to use them against you," he muttered. "I was only going to shoot some Poles . . ."

He drew himself up. "I want you to leave my house," he said firmly. "Go away—and leave us alone!"

The farmer Zollner was asking us to leave his house. But I strongly felt he meant we should get out of his country.

We—and the rest of us foreigners.

It was not long after the Zollner case that our CIC team left Kötzting. On 28 May, Corps had set up headquarters in Regensburg, some sixty miles to the west on the right bank of the Danube River, and we joined them there.

Regensburg has a long and bloody history of war and violence. Originally a pre-Christian Celtic settlement, it was conquered in A.D.179 by the Roman emperor Marcus Aurelius, who turned it into a Roman fortress and military camp, which he called Castra Regina. Parts of this ancient camp are still to be seen in today's Regensburg, such as the solid limestone blocks and slabs of Porta Praetoria and the massive walls.

The dukes of Bavaria made the city their capital in 530; Charlemagne captured the town in 788; and by the thirteenth century it had become the most flourishing town in southern Germany and an important station for the Crusaders on their way to the holy wars.

During the Thirty Years' War in the seventeenth century, Regensburg was captured by the Swedes and later by imperial troops, suffering pillage and plague, and by 1809 when Napoleon's invincible troops stood before its gates, the town had endured seventeen disastrous sieges in its strife-torn existence.

And now, once again, Regensburg had been ravaged by war.

The town had been the target of several massive Allied air raids, which had spared the historic landmarks including Saint Peter's Cathedral, Saint Jacob's Church, the Old Town Hall, and the *Ostentor*—the East Gate, part of the medieval fortifications—but leveled the great Messerschmidt aircraft factories and the vital railway yards as well as the main railroad station in downtown Regensburg. Some of the ancient structures were damaged, such as the twelfth-century stone bridge, the *Steinerne Brücke*, a medieval architectural marvel that was all but destroyed when SS troops blew up all the bridges over the river in a wanton and futile attempt to stem the American tide. But Regensburg, although war-ravaged and bomb-blasted, was in better shape than many of the other great German cities we had come through, such as Mainz and Frankfurt. A proud city, she wore her battle scars as proudly as a Heidelberg student his dueling scars.

When we arrived the town showed all the evidence of U.S. occupation: signposts on every street corner pointed the way to various units; "Kilroy" apparently had been everywhere, for his bald, round-eyed, long-nosed likeness peeked over fences and temporary barricades throughout the city; and army posters warning against VD and fraternization were tacked up all over the place—SOLDIER, DON'T FRATERNIZE. THE GERMAN PEOPLE IN GENERAL FEEL NO GUILT AGAINST OTHERS! DON'T BE A SUCKER! And with somewhat heavy-handed double entendre, a GI ogling a curvaceous *Fräulein,* with the admonition YOU'VE WON THE WAR—DON'T LAY THE GROUNDWORK FOR ANOTHER!

Corps CP, both forward and rear echelons, fused again once and for all, was housed in a complex of relatively undamaged gray stucco buildings on the outskirts of town that had served as *Kavallerie Kasernen* (cavalry barracks) for the Wehrmacht. It had formerly been the garrison of the German 10th Mounted Artillery Regiment and was in use as an Engineer officer candidate school when captured by U.S. troops. Corps officers were billeted in hotels in the city a couple of miles away, high-ranking brass occupying the plush Park Hotel Maximilian Hof, built on a grand scale inside and out.

When Cleo and I arrived in Regensburg, we had decided to stay in that same hotel and enjoy the luxury. Regensburg is a bustling, prosperous town, where the ancient and the modern rub shoulders in unselfconscious harmony.

Before we left Regensburg we visited another site east of the city, Walhalla, perched spectacularly on top of a hill on the bank of the Danube, just outside the little town of Donaustaf. I had been at Walhalla with Agent Franz Vidor when I was stationed in Regensburg in 1945.

According to Germanic mythology, Walhalla is the home of the Nordic gods into which only warriors chosen by the Valkyries may be admitted. The idea of creating a magnificent shrine to Germany's heroes—warriors, historical and cultural notables alike—dates back to a time of deep humiliation for Germany. In 1807, after the ignominious defeat of Prussia by Napoleon, then twenty-year-old Crown Prince Ludwig of Bavaria conceived a plan to collect sculptural images of

Germany's great to be housed in a temple of honor. "It must be grand," he decreed. "Not merely colossal."

Thirty-five years later, when Ludwig was King Ludwig I of Bavaria, on 18 October 1842, the opening ceremony of Walhalla took place.

Visible for miles, the striking building, shaped like a Greek temple, crowns the hill. A series of imposing broad marble stairways, 358 steps in total, lead down to the river below. Inside the temple, in one huge lofty hall ornamented with historical marble friezes, are 178 notables represented by marble busts and tablets, ranging from Otto von Bismarck and Frederick the Great to Ludwig van Beethoven, Richard Wagner, and Martin Luther, and—of course—Ludwig I of Bavaria, who is represented not merely as a bust like everyone else, but as a full seated figure.

As Cleo took my picture standing in the same spot on the broad steps in front of the templelike structure where Franz had photographed me forty-five years earlier, I suddenly had a disconcerting feeling that something was amiss. I felt sort of—naked.

And then I knew what it was. This time I was not wearing a shoulder holster and gun under my left arm!

In 1945 our CIC Headquarters in Regensburg had been set up in a small, relatively undamaged hotel on Maximilian Strasse next to a bombed-out movie theater. The ruined main railroad station was visible a few blocks away.

In 1990 the hotel was still there. At first I did not recognize the place—it had been radically remodeled—but soon I found myself standing in the little restaurant, which during the occupation had served as our main office area. The rooms upstairs had been used as interrogation rooms and our sleeping quarters. We had kept the red-and-white-check tablecloths on our work tables downstairs, thinking they looked cheerful and friendly. After the first day we took them off. Wrong message.

Here, forty-five years earlier, a man had come striding into the place, followed by a magnificent German shepherd dog that kept exactly two paces behind his master. In his forties, ramrod straight, well muscled, with penetrating pale gray eyes and close-cropped salt-and-pepper hair, the man was an imposing presence.

He marched up to my desk, made a short, almost spasmodic bow with his head, and all but clicked his heels.

"I am SS-Sturmbannführer Maximilian," he said in a clipped, sharp voice. He put his hand down along the seam of his right trousers leg and snapped his fingers. Immediately the dog leaped forward to sit at his side, fixing me unwaveringly with his alert eyes.

"That is Rolf," the man said crisply. "I am deputy chief, Gestapo, Regensburg. I wish to make a deal!"

CHAPTER 19

Unashamedly I gaped at the man. It was not every day that a mandatory arrestee—let alone a deputy chief of the Gestapo, among the most wanted on our list—came marching in to give himself up. In fact, it was unheard of.

"What do you mean—deal?" I asked, unable to keep the distaste out of my voice.

"It will be obvious to you," the major explained, as if lecturing a class of Hitler Youth recruits. "In my capacity of deputy chief of the Gestapo in this area, I possess more knowledge of people and activities than you will possibly be able to find out." He looked me straight in the eye; it was disconcerting. "I make you this proposition. I will deliver to you every day information about one of your—your *mandatory arrestees*." He showed his teeth in a quick, mirthless smile. "Such as I, myself. In exchange I will require immunity from being sent to a concen—an internment camp. Instead I will be put up in comparative luxury in town in a place of my choosing, with full maintenance for myself and Rolf, and with suitable transportation placed at my disposal. *And*—," he added with emphasis, a touch of arrogance creeping into his voice, "I will be allowed to operate without interference. That is my—deal."

It was quite a speech the major had made. I realized that his knowledge and collaboration could indeed provide a gold mine of information. He undoubtedly did know everyone in the Regensburg area who'd ever even heard the word *Nazi*. He most certainly could be more valuable to us as a stoolie than salted away in some internment camp. If! *If* he could deliver, and *if* he could be kept under control. I contemplated the man for a moment. So he didn't want to go to an internment camp. He undoubtedly had a vivid idea of what awaited him there, probably greatly exaggerated in his mind from his own observations of the Nazi concentration camps. And he undoubtedly also knew enough about investigation methods to realize that his chances of escaping us indefinitely were practically nil—now, or if he reneged on his proposed deal. No fool, this Major Maximilian.

"Wait here," I told him curtly. He inclined his head in brief acknowledgment.

I went to our files. The dossier we had on the deputy chief of Gestapo was big enough for two, but there were no major war crimes recorded. He probably would be released after an investigation and a short stay in an internment camp, an inconvenient and hardly luxurious experience but no major hardship. It was just as well he did not know that.

I walked back to him, a frown on my face. If he read it, and I'm sure he did, he showed no apprehension.

"If," I began, "if we were to agree with your—deal," I told him coldly, "let there be *no* mistake. First, your status as a mandatory arrestee remains unchanged, understood?"

The major nodded briefly.

"Second, if you fail to keep your part of the bargain—one mandatory arrestee each day—even for *one* day, you will at once be sent to an internment camp."

Again the man nodded.

"And finally, once we are finished with our work here and your usefulness has come to an end, there will be no guarantees." I looked squarely into his stony face as he confronted me unflinchingly. "However," I continued, "depending on how things work out, we shall strongly recommend leniency in your case. That is the best we can—or will—do. *Einverstanden*? Agreed?"

The major nodded. "I accept your conditions, eh—Captain. I have already selected my accommodations." He pulled a neatly folded piece of paper from his pocket and handed it to me, under the watchful eyes of Rolf. "Here is the address. I will return tomorrow with information about my first, eh—delivery and to accept assignment of a jeep for my purposes."

He drew himself smartly erect, turned abruptly, and with a short command, *"Zu Fuss!* Heel!" Gestapo Major Maximilian and his dog, Rolf, strode out of our office.

Thus began one of the strangest and most profitable collaborations of my job as a CIC agent. Every day Max and Rolf would show up at our office and hand us information, neatly written out, that would result in the arrest of someone we were looking for. And often Max was the key in cracking a tough case.

But more will always want more.

On a magnificent, secluded estate in the thick forests outside Regensburg had been located the Administrative Headquarters of the ruthless Waffen SS, the crack combat branch of the notorious Nazi Elite Corps. When U.S. troops overran the city and the estate shortly before VE Day, U.S. Intelligence operatives had made a beeline for this juicy plum, but the Waffen SS administrative staff, all records, papers, and personnel files had vanished completely. All that was left was a lone caretaker, a dour woman so close-mouthed that she wouldn't give you the time of day even if she had a wrist full of watches.

We had reason to believe that the records, which would be of immense value to Allied authorities, were still there, hidden somewhere on the huge estate. It was unlikely that the Waffen SS administration, in their haste to flee the area, had been able or willing to take the voluminous files with them. And the Nazis were always loath to destroy evidence of their "triumphs." But the whereabouts of all these invaluable documents was still a mystery. It would be quite a feather in the cap of any CIC team that could locate these vital records and clear up the enigma.

When next Max and Rolf showed up at the office, I sat him down with a cup of coffee.

"Max," I said. "You are familiar with the big estate up the river. In the forest?"

I felt him stiffen slightly, at once on the alert. *"Ja,"* he said noncommitally.

"During the last few years, what was it used for?"

A shadow seemed to cross the man's face. He shrugged. "I am not certain," he said. "It was not part of my jurisdiction. I believe the SS ran some sort of project there. Perhaps a school. Archives. I have no direct knowledge." He tried to dismiss the subject.

I looked at him with renewed respect for his cunning. He had given me just enough information. No more. No less. He had avoided the mistake of denying any knowledge of the place; that would have been unbelievable. Instead he had tried to give me an erroneous impression of the activities at the estate, belittle them, without my being able to catch him in a lie. And yet, I knew I had put him on edge. Uncharacteristically he let his coffee stand forgotten.

"We have reason to believe that certain records pertaining to the Waffen SS are buried on that estate," I informed him. "What do you know about that?"

"Nichts, nothing."

"Well, Max," I said. "I want to know about those records. If you have no information about them yourself, maybe you'd better come up with someone who does."

"I—I may not be able to do that," the major said uncomfortably.

"Oh?" I let my voice grow hard. "I was under the impression that that was exactly the kind of thing you were here to do."

"Yes, but this—"

"No *buts*, Major," I interrupted. "A *yes*—or, if you are prepared to give it, a *no*; in which case you can start packing."

Max fixed his cold, calculating eyes on me. I returned his gaze. I was well aware of being sized up. Was I really dead serious?

He looked away. He bent down and hooked a short leash onto Rolf's collar. It was something to do while his mind raced, I realized. I said nothing. Finally he looked up, his face flushed.

"It—it will take time."

"Fine," I snapped. "I'll give you two days."

He glared at me. His knuckles whitened where he clutched Rolf's leash.

"Two days," he repeated. He rose, his coffee cup still nearly full, and stalked angrily from the room.

As I looked after him, I wondered what he'd do. Take off? I doubted it. Come back and report failure? I doubted that too. Failure was a four-letter word in the major's vocabulary. What would he come up with?

Two days later to the hour, I was to find out.

Just after noon Max and Rolf appeared at our offices. With him he had a young woman who appeared to be in her early twenties. She looked terrified. She had obviously been crying; her eyes were red and puffy.

Max walked her up to my desk and pushed her down into a chair. He gave a short command to Rolf—"On guard!" At once the dog fixed his total attention on the petrified girl cowering in the chair. His lips drew back in a menacing snarl, and a low growl rumbled in his throat as he watched his charge. Max turned to me. He looked at his watch.

"Two days," he said stiffly. "As you ordered." He nodded, toward the girl. "This is Fräulein Ingeborg," he reported dispassionately. "She was for some time an office worker at the estate."

"Call your damned dog off!" I ordered. I motioned for one of the MPs on guard duty to come over. "Take that girl to one of the interrogation rooms upstairs," I told him. "Make her comfortable, but keep her there." As the MP walked off with the girl, I turned back to Max. "OK, Max," I said crisply, "what's the story? Has your Ingeborg information about the records from the estate?"

"Perhaps," the major shrugged. "She will not talk to me. But she is the only one who worked at the estate who is still in the area. Except for the caretaker." Flat-eyed, he looked at me, a hint of a sardonic smile on his lips. "But I understand that *she* already has told you all she knows."

The bastard is rubbing our noses in it, I thought. Again the Gestapo man looked at his watch. "Two days," he repeated. "I would have saved much time if you had told me that you already had questioned the caretaker," he finished reproachfully.

I chose to ignore him. For now. "I will talk to the Ingeborg girl," I said. "You will stay here. Hold yourself available. I will let you know if I need you." I was impersonal and curt. Deliberately so. I rose, turned on my heel, and walked away.

I found the MP on guard outside one of the interrogation rooms. I sent him away and walked into the room.

Ingeborg was crouched on the floor in a corner of the room, her eyes wild and wide in her ashen face, her arms tightly hugged around her drawn-up knees. She was trembling visibly. The room was typical for a small hotel: a chest of drawers with a mirror above it, a large closet, a table and two chairs that we used when interrogating a subject, and a large bed that dominated the room. Ingeborg was cringing in the corner farthest away from that bed, obviously terror-stricken.

Suddenly I knew why. Anticipation of rape, perhaps torture. I was convinced she fully expected me to rip her clothes off, hurl her onto the bed, and cruelly brutalize her. That was undoubtedly what she had been led to believe would happen to her if she were ever to fall into the hands of the *Ami* soldiers.

I knew it would be utterly useless to try to question her in this state of mind. She was on the verge of a complete nervous collapse, picturing herself as a ravaged prey. She wouldn't be able to think straight, let alone answer any questions intelligibly.

I stopped just inside the door. "Fräulein Ingeborg," I said, as gently as I could. "If you will please come with me, I'll take you downstairs to our little breakfast room. They've just made a fresh pot of coffee. *Real* coffee. You might like to have a cup." I opened the door wide and started to leave. "Please."

The girl stared at me. She stopped trembling. Slowly she rose to her feet.

"This way," I said, as I walked away.

She followed me.

The breakfast room was off the main dining area where we conducted our business. Through the open double doors I could see Max and Rolf waiting stoically at my desk. I placed Ingeborg with her back to the door so she could not see them.

As she sipped her black coffee, obviously enjoying it and quite as obviously puzzled at developments, I tried to put her at ease and be as calm and friendly as possible; gradually Ingeborg began to relax.

"Are you a native Regensburger?" I asked her conversationally.

She shook her head. "I was born in Munich," she told me. "But my parents moved to Regensburg when I was seven."

"You live with your parents?"

"With my mother. My—my father is a prisoner of war in Russia." She bit her lip.

"I'm sorry to hear that," I said. "I'm sure he'll be home soon."

She nodded. Not convinced—but hopeful. It was the wrong tack. I tried again.

"I like Regensburg," I said, comfortably leaning back in my chair. "And this little hotel is quite pleasant. Too bad the film theater next door was damaged. Did you ever go there?"

Ingeborg nodded. "Oh, yes," she said. "Many times."

"I like to go to the movies, too," I confided. "What are some of your favorite films?"

She frowned prettily in concentration. "Oh, there is *Opernball* (*Opera Ball*), with Paul Hörbiger. He is always so good. And *Schubert Serenade*, with Lilian Harvey. I loved the music." She was becoming quite animated. "And she is so wonderful."

"I've seen her," I nodded. "She *is* beautiful. I saw her in *Der Kongress Tanzt* (*The Congress Dances*)."

"Oh," she said with some astonishment. "You have seen German films?"

"Of course," I said. "Many of them. One of my favorites is *M*. With Peter Lorre."

"That is an old one," Ingeborg said. "I remember it. I was ten years old when I saw it." She gave a little laugh. "I was not supposed to. I was too young. But I sneaked in." She shuddered deliciously. "It—it was so—*schauderhaft,* so horrid." She sipped her coffee happily and smiled at me. I was no longer a menace.

It would change, I thought bleakly. Before we were done, it would change. It was time.

"How long did you work for the Waffen SS?" I suddenly asked her.

Ingeborg stiffened. Some of the old fear surged back into her eyes. But she answered.

"Almost two years."

"What did you do for them?"

"I—I was a secretary-typist. Sometimes I—I did some filing."

She sat rigidly on her chair, warily watching me.

"It must have been interesting work," I commented, trying to minimize her growing apprehension, however banal I had to be. "Tell me exactly what your duties were."

She did. She was a small cog in the scheme of things. She had indeed worked in the administration offices of the Waffen SS, but in a strictly nonsensitive capacity. She had held her job ever since she got out of the BDM, the Bund Deutscher Mädchen, the League of German Girls, the female counterpart of the Hitler Youth. She had handled logistic and administrative correspondence and filing, but she had not been involved with personnel, training, or any policy matters pertaining to the organization that occupied the estate. She knew that somewhere on the grounds of the estate there had been a school of some kind for young men, with whom she had been forbidden to fraternize. And she knew that everything had been strictly supervised by the SS. She had been dismissed when the operation had been shut down and the administration personnel had packed up and departed, shortly before the Americans arrived.

"As a typist and a file clerk you must have handled a lot of letters," I suggested. "And documents."

Ingeborg nodded.

I looked straight at her. "What happened to all those records and documents when the organization left the estate?"

The girl tensed visibly. She clutched her cup in front of her as if it were a life preserver. The fear was back.

"What was done with them?" I pressed. "You were there to the last. You must know. Tell me."

The girl stared at me. The color in her softly rounded cheeks, brought back by the hot coffee and the carefully nurtured sense of danger past, drained away as I watched.

"*Bitte,*" she pleaded pitifully. "Please. I do not know what was done with the documents. I do not know where they are. Please believe me." Tearfully she looked up at me. "Please do not hurt me," she begged. "I will do anything you ask, only—please do not hurt me! Please! I—I do not know." Tears of terror and self-pity welled up in her eyes.

Unsparingly, I persisted. "Tell me what you *do* know," I instructed her.

She shook her head slowly in frightened, silent indecision, as she felt her safety slip away. I wanted it that way.

I stood up and slowly walked over to her. I leaned down close to her, deliberately violating the private ego space she maintained around her. I let my voice take on a harsh note. "What was done with the records kept at the estate?" I demanded.

She strained away from me, pressing her body against the hard, straight back of the chair. "I—I think a lot of them were destroyed," she whispered. "Burned."

"All of them?"

"No—" She caught herself. "I do not know."

"Did *you* help dispose of any documents?"

"No."

"Did you help hide anything?"

It was a leading question. I knew it. It was a calculated risk. Like most suspects the girl was desperately anxious to find something to say that would please her interrogator. It was a common reaction. I only hoped her answers would have some truth in them and not be merely what she thought I wanted to hear. I glared at her. I waited.

"No—no—," she stammered. "I—I—Nothing." She stopped. She looked down. I knew she was lying. I slammed my hand down on the table. The girl started in shock. Her half-filled cup clattered to the table, rich brown coffee spreading in a dark stain on the tabletop. She was unaware of it, her eyes riveted in fear on me. Deliberately I walked around her, forcing her to turn with me until she had a good view of the area beyond—where Max and Rolf grimly waited. Involuntarily she shivered.

"I ask you again," I shot at her, the last vestige of my once-friendly manner now totally replaced by brusque exasperation. *"Did you help hide anything?"*

She shrank from me. "They—they made me swear not to tell." It was barely a whisper.

I drew back a little. "But you *will* tell, won't you," I said firmly.

"Please!" Her wounded eyes implored me.

"Now!"

She flinched. She sat in agonizing silence for a moment. I did not press her. Not now. Then slowly she began to talk, her voice trembling. "I—I helped the housekeeper, the caretaker. I helped her pack a large steel cabinet. From the office." Her voice broke. She gave a little sob. With difficulty she swallowed. I watched her in silence. "It—it was supposed to be buried," she finally sighed, "in the woods on the estate."

"Was it?" I could not help the excitement building in me.

"Yes."

"You know where?"

"Yes."

I straightened up. I was surprised how tense I had been. I had not been aware of how stiffly I'd carried my shoulders. I felt elated. At last!

"What was in the filing cabinet?" I asked her, unable to keep the excitement completely out of my voice. "You helped pack it. What was in it?"

The girl wet her bloodless lips. Her eyes flitted toward Max and Rolf in the other room. She looked imploringly at me. There was no reprieve. And finally the words came tumbling out.

"Silk," she said. "Silk and brocade from Paris. Silverware. Gold coins. And jewelry. Stockings. And perfume. And—but, please, nothing of it is mine. Nothing! I swear it. I only did what I was told. It all belonged to the commandant. *He* took it, when he was in Paris. Some of it was the woman's. Nothing is mine. Please! Please do not punish me. They made me swear. On my faith in the Holy Virgin. They made me swear not to tell!"

She buried her face in her hands, leaned her bare arms on the table, oblivious to the puddle of cold coffee that smeared her smooth skin. She cried softly, partly in relief, I thought, partly with fear of what was yet to come.

I looked at her. Loot! The disappointment tasted bitter in my mouth. Nothing but some damned SS officer's fucking loot! I bent down over the sobbing girl. I felt sorry for her, for what I'd had to put her through. She hadn't done anything to deserve it. I was sorry—but I had no regrets, and I had one more question to ask her.

"Ingeborg," I said quietly; "Do you know of any other place where something is buried on the estate?"

She shook her head. "No," she whispered.

I had known the answer. I believed her. Had she known anything, she would have talked.

I straightened up. It was over. I had failed. No Waffen SS documents for us. No feather in our cap. Nothing. I sighed. I watched the girl, weeping softly. So vulnerable. So miserable. Absentmindedly I stroked her hair. It felt silken. Somehow, I thought, somehow I'd make it up to her.

My eyes went beyond her to Max and Rolf, still waiting at my desk.

Rolf!

I suddenly drew myself up.

Rolf! Rolf, who had so terrified Ingeborg. I had an idea.

"Ingeborg," I said calmly. She looked up at me with tear-swollen eyes. "You have been of great help to us," I told her. "In a little while, I'll have you taken home," I assured her, "but first there's something I'd like you to do for me. Will you?"

Solemnly she nodded.

"Prima! And then we'll see if we can't round up a can of that coffee you spilled! For you and your mother."

The girl looked at me, her eyes wide. Then she lowered her head. And cried.

The following morning was gray and overcast as I drove my jeep toward the estate on the Danube outside Regensburg. I'd had a rough night. I'd spent most of it in painstaking preparations for the day, but I was so keyed up that my fatigue was forgotten. In a short while we'd find out if my efforts would pay off.

I glanced back. It was quite a convoy that followed my jeep. First came another jeep with my teammate Tom Winkler, Gestapo Major Maximilian—and Rolf. Then a 2½-ton truck crammed full of German PWs equipped with spades, shovels, and pickaxes, and bringing up the rear was a ¾-ton with six MP guards armed to the teeth, a couple of them carrying Thompson M1 submachine guns. With me rode our CO, Captain Kinsey.

We barreled through the long, tree-lined lane onto the estate and ground to a halt at the broad steps at the entrance to the manor house.

On the steps waited the taciturn caretaker flanked by two grim-looking MPs. At the foot stood a young engineer lieutenant and a small detail of men, their equipment lying on the ground before them. Good, I thought. Right on time.

I dismounted and with Tom I walked up to the bemused woman staring at us.

"Guten Morgen," I nodded curtly. "I shall come straight to the point. We are here to dig up the Waffen SS records hidden on the estate—and to give you one last chance."

She huffed in disdain: In her fifties, stocky of build, her gray hair pulled back and twisted into a tight bun at the back of her neck, she stood—feet firmly planted on the steps.

"We now have definite proof that the documents we want are, in fact, buried here," I informed her. I looked her straight in the eye, matching her scowl. "And we are convinced that *you* know where." I paused for dramatic effect. "We are giving you one last chance to show us where. If we are forced to find them without your cooperation, you will have to suffer the consequences. The *serious* consequences. It is your decision. I hope that is fully understood."

Again I paused significantly. Then I finished solemnly. "Make no mistake about it, this is your Last Chance." I gave the last two words unmistakable capital-letter importance.

I watched the woman closely. I hoped my performance had been properly impressive.

The woman returned my gaze. It was difficult to tell what she was thinking. Only one emotion showed on her stony face—contempt.

"I have nothing to say," she finally stated, her voice flat. "Nothing."

I nodded to Tom. He turned toward the MP detachment.

"Sergeant!" he called. "Dismount the prisoners!"

As the expressionless caretaker watched, the MP guards began to herd the German PWs from the truck. With shouts of *"Schnell! Schnell!"* and *"Los! Los!"* they formed the men into a column of twos, each man carrying a spade, a pick, or a shovel.

"As you can see, we have come prepared," I told the sullen caretaker and was rewarded with a look one might give a retarded five-year-old. "We will keep searching and digging," I continued, "until we find what we are looking for. And when we do . . ." I let the sentence hang and gave the woman an ominous look. Melodramatics are sometimes effective. But not this time. The woman's confident scorn did not change. She stood watching the proceedings with a slight smirk of aloofness on her face. She knew perfectly well that it would take a lifetime of digging before anything could be found on the hundreds of acres of land that made up the estate—unless the diggers knew exactly where and how deep to dig. And we did not.

I looked questioningly at her.

"I have nothing to say." She dismissed me.

I had expected it, of course. I turned toward the jeep where Max sat stiffly in the back with Rolf at his side.

"Major!" I called. "Will you please join us?"

The major dismounted. Leading Rolf on a long leash, coiled like a lasso in his hand so that the dog trotted close by his right leg, he walked over to us and faced the recalcitrant woman.

"This is Sturmbannführer Maximilian," I said importantly. I deliberately used his SS rank. "Formerly of the Gestapo." I thought I saw a brief flicker of alarm in the woman's flat eyes, but she said nothing. "The dog's name is Rolf," I went on. "He was trained by the Gestapo for a very special purpose." I lowered my voice and spoke with grave emphasis. "You see, we will not search aimlessly. We will not dig without method. Rolf will show us where to dig. He has been carefully trained by the Gestapo to smell out anything touched by human hands, even though it may have been buried for months."

I turned to the major. "Am I correct, *Herr Sturmbannführer?"*

"Ja." The Gestapo major's answer was curt and to the point.

For the first time the woman looked a little uneasy, a little uncertain. Her eyes involuntarily flitted to Rolf, who sat at Max's side fixing her with his ever-watchful eyes. Max gave a short yank on the leash, and Rolf bared his fangs and growled threateningly deep in his throat, never taking his eyes off the caretaker.

For a moment she was unnerved, but she stood her ground. Her peasant astuteness won out. I guessed that she correctly reasoned that *no* dog—Gestapo-trained or not—could possibly nose out old diggings in a fast-growing forest. I could almost see her smell the bluff. A thin, mocking smile played on her lips.

"Let the dog show you then," she said. "I cannot."

"Remember," I said. "It was *your* choice." I turned from her. "Ready to move out!" I called.

It was an impressive procession that lined up on the grounds before the manor house. At the head stood Major Maximilian holding the eagerly straining Rolf on a tight leash. Behind them was the column of PWs shouldering their spades, shovels, and picks, and guarded by the MPs. And bringing up the rear were Captain Kinsey and the engineer lieutenant with his detail of men carrying axes, ropes, pulleys, and hoisting equipment.

The woman took it all in. The open derision on her face had given way to a look of bemused uneasiness. But the set of her jaw was still stubborn and firm. I turned to her.

"Well?" I asked. "Have you anything to say?"

She did not answer. Stony-faced, she stared straight ahead.

I turned to the two MPs flanking her. "Bring her along," I ordered.

Tom and I, followed by the caretaker and her guards, marched to the head of the column. Tom grinned at me. "Curtain, Act One," he said sotto voce. "Let the play begin!"

We took up positions directly behind Max and Rolf. Max looked questioningly at me.

"Los!" I signaled. "Let's go!"

At once the major dropped the coiled leash from his hand, holding on only to the looped handle, giving Rolf full run. *"Such, Rolf!"* he commanded urgently. *"Such! Such!* Search! Search!"

With a yelp of excitement, nose to the ground, Rolf took off. Zigzagging, he searched and sniffed the ground before them in ever-widening loops. Suddenly he let out an eager bark, and tugging at the leash, he pulled his master toward the forest a short distance away.

Falling in behind Max and Rolf came Tom and I, the caretaker and her two guards, the column of German PWs and their MP guards, the engineer lieutenant and his detail of men, and Captain Kinsey—all of us half-trotting to keep up with the straining dog.

Through the woods wound the whole conglomerate procession, following the zigzag track of the dog. Deeper and deeper in among the trees and brush went the chase. From time to time Rolf would yelp as he pulled on his leash in an effort to leap ahead.

I gave the woman a quick glance. She seemed less sure of herself as we went on.

We were about four hundred feet into the woods when Rolf suddenly reared and barked sharply.

The major released him, and at once he streaked away. But only a short distance. At the edge of a small clearing he stopped. Furiously he began to scratch and claw at the ground.

Max ran to his dog. Clipping the leash back on, he held him back.

The caretaker had stopped dead in her tracks. She stood stock-still, rooted to the ground, staring with disbelief at the excited dog, her face drawn and deadly pale, her eyes wide in incredulous shock.

I took her firmly by the arm. Like an automaton she walked with me, never taking her eyes off the dog. I led her to the spot that showed the scratch and claw marks of the Gestapo dog. I turned to the dazed woman.

"Is there anything buried here?" I asked her sharply.

She did not hear me.

I stepped in front her, between her and Rolf. "Answer me!"

She shook her head. Whether in defiance or incredulity I couldn't tell. I grabbed a spade from one of the PWs and shoved it at her.

"Dig!"

She made no move. No sound. Her glazed eyes were riveted on the dog.

Rolf crouched before her as she stood—spade in hand—on the spot where he'd been clawing. Snarling and growling dangerously, he never took his eyes from her. Only the sturdy leash held by Max kept him in check.

"Dig!" I commanded. "Or are you afraid of what we'll find?"

The woman stood motionless, mesmerized, staring at the menacing dog as if she were looking at the devil himself.

I turned to Tom. "Tell the prisoners to start digging," I said loudly.

I looked at the caretaker. "You have made your choice," I said coldly. "You will now have to pay for it."

She shivered abruptly. She tore her gaze from Rolf. She grabbed my arm. "Wait!" she cried. "Wait!" She was obviously deeply shaken. Her eyes darted about in panic as if everything around her were unreal. She settled them on me, perhaps at that moment the only reality in her world.

"Der Hund hat rechts," she murmured. "The dog is right."

I stuck my face close to hers. Razor-eyed, I glared at her, holding her. I shot my questions at her like staccato bursts from a machine gun.

"There *is* something buried here?"

"Yes."

"There are other burial places?"

"Yes."

"You will show us where?"

She seemed to sag a little. Her ruddy complexion had gone sickly gray, her defiant eyes lackluster. She looked thoroughly cowed.

"Yes," she whispered hoarsely.

I took a deep breath. I needed to.

"How many other places are there?"

"Most of the papers were burned. Only the important ones were saved."

"How many other places are there?" I insisted.

"Twelve," she said tonelessly. "No. Thirteen. Thirteen."

"And you will take us to them?"

"Yes." She was barely audible.

And she did. Thirteen more places. For two days our PWs were busy digging up chests and boxes containing the entire records of the Waffen SS—personnel files; war activities and casualty losses; lists of foreign nationals pressed into service; the corps' proud achievements, some of which qualified as war crimes; and innumerable other documentation that made it possible for the American military authorities to compile complete and accurate data on the notorious Waffen SS, a treasure trove of information for the Nürnberg war crimes trials to come.

On our way back to Regensburg, Max and Rolf rode with Tom and me. Rolf had played his part like a trouper, even to the gratuitous defense of his "find." It was just as well the caretaker had not dug where we told her to. Had she done so, a foot down she would have unearthed the long, arm-thick Bavarian sausage I had buried there, after having spent half the night dragging it all over the estate, laying a trail for Rolf to follow leading to the only place where we *knew* from Ingeborg that something had been buried. The commandant's loot, the only place Rolf could possibly have found. But even though Rolf had merely followed the scent of a spicy, strong-smelling sausage, the dog had turned in an Academy Award performance.

The last hoard we dug up was the steel cabinet with the commandant's loot. We insisted that the caretaker be present. The look on her face when she saw the sausage and finally realized she'd been had was worth the price of admission.

The case of Gestapo Major Maximilian had an ironic ending. Shortly after we retrieved the Waffen SS records, Max had an accident with the jeep he was driving. It overturned, rolled over on him, and crushed his pelvis. He would spend the rest of his life as a pain-ridden invalid unable to walk.

Rolf escaped unhurt.

Our hotel headquarters was the site of other more pleasant visitors—an occasional Allied or U.S. intelligence officer, and once a most wonderful woman. She had been offered quarters in the swank accommodations of the grand luxury hotel, Park Hotel Maximilian Hof, which served as billet for high-ranking officers, but she had chosen to stay with us. She was with us for about a week.

Every morning when at the crack of dawn we came down for breakfast, she would greet us with a cup of steaming hot, fresh coffee and a radiant smile. She was fascinated by our work, and as she was born in Berlin, Germany, she spoke the language fluently. She sat in on several interrogations and often contributed perceptive questions. We even let her conduct a few preliminary routine interrogations—and she was good at it.

She always looked gorgeous, and I'm sure every one of the guys fell in love with her. I know I did. Her name was Marlene Dietrich.

It was not the first time Miss Dietrich had spent time with the XII Corps; she had been entertaining the troops in Europe both during and after the war. XII Corps history recounts an incident that took place in Pont-à-Mousson, some twelve miles north of Nancy, France, on 29 October 1944, when Miss Dietrich was performing for the 80th Infantry Division.

A short while after the show had gotten under way, German artillery began to come over. After a few minutes, Miss Dietrich turned to the audience and said, "The Nazis know I am here, and they don't like me. I'm sure they are shooting at me! Maybe we'd better cut this a little short before they find me!"

The show was cut by about ten minutes, during which time the artillery fire grew heavier—and came closer. The crew had barely gotten the piano and sound equipment out of the building when a direct hit demolished it—stage and all.

Every case in which I had been involved had begun in its own distinctive way—an unexplained shot fired in the forest, a florid tip from a former concentration camp inmate, a Gestapo officer looking for a good deal—but none was launched in a more melodramatic way than the case that would take us to a small village called Saint Johannsburg in the vicinity of Regensburg.

It began on a cloudy Friday morning. I was sitting with Capt. Benjamin Kinsey, CO of CIC Detachment 212, in the oak-paneled dining room in the hotel we'd taken over as our CIC Headquarters, finishing my morning coffee, when the telephone rang.

"Answer it, please," Ben said, biting into a fresh *Brötchen*, a warm roll, heaped with butter.

A soft female voice speaking English with an unmistakable German accent purred into my ear.

"Count your soldiers, *Ami*," the voice breathed seductively. "If you find that you are one short, you will find him lying near the road to Saint Johannsburg. Dead."

And with a click the tantalizing informer was beyond tracing, but she triggered a case that was to become one of the most unusual I had yet investigated.

My final case as a CIC agent.

CHAPTER 20

Saint Johannsburg was a small village about half an hour's drive from Regensburg. Franz Vidor, with whom I had worked before, joined me on the case, and within the hour we were in our jeep barreling down the forest-lined dirt road off the main Regensburg-Straubing highway that led to Saint Johannsburg.

I was driving. We could already see the village ahead of us when Franz suddenly sang out, "Hold it! Stop!"

I stomped on the brake, and the jeep skidded to a halt.

"Back up," Franz said. He pointed to the side of the road. "Bingo!" he called.

In the middle of a small clearing a few yards off the little-traveled road, we saw a large bundle wrapped in a soiled yellow tarpaulin. Next to it, hammered at an angle into the ground, stood a neat little wooden cross painted white. It puzzled us. Who had placed it there? The owner of the seductive voice on the telephone?

We dismounted and walked over to the tarpaulin bundle.

"Give me a hand," I said. "Let's see what we've got."

Together we carefully unwrapped the bundle.

The sight that met our eyes was horrible. I had seen a lot in the months of war behind me, but what I looked at now almost made me sick.

It was, or rather had been, an American soldier. He was dressed in field uniform except for his boots, which for some reason had been removed. We judged him to have been dead three or four days. The cause of death was easily established—a deep cut on the left side of his neck had severed his jugular vein. His uniform was blackish red with dried blood, and around his left arm a length of rope had been tied. But it was his face that held us fascinated with horror and revulsion.

It was not there.

Someone had carefully and methodically obliterated it—beaten it into a sickening, unrecognizable mass of raw flesh. There was absolutely nothing left that by the wildest stretch of imagination could be called a face, nothing but shapeless, crusted gore.

I looked at Franz. His face was ashen. I knew he was fighting to keep down the bile that rose in his throat. I was.

"The bastards," Franz muttered. "The fucking goddamned bastards!"

Automatically I nodded. Werewolves? I thought.

"Let's—let's find out who he is," I said. I hardly recognized my own voice.

Struggling to overcome our queasiness, and just barely succeeding, we systematically searched the body. When we were finished, we looked at each other. There was no need for words. We both knew why the GI had no face.

Someone had desperately wanted to conceal the identity of the corpse. It had been stripped of all identification—dog tags, wallet, papers; the pockets were empty. The shoulder patch, even the rank insignia, had been ripped from the uniform sleeve. We realized why the boots were missing: the victim's name or serial number must have been stamped or inked into the leather. His fingertips had been slashed—to obliterate his prints.

I watched Franz. He stood staring at the faceless GI, rubbing his hands along the sides of his pants, rubbing and rubbing, unaware of doing it, a frown on his face. I knew what that frown meant. I felt it too.

Something did not fit.

I looked around the little clearing. It was littered with trash. There might be something there that would give us a clue, I thought. At my feet lay a torn piece of newspaper. Not German. American. I picked it up. It was from a small-town Ohio tabloid dated 15 March 1945. Local news. Big help.

"There's a lot of junk lying around," I said to Franz. "Let's take a look at it." I pointed toward the little white cross. "Pile it over there. Perhaps—perhaps we can find some kind of lead—or something," I finished lamely.

Several minutes later we examined our hoard. A bunch of protective bottle sleeves made of straw; a U.S. Army field ration wrapper and a couple of empty OD C-Ration cans, one Ham and Lima Beans, one Pork and Beans; two soiled rags apparently torn from a woman's dress; two pieces of blue chalk; a length of tangled string; a broken wine bottle of recent vintage; a chewing gum wrapper; an empty, crumbled Lucky Strike cigarette pack and a few butts; and lying near the cross a large stone probably used to hammer the cross into the ground.

We looked at it. It was just a pile of rubbish. It meant nothing to us whatsoever.

The nagging feeling I had that something was seriously out of kilter would not leave me. I finally figured out what it was. Why would some vengeful German want to conceal the identity of his victim? I could think of no obvious reason. Was there a hidden one? If so, what? It made no sense.

Franz was gazing at the pile of trash. "Not much to go on," he observed.

I agreed. I looked toward Saint Johannsburg. "Let's see what they know in the village," I suggested.

"Why not?" Franz shrugged. "But I wouldn't count on anything. If they run true to form, they won't even tell you whether it's night or day."

"Gotta try," I said. "Somewhere along the line we might push the right button."

We covered the body with the tarp, mounted our jeep, and started for Saint Johannsburg a few hundred yards up the road.

Saint Johannsburg consisted of perhaps two dozen farms. The closest farmhouse had a direct view of the clearing with the cross, and we decided to begin our investigation there. If anyone in Saint Johannsburg had seen anything, the people on that farm might be the ones.

A huge, burly man with a weather-beaten, stubble-grown face, close-cropped graying hair, and fists the size of small hams was cutting and stacking wood near a ramshackle shed. He stopped his work and looked up, fixing us with a hostile glare as we drove into the farmyard.

Franz jumped smartly from the jeep and purposefully strode up to the farmer.

"Is this your farm?" he asked crisply.

The big man nodded.

I got out of the jeep and watched Franz question the sullen farmer. Franz had it down pat. If you acted with strength, self-confidence, and authority the Germans would accept that authority—that's what they were used to. But if you showed the slightest uncertainty or apprehension—watch out!

"There is the body of a dead American soldier lying at the road a short distance from here," Franz stated abruptly. "Do you know about it?"

The German was unfazed. "Yes," he said, an almost imperceptible tone of mockery in his voice. "And so does everyone else in Saint Johannsburg."

"Why did you not inform the American authorities?" Franz asked angrily. "There has been a Military Government office in Straubing for weeks."

The farmer shrugged indifferently. "We thought it none of our business," he said. "We are farmers here. Not soldiers, not policemen. Just farmers."

I could see the anger build in Franz, but he controlled it.

"How long has the body been there?" he asked.

"Three—four days," the man answered. He rubbed his nose with the back of his dirty fist. He nodded. "Yes. Three days it was."

"Three days!" Franz exploded. "And nobody reported it? What the hell did you think was going on?"

The German looked at him. Again he shrugged elaborately. "We thought surely the Americans knew," he explained.

Franz glared at the man. I knew he wanted to deck him. "Who else lives here?" I asked.

The farmer slowly shifted his gaze to me.

"My daughter," he said curtly. A sudden glint of hate flared briefly in his eyes. He looked down. "My wife was killed," he said. "In Regensburg. She had gone there to buy some clothing for us. It was an *Ami* air raid." He looked up, locking his cold eyes onto mine. "Neither of my two sons have yet returned from the war," he finished.

"Where is your daughter?"

"In the house. It will soon be time to eat." A sardonic smile suddenly split his face, moving only the upper lip and showing yellowed teeth behind it. "You should talk to her, *Herr Offizier,*" he smirked, "not to me. She saw what happened."

"What did happen?"

The farmer's shoulders once again heaved in one of his expressive shrugs. "She will tell you."

"Very well," I said. I pointed toward the house. "Move!"

The *Bauernstube* of the farmhouse was large and quite pleasant. Blue-and-white checked curtains at the windows; a large, sturdy wooden table with chairs and benches around it; a gaily painted cupboard; and the inevitable big, black wood-burning stove on which a pot of *Weisswürste*—the delectable Bavarian sausages—and another with potatoes were simmering. The warm air in the room smelled delicious. We were in no mood to enjoy it, however.

The farmer's daughter, a pleasingly plump blonde in her late teens, sat stiffly next to her father on a wooden bench against the wall, watching us fearfully.

"Okay," I said to her. "Start talking. What did you see?"

The girl stared at me with wide, frightened eyes. Instinctively she moved closer to her father.

"From the beginning," I said, softening my voice. No use scaring the girl into silence. "Just tell me the whole story." I pulled over a chair in front of her and sat down, leaning my elbows on the back of the chair, my eyes on her level, no longer looming over her. She seemed to relax a little.

"It—it was three days ago," she began timidly. "Early in the morning. I—I saw them from my window. I saw them throw the bundle next to the road." She stopped. Something was frightening her other than the questioning. What?

"Go on," I said kindly. "Who threw the bundle in the clearing? Did you get a good look at them?"

"They—they were far away," she said evasively.

"But you did see them?"

"Yes." It was more a sigh.

"Do you know who they were?"

In silence the girl nodded, her eyes uneasy.

"Who? Who were they?"

"They were—" her voice was barely a whisper. "They were—American soldiers."

I more felt than heard Franz sharply draw in his breath. My mind whirled. What did we have here?

"How do you know they were Americans?" I asked sharply.

The girl cringed. "They—they wore *Ami* uniforms."

I was aware of the smirk on the farmer's face as he sat next to his daughter. The bastard! He'd known, of course. I ignored him. I certainly was not going to give him the satisfaction.

My mind raced. I exchanged a quick glance with Franz. It was the wrong thing to do—it might signal our distress at hearing the girl's report—but I could not help it. Franz looked grim.

American uniforms! Was the girl telling us the truth? My hunch told me that she was, and I had long since learned to trust my hunches. Had they been enemy saboteurs in American uniforms? Like those Skorzeny jeep parties during the Bulge? Werewolves? Or had the men actually been Americans? Bleakly I knew it could have been the case. It was what had been bothering me. The whole thing wasn't consistent with a German strike. I looked at the apprehensive girl. She shrank against the wall. She had just told us that we, the *Amis*, were ourselves responsible for the atrocity in the clearing at the road, and now she was petrified, wondering what we'd do. I did not want to frighten her even further, but there was much I wanted to learn from her.

"How did the—how did they get the body, the bundle, there?" I asked as calmly as I could.

"They came by truck," the girl answered. "I heard it. Not many *Ami* trucks come to Saint Johannsburg, so I—I watched."

"Can you describe the truck?"

She nodded. Soberly I listened. From her description it was an Army ¾-ton. The description was unmistakable.

"What did they do?" I asked.

"The two soldiers opened the canvas in the back of the truck and pulled out the bundle. They threw it in the clearing. And then the others came out."

I stared at her. "Others? What others?"

"The girls."

"Girls? What girls?"

"There were two girls riding in the truck with the soldiers," she explained. "They came out."

This was a totally new wrinkle. Four of them. Two men. Americans? Germans? And two girls. How the hell were the girls involved? I could think of a million ways, but I had no immediate answer.

"There is a number painted in white along the hood of the truck," I said to the girl. "Did you see it?"

She nodded.

"Do you remember it?"

She shook her head. "I could not read it. Only the big white star."

"Did you see anything else?"

"No." She stopped. "Only—"

"Only what?"

"Only some boxes. Stacked in the back of the truck. I saw them when they took the—the bundle out of there."

"What kind of boxes?" I asked her.

The girl described them. The boxes could easily have been U.S. Class 1 supplies. Rations cartons. Dammit! It looked more and more as if this was not a CIC case at all but a case for the CID, the Criminal Investigation Detachment. Not our ballpark.

I had a good idea of what had happened. Three guys on the make and two willing Fräuleins; in this case five obviously made a crowd. A fight with a result that became a little too permanent—and a frantic attempt to conceal the crime by destroying the identity of the victim and putting the blame on the Krauts. If that wasn't the exact scenario, it would do till a better one came along. So far the scheme was certainly successful. We had not the slightest clue where to begin.

I contemplated the girl sitting tensely before me. I felt uneasy about her. That persistent hunch, that itchy feeling at the edge of the mind that something was being missed, was working overtime. What else did the girl know? What questions should I ask her to find out? I had no idea. I looked at Franz. He seemed to be adrift in the same boat.

Hell, we couldn't just drop the damned case. We had become involved. We were there. We might as well find out what we could. It *was* our job. Or was it? Of course, we could turn the case over to the CID; ultimately we'd have to anyway. Should we do it now? Bail out? Or follow through? Mentally I sighed. What the hell, we'd give it a shot. I admitted to myself that I was hooked. I wanted to know what had happened.

I turned to the girl. "What happened after the men"—I couldn't get myself to say Americans, not yet—"after the men put the body in the clearing?" I asked.

"They drove away."

"With the girls?"

"No, the girls walked back. The way they had come."

Figured, I thought; trouble—drop the broads.

"How did you know the bundle contained a—a corpse?" I asked the girl.

"I—we did not know," she said. She glanced at her father. "My father went to look. He told us."

"What do you know about all the trash lying in the clearing?"

It was the farmer who answered. "The *Amis*," he said, making the slightly derogatory word sound like an insult. "The *Amis* threw it there. When they first came to Saint Johannsburg. Many weeks ago."

So much for our Sherlock Holmes clues, I thought.

"And the cross?" I asked. "The white cross. Did you put that up?"

The man shook his head. "I would not do such a thing," he declared. Unsaid was the obvious "for an *Ami*."

Out of the corner of my eye I watched the girl. Did she suddenly look guilty? Had she put up the cross—without her father's knowledge? I decided to find out. Later.

"How long?" the farmer asked plaintively. "How long must we sit here? We have chores to do. A farm does not run itself."

"We're through with you," I said. "For now. Do your chores, but don't leave the farm. Either of you."

The farmer grunted. Whether in consent or displeasure I didn't know. And didn't care.

Before we did any further investigation or tried to find someone else in Saint Johannsburg who might know something, we made a quick run to the nearby town of Straubing and arranged for a graves registration crew to pick up the body of the dead GI in the clearing. We owed him that much. We returned to Saint Johannsburg with them and watched them load the grisly bundle into the ambulance and drive off.

Once again we stood in the now strangely empty clearing.

The white, wooden cross had been knocked askew. I was bothered by that cross. Who had put it there? The girl? Someone else? Who? I had the feeling that if we could find out, a big piece of the puzzle would fall into place.

We examined the road shoulder. We weren't really sure what we were looking for. Tire marks? Boot prints, other than the ones we and the graves registration boys had made? We found nothing.

I looked around at the surrounding woods. The underbrush was quite dense except in a spot just across the road from the clearing. There, about fifty feet away, a forest meadow could be seen through the trees.

A narrow path winding from the road through the underbrush led to it. I walked toward the meadow. Franz followed me. As I neared the open field I noticed animal tracks in the dirt. Small hoofs. And little hard, brown pellets scattered about. Goats.

Suddenly Franz called to me. "Hey! Look at this!"

Just off the path a few feet from the road Franz was squatting, looking at something on the ground. I walked up to him. Wordlessly he pointed to the ground.

There, scratched in the dirt, was a bizarre, strangely disturbing design. It could be the head of a bull or a goat, grotesquely, repulsively distorted. Or it could be the evil face of a devil, with fangs and horns and tufted ears.

I crouched down next to Franz and looked toward the clearing across the road. Although I was hidden by the underbrush I could clearly see the little white cross.

"Mean anything to you?" Franz asked.

I studied the repugnant image in the dirt. "The sketch itself doesn't mean a damned thing to me," I answered slowly. "But the fact that it is there sure does."

"Yeah," Franz mused. "Who drew it? But more important, *when?*"

I stood up and looked toward the clearing. "The body was lying there for three days," I thought aloud. "Since early Tuesday morning. We know that. It rained Monday, well into the night, so whoever drew that whatever-it-is must have done it after that, or it would have been washed away." I looked at Franz. "That means that whoever drew the thing must have seen the bundle with the body."

Franz looked down at the ugly devil's face scratched in the dirt. "I wonder what he was watching when he drew that damned thing," he said.

"If anything."

"If anything," Franz repeated thoughtfully. "Perhaps he's also the joker who put up the cross."

"Could be," I agreed. "He—or she. I think it's about time we had another little chat with our friendly neighborhood farmer and his daughter."

Once again the four of us were seated in the *Bauernstube*. The farmer and his daughter had had their meal; the big pots had been put away. Once again the farmer sat glowering at us, his daughter perched uneasily beside him.

"I ask you again," Franz barked at them, "who put up that cross in the clearing?"

The girl glanced quickly at her father, but neither answered.

"You!" Franz shot at the girl. "You know?"

Fearfully she shook her head.

"Who tends the goats around here?" I suddenly asked.

Involuntarily the girl drew in her breath. Her father gave her a quick angry glance. Then he looked straight ahead, sitting stonily on the bench.

I fixed my eyes on the girl. "Well?"

"Szarvas," the girl whispered.

Her father shot her a murderous look. I was surprised at the icy depth I saw in his eyes. His daughter avoided looking at him.

"Who is—Szarvas?"

"Szarvas is of no account!" It was the farmer. "He is Hungarian," he continued contemptuously, "not German. He does not even speak German well."

"What is his full name?"

The farmer shrugged churlishly.

"Is it his first name or his family name?" I persisted.

"It is not a name," the farmer grumbled. "It is the name we call him. It is the name of the town from which he came. It is the only thing he talks about. We do not know his name."

"Where is this Szarvas now?"

"Where he is supposed to be, I am certain. With the goats. In the field."

"Where?"

The farmer shrugged indifferently. "They are not my goats," he said. "I have none. Although Szarvas often lets them graze on my land," he said, his voice dripping with venom.

I turned to the girl. "Do you know where?"

She nodded, keeping her eyes averted from her father. "I believe so. It is today he tends the goats for the farmer Ziegler."

Her father gave a snort of disdain.

I gestured toward Franz. "You will go with the officer and bring Szarvas back here, understood?"

She nodded.

"I will not have Szarvas in my house," the farmer exclaimed heatedly. "He is nothing but a—a Hungarian *Gauner*, a Hungarian scoundrel and a liar! A good-for-nothing! He was in a *KZ Lager*—a concentration camp. For undesirables. Mauthausen he says it was called. He is not to be trusted. I will not have him set foot in my house!" *Ptui!* he made a spitting sound.

"That's too bad," I said icily. "*I* want him here, and he *will* be here. Is that understood?"

"Szarvas," the farmer said venomously, "is a *Trottel*, an imbecile!"

Suddenly the girl turned to her father, eyes ablaze. "No, *Vati,* he is not!" she exclaimed with unexpected fervor. "He is a kind man. A gentle man. He has had very bad times, but he is not an imbecile. I know you think he deliberately let the goats ruin your crop last year, but it was not his fault."

The farmer stared at his daughter, his mouth half open. It was obvious that she had never talked to him that way before. She met his gaze, eyes flashing, bosom heaving, and cheeks flushed. It was open rebellion. What had we wrought? With amusement I watched the family showdown unfold.

"I know you have forbidden me to speak his name in your house," the girl went on. "But it is *my* house, too, and you are wrong! You must not speak ill of Szarvas to the *Amis*. You will get him in trouble again, and that is unjust." She turned to me. It was amazing how attractive her anger and fervor made her.

"Once he was a great artist," she told me. "In Budapest. But he was not—not like other men, and things went bad for him. He was sent to a—a camp. It made him old. And it is—difficult for him to express himself now. But he has not forgotten. He is not an imbecile. He still draws. Often. And sometimes beautifully." She turned to her father, almost pleadingly. "You must not tell the *Amis* he is a bad man, *Vati*. He is not."

I stared at her. Szarvas. A goatherd. An artist making drawings. Often. Here was the creator of the devil in the dirt.

Franz and the girl left and returned twenty minutes later with the enigmatic goatherd.

Szarvas was a middle-aged man, small of stature, with graying, thinning hair and deep-set eyes that looked too large for his narrow, heavily furrowed face. He looked years older than his actual age, the result of his stay in Mauthausen, I thought, as a "pink"* (homosexual) prisoner in one of the most notorious concentration camps. His long, slender fingers toyed with the cigarette Franz had given him to win his confidence. Szarvas had taken the cigarette, but he had not yet lighted it. His German was halting and limited to words strung together without structure, and he obviously found it difficult to communicate—another legacy of his time in Mauthausen, no doubt. He seemed to take comfort in the presence of the girl, so we let her stay close to him. I finally pieced together his story.

Szarvas had indeed put up the cross for the dead American. He had made it from staves broken from a white picket fence at the garden at the Ziegler farm. He had been resting in the woods after having taken the goats to the meadow—it had been last Tuesday morning—when he saw the truck pull up and the soldiers unload the bundle. After they left, curiosity had gotten the better of him, and he had looked to see what was in the bundle. He had been sad—and he had made the cross.

I made him repeat his story, over and over, in an attempt to catch him in a contradiction. He made none. I was convinced he was telling the truth.

We had found an eyewitness.

From what Szarvas told us, and from what the girl had told us earlier, I now had the whole story.

Tuesday morning at about 0715 hours an American ¾-ton truck, covered, drove up to the clearing on the road to Saint Johannsburg. Two soldiers, in field jackets and without leggings, and two civilian girls dismounted. All of them helped unload a large tarpaulin-wrapped bundle from the rear of the truck. In the back of the truck were eight to ten large cardboard boxes fitting the description of ten-in-one U.S. rations. As soon as they had dumped their burden, the soldiers drove off in the direction of the Regensburg-Straubing highway, and shortly thereafter the girls walked away in the same direction. According to

*Concentration camp inmates wore triangular cloth patches of different colors to denote their category. Jews, the only ones to wear two patches, forming a star of David, wore *yellow*; political prisoners wore *red*; asocials and criminals, *green*; homosexuals, *pink*; Jehovah's Witnesses, *purple*. Unauthorized emigrants who had been caught wore *black*. The gypsies had no special color.

Szarvas's description of the two soldiers, one had worn the two stripes of a corporal; the other had no stripes.

Szarvas may have had difficulties communicating, but like a true artist his powers of observation were keen.

It seemed to be pretty much as I had thought. Three guys, two girls, a quarrel, a fight—and then two frantic GIs with a corpse on their hands and murder on their souls. Then the decision to dispose of the body quickly and far from his home grounds, and finally the removal of all identifying marks and the complete mutilation of the face and fingertips so that when the body was found it could not be recognized.

It fit. There was no doubt about it. It was a case for the CID, not for us. Dammit!

I looked at the Hungarian goatherd, still fidgeting with his unlit cigarette. Too damned bad. We had a bona fide eyewitness, and a good one, one who could unerringly pick out the murderers from any lineup. Hitch was—we had no lineup. We couldn't very well parade the whole U.S. Army before him.

Suddenly I sat bolt upright.

Of course! We *did* have a lineup. An unusual one, but a lineup nevertheless.

Quickly I turned to the girl. "I need some paper," I said urgently. "And a pencil. Can you get it for me?"

She nodded, puzzled, and hurried off. Presently she returned with pencil and paper.

For the next several minutes I was busy imitating Szarvas, the artist. When I was finished I had a series of twelve U.S. Army shoulder patches from units in the area—from the big *A* in the red circle of Third Army and the windmill of XII Corps to the 2d Cavalry Group—with a couple of imaginary patches thrown in for good measure.

I looked at Szarvas.

"Did the American soldiers wear patches?" I asked him. I touched my left shoulder. "Here," I said. "Shoulder patches? Pictures?"

Szarvas looked puzzled. He touched his own shoulder, uncomprehendingly. Suddenly he broke into a big grin. Eagerly he nodded. "Yes," he said. "Yes, yes, yes! Pictures. Much colors! Each man wear. Same."

I showed him the series of patches I had drawn. "Pick it out," I told him. "Which one?"

Szarvas's eyes searched the line of amateurishly drawn shoulder patches. Suddenly he jabbed a grimy finger at one of them. "That!" he cried. He put his hand on his left shoulder. "I see," he said. "I see!"

It was the shoulder patch of a small unit stationed in the Corps area.

With the leads we were able to give the CID, the case was quickly solved. All they had to do was locate a corporal and a private from a certain known unit stationed near Straubing who in the morning of a certain Tuesday in July, driving a ¾-ton truck, had been drawing rations for a small number of men. It was a mere matter of looking it up in the Orderly Room Detail Report of the outfit.

A few days later Captain Kinsey told me that the CID had conveyed their congratulations to our unit. They had got the two men, and one of them had confessed. It had happened pretty much as we'd figured. That rope around his arm, incidentally, was meant to make it look as if the poor bastard had been tied up and kept prisoner. Cute touch.

It had been an unusual and challenging case. I felt I'd come a long way since almost twelve months earlier when I had stood staring at a little old man with the runs, standing with his hands in the air and his pants bunched around his spindly legs. I felt we'd become professionals.

Shortly after the case of the GI without a face had been concluded, I was slated for my discharge, and following a brief stay in Camp Top Hat in Antwerp, Belgium, on 20 November 1945 I boarded the SS *Emma Willard* bound for New York.

Halfway there, I was convinced I wouldn't make it! We ran into a violent storm that lasted for days. Part of the ship's gear was lost; some of the passageways were awash; and a crack developed in the deck, so I thought we'd break in two. When the storm subsided we found that we were two hundred miles *south* of the Azores.

The trip home took sixteen days, but on 11 December I walked out of Fort Dix, New Jersey, with a brand-new "ruptured duck,"* in the lapel of my Eisenhower jacket.

I was once again a civilian.

*Nickname for the little pin given U.S. servicemen upon discharge.

AUTHOR'S NOTES

The foregoing account of my experiences in the ETO during World War II are based not only on my own recollections but also on certain documentation I was able to retain, such as XII Corps, G-2 Periodic Reports and copies of several cases submitted to headquarters MIS, ETOUSA in May of 1945, as well as copious notes and sketches set down immediately following my return to the United States in December 1945.

Dates, names, places, and historical facts and events were checked against such books as *XII Corps, Spearhead of Patton's Third Army*, by Lt. Col. George Dyer (The XII Corps History Association, 1947), *Patton*, by Maj. Gen. H. Essame (Charles Scribner's Sons, 1974), *A General's Life*, by Gen. Omar N. Bradley (Simon & Schuster, 1983), *Crusade in Europe,* by Gen. Dwight D. Eisenhower (Doubleday, 1948), as well as other historical reference books.

The dialogue is, of course, not verbatim, but it is factual and authentic in substance, meaning, and tone, and the action closely follows actual events.

Some of the cases related here in detail were reported in a different form immediately after the war in a couple of men's magazines in existence at the time or used in a fictional format in my early novels.

The journey in 1990 retracing the war route is based on day-by-day tapes made during the trip, on extensive photographic material, newspaper reports, and written notes.

ABOUT THE AUTHOR

Ib Melchior, a best-selling author, is also a motion picture and television writer-director-producer.

He was born and educated in Denmark, majored in literature and languages, and earned the degree of Cand. Phil. from the University of Copenhagen. He then joined as an actor a British theatrical company, The English Players, and toured Europe with this troupe, becoming stage manager and codirector of the company. Prior to the outbreak of World War II in Europe, he came to the United States with this company to do a show on Broadway.

He remained in the States when the company returned to Europe and joined the stage-managing department of Radio City Music Hall and the Center Theater Ice Show in New York. When Pearl Harbor was attacked, he volunteered his services to the U.S. armed forces. He served with the "cloak-and-dagger" OSS for a while, and when his area of operation was assigned to the British, he was transferred to the U.S. Military Intelligence Service. He spent two years in the European Theater of Operations as a military intelligence investigator attached to the Counter Intelligence Corps. For his work in the ETO he was decorated by the United States Army as well as by the king of Denmark, and was subsequently awarded the Knight Commander Cross of the Militant Order of Saint Brigitte of Sweden. He was also honored with the Medal of Merit by the venerable veterans' organization Old Guard, City of Philadelphia, in which organization he holds the rank of brigadier general.

After the war he became active in television and also began his writing career. He has directed over five hundred TV shows, from the musical "The Perry Como Show" to the dramatic documentary series *The March of Medicine.* Melchior has won several national awards for TV and documentary film short subjects that he wrote, directed, and produced, and he has written scripts for various TV series, including "Men into Space" and "The Outer Limits." He has also served as a director or in a production capacity on eight motion picture features including *The Time Travelers,* which he directed and for which he also wrote the original screenplay. In 1976 he was awarded the Golden Scroll for Best Writing by the Academy of Science Fiction.

Ib Melchior is the author of over a dozen best-selling, critically acclaimed novels based on his own experiences as a CIC agent in World War II. His novels are now published in twenty-five countries. His stories and articles have appeared in American and European magazines and anthologies. He has also written stage plays. For *Hour of Vengeance,* a dramatization of the ancient Amleth legend that was the original source for Shakespeare's *Hamlet,* he was honored with the Shakespeare Society of America's Hamlet Award for Excellence in Playwriting in 1982. He has also translated and narrated a cassette album of stories of Hans Christian Andersen.

Melchior is an avid collector of military miniatures and historical documents. He is the son of the late Wagnerian tenor, Lauritz Melchior.

His wife, Cleo, whose professional name is Cleo Baldon, is a partner in the prestigious Los Angeles–based landscape architectural firm Galper/Baldon Associates, which she and her partner founded in 1972. She is the firm's Design Director. She was born in Washington state and graduated from Woodbury College in Los Angeles.

Her landscape work includes design for residential and commercial spaces, even one of the Metro stations for the new Los Angeles subway system, and has been recognized by close to a hundred awards. She also designs interiors and indoor and outdoor furniture. In 1981 she designed a solar house that received much acclaim as the "House of the Decade" for its state-of-the-art technology and dramatic sculptural design.

With her husband she is the co-author of *Steps & Stairways,* an illustrated, large-format book tracing steps and stairs through time and cultures the world over in text and pictures, published by Rizzoli.

Cleo and Ib Melchior celebrated their silver anniversary in 1989. They have two grown sons, each from a previous marriage, and they live in the Hollywood Hills in Los Angeles, California.

INDEX